PAUL WINTER

ON THE TRIAL OF JESUS

# STUDIA JUDAICA

## FORSCHUNGEN ZUR WISSENSCHAFT
## DES JUDENTUMS

HERAUSGEGEBEN VON
E. L. EHRLICH
BASEL

BAND I

WALTER DE GRUYTER · BERLIN · NEW YORK
1974

# ON THE TRIAL OF JESUS

BY

## PAUL WINTER

SECOND EDITION
REVISED AND EDITED
BY
T. A. BURKILL
AND GEZA VERMES

---

WALTER DE GRUYTER · BERLIN · NEW YORK
1974

ISBN 3 11 002283 4
Library of Congress Catalog Card Number 73-94226
© 1974 by Walter de Gruyter & Co., Berlin 30
Printed in Yugoslavia

Satz und Druck: ČGP Delo, Ljubljana

TO  THE  DEAD

in

AUSCHWITZ
IZBICA
MAJDANEK
TREBLINKA

among  whom  are  those  who  were  dearest  to  me

# PREFACE

The present edition of the late Paul Winter's book, *On the Trial of Jesus,* incorporates a selection of the supplementary notes he assembled with a view to producing a revised version of the work. They were deciphered and assigned to their appropriate places in the text by T. A. Burkill. Both editors are responsible for the stylistic amendments and occasional *addenda.* Other improvements on the 1961 edition consist in the placement of the annotations as footnotes on the relevant pages, and the addition of a bibliography and an index. A biographical note on the author, as well as select lists of his publications and of reviews of the first edition, have also been included.

Our thanks are due to Lawrence E. Frizzell, of Linacre College, Oxford, for help in collecting Dr. Winter's scattered writings, and to the publishers, Messrs. Walter de Gruyter & Co., for encouraging us to introduce, despite the considerable extra costs, whatever changes we deemed desirable.

T. A. B.
G. V.

# FURTHER ACKNOWLEDGEMENTS

The basic revising of the monograph was done in Salisbury, and I am grateful to the Research Board of the University of Rhodesia for their financial support of the project; to colleagues in the Department of Theology, namely, Dr. Nigel Turner, Mr. M. H. Prozesky, Mr. E. C. Mandivenga, and Mrs. Jean Rex-Waller, and to Mrs. Ann Barnett, Lecturer in German, all of whom readily came to my aid in various connections; also to Bella, my wife, for secretarial assistance and for her share in the work of classifying a substantial part of Dr. Winter's literary remains.

T. A. B.

# CONTENTS

CONTENTS

# BIOGRAPHICAL NOTE

Paul Winter was born in 1904 at Straznice in Moravia. After reading philosophy and ancient languages at the University of Vienna and law at the University of Prague, he became a successful barrister. Jewish by birth and religious upbringing, he went underground in 1939, on the annexation of Czechoslovakia to the Third Reich, and managed to escape.

Following an adventurous journey through Hungary and the Balkans, he finally joined the Free Czech Army in Palestine and saw active service in North Africa (1941—43) and England (1944) under British Command, and in France and Germany with the American forces. In 1945 he served as senior liaison officer at the German Headquarters of the United States First Army, and was charged with the care of persons liberated from Buchenwald, Ohrdruf and Dora (Nordhausen). After the armistice, he became responsible for the repatriation of some eighty-thousand survivors of concentration and forced-labour camps. During this period he learned that his closest relatives, including his mother and his sister to whom he was deeply devoted, had perished in Nazi extermination centres.

On his demobilisation he returned to London, where he was assigned to the Central Tracing Office of the United Nations Relief and Rehabilitation Administration, an appointment which took him to Arolsen in Hesse. He was later made legal adviser for the Displaced Persons Operation, and before the establishment of the German Federal Republic participated in the deliberations of the Study Committee of the intergovernmental *Länderrat* (Stuttgart), a body concerned with drafting legislation designed to indemnify the victims of political or racial persecution.

From the end of 1947 he lived in London, eventually opting to take up British citizenship. For a short while he worked for the Overseas Service of the British Broadcasting Corporation, but the last two decades of his life were almost exclusively dedicated to the study of the New Testament, and particularly the trial of Jesus, a subject that had first captured his imagination in his youth. He pursued his research with whole-hearted devotion, enduring a solitary existence devoid of every comfort, working in libraries by day, and by night earning a bleak livelihood as a railway porter, a watchman at a hostel for epileptics, a post-office sorter, and the like.

A specialist in comparative law, Winter was quick to acquire exper-
tise in the domains of biblical philology and form-criticism, and his
provocative papers on the Fourth Gospel and the Lucan Birth Narratives, published in British, Continental and American learned periodi-
cals, soon placed him in the front rank of New Testament scholarship.
The first edition of the *Trial,* which appeared in 1961, revealed breadth
of knowledge, meticulous erudition and a sympathetic Jewish appreciation of Jesus of Nazareth. The book won world-wide acclaim —
more than a hundred-and-fifty reviews and notices were published on
various continents — and it was generally believed that it would
exercise a lasting influence on the historical understanding of Jesus'
trial, the emergence of the Church and the rise of Christian anti-Semi-
tism. The rumour goes that Cardinal Bea and his colleagues studied the
book, and that it had an impact on the pronouncement made by the
Second Vatican Council on the relation between Roman Catholicism
and the Jewish people.

It is a tragedy that Winter had to wait so long for recognition and
that he lived to the end in a state bordering on penury. After lengthy
delays, he did receive a small indemnity from the German Federal Republic, and the appearance of his book was rewarded by a grant from the
Bollingen Foundation of New York. But otherwise he was largely left
to fend for himself. Nonetheless, during his last few years he was
increasingly in demand for public engagements, and he took part in
Jewish-Christian discussions on German radio and television program-
mes and at Harvard University. He also lectured at various uni-
versities in Canada and the United States as well as in Germany — and
finally in Oxford itself. But by that time the years of struggle, isolation and poverty had taken their toll, and his health was irremediably
undermined. He died of a heart attack on the 9th October 1969.

Those acquainted with Paul Winter could scarcely have been unaware of his brave and combative spirit. Less well known was his capacity for affection towards his friends; perhaps equally unsuspected
was his deep religious sense and devotion to God, evident in the following poem found among his unpublished papers after his death.

זכרונו לברכה

May his memory be blessed!

# GOTTWANDLER

Ein anderer warst du, Gott, als ich noch Höhlen baute
Und in den nassen Fels mein dürftig Lager trug.
Wie wild du damals warst, du nackter Gast! — mir graute
Vor deinem Anblick mehr als wenn ich mich mit Bären schlug.

Doch immer zwangst du mich und riefst zum Kampf zu treten —
Und dann entrangst du dich und warst nicht hier.
Du lachtest hoch und fern, du flohst — in heissem Beten
Lag ich allein und Schweigen hing stumm über mir.

Ich wuchs, lebte fromm, gesättigt, bei den Meinen —
Da nahtest du mit schmeichelndem Betrug:
Du wurdest anders an den runden Ziegelsteinen,
Die ich zu meinem Herd zusammentrug.

Du bliebst, ein froher Gast. Du segnetest die Speisen,
Du kamst zum kranken Kind und wusstest meine Not.
Du lehrtest mich, ich liess mich gerne unterweisen.
Dem Feuer freundlich hütetst du das Haus und bukst das Brot.

So gingen Jahre hin. Ich kannte deine Züge
Und wusste immer: immer ist er nah.
Du wurdest alt, ich sah — ich sah! Du wurdest Lüge —
Dann bliebst du fort. Und einmal warst du da

Und fielst mich an, wie einst, mit einem Keulenschlage
— Ich kannte jäh dies flammende Gesicht —
Und ob ich zitternd rang und schrei und rief und klage,
Du schlugst nur einmal zu, ich hielt dich nicht.

Ich hielt dich nicht. Dumpf fiel, dumpf schlug der Kopf zu Boden,
Und rings umweint mich Zeit wie ein verlassenes Tier.
Du lachtest, gross und hoch, du schwebtest oben —
Ich lag allein und Schweigen hing stumm über mir.

Doch kommst du wieder. Dass ich wieder dich bekriege,
Du ewiger Feind, mein Gott — o Jobel fern von Ruh! —
Wenn ich einst Brust an Brust mit dir in einem Atem liege —
Du würdest klein wie ich, werd ich erst gross wie du.

Ein anderer wirst du, Gott, vor dem mir einstmals graute:
Du steigst in meinen Tag und machst mich reich und froh.
Du bist um mich, den ich in wandelnden Gestalten schaute,
Du bist und ich. Wir beide sind in einer Loh.

Paul Winter

## MY CHANGING GOD

You were another, God, when I was hollowing caves
And making meagre camp among damp rocks.
How fierce you were, my naked guest! I shuddered more
Before your face than when I fought with bears.

But always you compelled me, you challenged me to fight —
And then escaped and were no longer there.
You laughed aloud and far, you fled. In burning prayer
I lay alone, with quiet silence over me.

I grew, I lived contented and devout among my people.
You then approached with honey-mouthed deception,
Became another by the rounded stones
I brought together for my fireplace.

You stayed, a happy guest. You blessed my meal-times,
Visited an ailing child and knew my woe,
You taught, and willingly I learnt from you.
Fire's friend, you were the house's guardian, the baker of its bread.

Thus years passed by. I knew your features.
Always I knew: he is always near.
You aged. I saw — I saw — you were a lie.
And then you stayed away. — But once again you came

And fell on me, as formerly, with crushing blow
— I recognised at once that flaming countenance —
And whether I struggled, cried, called out to you and wailed,
You struck but only once; I did not hold you.

I did not hold you. My head fell heavily and struck the ground,
Time wept about me like a beast forsaken.
Great and on high you laughed; you soared above me.
I lay alone, with quiet silence over me.

And yet you come again. Again I battle with you,
O everlasting foe, my God — O joy remote from calmness! —
If, breast to breast, and with one breathing, I could lie with you,
You would grow small as I, and I, at last, grow great as you.

You are another, God, from him who caused me once to shudder.
You climb into my day and make me rich and happy.
You, whom I saw in changing forms, are all about me,
You are, and I; together now in one fiery glow.

# SELECT LIST OF PAUL WINTER'S PUBLICATIONS

### 1953

μονογενὴς παρὰ πατρός. *Zeitschrift für Religions- und Geistesgeschichte*, vol. 5, pp. 335—365.
»Some Notes on Luke (1:78, 2:13) with Regard to the Theory of ›Imitation Hebraisms‹«. *Studia Theologica*, vol. 7, pp. 158—165.

### 1954

»Notes on Wieder's Observations on the DWRŠ HTWRH«. *Jewish Quarterly Review*, vol. 45, pp. 39—47.
»Jewish Folklore in the Matthaean Birth Story«. *Hibbert Journal*, vol. 53, pp. 34—42.
»Isa. lxiii 9 (Gk) and the Passover Haggadah«. *Vetus Testamentum*, vol. 4, pp. 439—441.
»Some Observations on the Language in the Birth and Infancy Stories of the Third Gospel«. *NTS*, vol. 1, pp. 111—121.
»Zum Verständnis des Johannes-Evangelium«. *Vox Theologica*, vol. 25, pp. 149—159.
»Luke II 49 and Targum Yerushalmi«. *ZNW*, vol. 45, pp. 145—179.
»Magnificat and Benedictus — Maccabaean Psalms?«. *Bulletin of the John Rylands Library*, vol. 37, pp. 328—347.
»The Cultural Background of the Narrative in Luke I and II«. *Jewish Quarterly Review*, vol. 45, pp. 159—167; 230—242; 287.

### 1955

»Ben Sira and the Teaching of ›Two Ways‹«. *Vetus Testamentum*, vol. 5, pp. 315—318.
»The Treatment of his Sources by the Third Evangelist in Luke XXI—XXIV«. *Studia Theologica*, vol. 8, pp. 138—172.
»Lc 2, 49 and Targum Yerushalmi again«. *ZNW*, vol. 46, pp. 141—142.
»Der Begriff ›Söhne Gottes‹ im Moselied«. *ZAW*, vol. 67, pp. 40—48.
»ὅτι recitativum in Luke I 25, 26, II 23«. *HTR*, vol. 48, pp. 213—216.
»Luke XXII, 66b—71«. *Studia Theologica*, vol. 9, pp. 112—115.

### 1956

»Simeon der Gerechte und Caius Caligula«. *Judaica*, vol. 12, pp. 129—132.
»Sadoqite Fragments IV 20, 21 and the Exegesis of Genesis 1:27 in Late Judaism«. *ZAW*, vol. 68, pp. 71—84, 264.
Review of W. D. Davies, *Paul and Rabbinic Judaism* (2nd ed.). *Theologische Literaturzeitung*, vol. 81, col. 677.

»Matthew XI, 27 and Luke X, 22 from the First to the Fifth Century: Reflections on the Development of the Text«. *NovT*, vol. 1, pp. 112—148.

»The Proto-Source of Luke I«. *NovT*, vol. 1, pp. 184—199.

»Nazareth and Jerusalem in Luke chs. I and II«. *NTS*, vol. 3, pp. 136—142.

Review of H. Conzelmann, *Die Mitte der Zeit. Theologische Literaturzeitung*, vol. 81, cols. 36—39.

»Twenty-six Priestly Courses (IQM II:2)«. *Vetus Testamentum*, vol. 6, pp. 215—217.

»On Luke and Lucan Sources«. *ZNW*, vol. 47, pp. 217—242.

Review of C. K. Barrett, *The Gospel according to St. John. Gnomon*, vol. 28, pp. 310—311.

»Reflections on Bultmann's Commentary on John«. *Hibbert Journal*, vol. 54, pp. 176—183.

## 1957

»Das aramäische Apocryphon«. *Theologische Literaturzeitung*, vol. 82, cols. 257—262.

»Das Neue Testament und die Rollen vom Toten Meer: Bemerkungen zu einem Sammelband«. *Theologische Literaturzeitung*, vol. 82, cols. 833—840.

Review of H. J. Schoeps, *Urgemeinde, Judenchristentum, Gnosis. NovT*, vol. 2, p. 154.

Review of R. S. Wallace, *Many Things in Parables. Theologische Zeitschrift*, vol. 13, pp. 229—230.

Review of B. Kraft, *Die Zeichen für die wichtigeren Handschriften des griechischen Neuen Testaments* (3rd ed.). *NovT*, vol. 2, pp. 154—155.

Review of P. M. Bič and J. B. Souček, *Biblická Konkordance. NovT*, vol. 2, p. 155.

»Eine vollständige Handschrift des palästinischen Targums aufgefunden«. *ZNW*, vol. 48, p. 192.

Review of F. C. Grant, *The Gospels: Their Origin and their Growth. NovT*, vol. 2, pp. 156—157.

»I Corinthians XV, 3 b—7«. *NovT*, vol. 2, pp. 142—150.

»Note on Salem-Jerusalem«. *NovT*, vol. 2, pp. 151—152.

»Miszellen zur Apostelgeschichte (5 : 36; 15 : 14)«. *Evangelische Theologie*, vol. 17, pp. 1—9.

## 1958

»Genesis 1:27 and Jesus' Saying on Divorce«. *ZAW*, vol. 70, pp. 260—261.

Review of D. Howlett, *The Essenes and Christianity. Orientalistische Literaturzeitung*, nos. 11—12, cols. 557—558.

»On the Margin of Luke I, II«. *Studia Theologica*, vol. 12, pp. 103—107.

»Lukanische Miszellen«. *ZNW*, vol. 49, pp. 65—77.

Review of E. Stauffer, *Jerusalem und Rom. NovT*, vol. 2, pp. 318—319.

»The Main Literary Problem of the Lucan Infancy Story«. *Anglican Theological Review*, vol. 40, pp. 257—264.

## 1959

»Two Non-allegorical Expressions in the Dead Sea Scrolls«. *Palestine Exploration Quarterly*, vol. 91, pp. 38—46.

»Back to the Caves«. *Palestine Exploration Quarterly,* vol. 91, pp. 132—134.
»Anlässlich eines neuen Jesus-Buches« — W. Grundmann, *Die Geschichte Jesu Christi. Zeitschrift für Religions- und Geistesgeschichte,* vol. 11, pp. 165 —168.
Reviews of R. Bultmann, *Theologie des Neuen Testaments* (3rd ed.) and *Glauben und Verstehen: Gesammelte Aufsätze* (2 vols. 3rd ed.). *NTS,* vol. 6, pp. 174—177.
Review of J. Leal, *Sinopsis Concordada de Los Cuatro Evangelios. Theologische Literaturzeitung,* vol. 84, cols. 430—431.
Review of W. F. Arndt, *Bible Commentary: The Gospel according to St. Luke. Theologische Literaturzeitung,* vol. 84, col. 673.
»Marginal Notes on the Trial of Jesus I—II«. *ZNW,* vol. 50, pp. 14—33, 221—251.
»The Holy Messiah«. *ZNW,* vol. 50, p. 275.

## 1960

Review of C. E. B. Cranfield, *The Gospel according to Saint Mark. Theologische Literaturzeitung,* vol. 85, cols. 744—746.
»The Wicked Priest«. *Hibbert Journal,* vol. 58, pp. 53—60.
Review of H. Lietzmann, *Kleine Schriften* I. *Deutsche Literaturzeitung,* vol. 81, cols. 106—108.
Review of H. Conzelmann, *Die Mitte der Zeit* (3rd ed.). *Theologische Literaturzeitung,* vol. 85, cols. 929—931.
Review of E. Hennecke, ed., *Neutestamentliche Apocryphen in deutscher Übersetzung* (3rd ed.). *Palestine Exploration Quarterly,* vol. 92, pp. 79—81.

## 1961

*On the Trial of Jesus* (Berlin). — Over 150 notices and reviews of this work were published during the early sixties; 75 of these are listed below, pp. XXI—XXII.
Reviews of Marcel Simon, *Les sectes juives au temps de Jésus* and *St. Stephen and the Hellenists in the Primitive Church. Deutsche Literaturzeitung,* vol. 82, cols. 789—792.
Review of M. Goguel, *Jesus and the Origins of Christianity* I, II (Translated by Olive Wyon with an introduction by C. L. Mitton). *Theologische Literaturzeitung,* vol. 86, col. 276.
Letter to *The Tablet* (re the trial of Jesus), 27th May, pp. 519—520.
Review of Otto Betz, *Offenbarung und Schriftforschung in der Qumransekte. Revue de Qumran,* vol. 3, pp. 292—296.
Review of H. Lietzmann, *Kleine Schriften* II. *Deutsche Literaturzeitung,* vol. 85, cols. 209—211.

## 1962

»Judith«, »Philo, Biblical Antiquities of« and »Psalms of Solomon«. *The Interpreter's Dictionary of the Bible* (ed. G. A. Buttrick).
»Markus 14:53b, 55—64 ein Gebilde des Evangelisten«. *ZNW,* vol. 53, pp. 260—263.

Review of *New Testament Essays: Studies in Memory of T. W. Manson 1893—1958* (ed. A. J. B. Higgins). *Deutsche Literaturzeitung,* vol. 83, cols. 205 —206.

## 1963

»Une lettre de Ponce-Pilate«. *Foi et Vie,* vol. 62, pp. 101—108.

»News from Pilate in Liverpool«. *Encounter,* vol. 21, pp. 68—70.

Review of G. Vermes, *Scripture and Tradition in Judaism. Durham University Journal,* vol. 55, pp. 89—91.

Reviews of R. J. H. Shutt, *Studies in Josephus* and N. N. Glatzer, *Jerusalem and Rome. Theologische Literaturzeitung,* vol. 88, cols. 347—349.

»The Marcan Account of Jesus' Trial by the Sanhedrin«. *Journal of Theological Studies,* n. s., vol. 14, pp. 94—102.

Review of H. J. Kraus, *Gottesdienst in Israel* (2nd ed.). *Anglican Theological Review,* vol. 45, pp. 414—416.

Review of B. Gerhardsson, *Memory and Manuscript. Anglican Theological Review,* vol. 45, pp. 416—419.

Review of R. Bultmann, *The History of the Synoptic Tradition* (Translated by J. Marsh). *NTS,* vol. 10, pp. 523—525.

»Nochmals zu Deuteronomium 32:8«. *ZAW,* vol. 75, pp. 218—223.

Review of F. W. Beare, *The Earliest Records of Jesus. Theologische Literaturzeitung,* vol. 88, cols. 595—596.

»Zum Prozess Jesu«. *Das Altertum,* vol. 9, pp. 157—164.

»Heimholung Jesu in das jüdische Volk«. *Communio Viatorum,* vol. 6, pp. 303—307.

## 1964

»The Trial of Jesus«. *Commentary,* vol. 38, no. 3 (Sept.), pp. 35—41.

»A Letter from Pontius Pilate«. *NovT,* vol. 7, pp. 37—43.

Reviews of R. Hummel, *Die Auseinandersetzung zwischen Kirche und Judentum im Matthäusevangelium;* H. W. Bartsch, *Entmythologisierende Auslegung* and *Wachet aber zu jeder Zeit;* N. Wieder, *The Judean Scrolls and Karaism;* and K. Rudolph, *Die Mandäer. Anglican Theological Review,* vol. 46, pp. 119 —123.

Review of Gert Jeremias, *Der Lehrer der Gerechtigkeit. Anglican Theological Review,* vol. 46, pp. 322—323.

Review of H. Lietzmann, *Kleine Schriften* III. *Deutsche Literaturzeitung,* vol. 85, cols. 978—979.

Review of Gert Jeremias, *Der Lehrer der Gerechtigkeit. Revue de Qumran,* vol. 5, pp. 145—147.

»The Trial of Jesus and the Competence of the Sanhedrin«. *NTS,* vol. 10, pp. 494—499.

Review of T. A. Burkill, *Mysterious Revelation: An Examination of the Philosophy of St. Mark's Gospel. Gnomon,* vol. 36, pp. 210—212.

## 1965

Reply to readers' comments on »The Trial of Jesus« (Sept. 1964). *Commentary,* vol. 39, no. 3 (March), pp. 20—28.

Reviews of E. Jüngel, *Paulus und Jesus* (2nd ed.); K. Aland, ed., *Synopsis Quattuor Evangeliorum;* J. C. McRuer, *The Trial of Jesus;* W. D. Davies, *The Setting of the Sermon on the Mount;* and W. Trilling, *Das Wahre Israel. Anglican Theological Review,* vol. 47, pp. 111—115, 120—121, 302—308.

### 1966

Review of H. E. Tödt, *The Son of Man in the Synoptic Tradition* (Translated by D. M. Barton). *Communio Viatorum,* vol. 9, pp. 199—200.

Letter re the Court of the Gentiles (Herodian Temple at Jerusalem). *Commentary,* vol. 40, no. 3 (March), pp. 22—23.

»Sadduzäer und Pharisäer« in *Die Zeit Jesus* ed. H. J. Schultz (Stuttgart, 1966), pp. 43—50. Engl. trans. *Jesus in his Time* (Philadelphia, 1971), pp. 47—56.

Review of W. D. Davies, *The Setting of the Sermon on the Mount. Gnomon,* vol. 38, pp. 102—103.

Review of S. Wagner, *Die Essener in der wissenschaftlichen Diskussion vom Ausgang des 18. bis zum Beginn des 20. Jahrhunderts. Helikon,* vol. 6, pp. 381—383.

### 1967

Werner Koch, *Zum Prozess Jesu,* mit Beiträgen von: Josef Blinzler, Günter Klein, Paul Winter. Weiden — Cologne.

Review of P. Vielhauer, *Aufsätze zum Neuen Testament. Palestine Exploration Quarterly,* vol. 99, pp. 121—122.

»Sadoqite Fragments IX, 1«. *Revue de Qumran,* vol. 6, pp. 131—136.

»Zum Prozess Jesu« in W. Eckert, ed., *Antijudaismus im Neuen Testament* (Munich), pp. 95—101.

»Tacitus and Pliny: The Early Christians«. *Journal of Historical Studies* (Princeton Univ. Press, N. J.), vol. 1, pp. 31—40.

### 1968

»The Trial of Jesus as a Rebel against Rome«. *Jewish Quarterly,* vol. 16, pp. 31—37.

Review of N. Perrin, *Rediscovering the Teaching of Jesus. Deutsche Literaturzeitung,* vol. 89, cols. 783—785.

»Josephus on Jesus«. *Journal of Historical Studies,* vol. 1, pp. 289—302.

Reviews of S. Sandmel, *We Jews and Jesus* and H. Schonfield, *Those Incredible Christians. Journal of Historical Studies,* vol. 1, pp. 370—375.

### 1969

Review of K. H. Rengstorf and S. von Kortzfleisch, eds., *Kirche und Synagoge: Handbuch zur Geschichte von Christen und Juden: Darstellung mit Quellen* (vol. 1). *Journal of Historical Studies,* vol. 2, pp. 242—244.

# SELECT LIST OF REVIEWS OF »ON THE TRIAL OF JESUS«

## 1961

Abdullah, M. S., *Der Islam,* vol. 13 (May), pp. 5—6.
Arnaldich, L., *Revista Espanola de Derecho Canonico,* vol. 16, p. 274.
Benoit, P., *Revue Biblique,* vol. 68, pp. 593—599.
Brandon, S. G. F., *The Guardian,* 3rd Nov., p. 6.
Bruns, J. A., *Catholic Biblical Quarterly,* vol. 23, pp. 360—363.
Crehan, J., *The Catholic Herald,* 15th Sept., p. 8.
—, *Catholic Gazette,* vol. 52 (Nov.), pp. 322—323.
Flusser, D., *The Jerusalem Post,* 26th May. p. vi.
Grant, R. M., *JBL,* vol. 80, pp. 185—186.
Hahn, F., *Monatschrift für Pastoraltheologie,* vol. 50 (Dec.), pp. 524—525.
Hollis, C., *The Tablet,* 1st April, pp. 297—298; 15th April, pp. 352—353.
Isaac, J., *Revue Historique,* fasc. 459, pp. 127—137.
Lesser, J., *Jewish Chronicle,* 24th March, p. 31.
Lohse, E., *Gnomon,* vol. 33, pp. 624—626.
Maier, J., *Ha-'arez,* 3rd Nov., p. 10.
—, *Judaica,* vol. 17, pp. 249—253.
Matthews, W. R., *The Daily Telegraph,* 7th Feb., p. 12.
Michaelis, W., *Theologische Zeitschrift,* vol. 17, pp. 226—227.
Oyen, H. van, *Christlich-jüdisches Forum,* no. 26 (May), pp. 1—3.
Smit Sibinga, J., *Woord en Dienst,* 22nd July, p. 243.
Soper, D., *Tribune,* 10th March, p. 11.
Schweizer, E., *Neue Zürcher Zeitung,* 4th May, pp. 1—2.
—, *Evangelische Theologie,* vol. 21, pp. 238—240.
Trevor-Roper, H. R., *The Sunday Times,* 13th August, p. 22.
Zerafa, P., *Angelicum,* vol. 38, pp. 455—458.

## 1962

Bruce, F. F., *Book List 1962* (ed. G. W. Anderson — The Society for Old Testament Study), p. 80.
Burkill, T. A., *NTS,* vol. 8, pp. 174—175.
Davies, W. D., *Commentary,* vol. 33 (June), pp. 540—541.
Dewailly, L.-M., *RHR,* vol. 161, pp. 251—252.
Dell'Orca, R., *Revista Biblica,* vol. 24, p. 184.
Evans, O. E., *London Quarterly and Holborn Review,* no. 187, pp. 69—70.
Finegan, J., *Interpretation,* vol. 16, pp. 102—104.
Finley, M. I., *New Statesman,* 2nd Feb., pp. 165—166.
Flusser, D., *Tarbiz,* vol. 31, pp. 107—117.
—, *Christian News from Israel,* vol. 12, pp. 28—32.
Fohrer, G., *ZAW,* vol. 74, p. 367.

Hoffman, J.-G.-H., *La Revue Réformée*, vol. 13, no. 52, pp. 42—43.
Mikat, P., *Biblische Zeitschrift*, vol. 6, pp. 300—307.
Nineham, D., *Journal of Theological Studies*, vol. 13, pp. 387—392.
Orlinsky, H. M., *In Jewish Bookland* (March), p. 1.
Parkes, J., *The Jewish Journal of Sociology*, vol. 4, pp. 130—131.
Potterie, I de la, *Biblica*, vol. 43, pp. 87—93.
Prado, J., *Sefarad*, vol. 22, pp. 168—178.
Prigent, P., *Église et Théologie*, vol. 25 (March-June), pp. 81—82.
Rasco, E., *Gregorianum*, vol. 43, pp. 776—778.
Ruef, J. S., *Anglican Theological Review*, vol. 44, pp. 92—93.
Sandmel, S., *Journal of the American Oriental Society*, vol. 82, pp. 386—387.
Schalit, A., *Kirjath Sepher*, vol. 37, pp. 333—341.
Simon, M., *Revue d'Histoire et de Philosophie Religieuses*, vol. 42, pp. 250—252.
Simpson, W. W., *The Observer*, 22nd April, p. 8.
Smith, L. P., *Jewish Currents* (October), pp. 37—40.
Suarez, P. L., *Estudios Biblicos*, vol. 21, pp. 100—102.

*1963*

Barrett, C. K., *Durham University Journal*, vol. 55, p. 89.
Bartsch, H. W., *Theologische Literaturzeitung*, vol. 88, cols. 97—102; *NovT*, vol. 7, pp. 210—216.
Beare, F. W., *Canadian Journal of Theology*, vol. 9, pp. 292—296.
Eisenstadt, S., *Deutsche Literaturzeitung*, vol. 89, cols. 820—821.
Grant, R. M., *Christian Century*, vol. 80, p. 1338.
Gruenler, R. G., *Encounter* (Spring), pp. 252—254.
Hartke, W., *Helikon*, vol. 3, pp. 744—746.
Léon-Dufour, X., *Recherches de Science Religieuse*, vol. 51, pp. 608—611.
Schalit, A., *Annual of the Swedish Theological Institute*, vol. 2, pp. 86—101.
Snyder, G. F., *Journal of Bible and Religion*, vol. 31, p. 338.
Souček, J. B., *Communio Viatorum*, vol. 6, pp. 197—202.
Stauffer, E., *Theologische Literaturzeitung*, vol. 88, cols. 97—102.
Zeitlin, S., *Jewish Quarterly Review*, vol. 53, pp. 77—88.

*1964*

Betz, O., *Journal of Religion*, vol. 44, pp. 181—182.
Grant, F. C., *Journal of Religion*, vol. 44, pp. 230—237.
Hamerton-Kelly, R. G., *Union Seminary Quarterly Review*, vol. 19, pp. 242—246.
Leimbeck, M., *Bibel und Kirche*, vol. 19, pp. 32—33.
Pitman, R., *The Sunday Express*, 29th March, p. 6.
Radermakers, J., *Nouvelle Revue Théologique*, vol. 86, pp. 426—427.
Weise, M., *Zeitschrift der Deutschen Morgenländischen Gesellschaft*, vol. 114, pp. 421—423.

*1965*

Gordis, R., *Jewish Social Studies*, vol. 27, pp. 185—187.
Treves, M., *La Rassegna Mensile di Israel*, vol. 31, pp. 192—193.

# ABBREVIATIONS

CSEL = Corpus Scriptorum Ecclesiasticorum Latinorum (Vienna)
GCS  = Die griechischen christlichen Schriftsteller der ersten Jahrhunderte (Leipzig and Berlin)
*HTR* = The Harvard Theological Review (Cambridge, Mass.)
*JBL*  = Journal of Biblical Literature (Philadelphia, Pa.)
MPG = Patrologiae Graecae Cursus Completus (Paris)
MPL = Patrologiae Latinae Cursus Completus (Paris)
*NovT* = Novum Testamentum (Leiden)
*NTS*  = New Testament Studies (Cambridge)
*RHR* = Revue de l'histoire des religions (Paris)
T. B. = The Babylonian Talmud
T. Y. = The Palestinian Talmud
*ZAW* = Zeitschrift für die alttestamentliche Wissenschaft (Berlin)
*ZNW* = Zeitschrift für die neutestamentliche Wissenschaft (Giessen and Berlin)

# INTRODUCTION

Jesus of Nazareth was tried and sentenced to die by crucifixion.
These are historical facts, attested by Roman, Jewish and Christian
authors in extant documents. As facts, they are a subject for historical
investigation regarding the charge on which he was tried, the grounds
for the prosecution, and the course of the proceedings. Sufficient to
sustain the fact of the trial, so far as these questions are concerned our
sources all but elude us.

In second century literature there are sporadic allusions to minutes,
*acta*, supposed to have been taken at Jesus' trial on Pilate's order. Such
references are of an apologetic nature and do not merit serious consideration. The writers making such allusions made them without having
access to any official archives.

What survives of pagan and Jewish records of the trial and subsequent execution of Jesus is of too late a date, too secondary a character,
too fragmentary a nature, and too tendentious to be of more than supplementary value in a systematic attempt to reconstruct the history of
the case. The accounts from Christian sources — chiefly the Gospels —
are both earlier in date and fuller in their description. Paraphrasing the
words of Origen, we may be tempted to say οὐδὲν ἔχομεν ἔξωθεν τοῦ
εὐαγγελίου[1] if we embark upon the task of tracing the precise course of
events. Yet without historical analysis, even the Gospels do not yield
the necessary data. For while they furnish us with information of a kind,
the Gospels were not written for the purpose of guiding historians. The

---

[1] Contra Celsum II 13 (GCS Origenes vol. 1, p. 141; MPG 11, col. 820).

use which their authors intended for the Gospels was religious, not historical. When the evangelists wrote down their accounts of Jesus' trial, they did so not with a view to preserving a record for historical research, but in order to convey a religious message. In this, they were not without forerunners. The earliest Christian preaching revolved around the theme of Jesus' passion and resurrection. »[Das Evangelium] hat ... den Inhalt, daß Jesus nicht ... durch die Kreuzigung vernichtet, sondern zum Himmel erhoben ist, von wo er dann auf die Erde zurück kommen wird, um sich als der Christus in Herrlichkeit zu zeigen und sein Reich unter den Seinen aufzurichten«[2].

When the Gospels are referred to as *our primary sources* for an investigation of the trial of Jesus, the word *primary* requires qualification. They are primary sources insofar as they reflect the situations in which their authors — members of certain early Christian communities — found themselves, and insofar as they express the beliefs current in those communities. They are not primary sources in the sense that they provide first-hand evidence of the events which they describe. They are direct evidence only for the significance attached to the actions, sayings, and the death of Jesus at the time the Gospels were written. They may be used as a source of information on certain happenings in the life of Jesus, provided we examine how it came about that this significance was attributed to the events described, and how the records themselves had originated.

The forerunners of the evangelists, whether they were transmitting types of early preaching orally or whether they had attempted to collect such preaching in written form, were moved by aims of their own — aims not always identical with those of the authors of the canonical Gospels. Hence we are required, as it were, to break through the Gospel accounts to the traditions behind them, to sift those traditions with a view to determining their sources and relative antiquity, to separate what is editorial accretion from early tradition and, finally, to infer from the most primitive form of tradition the historical event which occasioned it. In the words of Wilhelm Brandt, »Die Untersuchung ... [der evangelischen] Berichte liefert uns ..., nicht Angaben über das wirkliche Leben Jesu, aber solche über die Motive des Glaubens und der Politik, kraft deren die dürftige ursprüngliche Überlieferung zu dem ... evangelischen Geschichtsbild aus- und umgestaltet worden ist«[3]. What Brandt noted of the Gospels *qua Gospels*, has been restated more precisely with regard to the evangelical Passion Narratives by Martin Dibelius: »Bei den Vernehmungen Jesu vor dem Hohenpriester und vor Pilatus ist eine Überlieferung des Hergangs durch Augenzeugen

---

[2] Julius Wellhausen, *Das Evangelium Johannis* (Berlin 1908), p. 121.
[3] Wilhelm Brandt, *Die Evangelische Geschichte und der Ursprung des Christenthums* (Leipzig 1893), p. X.

ausgeschlossen«[4]; »Die Frage nach der Geschichtlichkeit der evangelischen Berichte über den Prozeß Jesu kann . . . erst behandelt werden,
wenn der Sinn der Berichte klargestellt ist. Erst wenn man gesehen hat,
unter welchem Gesichtspunkt die Erzähler berichten wollten, kann man
fragen, was sie auf Grund der Überlieferung berichten konnten«[5].

Neither the tradents of early preaching nor the evangelists who succeeded them were interested in the events for the sake of their historical
actuality. Their interest lay in different fields. What the Gospels tell us
of the life, and in particular of the trial, of Jesus is not a historical account of what actually took place, but is a representation of the manner
in which the Passion of the Lord was interpreted in certain early Christian circles. Not written with any historical aim but with a religious
one, the Gospels may affect the outward form of a biography, but they
are much rather theological treatises, based on collective traditions and
incorporating communal preaching about Jesus as it had developed
over a period of several decades. Yet the tradition also contains statements which derive from historical fact. To the theologian the distinction between fact and preaching may be unimportant; to the historian
it is all-important. When attempting a historical examination of Jesus'
trial, attention is drawn in the first place to the Gospel according to
Mark, which is the earliest of the four canonical Gospels and hence the
least affected by aims and influences belonging to a later period of
Christian development. Yet even Mark is by no means a biographical
record of Jesus' life, but a work composed under the pressure of the
author's theological concerns; the writer collects and reinterprets factual accounts and kerygmatic pronouncements regarding the activities
of Jesus in such a manner as to bring out the significance of those activities as he sees them. »Über den unbiographischen Charakter der evangelischen Überlieferung herrscht . . . Einigkeit in der Forschung. Die
evangelische Überlieferung ist Glaubenszeugnis, nicht Geschichtschreibung. Es gibt kein Jesuswort, keine Einzelgeschichte in den Evangelien,
die aus einem rein geschichtlichen Interesse tradiert wäre«[6]. The arrangement of successive sections in the Gospels is governed by pragmatic,
not by chronological considerations, yet the presentation as a whole is
superficially disguised in the form of a continuous narrative[7]. Hence, to

---

[4] Martin Dibelius, *Die Formgeschichte des Evangeliums* (Tübingen [3]1959, p. 214;
English edition *From Tradition to Gospel* (London 1934), p. 213. Cf. »Kein Augen-
oder Ohrenzeuge stand der Gemeinde . . . zu Diensten bis zu der in aller Öffentlich-
keit vorgenommenen Kreuzigung auf dem Golgatha«, Brandt, *o. c.*, p. 88.

[5] Dibelius, *o. c.*, p. 205: *cf.* p. 218; Engl. ed., p. 204: *cf.* p. 217.

[6] Erik Sjöberg, *Der verborgene Menschensohn in den Evangelien* (Lund 1955),
p. 216.

[7] This *form*, that is to say, the arrangement of various traditional elements so
as to give to the entire work *the appearance of a life story*, is not of Palestinian
origin.

arrive at the underlying traditions, we must disregard the framework given to the 'elements' of the gospel by the writers of the Gospels. But even if we succeed in arriving at the most primitive traditional units, we have not yet separated history from interpretation. »The tradition that reached the evangelists was already an interpreted ... tradition ... We cannot find a tradition innocent of interpretation; as far back as we can track them down the units of tradition bear the marks of Christological interpretation. Those who handed them down [did so] in the conviction that the history ... they were narrating alone gave meaning to all history ... the historical tradition was from the beginning ... used in the interests of the conviction 'Jesus is Lord'«[8]. Our task therefore is to make an historical investigation on the basis of documents that were neither written for historical purposes nor by persons used to thinking in historical terms.

Even so, the Gospels can yield considerable historical information provided the historian knows how to read them.

It is characteristic of the gospel traditions that *theological propositions* and *apologetic argumentations* are on occasion set forth in narrative form, and thus assume the appearance of *statements of fact*. A process of this kind finds illustration, for example, in the healing-stories of Mc 7, 24 b, 25, 26 b—29, 30 and of Mt 8, 5—12, 13 (cf. Lc 7, 1, 2, 6 b—9, 10; Jn 4, 46—53). In each of these instances an isolated saying, ascribed to Jesus, circulated in a certain community. The saying had no ›situation‹[9]. To supply it with the missing situation, a frame was provided, and this now became the focus of attention. The characteristics of the frame furnish us with the clue in an endeavour to ascertain under what conditions, and with what aim, the narrative assumed its present form. The constituent elements of the stories as related in the passages referred to are the following:

(1) Jesus demonstrates his power of healing from a distance
(2) on the child (*in Mark*) or servant (*in Matthew and Luke*) of a Gentile.

Whatever the version given to it by the evangelists, the 'story' comes from a situation in which the relation of Gentiles to the gospel was

---

[8] C. Kingsley Barrett, *Yesterday, Today, and For Ever: The New Testament Problem. Inaugural Lecture* (Durham 1959), p. 7.

[9] Johannes Weiss, *Das älteste Evangelium* (Göttingen 1903), noted: »die Geschichte [groupiert sich] um ein bemerkenswertes Logion« (p. 225). Rudolf Bultmann, *Die Geschichte der synoptischen Tradition* (Göttingen ²1931), p. 38, remarks: »Das Wunder wird nicht um seiner selbst willen erzählt, sondern Jesu im Gespräche sich entwickelndes Verhalten ist die Hauptsache«; English edition *The History of the Synoptic Tradition* (Oxford ²1968), p. 38. Similary Martin Dibelius, *o. c.*, p. 53, note 1: »eine Perikope, ... deren eigentlichen Körper ein Dialog bildet«; p. 261: »ursprünglich nicht als Erzählung, sondern als Redestück überliefert« (*cf.* p. 245 on Mt 8, 5—13); Engl. ed., pp. 55, 261: *cf.* pp. 244 f.

a matter of concern — the interest of Gentiles in the saving (healing) power of Jesus, the κύριος, had been roused and Gentiles embraced the belief in him as σωτήρ. Jewish adherents to the faith had to come to terms with this contingency. They accepted the proposition to admit Gentiles within their conventicles, and the result of protracted deliberations found expression in simple narratives which, moreover, were thrown back into the life of Jesus. Yet even in such a creative reinterpretation those among whom the stories originated remained sufficiently true to historical fact to remember that Jesus himself had not come into direct contact with Gentiles during his preaching activities — hence the stories present him as exercising his saving, or healing, power on Gentiles from a distance[10].

Another example from which it may be seen how theological argument can be covered up in the Gospels by a narrative, is provided by the story of Dives and Lazarus (Lc 16, 19—31) in its conclusion (vv. 29—31). The tremendous claim of Jesus' resurrection left the great majority of his compatriots unconvinced. To blunt the argument that the proclamation had little effect on the people generally, recourse is made to Moses and the prophets: *they will not be persuaded to repentance if one rise from the dead,* so Abraham is made to say, *if Moses and the prophets have failed to make them hear.* We have to understand: *if they do not accept that interpretation of holy writings which apostolic preachers were wont to put forward when they quoted Moses and the prophets.*

It is in such an oblique fashion that historical data can be conveyed in seemingly artless parables and narratives which the Gospels connect with Jesus.

Rarely in the New Testament do we find such a wide variety of description of the same event as is displayed in the Passion Narratives of the four Gospels. This indicates that changing motives governed the formation of the tradition. Hence before an assessment can be made of the historical value of the various reports of Jesus' trial in the Gospels, we have to consider the circumstances in which the Gospels came to be written, for whom they were intended, and to the special needs of the prospective readers. As it was already many decades after the events that the evangelists wrote their accounts, we must ask: What were the sources on which they based their own narratives, and what were the

---

[10] A certain reluctance to admit Gentiles lingers perceptibly on in Lc 7, 1—10 (an independent Judaeo-Christian rendering of the story, but not necessarily of earlier date), where the exercise of Jesus' saving grace is recommended in view of the Gentile's generosity towards Jewish (i. e. Jewish Christian!) believers; he is not admitted for his own sake, but rather on the ground of his merits as a benefactor of the congregation. Similarly, some reserve on the Gentile question makes its presence felt in the word πρῶτον in Mc 7, 27 and, of course, in Mt 15, 24.

purposes for which they used such sources of information as were available to them?

If there were anything like an axiom in New Testament scholarship, it would be that some account of the circumstances leading to the death of Jesus was among the oldest recollections that were preserved by his adherents. The Gospel — meaning by this expression a narrative of the life and teaching of Jesus, of his death and resurrection — grew backwards: the end was there before the beginning had been thought of. The last things were remembered first. Early preaching, the oldest traditions, centred around the theme of the Messiah's suffering and glory. Only later, when the Gospel had grown, was the Story of Jesus' Passion prefaced, as it were, by reminiscences of events in his life. The point at which the Gospel begins was traced retrogressively from the time of his death to the time of his baptism; later to his birth; and finally — to begin with the Very Beginning — to the Word that Was with God.

If some account of the events immediately preceding Jesus' death had been drawn up before anything was formulated concerning his teaching and activities, we would assume that such an account was handed on unchanged to subsequent generations and that its form, once fixed, was retained in outline during the process of oral and literary transmission. A glance at the New Testament shows that this is not the case. Seldom is there in the Gospels such a variety of diverging and repeatedly con-flicting accounts of the same events as in the narratives describing the arrest, trial, crucifixion and resurrection of Jesus. This may seem para-dox — yet is it really surprising? The Passion, as a prelude to the Re-surrection, was a theme of momentous importance in the Christian proclamation. Everything connected in the remotest way with this event was pondered over in the believers' minds, was told and retold many times. New significances emerged as the event was mentally re-enacted, and a new understanding required progressive reformulation of the primitive original story.

No testimony was available of eye-witnesses present either at a pre-liminary examination of Jesus or at the court session in which sentence of death was passed. Lack of direct first-hand evidence was of itself conducive to an expansion of reports such as were being circulated. The people who transmitted these reports, first from mouth to mouth, later from pen to pen, were not historians. To them the trial of Jesus was part of his Passion, not an object for legal, or historical, enquiry but an experience of intense religious import. Historical interest, if any, was submerged in a complex pattern of more urgent needs: concerns of a cultic, missionary, apologetic and polemical nature provided the mo-tive for disseminating the message in which all that was known of Jesus' trial had come to be embedded. Even if actual minutes taken at the proceedings had been at the disposal of Jesus' followers, their interest would not have been satisfied by the mere preservation of such minutes or the transmission thereof as a disinterested record. The event was not memorable for historical reasons, but for what it signified. Whatever memories of the arrest and crucifixion had been preserved by contemporaries, the report soon gathered speed, grew in volume, and spread — not in one direction, but in many.

In addition to the scanty information that existed in the early days, secondary traditions took shape. These traditions did not entirely supplant reminiscences from people who had been alive at the time of the crucifixion, but an amalgamation of primary and secondary strands came into being. Let us not assume that the elements of the earliest rendering were substantially changed in this process, or that free imagination displaced actual recollections. What happened rather was that in the course of oral transmission motifs which had formed part of the trial story from the outset were transposed from their germane original setting and assigned to a new context. A multiplication of the same themes took place, there was a shift in emphasis, and inevitably, descriptive details were added to enhance the vividness of the refashioned narrative. The same event, instead of being narrated once, was narrated several times, in different places. New persons were introduced into the story, new situations were created — but the basic motifs remained constant and were merely adapted to fit their new context. Tradition expanded.

When individual evangelists collected what had been related and assumed the task of arranging their material to provide a framework of their own theological notions, they found not o n e, but s e v e r a l relevant traditions. Side by side with what we may call ›primary tradition‹ there now were a number of secondary traditions which had developed from the former. Rather than omit anything they considered of importance, the evangelists assembled all they could collect, combining secondary and primary traditions, and reanimating the narrative for purposes of illustration, exposition, exhortation and apologetics. Successive stages in the development of the tradition, in which later forms had grown up from the earlier, now became co-ordinated. Thus the Gospels contain no less than seven different descriptions of a scene of a judicial or quasi-judicial character, together with five descriptions of a scene of the maltreatment and mockery of Jesus. The original themes had been multiplied in the secondary tradition assigning to them new and different contexts. Each evangelist retained what he himself had found, and enlarged it by his specific contribution. In this way a discrepancy came about between the various evangelical accounts. The point in time occupied in one Gospel by a certain event is in another assigned to quite a different one. The narrow shape of the primary tradition is distorted; here and there bulges have occurred; the same incidents are reported over and over again, with modifications, in different places. The sequence of events now recorded in the four Gospels could not possibly have taken place within the space of six or seven hours, the actual time-lag between Jesus' arrest and crucifixion. Hence modern writers have attempted to stretch this span of time by postulating a period of several days, thereby hoping to accommodate all the details about the trial contained in the Gospels. Yet it is impossible to weave together all these disconnected facts into one harmonized account of the trial of Jesus, whether we assume that it lasted a few hours or several days. The writers who have tried to make room for every scene and detail in the various descriptions act in disregard of the evangelists' intentions. Each evangelist aimed at giving a complete and unbroken account of the proceedings. It is illegitimate to interpose an interval of two days between the 'events' reported in successive lines of a certain Gospel, and fill this interval with descriptions taken from another Gospel.

Our first question is: What was the aim of a particular evangelist? When we have satisfied ourselves as to the viewpoint from which he wrote his Gospel, we may ask what traditions were available to him in carrying out his task.

In the various accounts of Jesus' trial all the evangelists combined traditional themes with their own elaborations. It is not beyond the means of scholarship to separate the editorial elements, due to a particular evangelist, from the traditional residue. To do so we have to find out his object, his main interest, his theological position, and his literary characteristics. If we succeed — and we can succeed — in separating editorial additions from the traditional elements, the picture is much simplified. The overgrowth, planted by pious and studious hands, has been scraped away, and we are left with rocks and pebbles of tradition.

Such a procedure, however, is only the first stage in our task. The second is to distinguish between the traditions, and to separate the secondary from the primary. This is a more difficult undertaking than the first where we were guided by the specific theological interests and literary proclivities of the authors of the Gospels. No such guidance is available when we try to distinguish between elements of tradition and determine which of them may be primitive and which secondary. Yet even this task is not entirely hopeless. For, as has been said, secondary traditions were brought about mainly by a process of rearranging the motifs, by the duplication or multiplication of the same themes, now assigned to different contexts. Individual judgment may not be free from some subjectivism when we decide what is secondary and what primary; but even this object in our search for the oldest report of Jesus' trial can be achieved with some degree of certitude.

When breaking through the extant evangelical accounts to the underlying traditions, we discern different stages of a tradition, already developed, yet still retaining the earliest elements of an account drawn up by men who were contemporaries of Jesus. And only this account, combined though it may be with an interpretation of the events recorded, is likely to yield historically valuable information. Successive separation of editorial from traditional, secondary from primary elements, will obviate the need for spreading the events described in the four Gospels over a period of several days. Instead of seven scenes of a judicial sitting, we are left with one. Instead of five descriptions of the mockery of Jesus, one emerges to correspond to the very earliest setting.

When it was asserted on a previous page that non-Christian documents have, at their best, only a supplementary value for an assessment of the juridical proceedings against Jesus, it was not to be understood that they could be disregarded altogether. As far as concerns the legal system obtaining in Judaea in the time of Jesus, the evidence of non-Christian records is of greater value than that of the Gospels. Yet such evidence is far from complete. We have detailed accounts of R o m a n L a w in force at the time, but the rulings applied in outlying provinces were hardly identical with those observed *in Urbe* or in such senatorial provinces as had been under Roman administration for a relatively long period. We have ample descriptions of the injunctions of J e w i s h L a w , yet these belong to a time posterior to that of Jesus. Some of the enactments regulating Roman judicial procedure were certainly applied in the provinces no less than in the capital city itself; some of the ordinances enumerated in the treatise Sanhedrin of the Mishnah were already valid in the time of Jesus. Yet much latitude is allowed for surmises[11].

There are scholars who, holding that Jesus was sentenced for political reasons by the Roman authority and consequently put to death in accordance with Roman penal procedure, are inclined to brush aside the question whether in the period concerned the Jewish judicial authorities possessed the right to pass death sentences and to have them carried out without reference to the prefect. Oscar Cullmann, for instance, expresses this view in the following form: ». . . the whole controversy got off on a sidetrack. The discussion centered exclusively on the juridical question of the right of the Jews to carry out capital punishment on their own authority. The discussion of this specialised question yielded no result, and in all probability the question is insoluble. But the principal question — whether Jesus was condemned by the Romans or by the Jews — was thus lost to view. Yet its answer does not depend on this side-issue«[12].

---

[11] Sections of this, as well as some of the following divisions, were published in the *Zeitschrift für die neutestamentliche Wissenschaft (ZNW)*, volume 50, 1959. My thanks are due to the editor of the Zeitschrift, Professor D. Walther Eltester, for kindly permitting me to reproduce them in this book.

[12] *Der Staat im Neuen Testament* (Tübingen 1956), p. 29; French edition *Dieu et César* (Neuchâtel 1956), p. 45; English edition *The State in the New Testament* (London 1957), p. 42. Compare Bennett Harvie Branscomb, *The Gospel of Mark (Moffatt New Testament Commentary;* London 1937), pp. 283—288, 292—295.

Cullmann's conclusion is indisputable. Whatever the competence of the Jewish judicial authorities in capital cases might have been in the time of Jesus, it remains that Jesus was executed in the Roman fashion, as laid down by Roman law. The fact that this punishment was restricted to certain classes of persons — to which Jesus belonged — and was confined to certain categories of crimes — amongst which the charge laid against Jesus was included[13] — makes the conclusion inevitable that the court whose sentence was carried out in this manner was a Roman court. So far, Cullmann's opinion is sound. Yet the discussion of the Sanhedrin's competence should not be lightly dismissed. Examination of the extent of the Sanhedrin's judicial authority is relevant to the issue. Admittedly it is not the only, or the decisive, point on the clarification of which the solution to our problem depends. Even if it were established that the Sanhedrin did possess the right to try Jewish defendants in capital cases, and did have the competence to ensure that the sentences of death pronounced were carried out, we would still be without definite knowledge of the grounds and judicial procedure by which Jesus of Nazareth was put to death; but we would have considerably narrowed the field of enquiry and have gone some way towards disentangling the knotted threads of the rendering of Jesus' trial given in the Gospels. The question of the Sanhedrin's juridical authority is therefore of importance since the answer to that question will necessarily reflect on the historical reliability of the scriptural Passion Narratives. It may not solve all the problems which those narratives place before the historian, but it will be of assistance in an attempt to arrive at a more valid assessment of the relevant issues if and when we come to some assurance with respect to the Sanhedrin's competence.

Two papers by T. A. Burkill deal with the questions of the juridical competence of the Jewish Judiciary to inflict capital punishment upon persons tried for religious offences, and of the legal proceedings against Jesus, respectively[14]. In these, the author arrives at the conclusion that

---

[13] *Legis Corneliae de sicariis et veneficis [poena adficitur:] ... qui auctor seditionis fuerit,* Digesta XLVIII viii 3 (4).

*Auctores seditionis et tumultus vel concitatores populi, pro qualitate dignitatis, aut in crucem tolluntur aut bestiis obiiciuntur aut in insulam deportantur,* Sententiae Pauli, liber V, titulus xxii (De seditiosis), 1.

*Auctores seditionis et tumultus populo concitato pro qualitate dignitatis aut in furcam tolluntur aut bestiis obiiciuntur aut in insulam deportantur.* Digesta XLVIII xix 38, 2.

[14] Burkill, »The Competence of the Sanhedrin«, *Vigilae Christianae,* vol. 10, 1956, pp. 80—96, and »The Trial of Jesus«, *Vigiliae Christianae,* vol. 12, 1958, pp. 1—18. See also the same writer's monograph *Mysterious Revelation* (Ithaca, New York, 1963), pp. 280—318, and his articles »Sanhedrin«, *The Interpreter's Dictionary of the Bible* (ed. G. A. Buttrick; Nashville, Tennessee, 1962), vol. 4, pp. 214—218, and »The Condemnation of Jesus: A Critique of Sherwin-White's Thesis«, *Novum Testamen-*

the Jewish Law Court had the authority to pass, and carry out, capital sentences, yet that Jesus was not condemned to death by the Sanhedrin. Such is the general thesis that will be sustained in the present work.

*tum*, vol. 12 (1970), pp. 321—342. [*Revisers' addendum:* Winter saw the MS of this latter article before its publication.]

# 1. JEWISH-ROMAN RELATIONS

It is often overlooked that Mark nowhere mentions any restriction of the Sanhedrin's authority to carry out the judgments it had passed. We must be wary of constructing an artificial composite picture from the descriptions of Jesus' trial in the four Gospels. To read into the Marcan account a statement which comes from John rather than making for clarification adds to confusion[1]. There is nothing in Mark to the effect that the supreme council of the Jewish nation lacked the authority to carry out the sentence pronounced in Mc 14, 64 b. If the Second Evangelist had possessed such information as is provided in Jn 18, 31 b, he would have passed it on to his readers so as to motivate his story and explain why Jesus, already sentenced to death, was arraigned for further trial before the governor. He would have clarified why Jesus, if sentenced ὑπὲρ τῆς βλασφημίας, was actually executed on the basis of a different charge. As it stands, the Marcan account is wanting in coherence; it remains unexplained why the prisoner was handed over to Pilate if sentence had already been passed. We must credit the Second Evangelist with enough perspicacity to have noticed this lack of cohesion. As he does not mention any legal impediment attaching to the Sanhedrin's authority, we have to presume that he knew of no such impediment.

We possess no records on which to base a continuous representation of the development of Jewish Law. Doubtless the regulations varied from period to period. In ancient times there appears to have been a certain recognition that executive and judicial power should not be combined in the same office — as we may deduce from the proceedings initiated against Naboth[2] by the king and his wife. The Judiciary, at the time from which the story comes, was not in the hands of the poli-

---

[1] The trial of Jesus in Mark and that in John are two quite different matters. The Jesus in Mark is not the same as the Jesus in John — they speak differently, act differently, die differently. The Jesus in Mark is arrested on the 15th Nisan, sentenced to death at night, is bound after trial, sentenced a second time, is raised to the cross at 9 a. m., and dies at 3 p. m. The Jesus of John is arrested on the 14th Nisan, put into fetters immediately, sentenced at about midday, led to his execution in the afternoon, and dies towards evening. The Jesus of Mark has his cross carried by Simon of Cyrene; the Jesus in John bears it himself. The one cries out from the cross »Why hast thou forsaken me?«; the other converses with bystanders and dies contented in the knowledge that »it has been accomplished«. The Marcan Passion Narrative scarcely admits of being 'supplemented' with items derived from John.

[2] 1 Kings 21, 8—13.

tical ruler, but was entrusted to »the elders and nobles« of each locality in Israel. According to Jer 26, 10—24, Jeremiah was brought before the princes and the people for prophesying against the Temple and the city of Jerusalem. Not infrequently, however, the kings exercised judicial authority.

To ascertain exactly what conditions obtained in Judaea when the country was ruled by Roman procurators is a task beset with difficulty. Before the year 70 CE Judaea (or Palestine) was not completely integrated into the Roman Empire. Foreign and military affairs were in the hands of the representative of the sovereign power; the maintenance of public order was partly a Roman, partly a Jewish responsibility; most other matters of a purely internal character remained in the hands of the local Jewish authorities. This distribution of power was not explicitly laid down in any written constitution or contractual agreement between the two nations, and the way in which the general convention was observed was subject to variation in detail according to the policy of the goverenor in office. Progressively, as the Roman hold in the country became stronger, the procurators were all the more liable to arrogate to themselves rights which the native Jewish authorities considered properly to belong to their own domain. This development ultimately led to the rising against Rome in the year 66 CE. Generally speaking, however, the Romans who were masters in the art of indirect rule were content to allow the established local authorities, headed by the Supreme Sanhedrin, to function without interference in matters with no bearing on Roman interests. There is evidence from the period between the years 6 and 66 CE of individual judicial cases of prosecution for capital offences — by Roman as well as Jewish tribunals — but we lack a précis outlining in systematic form the ordinances then in force and especially setting forth the criteria decisive for the distribution of power between the Roman and the Jewish judiciary. To arrive at safe premises for determining the criteria in question, we must take note of the situation as it existed before the time when the Romans became political masters in Judaea and the conditions under which the country was placed during their rule.

The Roman Empire, at the beginning of our era, was an association of city states, each with its own indigenous judicial institutions. Judaea was no exception. The Jews enjoyed autonomy in legal affairs, save in the case of political offences. Uninterested in the religious concerns of the subject and associate populations, the Romans fastidiously refrained from interfering in the area of jurisdiction relative to matters of Jewish religious law. It was, in fact, an undertaking on the part of Rome that the ancestral Jewish law should continue to be applied and should be protected by the imperial representative[3].

---

[3] The history of their relations with Rome led the Jews to believe that their own national institutions would enjoy a greater measure of autonomy under Roman

The problem is one of interpreting the stipulation concerning the applicability, under Roman rule, of Jewish »ancestral laws«. In our search for a solution, we have to consider conditions as they obtained in the Second Jewish Commonwealth, prior to and during the reigns of Hasmonaean and Herodian rulers. The Sanhedrin — an institution which wielded judicial and other powers — is of greater antiquity than the royal prerogative in the period of the Second Temple. The Sanhedrin antedated the monarchy; it continued to exist beside it and it outlasted the kings or ethnarchs. In a letter of Antiochus III, the Great, the Jewish representative assembly, composed of priests and other persons of rank, is denoted by the name γερουσία[4] — the people's senate. When the Hasmonaeans assumed the political government, the Sanhedrin was not abolished; decrees issued by the high-priests and the kings were co-signed by the Senate[5]. Even Jewish coins from this period mention the Senate. In late Hasmonaean times, particularly under Alexander Jannaeus, friction arose between the King and the Sanhedrin who complained about the king's frequent infringement of its rights. When the Romans first appeared on the scene and the contending Hasmonaean brothers Hyrcanus II and Aristobulus II made Pompey an arbiter in their dispute, the latter held consultations not only with these pretenders to royal dignity, but also with a deputation from the Jewish Senate. "The nation was against them both" and accused the two claimants to the throne of seeking to change the constitution, thereby enslaving the people[6]. This presupposes the existence of the Sanhedrin as an institution independent in some degree of the priestly-royal house and endowed with sufficient power to make itself heard by the triumvir. The Jews — we have to understand, the spokesmen of the Sanhedrin — requested Pompey to abolish the monarchy, depose the Hasmonaean dynasty, and restore the Sanhedrin's rule. Pompey did not entirely accede to this request, but he limited the authority of the Hasmonaean ruler whilst leaving the powers of the Sanhedrin untouched[7]. These

---

political protection than under Herod the Great and his sons. After ten years of Archelaus' rule, his own brother, in league with the principal leaders of the Jews in Jerusalem, accused him in Rome. The Jewish deputation requested that Archelaus should be deposed. Herod Antipas hoped that he would be made ethnarch in his brother's place, but he was to be disappointed. The territory over which Archelaus had ruled was now reduced to a province, and was put under the political administration of a Roman prefect (B. J. II 117, Ant XVIII 2).

[4] Ant XII 142; for the whole letter see Ant XII 138—144.

[5] The decree quoted in 1 Macc 14, 27 b—45 (—47) seems to have been passed by the assembled people, not just by members of the γερουσία who were somewhat decimated at the time.

[6] Ant XIV 41.

[7] »The nation ... asked not to be ruled by a king, maintaining that it was their country's custom to obey the priests«, Ant XIV 41; cf. Ant XX 244.

powers were evidently not inconsiderable as may be gauged from the fact that the Romans, a little later, thought it advisable to carry out a measure of decentralisation[8].

From the time of Julius Caesar we possess data that enable us to form a positive assessment concerning the continuance of the Sanhedrin's functioning and authority. Caesar upheld the Sanhedrin's rights when he confirmed Hyrcanus II as ethnarch and high-priest. He stipulated that the ethnarch should exercise such powers and enjoy such privileges as were compatible with the country's legal system[9]. Later, when Mark Antony and the Roman Senate conferred the royal title upon Herod[10], the Sanhedrin in principle suffered no diminution of its constitutional privileges, although Herod, as a matter of fact, on more than one occasion treated it with indifference or liquidated such of its members as were opposed to his government. Herod the Great appropriated the right of adjudicating legal cases of a political character. He did not interfere with the Sanhedrin's authority in matters of religious law. Throughout the period of Herodian rule the Sanhedrin still exercised certain powers, including that of jurisdiction, and was in a position to send deputations to Rome and express wishes contrary to those of the royal dignitary or of the claimant to royal power. So in the year 4 BCE, when Herod the Great died, the Sanhedrin despatched its envoys to Rome to inform the Romans that the Jewish leaders preferred autonomy under Roman rule to being governed by any of Herod's sons[11]: »they were desirous of gaining their liberty and to be put under

---

[8] B. J. I 169, 170; Ant XIV 91.

[9] κατὰ τοὺς ἰδίους αὐτῶν νόμους, Ant XIV 195; cf. B. J. I 199.

[10] B. J. I 284, Ant XIV 385; cf. Ant XX 247.

[11] B. J. II 22, Ant XVII 227, 304—317.

»Gerade um den freieren Gebrauch ihrer Gesetze zu haben, begehrten die Juden nach dem Tode des Herodes..., daß ihr Land zur Provinz Syrien geschlagen und ihnen eigene Römische Procuratoren gegeben würden. Sie hofften bezüglich ihrer Gesetze und Magistrate selbständiger zu werden, als sie unter Herodes gewesen waren [Ant XVII 227, 342]. Wäre [, als Judaea römische Provinz wurde,] diese Hoffnung der Juden vereitelt und die Autonomie ihnen genommen worden, so würde dies Josephus wohl erwähnt haben. Aber... [er läßt] den Hohenpriester Ananus und den Titus selbst es aussprechen, daß die Römer die Gesetze der Juden bestätigt, die freie Handhabung derselben ihnen gewährt hätten [B. J. VI 333]. Selbst nach Ausbruch des Krieges bot Titus den Juden noch die Autonomie an, wenn sie sich unterwerfen wollten, die ihnen also sicher vorher nicht entzogen worden war«, Ignaz Döllinger, *Christenthum und Kirche in der Zeit der Grundlegung* (Regensburg 1860), pp. 454, 455; (²1868), pp. 457, 458; English edition *The First Age of Christianity and the Church* (London 1866), Second Book, pp. 305, 306. Cf. below, Chapter 2, note 6.

»Auguste n'amoindrit sûrement pas les pouvoirs des autorités juives. L'on peut même supposer que dans la nouvelle constitution [de l'an 6 après Jésus-Christ] ces pouvoirs furent plutôt étendus que restreints«, Jean Juster, *Les Juifs dans l'Empire romain. Leur condition juridique, économique et sociale*, tome 2 (Paris 1914), p. 132.

a Roman governor«. This presupposes that they hoped a representative of the Empire would show more consideration for their traditional rights than Herod had done. There was a recurrence of this situation ten years later, in the year 6 CE, when the Jews sent deputies to Octavius Augustus and denounced Archelaus' misrule[12], this time with the effect that Archelaus was deposed and Judaea put under a prefect[13]. We have a report from Josephus that even during the last stage of the siege of Jerusalem, in the year 70 CE, Titus, appalled by the ravages of war, protested that he had offered to restore Jewish self-rule (αὐτονομία) if the rebels laid down their arms[14]. Such a declaration presupposes that the Jews in Palestine — prior to the outbreak of the revolt — a c t u a l - l y   d i d   e n j o y   t h e   r i g h t s   o f   s e l f - d e t e r m i n a t i o n  in affairs of an internal character.

Here we may pause to sum up the results of our survey. The Sanhedrin, disgruntled by encroachments upon its rights under Alexander Jannaeus, fared no better under Herodian rule. The hope that the authority of the Sanhedrin in its various echelons as the sole judicial institution in Jewish lands would be restored was disappointed. In numerous instances Herod the Great circumvented the jurisdiction of the Sanhedrin and took it upon himself to try such persons as he suspected of disloyalty[15]. When Archelaus was deposed, the Roman governor stepped into the place of the ethnarch. Judicial conditions were not restored to their pre-Herodian state; the changes which had been instituted could not entirely be set aside. Political offences were dealt with as belonging to the prefect's domain, while the Sanhedrin's right to deal with other juridical matters was not assailed. As they had previously been adjudicated by Herod and his son, legal matters of a political nature were now referred to the governor; yet the Sanhedrin continued to exercise authority *inter alia* as a court in matters of a non-political character. The Romans were not interested in internal Jewish jurisdiction. When, reluctantly enough, they sent a governor to Judaea, they

---

»... the Romans restored to the Sandhedrin [its power] in greater measure than [it had under] the Herodians«, Josef Pickl, *Messiaskönig Jesus in der Auffassung seiner Zeitgenossen* (München ²1935); English edition *The Messias,* translated by Andrew Green (St. Louis, Mo., and London 1946), p. 9; »after the overthrow of Archelaus the Romans restored its influence to the Sanhedrin« (*ibidem,* p. 30).

[12] B. J. II 111, Ant XVII 342; *cf.* B. J. I 670.

[13] See above, note 12.

[14] B. J. VI 215.

[15] Resentment of this situation finds expression in the speech, composed by Josephus and attributed to members of the Sanhedrin who were offended by Herod the Great's dispensation of justice (Ant XIV 167) and in Mishnah Sanhedrin ii 2: »The king may neither judge nor be judged«. There are, however, records in which the judicial authority of the Sanhedrin over the king is asserted, *e. g.* the report in T. B. Sanh 19 a of Shimeon ben Shetaḥ's reproof administered to Alexander Jannaeus.

did so solely for the purpose of pacifying the territory and safeguarding the land-route from Syria to Egypt. They were anxious to prevent a situation in which discontented Jewish factions might seek the support of powers outside the Empire, as had happened during the struggle between Hyrcanus II and Aristobulus II when the Parthians were called in. Herod the Great had secured the safety of the lines of communication for the Romans during his reign in Judaea. When Herod's successor failed to keep the country pacified, and popular discontent threatened to result in a disruption of the political order, a governor was sent to Judaea. His powers were not point by point defined in relation to those of the local authorities, but he was expected to respect Jewish customs and to refrain from any interference with matters of religious law. »Under the procurators, the Jews had larger room to manage their own affairs in their own way than under Herod. The Roman administration had need of a representative and responsible intermediary between it and the people, and found such an organ in the Council, or Sanhedrin . . . Cases between Jew and Jew were left to the adjudication of their own tribunals, from the village judges up to the high court in Jerusalem«[16]. »It was the general policy of Rome to leave local matters . . . to be settled in native courts by native law . . . Religious issues would certainly be . . . referred to the Sanhedrin . . . The Romans . . . allowed the native court considerable latitude, including civil and criminal competence as well as merely religious. The limitation on Jewish authority in cases affecting non-Jews, especially Roman citizens, would doubtless be found in matters involving capital punishment, and in what we may class as offences against the Roman State or Emperor«[17].

In the Acts of the Apostles we read of legal cases dealt with by the Sanhedrin, and they all concern religious offences. When Paul is accused in Corinth and the proconsul decides that it is a religious matter[18], he refuses to try the case; yet when the Apostle is accused of a political offence in Philippi[19], the praetor takes action. Roman officials were generally anxious to respect the autonomy of *peregrini* in the provinces. In Palestine Greeks as well as Jews had jurisdiction in non-political matters over their respective citizens, and the Romans were as a rule careful not to encroach upon these prerogatives[20]. Josephus

---

[16] George Foot Moore, *Judaism in the First Centuries of the Christian Era*, vol. 1 (Cambridge, Mass., 1927), p. 82.

[17] Henry Joel Cadbury, »Roman Law and the Trial of Paul« in *The Beginnings of Christianity*, vol. 5 (London 1933), pp. 297—338, on pp. 301, 302. Cf. Jean Juster, o. c., pp. 110—112, 132—142; also, M. S. Enslin, *The Prophet from Nazareth* (New York 1961), p. 175.

[18] Acts 18, 12—17.

[19] Acts 16, 20, 38.

[20] Note the polite tone in Petronius's letter to the Municipal Council of Doris and his reluctance to interfere (Ant. XIX 308—311).

on the whole looks unfavourably on the activities of Roman procurators in Palestine, but he never suggests that any of them assumed jurisdiction over Jews in a case of religious significance; the cases he records of Jews having been put to death at the order of a procurator invariably involve political, never religious, offenders[21].

Apart from offences of a political character Roman jurisdiction in Palestine in the first seven decades of our era was confined to persons who enjoyed the privilege of Roman citizenship. The provincial population, including most of the Jews, were subject to their own legal institutions. Although recognizing this to be so, many scholars make an exception insofar as the infliction of the extreme penalty, the administration of a death sentence, is concerned. They maintain that the right to inflict capital punishment was reserved to the governor. This they deduce from the statement in B. J. II 117 where Josephus reports that Coponius, on his despatch to Judaea, was entrusted with full powers by Augustus, and from Jn 19, 10. But the deduction is unsound. When Josephus says that the governor was empowered by the emperor to the extent of inflicting capital punishment — μέχρι τοῦ κτείνειν λαβὼν παρὰ καίσαρος ἐξουσίαν — he refers to the political and executive authority which Augustus, in his capacity as the Head of the Roman State, had delegated to Coponius. Josephus does not thereby imply a limitation of the Sanhedrin's former powers, nor does he report anywhere else that the Sanhedrin's right to try Jews for capital offences and carry out such sentences as it had passed was in any way curtailed by Augustus or his successors. There is abundant evidence that even in the period *after* the death of Jesus the supreme council of the Jewish nation exercised the function of a judicial tribunal in trying Jews on charges which involved capital punishment[22] and inflicting the death penalty[23].

---

[21] E. g. the λῃσταί whom Festus and Albinus ordered to be put to death; the examples are numerous. »... tous les cas connus de juridiction procuratorienne en Palestine sont relatifs aux séditieux et aux brigands«, Jean Juster, Les Juifs dans l'Empire romain. Leur condition juridique, économique et sociale, tome 2 (Paris 1914), p. 147.

[22] The fact that executions were carried out may be deduced from the rule »The property of those executed by the State falls to the king; the property of those executed by the Law Court belongs to their heirs« (Mishnah Sanh ii 3, T. B. Sanh 48 b).

Philo — quoting a letter of Agrippa I — records that even a high-priest who entered the Holy of Holies, unless he did so in the exercise of his sacerdotal duty, was liable to the death penalty (Legatio ad Gaium 307).

A Roman citizen who transgressed Jewish Law by entering the inner area of the Temple was put to death in accordance with that law (Philo, Leg. ad Gaium 212; Josephus, B. J. V 194, VI 125, 126, Ant. XV 417; cf. Acts 21, 28 b, 29; Mishnah Kelim i 8). Illustrative of the consideration shown, as a rule, for the Jewish law by responsible Roman officials is Josephus's report in B. J. II 341. (Some sort of restriction for non-Jews, to enter the enclosure on the Temple Mount, was already in force in the

It has every appearance of special pleading if all these instances are either represented as irregularities, tacitly tolerated by an indulgent Roman government, or are dated in the short interval of the reign of

time of the Seleucid king Antiochus III the Great, as appears from Ant XII 145). A slab of limestone bearing an inscription which supports Josephus's report was discovered by Clermont-Ganneau in 1871 in Jerusalem. The inscription reads: Μηθένα ἀλλογενῆ εἰσπορεύεσθαι ἐντὸς τοῦ περὶ τὸ ἱερὸν τρυφάκτου καὶ περιβόλου· ὅς δ'ἂν λήφθῃ ἑαυτῷ αἴτιος ἔσται διὰ τὸ ἐξακολουθεῖν θάνατον (see Charles Clermont-Ganneau, »Une stèle du Temple de Jérusalem«, Revue archéologique ou Recueil de documents et de mémoires relatifs à l'étude des monuments, à la numismatique et la philologie de l'Antiquité et du Moyen Age, nouvelle série, 13e année, 23e tome; Paris 1872, pp. 214—234, 290—296). The stone with the inscription is now in the Činili Kiöšk Museum in Istanbul. (According to the Greek text of B. J. V 194 the inscription was in Greek or Latin; according to the Slavonic Josephus it was trilingual). It is unbelievable that Jewish magistrates had less authority in respect of Jewish offenders than in respect of Romans. A report on Rabban Yoḥanan ben Zakkai's procedure of testing the trustworthiness of witnesses in capital cases implies that there were occasions when this procedure was followed (Mishnah Sanh v 2; T. B. Sanh 9 b, 41 a).

[Revisers' addendum: Of course Winter rejected the view that the ordinance on the Clermont-Ganneau inscription permitted lynching (see, for example, A. N. Sherwin-White, Roman Society and Roman Law in the New Testament, Oxford 1963, p. 38, note 2 and p. 43, note 1), and also the view that it was not forensic but imprecatory after a manner well known in ancient times, warning visitors to holy places of the danger of incurring divine wrath should they, unpurified and uninitiated, profane the sacred precincts by passing beyond prescribed limits (see, for example, F. C. Grant, The Journal of Religion, Chicago, vol. 44, 1964, pp. 234—235). See Winter's statement in Commentary, New York, March 1965, pp. 20—28; cf. Burkill, Novum Testamentum vol. 12, 1970, p. 338, note 2.]

[23] Incontestable evidence has survived of three actual trials:

    a) the trial and execution by stoning of Stephen (Acts 6, 12; 7, 58);

    b) the execution by burning of a priest's daughter — reportedly of the name Imarta bath Tali — convicted of adultery (Mishnah Sanh vii 2; Tosefta Sanh ix 11; T. Y. Sanh vii 224 b; T. B. Sanh 41 a); from the wording in the Babylonian Talmund (Sand 52 b) it would appear that Eleazar ben Ṣadoq recollected two instances in which the death penalty had been carried out by burning, but this may be due to a misapprehension on the part of the late rabbinical recorder;

    c) the trial and execution by stoning of James (Ant XX 200).

A further case, though the evidence is disputable, is that of the trial and execution by stoning of Ben Stada, or Sotada (Tosefta Sanh x 11; cf. T. Y. Sanh vii 16, 25 d, T. Y. Yeb XV 6, 15 d, T. B. Sanh 67 a). Of interest are the differences, concerning points of law, between the report from the Tosefta and the rules of the Mishnah relating to the infliction of capital punishment: sentence of death was pronounced on the same day on which the trial took place; a majority vote of one was considered sufficient to arrive at a verdict of guilt; judges who had voted for acquittal were in cases like that of Ben Stada considered justified in retracting their vote to the detriment of the accused.

Agrippa I between the governorship of Marullus and that of Cuspius
Fadus.

Owing to the character of our sources, it is advisable to examine
separately certain issues that have a bearing on the gospel accounts
concerning Jesus' trial, before attempting to reconstruct in outline the
actual course of events.

## 2. THE HIGH-PRIEST'S INSIGNIA OF OFFICE

There is an item in the complex interrelationship between Roman and Jewish administration in Judaea during the period in which the trial and execution of Jesus took place, that may be of little significance in itself, and yet it is illustrative of the divison of powers which resulted from Roman indirect rule and the nominal continuance of Jewish national institutions. From the arrival of Coponius to the departure of Pontius Pilate, Roman governors had the custody of the high-priest's official vestments[1]. The practice was not instituted by the Romans, but had been carried over by them from Herodian times, Herod the Great and his son Archelaus having had good reason to be suspicious lest a high-priest, the Anointed of the Lord, should show signs of an independent spirit. The costly stole and other insignia[2] of the hierarch were kept in a stone-chamber in the Antonia under a triple seal, affixed jointly by priests, Temple officials, and the Roman military commander. From there they were removed and handed over to the high-priest before any occasion on which he was required to wear the formal dress and other insignia of his office; after each such occasion they were returned to Roman custody. Josephus mentions that this procedure was observed before and after the annual three high festivals, Passover, Pentecost and the Feast of Booths — and the Day of Atonement[3]. There is no reference to other occasions in his writings. Under Roman suzerainty the practice lasted in fact only for about thirty years, from 6 to 36 CE. Vitellius, anxious to regain Jewish confidence in the Roman political administration of the country, requested and obtained the Emperor's consent to restore the high-priest's vestments to Jewish custody[4].

Keeping the stole and other apparels of the highest Jewish dignitary under military custody, and handing them over to him only on certain

---

[1] Ant XV 408, XVIII 93; cf. Ant XX 6, 7.

[2] In Ant XV 403 Josephus speaks only of the stole worn by the high-priest when he offered sacrifices; in Ant XVIII 90, however, Josephus explicitly refers to other appurtenances of his apparel: ἡ στολὴ τοῦ ἀρχιερέως καὶ πᾶς ὁ αὐτοῦ κόσμος, leaving thus no doubt as to the fact that all insignia had to be deposited for safekeeping by the Roman authorities; in Ant XX 6 Josephus mentions the χιτών of ankle-length and the sacred stole. A description of the various appurtenances of the high-priest's apparel is given in Ant III 151—178.

[3] Ant XVIII 94.

[4] Ant XV 405, XVIII 90, 95.

pre-arranged occasions, was a precautionary measure designed to retain
control of the hierarch's actions and to guard against any surprise move
he might make in his official capacity. Small as the matter was in itself
— though, no doubt, rankling to the high-priest's pride — it made sure
that the Jewish high-priest who as such presided over the nation's
senate, the Great Sanhedrin[5], would not exercise his authority without
being strongly reminded of Rome's military presence.

What precise purpose was served by a precautionary measure of
this sort? It cannot have been intended to impede the Jewish priesthood
in their sacerdotal ministrations in the Temple. Never at any time before the year 70 CE was it Roman policy to put obstacles in the way
of Jewish worship and prevent the high-priest from fulfilling his cultic
obligations. On the contrary, the Julian and Claudian emperors sought
to facilitate the observance of Jewish religious customs as best they
could. The Emperor himself set an example by sending his gifts to the
sanctuary in Jerusalem. Hence the custody of the high-priest's insignia
could not have been meant to prevent him from exercising purely religious functions or from attending to his ceremonial duties in the
Temple. The reasons must lie elsewhere.

We cannot say, on the basis of information at our disposal, on what
occasions other than the performance of sacerdotal duties Jewish high-
priests were required to wear the insignia of their office. It is probable
that they did so on occasions of State such as a visit from some foreign
prince or Roman legate, and also when presiding over the Senate of

---

[5] Many Jewish scholars deny that there was any connection between the high-priest
and the Jewish Law Court, and maintain that we have to differentiate between the latter, the בית דין which exercised jurisdiction in religious matters, and the συνέδριον or
γερουσία which dealt with political affairs only. (See Adolf Büchler, *Das Synedrion
in Jerusalem und das große Beth-Din in der Quaderkammer des jerusalemischen
Temples*, IX. *Jahresbericht der israelitisch-theologischen Lehranstalt in Wien*,
Vienna 1902. Büchler is followed by Solomon Zeitlin and Sidney Benjamin Hoenig,
and more recently by Hugo Mantel, *Studies in the History of the Sanhedrin*, Cambridge, Mass. 1961, pp. 92—101). Although the evidence is problematical, on the
whole the picture in the New Testament and Josephus appears closer than later
rabbinical records to the realities of the first century. Even the Mishnah contains
evidence to this effect. It records, for instance, that the Sanhedrin was competent to
declare war and to set up subordinate sanhedrins "for the several tribes" (Mishnah
Sanh i 5). The body that had such authority could not have been an institution that
was exclusively concerned with ensuring compliance with religious legislation, but
the Supreme Council of the nation, and was as such presided over by the high-
priest, who in pre-Herodian times had been the Head of State.

[*Revisers' addendum:* Y. Ephron has recently argued that the Central Sanhedrin
described in the Palestinian Talmudic sources was an ideal institution, and not a
fully realised one. See *Benzion Katz Jubilee Volume*, Tel Aviv 1967, pp. 167—204;
*World Congress of Jewish Studies 4 (1965) Papers*, vol. 1, Jerusalem 1967, pp. 89—93.
For an English summary, see *Immanuel* No. 2, 1973, pp. 44—49.]

the Jews, the Sanhedrin of 71 members. There is no doubt whatever that the Sanhedrin enjoyed under procuratorial administration autonomous rights over a wide range of internal affairs, which certainly included jurisdiction in accordance with the religious law of the land[6].

---

[6] It is now more than a hundred years ago that Johann Joseph Ignaz von Döllinger recognized from his examination of the New Testament and of the writings of Josephus that Jewish law courts possessed in New Testament times the competence to pass and carry out sentences of death for religious offences. After having in his book *Heidentum und Judenthum* (Regensburg 1857) on pp. 767 and 780 expressed the oft-repeated opposite opinion, Döllinger came to realize in 1860 that there is strong evidence for the right of Jewish courts to execute capital sentences: »[Zieht man in Betracht,] daß selbst Nicht-Juden, wénn sie ... in den inneren Tempelhof eindrangen, den Tod erlitten, und zwar durch die jüdische Behörde, so wird es umso unglaublicher, daß ihnen die Befugniß, ihren Gesetzen gemäß über ihre eigenen Volksgenossen zu richten, entzogen worden sein sollte. Die Römischen Statthalter hatten die Macht, in allen Fällen, welche als Aufruhr, Hochverrath und Störung der öffentlichen Ordnung zu betrachten waren, zu richten und zu strafen, aber in religiösen Dingen und in den durch das Mosaische Gesetz vorgesehenen Fällen blieb das Recht der Jüdischen Behörden, über Leben und Tod zu entscheiden, und das Urtheil vollstrecken zu lassen, ungeschmälert«, Ignaz Döllinger, *Christenthum und Kirche in der Zeit der Grundlegung* (Regensburg [1]1860), pp. 455, 456; ([2]1868), pp. 458, 459; English edition *The First Age of Christianity and the Church* (London 1866), Second Book, p. 307.

It was due to the influence of Emil Schürer that scholars lost sight of the important fact concerning the Sanhedrin's competence. By a critical analysis of the New Testament reports, Alfred Loisy — from *Les évangelies synoptiques* (Paris 1907/08) to *Les Actes des Apôtres* (Paris 1920) — perceived the reality of the Sanhedrin's autonomy. But it remained for Jean Juster in his book *Les Juifs dans l'Empire romain* (Paris 1914) to assemble the pertinent evidence demonstrating anew that the Sanhedrin actually exercised rights in this connection. In 1931, Hans Lietzmann took up Juster's position, and the validity of Döllinger's argument has since regained recognition.

»Auch in der Zeit der ... Römer ward der Rest von Autonomie, welcher der Nation verblieben war, durch das Synedrium ausgeübt«, Julius Wellhausen, *Die Pharisäer und die Sadducäer. Eine Untersuchung zur inneren jüdischen Geschichte* (Greifswald 1874), p. 28. »En matière capitale, le compétence semble, d'après la loi juive, avoir appartenu exclusivement aux Sanhédrins juifs locaux ou au Grand-Sanhédrin«, Jean Juster, o. c., tome 2, pp. 127, 128. »Le Sanhédrin jugeait ... les affaires religieuses. Il pouvait appliquer toutes les peines prescrites par les lois juives, inclusivement les différentes sortes de peines capitales, et les faire exécuter lui-même«, Jean Juster, o. c., tome 2, p. 133; cf. pp. 139—142. »Le sanhédrin, sous la domination romaine, conservait l'intégrité de sa juridiction religieuse sur le sol palestinien, et il pouvait rendre des sentences de mort; il va sans dire que cette juridiction juive n'atteignait que les Juifs, non les étrangers, sauf le cas ... de l'étranger qui aurait pénétré dans l'enceinte sacrée du temple, et que l'autorité juive avait faculté de mettre à mort, fût-il citoyen romain. Les évangiles synoptiques ne nient pas ce droit: la tradition paraît s'être trouvée en présence de ce fait embarrassant, la condamnation de Jésus par Pilate pour cause de sédition, et en avoir atténué

Because of the Sanhedrin's important position it was reasonable from the Roman point of view to protect themselves against the possibility that the Sanhedrin's powers would be used in a manner contrary to Roman interests. The custody of the high-priest's insignia — if the high-priest were required to wear some of these in his capacity as the president of the senatorial assembly — would ensure that the governor would have ample notice in advance when the Sanhedrin was going to meet. We have no definite evidence that Jewish high-priests were required by custom to wear their official insignia when they presided over the Great Council, but it is arguable that on solemn occasions they would do so, especially in a law case considered to be of such importance that the decision was referred to the supreme judicial institution of the nation.

By holding the high-priestly insignia under seal, the governor would then be in a position to keep check on the Sanhedrin's official meetings and perhaps make sure as far as possible that the Council would discuss only such agenda of which he had prior knowledge. The supposition that the high-priest had to wear his insignia on other occasions also than those incumbent on him in his sacerdotal capacity is to some degree supported by the report that, at a time when the country was in upheaval the procurator, Cuspius Fadus, demanded the return of these insignia to Roman custody[7]. Perhaps another report from the same source, concerning the complaint by Jewish citizens of the high-handedness of Ananus II, helps to clarify the situation. This complaint, though rooted in disapproval of the execution of Jesus' brother James[8], was formally directed not against the execution as such, but against the fact that Ananus had convoked the Council without due authorization: ὡς οὐκ ἐξὸν ἦν Ἀνάνῳ χωρὶς τῆς [τοῦ ἐπάρχου] γνώμης καθίσαι συνέδριον[9]. The illegality of Ananus's action lay not in the fact that he had

---

la portée dans une intention apologétique, en imaginant que la sentence de mort avait été rendue en réalité par le sanhédrin, qu'on l'avait seulement notifiée à Pilate et que celui-ci, ayant vainement cherché à sauver Jésus par moyen de grâce, s'était vu contraint de l'exécuter...«, Loisy, *Les Actes des Apôtres* (Paris 1920), p. 876. »Le sanhédrin conservait une juridiction complète en matière rerligieuse sur les Juifs de Palestine et sa compétence n'était limitée qu'en matière politique... C'est seulement après la ruine de Jérusalem que l'autorité rereligieuse du judaïsme a perdu, avec son conseil national, le droit de condamner à mort pour délit de religion«, Loisy, *ibidem*, pp. 309, 310.

[7] Ant XX 6, 7.

[8] Ant XX 200—203.

[9] Whilst not attaching undue force to purely speculative arguments, we may consider the possibility that Ananus II had filled vacancies on the Sanhedrin without awaiting the procurators's *placet*. The Romans did not abolish the Council's authority in internal Jewish affairs, yet they were anxious to have control of its activities. The custody of the official vestments of the president would have been a convenient way of preventing the Jewish Senate from meeting without the consent and appro-

James executed, but in the circumstance that he convened the Council without authorization from either his Roman or his Herodian political superiors[10].

Admittedly, one can scarcely interpret the words οὐκ ἐξὸν ἦν... καθίσαι συνέδριον with confident assurance. They cannot mean that the high-priest had to obtain the procurator's permission before the members of the Great Sanhedrin could be called together on any particular occasion. The most probable explanation of the words used by Josephus is that on the arrival of a new procurator the high-priest, in his capacity as Head of the Local Administration, was obliged to renew Roman authorization for the functioning of the Jewish senatorial assembly. Permission might have been valid only for the duration of the procurator's term of office. If given, it would cover the whole period during which the procurator was in power. From the Roman point of view, it would have been reasonable to insist that the high-priest should request any newly-appointed procurator to confirm the Council's rights and privileges. Such a request would imply a recognition of the procurator as the Emperor's representative. The Romans particularly would have looked askance at convocations of the Great Sanhedrin during an interregnum, when no procurator was present in Judaea, for decisions taken at such times might easily have proved contrary to their interests.

The illegality of the act of Ananus II did not lie in the fact that he ordered James to be executed. Had this been the accusation, the Romans would certainly not have been satisfied with merely noting that the high-priest had been deposed from his office by Agrippa, the king of Chalcis, but they would have charged Ananus — and all members of the Council who had taken part in the proceedings against James — with murder. As no proceedings whatever were taken against any member of the Sanhedrin except the high-priest who had summoned the court to its session, and as Ananus II was merely removed from office without the preference of any charge of murder against him and his associates, the Romans clearly did not consider the execution of James illegal, but they objected

---

val of the representative of the Imperial Government. Although not prevented from exercising its judicial and other functions in accordance with national custom, the Sanhedrin was nevertheless carefully watched by the procurators.

[10] In Ant XX 216—218 we read that king Agrippa II convened the Sanhedrin for the purpose of passing a new ordinance. It would appear that after the year 36 CE supervision over the activities of the Sanhedrin passed to a certain extent to the last members of Antipater's House. Agrippa II did not assemble the Sanhedrin for a juridical matter. But Josephus, in reporting the case, again asserts that obedience to law was strictly enforced by the Sanhedrin; persons found to have transgressed the Law were liable to punishment.

to an unauthorized convocation of the Great Sanhedrin during the absence of the Emperor's representative. Even so, they remained remarkably passive during the affair, leaving it to an allied Jewish king to deal with the situation. Ananus, beyond being removed from his high office, suffered no punishment of any kind.

From the wording of Mc 14, 63 it might appear that the high-priest, at a nocturnal session of the Jewish Senate, was wearing the χιτών which according to Ant XX 6 was kept under lock and seal in Pilate's days of governorship. No positive conclusion can be based on the occurrence of the word χιτῶνες in the Marcan trial account. It is an old Greek word[11], meaning originally the linen undergarment worn by a male person, later also used of linen undergarments for women, and still later of undergarments made from any material[12]. Hence χιτῶνες in Mc 14, 63 is not a *terminus technicus* for the official robes worn by Jewish high-priests on solemn occasions. Noteworthy, however, is the fact that in the passage under review it occurs in the plural and refers thus also to the outer garments for which the word τὰ ἱμάτια[13] might have been used, an expression not unknown to the Second Evangelist, as its occurrence in Mc 5, 30; 10, 50; 15, 24 shows. The employment of the word χιτῶνες in Mc 14, 63 may have been intentional; whoever was responsible for the report may have chosen this expression because of its similarity in sound with כיתונא, transliterated by Josephus as χέθον or χεθομένη[14].

It is well to repeat that our information does not allow us to say with certainty how the high-priest was robed when the Sanhedrin met. We may, however, legitimately assume that he wore on such occasions at least some of the insignia appertaining to his status.

It is a curious circumstance that just at the moment when the governor who had been in office when Jesus was tried and sentenced was recalled from Judaea[15] — and soon after the then officiating high-priest, Yosef Qayyafa, was deposed[16] — the custody of the priestly vestments was restored to Jewish hands. An intriguing coincidence, indeed.

---

[11] Ionic κιθών, Doric κιτών. The word occurs in the Odyssey I 437, XIV 72, XV 60, and variously in Herodotus.

[12] The word may have come into the Greek language by way of Asia Minor, by ›Aegaean‹ on ›Minoan‹ contacts. Cf. J. Huber, *De lingua antiquissimorum Graeciae incolarum (Commentationes Aenipontanae,* tomus IX, Vienna 1921), p. 31.

[13] Cf. Mt 26, 65; the First Evangelist is aware of the arbitrary use of the term in Mc 14, 63; he distinguishes between χιτών and ἱμάτιον (Mt 5, 40).

[14] Ant III 153.

[15] Ant XVIII 89.

[16] Ant XVIII 95.

## 3. THE MEETING-PLACE OF THE SANHEDRIN AND MARK'S NOCTURNAL SESSION

During the life-time of Jesus the Great Sanhedrin conducted its official business in a building especially assigned for that purpose — as would befit the highest legislative, administrative and judicial institution of a fairly populous nation. The members of the Supreme Council assembled in a place, variously named in our sources βουλή, βουλευτήριον, συνέδριον, לשכת הגזית = the Council-Hall, or Council-Chamber. Owing to differences in our sources[1] modern scholars vary considerably in their opinions regarding the location of this meeting-place[2]. It is not necessary to investigate here the topographical question; suffice it to bear in mind that our sources, with the exception of Mark and Matthew, agree that the Sanhedrin held its sessions in a building specifically devoted to that purpose.

The Gospels report that Jesus was led from the place of his arrest to the house of the high-priest (Mc 14, 53 a; Mt 26, 27; Lc 22, 54; Jn 18, 13, 24). Their unanimity on this point is the more noteworthy in view of the fact that they differ in their descriptions of subsequent events.

---

[1] Josephus, B. J. V 144, VI 354; Mishnah Sanh xi 2 Middoth v 4; Tosefta Sanh vii 1; T. Y. Sanh i 4 19 c; T. B. Shabb 15 a, Rosh hashanah 31 a, Sanh 12 a, 41 a, 88 b, Abodah zarah 8 b.

[2] Joseph Derenbourg, *Essai sur l'histoire et la géographie de la Palestine, d'après les Thalmuds et les autres sources rabbiniques* (Paris 1867), pp. 465—468; Emil Schürer, »Der Versammlungsort des großen Synedriums. Ein Beitrag zur Topographie des Herodianischen Tempels«, *Theologische Studien und Kritiken*, vol. 51, 1878, pp. 608—626; the same, *Geschichte des jüdischen Volkes im Zeitalter Jesu Christi*, vol. 2 (Leipzig ⁴1907), pp. 263—265, vol. 1 (Leipzig ³1901), p. 633; Engl. ed. *A History of the Jewish People in the Time of Jesus Christ*, Second Div., vol. 1 (Edinburgh 1885), pp. 190—193, First Div., vol. 2 (Edinburgh 1890), p. 246; Adolf Büchler, *Das Synedrion in Jerusalem und das große Beth-Din in der Quaderkammer des Jerusalemischen Tempels* (Vienna 1902), pp. 5, 6; Gustaf Dalman, *Orte und Wege Jesu* (Gütersloh 1919), pp. 304, 272; the same, *Jerusalem und sein Gelände* (Gütersloh 1930), pp. 193, 194; Hermann L. Strack and Paul Billerbeck, *Kommentar zum Neuen Testament aus Talmud und Midrasch*, Vol. 1: *Das Evangelium nach Matthäus* (Munich 1922), p. 998; Joachim Jeremias, *Jerusalem zur Zeit Jesu*, vol. 2 (Göttingen ³1962), p. 78; Engl. ed. *Jerusalem in the Time of Jesus* (London 1969), p. 214; Sidney Benjamin Hoenig, *The Great Sanhedrin* (Philadelphia 1953), pp. 74—84, 198, 200 to 203; Hugo Mantel, *Studies in the History of the Sanhedrin* (Cambridge, Mass. 1961), pp. 95—96.

According to Mc 14, 53 b (Mt 26, 27) the Jewish Senate met during the night immediately after Jesus' arrest in the high-priest's residence. This conflicts with all the information available concerning the procedural activities of the senatorial assembly. Josephus and the Talmud cover many centuries of Jewish history; they contain the data in respect to public affairs in first-century Palestine against which the Gospel Narratives have to be checked when their historical character is called in question. Nowhere in the writings of Josephus and nowhere in rabbinical literature[3] do we find any reference to the Sanhedrin's ever holding a meeting in the residence of a high-priest. Not only does Mc 14, 53 b conflict with information derivable from the works of Josephus, from the Mishnah, the Tosefta, and the Talmudim, but it also contrasts with certain other evidence supplied by the New Testament. The wording in Lc 22, 66 καὶ ἀπήγαγον [the reading ἀνήγαγον is presupposed in the Old Syriac Version] αὐτὸν εἰς τὸ συνέδριον αὐτῶν = *and they led him away into their council-chamber[4]* implies that the πρεσβυτέριον τοῦ λαοῦ did not assemble in the place where Jesus had been held in custody after his arrest. The session of the Sanhedrin, according to the Third Gospel, was held in the official Council-Hall.

Evidently, Lc 22, 66 does not correspond to Mc 14, 53 b, but to Mc 15, 1 a. In this latter passage we are informed that the Sanhedrin met in the morning — without reference, however, to there having been an earlier noctural meeting (Mc 14, 53 b, 55—64). The statement in Mc 15, 1 a could be understood in the sense that the morning session was held in a different place from that in which the narrative of Mc 14, 53—72 is set, namely, where Lc 22, 66 puts it. But as Mc 15, 1 displays no knowledge whatever of an earlier session, no inference can be drawn as to the Second Evangelist's intention concerning the topographical relation between Mc 15, 1 a and Mc 14, 53 b. The Third Gospel is explicit: the localization of the council-meeting, Lc 22, 66, is different from that of the scenes in Lc 22, 54—65. The Third Evangelist could not have drawn the information that Jesus was led away from the house of the high-priest to be confronted by the πρεσβυτέριον τοῦ

---

[3] »Synedrialsitzungen im Hause des Hohenpriesters werden in der rabbinischen Literatur ... nicht erwähnt«, Billerbeck, o. c., p. 1000.

[4] συνέδριον in Lc 22, 66 signifies the hall, the building — not the Council as such; so with βουλή in Josephus B. J. V 144. As the Third Evangelist uses in Lc 22, 66 for the Council as such the expression τὸ πρεσβυτέριον τοῦ λαοῦ, it is obvious that the words τὸ συνέδριον αὐτῶν refer to the building in which the Council assembled. The same terminology recurs in Acts 6, 12, possibly also in Acts 4, 15; 23, 6, 20, 28. Lagrange, *Évangile selon Saint Luc* (Paris 1921), p. 571, expressed a different opinion, and Loisy, *L'évangile selon Luc* (Paris 1924), p. 540, agreed with him on this point. Yet Lc 22, 66 does not state that Jesus was led *before* the Council, but *into* (εἰς) the συνέδριον.

λαοῦ from Mark — in all likelihood, Lc 22, 66 i s  b a s e d  o n  a
n o n - M a r c a n  r e c o r d⁵.

The assumption that in the words ἀπήγαγον αὐτὸν εἰς τὸ συνέδριον
αὐτῶν (but not λέγοντες κτλ.) there comes to light an old tradition of the
same provenance as that reproduced in Mc 15, 1 — a tradition, however, which must have been transmitted to the author of the Third
Gospel through channels other than Mark — finds confirmation when
we examine the relationship between the accounts of Mc 14, 65 and
Lc 22, 63—65. Here also the same tradition is ultimately discernible
behind both renderings. Yet the Lucan version is free from Marcan
influence. Not only are the setting and timing different, but the vocabulary varies to such a degree as to make it *a priori* improbable that
the Third Evangelist had in this case used the Second Gospel as his
source. According to Luke, Jesus was mocked and maltreated after his
arrest yet before the Sanhedrin's session; the mockers were the jailers.
According to Mark, the mockery takes place after the session of the
Sanhedrin in the hierarch's palace, and it is certain members of the

---

⁵ The extant Passion Narrative of the Third Gospel is of a composite character,
consisting of pre-Marcan, Marcan, post-Marcan elements, of Lucan editorial modifications, and of post-Lucan insertions. Only the words from καὶ ὡς ἐγένετο ἡμέρα
to εἰς τὸ συνέδριον αὐτῶν in Lc 22, 66 can be considered as being derived from an
old, pre-Marcan, record or tradition; on the ensuing passage see my article »Luke
XXII 66 b—71«, *Studia Theologica* vol. 9, Lund 1956, pp. 112—115.

»[Es ist wahrscheinlich] dass [Lukas] einer... älteren Überlieferung n e b e n
Markus einen Einfluss auf seine Darstellung verstattet [hat]«, Johannes Weiss, *Das
älteste Evangelium* (Göttingen 1903), pp. 332, 333.

»...den Hauptteil der Erzählung [in Lukas 22 und 23] bilden nicht mehr die
aus Markus genommenen Stücke [, sondern teils ganz neue Stoffe, teils Umbildungen
an dem mit Markus parallelen Sätzen] ... Nach Absonderung der aus Markus ge-
holten Sätze [bleibt] ein nahezu lückenloser Bericht«, Adolf Schlatter, *Die beiden
Schwerter, Lukas 22, 35—38. Ein Stück aus der besonderen Quelle des Lukas (Beiträge zur Förderung christlicher Theologie,* Jahrg. 20, 1916, Heft 6; Gütersloh
1916), p. 7.

*Cf.* Rudolf Bultmann, *Die Geschichte der synoptischen Tradition* (Göttingen
²1931): »Ich halte den ganzen Bericht des Markus [*sc.* Mc 14, 53 b, 55—64] für eine
sekundäre Ausführung der kurzen Angabe 15, 1. Die Einfügung des Stückes in den
geschlossenen Zusammenhang der Petrus-Geschichte, *das mutmaßliche Fehlen der
Nebenquelle des Lukas* [italics supplied], die Unwahrscheinlichkeit der Beschaffung der
Zeugen und der nächtlichen Verhandlung beweisen es« (pp. 290, 291); »Von der...
Synedriums-Verhandlung hat Mk... keinen älteren Bericht erhalten als 15, 1, und
vielleicht ist die Parallele Lk 22, 66 noch älterer Herkunft« (p. 294); »Lk 22, 66—71
kombiniert den Mk-Bericht über die Verhandlung mit seiner Quelle, die in v. 66 zum
Vorschein kommt« (p. 292; *cf.* p. 387); »Sehr wahrscheinlich ist..., daß die Verhaftung [Mc 14, 43—52] ursprünglich eine Fortsetzung hatte, in der Jesu Abführung
und Verurteilung erzählt wurde. Diese könnte 14, 53 a und vielleicht auch 14, 65
enthalten haben und jedenfalls den Grundbestand von 15, 1—5 ...« (p. 301); English
edition (²1968), pp. 269, 270, 272, 279; see also p. 363.

Supreme Court itself who take part in the cruel farce. The actions of the Council members are defined as ἐμπτύειν, περικαλύπτειν, κολαφίζειν in Mark, whilst the infliction of ῥαπίσματα describes the participation of subordinate officials. In Luke we find the verbs ἐμπαίζειν, δέρειν, περικαλύπτειν and βλασφημεῖν, all of which refer to the behaviour of the jailers. Neither the setting of the story nor the phraseology is the same as in Mark[6]. The differences are too great to be fortuitous, and they cannot be attributed to a Lucan redrafting of the Marcan account. The Third Evangelist drew on a pre-Marcan Passion Narrative[7]. In fact, if the intruding lines Mc 14, 53 b, 55—64 are removed, it will be seen that the Lucan order approximates to the Marcan sequence of events with which at present it conflicts irreconcilably. The matter may be set forth as follows: (1) Jesus is brought to the residence of the high-priest (Mc 14, 53 a; Lc 22, 54); (2) Jesus is mocked (Mc 14, 65; Lc 22, 63—65); (3) Peter denies the Master (Mc 14 [54] 66—72; Lc 22, 55—62); (4) The Sanhedrin assembles (Mc 15, 1 a; Lc 22, 66 a). The only difference in the order of the two renderings now concerns the transposition of items (2) and (3);

---

[6] In the gospel reports of the second mockery, by Pilate's soldiers and the entourage of Herod Antipas, respectively, we find in Mc 15, 19—20 the verbs ἐμπτύειν and ἐμπαίζειν; in Lc 23, 11 again ἐμπαίζειν. Can we deduce from this observation that the pre-synoptic record (which probably mentioned only one occurrence of the scene) contained the vocable ἐμπαίζειν even though the Second Evangelist has not retained it in Mc 14, 65? If so, the originality of Lc 22, 63 would be apparent.

Besides in Mc 15, 20, the verb ἐμπαίζειν also occurs in Mc 10, 34. In this passage Jesus predicts that it will be pagans (τὰ ἔθνη, here a designation of individuals of non-Jewish descent, in the same manner as הגוים in rabbinic literature; normally we would expect to read οἱ ἐθνικοί) who will mock him (ἐμπαίξουσιν αὐτῷ) and spit upon him (ἐμπτύσουσιν αὐτῷ); in Mc 14, 65 it is members of the Jewish court who fulfil this prophecy (cf. also Mt 20, 19 with Mt 26, 67).

[7] »[Es ist wahrscheinlich,] daß Lukas eine... Redaktion der Vorlage der Passionsgeschichte des Markus neben Markus benutzte«, R. Bultmann, o. c., p. 303; English edition, p. 280.

Cf. Pierre Benoit, O. P., »Jésus devant le Sanhédrin«, Angelicum, vol. 20, Rome 1943, pp. 143—165: »... l'ordre de Luc... est vraisemblable tandis que celui de Matthieu et Marc est très difficile à concevoir« (p. 150, 151); »Il n'y a d'ailleurs aucune difficulté à penser que Luc doit ce meilleur arrangement des choses à une tradition originale« (p. 151).

»... the non-Marcan tradition... forms the main basis of the Lucan Passion narrative«, Charles H. Dodd, The Interpretation of the Fourth Gospel (Cambridge 1953), p. 451.

Also Walter E. Bundy, Jesus and the First Three Gospels. An Introduction to the Synoptic Tradition (Cambridge Mass. 1955): »It seems probable that Luke is using an earlier version... which he had before him in written form. Luke may have used the pre-Markan passion story used by Mark with incidental use of the form now in Mark« (p. 480); »Luke's version... has greater probability... In Luke this morning session is not a formal trial but a preliminary hearing« (p. 523).

whilst in Luke Peter's denial precedes the scene of Jesus' mockery, the reverse is the case in Mark. If we may be allowed to consult the Fourth Gospel[8] in an endeavour to reconstruct *an earlier form of the tradition*, it would appear that on this point Mark stands closer to a more primitive form. Intended to be related as more or less simultaneous happenings, the mockery of Jesus might nonetheless have been recorded before the account of Peter's denial.

Though we may not always be able safely to identify the various constituents of the Passion Stories that come from different backgrounds, we are in a position to distinguish between the later and the earlier strata. In all four Gospels there are elements of the narrative that have remained unaffected by developments which the tradition underwent in the process of literary formulation. To these 'constants' belong the reports of the despatch of Jesus to the residence of the highpriest (Mc 14, 53 b; Lc 22, 54; Jn 18, 13) and of the subsequent buffetting (Mc 14, 65; Lc 22, 63—65; Jn 18, 22). It is these stable or recurrent features that undoubtedly were part of a fairly old form of tradition — t r a d i t i o n   i n   t h e   p r o p e r   m e a n i n g   of the word. The amplification of scanty traditional pieces of information about what happened during the night when Jesus was delivered belongs to   t h e   e d i - t o r i a l   p r o c e s s   by which tradition was moulded for the purposes of literary presentation. The places which the traditional pieces — the 'stable features' — now possess in the present framework of a particular Gospel belong to the latest stage of gospel formation; the assignment of these positions was due to the use which individual evangelists made of the traditional elements. By disregarding their present positions in the Gospels and concentrating upon the items themselves we may hope to arrive at an appreciation of the earliest form of the tradition. The context may have been altered, the emphasis shifted, new 'situations' created, new persons introduced, the wording vastly modified — and yet, the main themes remained constant and still give some indication of the nature and the contents of an early pre-synoptic Passion Narrative. Comparative analysis of Mark, Luke and John shows that the item concerning Jesus' mockery and maltreatment had a place in a pre-evangelical tradition of his arrest. The evangelists incorporated this item and assigned it to contexts that suited their several literary purposes. It seems that in Lc 22, 63—66 a the earlier tradition has been best preserved even if in the original order the event recorded in Lc 22, 55—62 occupied a place between the events now related in Lc 22, 63—65 and Lc 22, 66.

We are thus led to the conclusion that Lc 22, 54—66 (ending before λέγοντες) is, from an historical point of view, preferable to the narration

---

[8] John 18, 22 (ἔδωκεν ῥάπισμα) and 23 (τί με δέρεις;) contain verbal agreements with Mc 14, 65 and Lc 22, 63.

in Mc 14, 53—15, 1 a (of which Mt 26, 57—27, 1 is a replica)[9]. According to the Second Gospel, Jesus was found guilty of blasphemy[10]; the Council unanimously pronounced him worthy of death. The penalty for blasphemy is prescribed in Lev 24, 16 and Mishnah Sanh vii 4; it is death by stoning. Yet the members of the tribunal who have just condemned Jesus take no action in consequence of their decision[11]; the Council meets again in the morning (Mc 15, 1 a) and proceeds as if nothing had happened the night before. The result of the morning consultation is that Jesus is extradited to Pilate to be tried. But it is impossible to understand from Mark why Jesus should stand trial before Pilate if he had in fact already been tried by the Sanhedrin and sentence had been passed.

We have come to a stage in our examination when it is needful to consider under what conditions and with what aim in the writer's mind the story related in Mc 14, 53 b, 55—64 was composed.

The Marcan report of Jesus' trial by the Sanhedrin is intersected with the story of Peter's denial. Both are told in such a manner as to give the impression that the two sets of occurrences eventuate simultaneously in different parts of the high-priest's residence. It is rather like the old cinema technique when the screen is divided in the centre, and two different scenes are unfolded before the eyes of the onlooker to make him aware of the fateful connection of two courses of events. Intercalations of this sort are not infrequent in the Second Gospel. It is the combination, the confrontation of the two series, which contains 'the moral' and provides the clue to the narrator's motive. We are called upon to understand that whilst Peter was importuned by domestics of an influential personage, and succumbed in face of hostile interrogation, Jesus himself kept his faith and maintained his composure before the highest authority of the land irrespective of the consequences. The Evangelist is not concerned with simple chronological considerations such as the fact that Peter's discourse with his questioners could easily be accommodated within the time-limit of perhaps half-an-hour, whilst a complex legal action would have taken much longer. Witnesses are interrogated; their evidence is found wanting and

---

[9] »In all the circumstances, while there may have been an earlier inquiry, the Lukan date is to be preferred«, Vincent Taylor, *The Gospel according to St Mark* (London 1952), p. 646.

[10] Which conflicts with Mishnah Sanh vii 5: The blasphemer is not culpable unless he distinctly pronounces the [divine] Name.

»Nach jüdischen Begriffen lag darin unmöglich eine Gotteslästerung, daß jemand sagte, er sei der Christus, der Sohn Gottes«, Julius Wellhausen, *Das Evangelium Marci* (Berlin 1903), p. 132.

[11] Once a final sentence of death had been pronounced, and no new evidence was offered, the sentence was carried out immediately (Mishnah Sanh xi 4). This provision was in force in the time of Jesus; cf. Acts 7, 57—58.

rejected; the proceedings turn to another charge; the accused himself is closely examined; the verdict is pronounced; sentence is passed by a court of 71 members; the senators indulge in undignified mockery of a man whom they have just condemned to death. The discrepancy between the chronological requirements of the two sets of events makes it clear that the motive for the intersection in the Marcan Trial Narrative is not of an historical character[12]. The reasons for the combination are probably of a complex nature. The main factor, however, lies in the confrontation of an account of weakness displayed by a member of the Church when being questioned by his enemies with an account of the imperturbable steadfastness exemplified by him to whom the Church owed allegiance. The juxtaposition testifies to a hortatory interest on the part of the story-teller, easily understandable in the Second Evangelist's time when the profession of the Christian faith was liable to involve the believer in dire consequence. *The Evangelist here exhorts his readers to follow the example given by Jesus, not that given by Peter.* If your endurance brings you suffering, it also brings you glory[13].

Besides the hortatory interest we discern an apologetic motive. The Second Evangelist — writing probably in Rome — wishes to emphasize the culpability of the Jewish nation for the death of Jesus, particularly of its leaders[14]; they, not the Romans, are to be held responsible for

---

[12] In the Fourth Gospel the story of Peter's denial is also told in conjunction with a report of legal proceedings against Jesus — though here it is not a session of the Sanhedrin that takes place at the time, but a preliminary interrogation (the interrogator being identified with Annas). Such an interrogation might conceivably be accommodated within approximately the same time as it took Peter to make his disavowals.

[13] The combination of the story of Peter's denial with that of Jesus' conduct at a fictitious session of the Sanhedrin is designed by the Evangelist to convey an exhartation members of the *ecclesia* to remain true to their convictions if and when faced by official inquisition. The report of an event of major consequence — the trial of Jesus — is parenthetically inserted into the report of an event of minor consequence — Peter's wavering and his repudiation of the Lord — and this betrays the narrator's contrived manner. Johannes Weiss, *o. c.*, p. 349, characterized this editorial procedure in the following way: »... die Verleugnungsgeschichte, in die die Versammlung und Beratung des Synedriums gewaltsam eingefügt wurde«. »Mark's... version of the nacturnal trial is very much in the interests of his dramatic story of the Denial of Peter, to which it takes an almost subordinate place«, Matthew Black, »The Arrest and Trial of Jesus«, in *New Testament Essays. Studies in Memory of Thomas Walter Manson*, edited by A. J. B. Higgins (Manchester 1959), pp. 19—33, on p. 25 See also my paper »The Treatment of His Sources by the Third Evangelist in Luke XXI to XXIV«, *Studia Theologica* vol. 8, Lund 1955, pp. 138—172, on pp. 161, 162.

[14] *Cf.* T. A. Burkill, »L'antisémitisme dans l'évangile selon saint Marc«, *RHR* tome 154, 1958, pp. 10—31. »Marc, en dépit de sa doctrine..., essaie de montrer que les Juifs doivent être tenus directement ou indirectement (en la personne de leurs chefs contemporains des faits) responsables du plus odieux des crimes, savoir

the crucifixion. It is not to be assumed that the Evangelist was moved by positively anti-Jewish sentiments; his tendency was defensive rather than aggressive. He was concerned to avoid mentioning anything that would provoke Roman antagonism towards, or even suspicion of, the ideals for which he stood. The materials from which the Second Gospel was made up had to a considerable extent developed in a Palestinian-Jewish ambit, but the Evangelist was addressing himself to a predominantly Gentile Christian community which was exposed to attack from pagan quarters. He shaped 'the gospel' so as to adapt it to the particular needs of readers in a Roman environment, and came to realize that he should omit anything that might be taken to suggest to the mind of the reader that the case of Jesus, who had been put to death by a Roman governor in Judaea, could be compared to any of the cases of capital punishment — innnumerable as they were — that had been carried out by Roman authorities during the years 66—70 CE. No grounds must be given for the inference that Jesus was in any way connected with subversive activities such as those which had resulted in the recent uprising. The Evangelist therefore contrived to conceal that Jesus had been condemned and executed on a charge of sedition. The argument runs that he was not arrested by Roman troops, not sentenced for political reasons by a Roman magistrate, but that his condemnation and subsequent execution were due to some obscure cause of the Jewish Law which, of course, would be devoid of relevance in the eyes of a Roman reader after the year 70 CE. The insertion of the passage Mc 14, 53 b, 55—64 into an old tradition — so as to combine the record of Jesus' removal to the high-priest's residence and of Peter's weakness in face of personal danger with an account of Jesus' interrogation by the Jewish Senate, *introduced by the Evangelist ad hoc* — h a s its *Sitz im Leben* i n t h e h i s t o r y o f t h e e a r l y C h u r c h, n o t i n t h e h i s t o r y o f J e s u s' l i f e. The insertion was made without noticeable literary skill and without much effort to produce a coherent logical sequence. The Marcan Passion Narrative gains in clarity if Mc 14, 53 b, 55—64 is eliminated. In all probability the insertion was made by the Second Evangelist who supplemented his source with a depiction of the Sanhedrin's nocturnal session in the high-priest's residence — inspired by hortatory and apologetic interests[15].

---

le rejet du Fils unique de Dieu venu parmi les hommes...« (p. 11). »...il entre dans les intentions doctrinales de Marc de montrer clairement à ses lecteurs que le mauvais vouloir des propres compatriotes de Jésus fut le facteur déterminant derrière la crucifixion...« (p. 15).

[15] Wilhelm Brandt, in his *Die Evangelische Geschichte und der Ursprung des Christenthums* (Leipzig 1893), pp. 53—68, characterized the account given in Mc 14, 53 b. 55—64 aptly by calling it *Eine Dichtung des Marcus*.

*Cf.* Benjamin Wisner Bacon, *The Beginnings of Gospel Story* (New Haven, Conn., 1909): »...we have... evidence of redactional recasting of the story, and

In Mc 15, 1 the members of the Great Council are introduced to the reader in a very elaborate manner. The enumeration οἱ ἀρχιερεῖς μετὰ τῶν πρεσβυτέρων καὶ γραμματέων καὶ ὅλον τὸ συνέδριον would be intelligible if now for the first time the reader were being informed of the councillors' meeting together. If an earlier meeting had been mentioned in the narrative shortly before Mc 15, 1, there would have been no point in giving a renewed description of the Council's composition. The words καὶ ὅλον τὸ συνέδριον are probably an addition made by the

---

the interest of [the Evangelist]... is rather apologetic... [than] historical« (p. 195); »As regards the trial scene, it is only too apparent that the Church had no witness to whom it could refer, while the description itself reflects much more of anti-Jewish apologetic than of the actual historical conditions« (p. 198); »[Mc 14, 53 b] is an addition [of the editor] preparatory to the trial scene of verses 55—64... The story which [the editor]... interjects [i. e. Mc 14, 55—64] not only interrupts the context... but is historically impossible as well as logically useless« (p. 210).

»That there was any meeting of the full Sanhedrin is most doubtful«, Claude Goldsmid Montefiore, The Synoptic Gospels (London 1927), p. 346.

»[Le verset 53 b] paraît intercalé dans un récit plus bref où le reniement de Pierre était... le seul fait mentionné entre l'arrestation de Jésus et la consultation tenue le matin par les principaux membres du sanhédrin avant de livrer le prisonnier à Pilate«, Alfred Loisy, L'Évangile selon Marc (Paris 1912), p. 426. »Trois scènes vaguement dessinées et encore plus vaguement reliées entre elles vont se succéder:... ces éléments ont été pris de divers côtés et mal soudés ensemble... [La parole contre le temple] fut matière à discussion dans les premiers démêlés de la communauté apostolique avec les Juifs. La... scène... [d'] aveu de messianité... se rencontre sous une autre forme dans le procès public (xv, 2)... devant Pilate. Enfin les mauvais traitements que l'on inflige au Christ chez le grand-prêtre correspondent aux coups et à la dérision des soldats dans le prétoire (xv, 16—20). Ce procès nocturne, qui paraît fictif, double donc le procès réel et contient des traits qui ont eu leur place dans celui-ci, ou qui s'y rapportent directement« (o. c., pp. 427, 428).

Hans Lietzmann, »Der Prozess Jesu«, Sitzungsberichte der Preussischen Akademie der Wissenschaften, Phil.-Hist. Klasse, 1931, xiv, Berlin 1931, pp. 313—322. »In die Verleugnungsgeschichte, die mit v. 54 abbricht und mit v. 66 weitergeführt wird, ist das Verhör Jesu vor dem Hohenpriester wie ein Fremdkörper hineingesteckt worden«; »Zweifellos ist, dass apologetische Phantasie einen Verbindungsweg zwischen dem Palästinnern und der christlichen Gemeinde ausdenken kann..., für den Historiker [aber] steht die Geschichte frei in der Luft« (p. 315); »... nichts [ist] sicherer, als dass Jesus gekreuzigt worden ist: das ist eine typisch römische Strafe, aus deren Vollzug sich der selbstverständliche Schluss ergibt, dass Pilatus das entscheidenden Urteil gesprochen hat. Also kann er nicht vom Synedrion verurteilt sein« (p. 317); »Das Wesentliche ist, dass der römische Prokurator Jesus als ›Judenkönig‹ zum Tode verurteilt und ans Kreuz schlagen lässt: das war die gewöhnliche Todesart für Landfriedensbrecher« (p. 320). Cf. Hans Lietzmann: »Bemerkungen zum Prozess Jesu«, ZNW vol. 30, 1931, pp. 211—215, vol. 31, 1932, pp. 78—84. (See also his Kleine Schriften, vol. 2 [Berlin 1958], pp. 251—263, 264—268, 269—276).

Jack Finegan, Die Überlieferung der Leidens- und Auferstehungsgeschichte Jesu (Beiheft 15 zur ZNW, Giessen 1934): »Das eigentliche Verhör Jesu vor dem Syn-

Second Evangelist to the source he used. The source — consonant with Lc 22, 66 — is o l d e r than Mc 14, 53 b, 55—64 for there is no reference back im Mc 15, 1 to an ealier deliberation, or earlier session, by the members of the Sanhedrin. Hence, despite Elias Bickermann's contention that it is impossible to identify the different traditions that lie behind the extant Passion Narratives[16], in this instance one can safely assert that the report of a night session in Mc 14, 53 b, 55—64 is an importation into the earlier tradition. The apparent repetition of the enumeration of the members of whom the Sanhedrin was constituted (Mc 15, 1) proves beyond doubt that what we now find in the Second Gospel is not all of a piece, and was not the production of a single writer. The enumeration in Mc 15, 1 is in its correct place, except for the redundant words καὶ ὅλον τὸ συνέδριον — only through the insertion of Mc 14, 53 b, 55—64 does it now appear superfluous[17]. M a r k  15, 1

---

edrium Mc 14, 55—65 ist auszuschalten. Wir können keinen Gewährsmann dafür nennen. Der Bericht ist deutlich in die einheitliche Verleugnungsgeschichte v. 54, 66—72 eingeschoben ... Hätte das Synedrium wirklich Jesus für schuldig der Lästerung erklärt v. 64, so hätte man ihn sofort gesteinigt« (p. 72).

Further Martin Dibelius, »Das historische Problem der Leidensgeschichte«, ZNW vol. 30, 1931, pp. 193—201, who maintains that »die Ausgestaltung [des Jesuswortes wider den Tempel] zu Szenen auf literarischer Steigerung beruht« (p. 199); »[eine] Komposition, die ... Worte Jesu in eine vom Alten Testament vorgezeichnete Situation hineinsetz[t]« (p. 199). »Dem Verfasser des Markusevangeliums lag bereits ein alter Bericht vor, der an ein paar Stellen Augenzeugenangaben verwertete, im übrigen aber ... bereits legendärisch gefärbt [war]; nur eine solche Stilisierung entsprach dem Bedürfnis der Gemeinde« (p. 200). »Eine Verhandlung vor dem Synedrium, ein wirklicher jüdischer Prozess, [hat] nicht Stattgefunden ...« (p. 200); see also his Botschaft und Geschichte. Gesammelte Aufsätze. Band 1: Zur Evangelienforschung (Tübingen 1953), pp. 248—257, on pp. 255, 256. And cf. his Die Formgeschichte des Evangeliums (Tübingen ³1959), pp. 178—218; English edition, pp. 178 —217.

Also Erich Klostermann, Das Markusevangelium (Handbuch zum Neuen Testament; Tübingen ³1936), pp. 154—157, where the pericope of a nocturnal trial of Jesus by a Jewish Law Court is pertinently called »ein Einschub ..., um zugleich die Juden zu belasten und Jesus als Messias sterben zu lassen« (p. 155).

Albert ten Eyck Olmstead, Jesus in the Light of History (New York 1942): »... accounts, involving a ... night trial before the Sanhedrin, are on their face impossible« (p. 228).

Walter E. Bundy: »Mark's ... version of the night session of the Sanhedrin seems to be the result of a process of later retouching« (o. c., p. 519).

[16] See his article, »Utilitas crucis. Observations sur les récits du procès de Jésus dans les Évangiles canoniques«, RHR tome 112, 1935, pp. 169—241. »L'incorporation de matériaux de provenance diverse dans les récits de la Passion demeure bien probable, mais elle échappe à une appréciation précise« (l. c., p. 169).

[17] »Ich verstehe ... den Text des Markus so, dass er hier eine Überlieferung mitteilt, die von der nächtlichen Synedriumssitzung nichts enthielt und auch über den Inhalt der Morgensitzung nichts wusste. Sie erzählte nur, dass am frühen Morgen

is based on a tradition, apparently already in written form, which knew nothing of the report given in Mc 14, 53 b, 55—64.

Perhaps the most spirited attempt to defend the Marcan description of Jesus' trial by a Jewish court sitting at night has been made by Bickermann[18]. He maintains that the objections against regarding Mc 14, 53 b, 55—64 as being based on a reliable report of what actually happened lie not in what the Second Evangelist wrote, but in a mistaken interpretation of the Marcan text. The contention is that βλασφημία in v. 64 does not carry the meaning of 'blasphemy' in the technical sense of Jewish Law[19], but was used by our writer in the sense of *énormité, outrage, gross impropriety*[20]. Bickermann further argues that the words οἱ δὲ πάντες κατέκριναν αὐτὸν εἶναι ἔνοχον θανάτου signify *se prononcer contre* and do not relate the passing of a final sentence of death, but merely imply a decision to commit the prisoner for formal trial on a capital charge before the competent authority[21]. In other

---

das Synedrium eine Sitzung gehalten habe (natürlich war diese höchst geheim), nach deren Beendigung Jesus zu Pilatus abgeführt wurde«, Johannes Weiss, *o. c.,* p. 312.

[18] See above, note 16.
[19] See above, note 10.
[20] *Cf.* Lc 22, 65.
[21] *L. c.,* pp. 182, 183.

Consequently, Bickermann sums up his exposition of the Marcan Trial Account by saying: »... le jugement est rendu seulement par le procurateur. Car le Sanhédrin n'a pas prononcé une sentence, mais ayant constaté un crime comportant la mort, [il traduit] l'inculpé devant le tribunal romain, comme c'était d'usage dans la juridiction provinciale« (p. 199).

With some obvious hesitation Père Pierre Benoit, O. P., seems to endorse this view when he remarks: »... il est permis de voir dans la séance du Sanhédrin une réunion délibérative qui n'avait pas à observer toutes les formes légales, et dans sa sentence finale une décision véritable, mais qui n'avait pas de soi valeur de condemnation formelle«, *Angelicum* vol. 20, 1943, p. 163.

Maurice Goguel anticipated the conclusions of both Bickermann and Benoit when he wrote: »In reality, Jesus was not tried by the Sanhedrin. None of the rules of procedure which are laid down in the treatise *Sanhedrin* was observed, and, although there are excellent reasons for thinking that they did not exist at the time of Jesus as they were formulated in that book, something must have been in existence all the same. There was no trial before the Sanhedrin. At the moment when Jesus appeared before the high priest, he was not his prisoner at all, but the prisoner of Pilate ... Jesus was taken before the Jewish authorities because the Procurator wished it ...«, Maurice Goguel, *La vie de Jésus* (Paris 1932), p. 495; Engl. translation *The Life of Jesus* (London 1933), pp. 511, 512. Goguel's book is quoted here from the first edition, as only this is available in an English translation. A second edition was published under the title *Jésus: Histoire des vies de Jésus* (Paris 1950). Other studies by the same author, of relevance to our subject, are: *Les Chrétiens et l'Empire romain à l'époque du Nouveau Testament* (Paris 1908), *Les sources du récit johannique de la Passion* (Paris 1910), »Juifs et Romains dans l'histoire de la Pas-

words the Sanhedrin decided that there was a case to answer, but did not judge.

We must differentiate between what was historical fact and what was the Evangelist's intention — between what actually could have happened and what the author of the Second Gospel wished to convey. Bickermann's exposition would give a more tidy appearance to the description of Jesus' trial in Mark, but the criterion of tidiness, or coherence, is a doubtful guide when trying to establish the Marcan meaning. To attempt to determine the meaning of Marcan words from the use of the same vocabulary in the writings of pagan authors is a questionable enterprise. Leaving then the meaning of ἡ βλασφημία aside, the correct understanding of the passage hinges on the words κατέκριναν αὐτὸν εἶναι ἔνοχον θανάτου.

The meaning the Evangelist wished to convey in these words is most likely to be arrived at by comparing the construction with other passages in the New Testament. The formulation ἔνοχος τῇ κρίσει (Mt 5, 21, 22 a) and ἔνοχος τῷ συνεδρίῳ (Mt 5, 22 a) appear to lend some support to Bickermann's contention, though κρίσις (משפט) — and συνέδριον (בית דין) — could, in the light of Rev 18, 10, Heb 10, 26, imply judicial punishment rather than arraignment for trial. If the two references cited do not allow us to decide dogmatically one way or the other whether the actual meaning is "committal for trial before the court" or "punishment by the court", there are other less ambiguous instances of the use of the phrase: Mt 5, 22 b ἔνοχος εἰς τὴν γέενναν τοῦ πυρός — and Mc 14, 64 b itself. The actual penalty is explicitly stated in these cases; the meaning can be only the passing of a final sentence. The word πάντες is not without significance. The Supreme Court would hardly have met in full session merely to decide whether or not there was a prima facie case to answer and whether an indictment should be drawn up. Yet the Marcan text states that there was a full session, and that all members of the Sanhedrin came to a unanimous decision regarding the death-worthiness of Jesus. The vocable πάντες, therefore, also provides a clue that assists us in our effort to ascertain the meaning of Mc 14, 64 b and thereby to grasp the point which the Evangelist wished to make.

Lastly, there is the formulation of the three Marcan predictions of Jesus' Passion (Mc 8, 31; 9, 31; 10, 33—34) of which the final passage, Mc 10, 33, is an authentic commentary on the implied meaning of Mc 14,64. Regardless of what happened, or what could have happened, as a matter of historical fact, it was the purpose of the writer of Mc, 14,

---

sion«, *RHR* tome 62, 1910, pp. 165—182, 295—322, and his *Introduction au Nouveau Testament* (Paris 1923—1926).

The present writer holds that there was no night-session, and hence not even *une déclaration de culpabilité* without formal sentence.

64 b to assert that a formal sentence of death had been passed by the entire Jewish Senate[22].

If Bickermann's exposition fails to take into account the Second Evangelist's intention, it remains, however, to consider the possibility that the ambiguous expression in Mc 14, 64 b could have been due to the fact that the Evangelist — in fabricating the night-session — utilized an older tradition connected with the report of the morning-meeting (Mc 15, 1 a; Lc 22, 66 a), transposing and adapting it to the requirements of a new context. The tradition perhaps reported that t h e S a n h e d r i n, a t i t s  m o r n i n g - s e s s i o n, d e c i d e d t o a p p r o v e a w r i t o f i n d i c t m e n t d r a w n u p d u r i n g t h e n i g h t, a n d t o h a n d J e s u s o v e r t o t h e a u t h o r i t y c o m p e t e n t t o p r o s e c u t e i n p o l i t i c a l c a s e s. In any attempt to determine the nature of the morning-meeting we are at once in difficulty because we do not possess a complete description of the Sanhedrin's functions and procedure. The Mishnah tractate Sanhedrin describes only the rules of procedure in *judicial* matters. In the time of Jesus, however, *the Sanhedrin exercised authority also as a legislative and administrative organ* of the nation. Rules of procedure determining the Sanhedrin's executive functions might conceivably have differed from those operative when the Senate acted as a court[23]. The meeting that is mentioned in Mc 15, 1 a and Lc 22, 66 a seems to have dealt with *an administrative question within the Council's competence,* namely, the delivery of a person suspected of sedition to the procurator.

The tradition from which the words in Mc 14, 64 b may have been borrowed by a process of transposing could thus have contained words

---

[22] »Es kann kein Zweifel sein, dass [Markus] ein förmliches Gerichtsverfahren und eine rechtsgültige Verurteilung erzählen will ... Es entspricht dies der Gesamtanschauung des Markus, wonach die Juden die Schuld am Tode Jesu tragen«, Johannes Weiss, *o. c.,* p. 315.

»Im Falle ... Mc 14, 64 [haben wir] ein regelrechtes Urteil. Aber ... als ob nichts geschehen wäre, wird Jesus dem Pilatus überliefert, ... ›verklagt‹ und ... aufs neue verurteilt, und zwar als βασιλεὺς τῶν Ἰουδαίων«, Hans Lietzmann, *ZNW* vol. 31, 1932, p. 83. (also *Kleine Schriften,* Band 2, p. 275).

[23] *Cf.* Gustaf Dalman, *Jesus-Jeschua. Die drei Sprachen Jesu. Jesus in der Synagoge, auf dem Berge, beim Passahmahl, am Kreuz* (Leipzig 1922): »... die Sitzungen [hätten vielleicht nicht] als offizielle Sitzungen ... bezeichnet werden dürfen« (pp. 91, 92).

»... cette délibération n'aurait pas été une séance officielle, mais une réunion privée dans laquelle aurait été concertée l'accusation«, Alfred Loisy, *L'Évangile selon Luc* (Paris 1924), p. 539.

»The trial and conviction [of Jesus] are ... the affair of the Romans only ... the hearing before the high-priest was not a regular session of the Sanhedrin«, Oscar Cullmann, *o. c.,* p. 44; »... [the proceedings before the high-priest] did not have the character of a trial, but of an unofficial investigation by the authorities, from which ensued the accusation before the Romans«, *ibidem,* pp. 45, 46.

possibly rendered by ἔνοχος τῇ κρίσει[24] or some similar expression — without explicit indication of the formal passing of a death sentence. A procedure of this sort would be in complete accord with what Josephus records. The much disputed Testimonium Flavianum includes the following phrase:

$$αὐτὸν ἐνδείξει τῶν πρώτων ἀνδρῶν παρ' ἡμῖν$$
$$σταυρῷ ἐπιτετιμηκότος Πιλάτου....$$

This passage appears to be genuine[25]. The balanced distinction between ἔνδειξις (a verbo ἐνδείκνυμι) writ of indictment, attributed to Jewish leaders[26], and the act of awarding sentence (ἐπιτιμᾶν σταυρῷ) is not likely to be the work of a Christian interpolator from post-Origenian times[27]. Such an interpolator would scarcely have been content with reproaching Jewish leaders for drawing up an indictment against Jesus whilst stating that the imposition of sentence by crucifixion was an act of Roman justice. The words above referred to are in agreement with the results of a critical analysis of the gospel records.

It is arguable that some confirmation of the fact that the Sanhedrin did n o t pass sentence upon Jesus may be obtained from Luke. Not

---

[24] Cf. Gustaf Dalman, Jesus-Jeschua, pp. 66, 67; Engl. translation Jesus-Jeshua. Studies in the Aramaic Gospels (London 1929): »The phrase ἔνοχος τῇ κρίσει... cannot be rendered literally into Hebrew or Aramaic«; »There is a Jewish phrase in Jewish legal terminology: meḥuiyebē mītōt bēt dīn, i. e. such who deserve punishment of death by a court of justice (T. Y. Meg 71 a, Ket 27 b)... and ḥaiyābin mītōt bēt dīn, ›those deserving capital punishment by a court of justice‹ (T. Y. Yeb 6 b)« (p. 71).

[25] Alfred von Gutschmid, »Vorlesungen über Josephos' Bücher gegen Apion«; see A. v. Gutschmid, Kleine Schriften, hrsg. von Franz Rühl, vol. 4 (Leipzig 1893), pp. 336—589, on pp. 352, 353. Cf. Peter Corssen, »Die Zeugnisse des Tacitus und Pseudo-Josephus über Christus«, ZNW vol. 15, 1914, pp. 114—140, on pp. 132—134 (The arguments that it was the Jews in Rome who denounced the Christians for having set fire to the city, and in particular that it may have been Josephus who used his influence on Popaea Sabina to goad Nero, are pure phantasy). See also Joseph Klausner, Jesus of Nazareth. His Life, Times, and Teaching (London 1925), pp. 55—58, and my article »Josephus on Jesus«, Journal of Historical Studies, vol. 1, Princeton, N. J., 1968, pp. 289—302. [Revisers' addendum: cf. Emil Schürer, The History of the Jewish People in the Age of Jesus Christ (revised and edited by Geza Vermes and Fergus Millar), vol. 1 (Edinburgh 1973), pp. 428—441.]

[26] The πρῶτοι παρ' ἡμῖν ἄνδρες are the priestly aristocracy. Compare ἀριστοκρατία μὲν ἦν ἡ πολιτεία, τὴν δὲ προστασίαν τοῦ ἔθνους οἱ ἀρχιερεῖς ἐπεπίστευντο. (Ant XX 251).

[27] C. Celsum I 47, II 13 (GCS Origenes t. I, p. 97, 143; MPG 11, cols. 745, 748, 824), Commentarium in Evangelium secundum Matthaeum, tomus decimus XVII (GCS Origenes t. X p. 22; MPG 13, col. 877).

even in the pericope Lc 22, 67—71[28] is there any mention of a formal sentence passed by the Council. This is significant as the Third Evangelist undoubtedly had read Mark. There are recent writers who explain the absence as being due to the Evangelist's carelessness in his copying of Mark. The Third Evangelist however did not copy Mark in his Passion Narrative — although he used Marcan topics — and he was not careless. The absence of a report of a death sentence passed by the Sanhedrin must have been deliberately intended. This comes out in Acts 13, 27—28 where the author of Luke-Acts allows Paul to say: »The inhabitants of Jerusalem and their rulers ... finding no cause of death (μηδεμίαν αἰτίαν θανάτου εὑρόντες) [in Jesus], asked Pilate that he should be killed". Allowing for the apologetic colouring of the formulation in the second half of this statement, we find here a definite assertion that the rulers (= the Sanhedrin) had neither found Jesus guilty nor passed sentence upon him. Thus Acts 13, 27—28 provides the explanation as to why the Third Gospel nowhere mentions that the Sanhedrin sentenced Jesus to death.

No less significant than the passage in the Acts of the Apostles is the wording of Lc 18, 32—33; it contains no prediction of any participation by the Sanhedrin in the act of condemning Jesus to death[29]. The difference between the Lucan wording and that of Mc 10, 33—34 can best be accounted for by presuming that the Third Evangelist either did not know what we know from our Second Gospel, or that, although he knew it, he also knew another source in the trustworthiness of which he put greater confidence than was the case with Mark.

It is illuminating to note the contrast between the procedure adopted by the Third Evangelist when recording the first two predictions of Jesus' Passion given in Mark, and that adopted by him in the case of the third prediction. In Lc 9, 22 he repeats with little alteration what he found in Mc 8, 31, namely, the statement that Jesus would be rejected by the elders, chief priests and scribes. The Marcan wording does not imply here that the Sanhedrin would pass a death sentence upon Jesus, and the Third Evangelist could easily have understood that the

---

[28] *Cf. Studia Theologica*, vol. 9, pp. 112—115.

[29] »Luc ... devait se conformer au document fondamental de Marc, sachant fort bien d'ailleurs que Jésus n'avait pas été jugé ni condamné par le sanhédrin«, Alfred Loisy, *L'Evangile selon Luc* (Paris 1924), p. 539. This is correct in the sense that the writer of the Third Gospel could not afford to dispense entirely with the account of the proceedings against Jesus he had found in Mark; yet the fact that the Third Gospel is not throughout conformant with the Second, so far as the trial narrative is concerned, warrants the conclusion that its author had at his disposal certain information — in all probability documentary information — which differed from the Marcan account.

Loisy, and afterwards Martin Dibelius, thought that the differences between the Marcan and the Lucan Trial Narratives were due solely to editorial modifications on the part of the Third Evangelist.

'rejection' came to expression in the Council's decision to hand Jesus over for trial to Pilate. Equally, in Lc 9, 44 b there is no substantial alteration of the words presented in Mc 9, 31 a. When reproducing the third prediction of the Passion, however, the Third Evangelist's procedure is quite different: whereas Mc 10, 33 reads "The Son of Man shall be delivered to the chief priests and the scribes, and they *shall condemn him to death and* shall deliver him to the pagans", the words referring to the Council's pronouncement of a capital sentence are significantly absent from Lc 18, 32.

The Gospels report that Jesus spent the interval between his arrest and the morning-session in the residence of the high-priest. There is no reason to doubt that this report is based on historical recollection. The high-priest, as the chief of the local Jewish administration, was responsible to the governor for the maintenance of public order. It was part of his duty to render assistance in the apprehension of political suspects and in the preparation of proceedings against political offenders, even in cases which came up for trial before the Roman representative. It could be that we have here an explanation for the detention of Jesus in the high-priest's palace. Support for such a view may be found in Jn 18, 12—27 which seems to contain a highly elaborated account of an early tradition.

The Fourth Evangelist who dramatizes the summary Roman military court proceedings[30] out of all proportion, has a tendency to overstate the importance of Jesus' opponents. It was more likely a *decurio* than a *tribunus militaris* that arrested Jesus, and more likely one of the high-priest's subordinate clerks than the high-priest's father-in-law who examined him — and yet, a historical substratum of the story in Jn 18, 12 —27 is not improbable. While no χιλίαρχος took part in the arrest and probably no Annas in the investigation, even if title and name are the Fourth Evangelist's creation, the tradition he used apparently reported that Jesus was arrested by Roman soldiers and subsequently taken by them to the residence of the high-priest to be interrogated there by some Jewish official and afterwards to be handed back to the Romans for trial. Jesus could sarcely have been brought before Pilate in the early morning unless the governor had prior knowledge of his arrest and the accusation against him. There is nothing incredible in the account of Jn 18, 12—13 a, 28 which states that a Roman military commander, having arrested Jesus, conducted him to a local Jewish official with the

---

[30] We know from Roman sources (Tacitus, Annales XV xliv 4) that Jesus was put to death by Pilate, but of the legal proceedings leading up to the death sentence we know next to nothing. It was certainly not the procedure observed in Rome, the capital city of the Empire, but a summary military procedure such as characterized the dispensation of justice by Roman provincial governors: »... militaribus ingeniis subtilita[s] de[est], quia castrensis iurisdictio secura et obtusior ac plura manu agens calliditatem fori non exerceat«, Tacitus, Agricola ix 2.

order to prepare the judicial proceedings for the governor's court and, this done, to hand him back to the imperial authority. A preliminary examination was required prior to the trial before Pilate. There was the necessity to question Jesus, interrogate witnesses, translate their depositions, and prepare the charge-sheet. Pilate apparently knew what the charge was (Mc 15, 2; Mt 27, 11; Lc 23, 3; Jn 18, 33) though with the exception of Lc 23, 2 no evangelist specifies the charge or a charge-sheet. Differences of language, custom and conventional habits between the Roman officers and the indigenous population would necessitate that the preparation of the case should be entrusted to Jewish officials on the high-priest's staff. Even if in political cases the actual trials were reserved for the imperial representative, the Romans in the provinces were compelled to make use of local institutions for their own ends. We have in John an account of a preliminary investigation. As for the description of Jesus' interrogation in Jn 18, 13, 19—24, 28, we cannot be certain of the reliability of the Evangelist's notice with regard to the personal identity of the interrogator nor of his information concerning the course of the interrogation itself. The magnification of the importance of those who played an adverse part in the final proceedings against Jesus would be calculated by the Evangelist to enhance the significance of the prisoner. It need not have been an entire σπεῖρα (or cohort) under the command of a military tribune that arrested Jesus, nor need it have been the acting high-priest's father-in-law who conducted the subsequent interrogation. Such features are accretions due to the Evangelist. But the tradition used by the author of the Fourth Gospel, namely, that Jesus was arrested by the Romans and interrogated by a Jewish official before he was handed back to the Romans for trial, might well be rooted in historical fact.

The Johannine tradition is not irrelevant for the examination of Mc 14, 53—72. The interrogation by Annas (Jn 18, 12—14; 19—24) is intercalated into the story of Peter's denial as is the case with the nocturnal trial in Mark. The primitive tradition may have reported that Jesus, after his arrest was questioned in the high-priest's residence by some Jewish official. The Second Evangelist made of this a nocturnal session of the Senate, and the Fourth Evangelist a preliminary investigation conducted by Annas[31].

---

[31] [Revisers' addendum: Concerning Winter's understanding of the Lucan narrative, see D. R. Catehpole, The Trial of Jesus, Leiden 1971, pp. 208—220. In general, cf. W. R. Wilson, The Execution of Jesus, New York 1970, pp. 215—226.]

# 4. »THE HIGH-PRIEST OF THAT YEAR«

Traditions formed and handed down by the contemporaries and immediate followers of Jesus contain no trace of the name of the highpriest who, according to the Gospels, played such an outstanding rôle in the events that resulted in Jesus' crucifixion.

The earliest of the Gospels, Mark, mentions in several places[1] the Roman governor by his *cognomen* but does not in a single instance give the name of the high-priest then in office. This in itself indicates that what we read in Mc 14, 53 b, 55—64 does not stem from tradition, but rather represents a later accretion. Had tradition assigned to the Jewish high-priest such a prominent part as he now takes in Mark, those who handed the tradition down would hardly have failed to record beside Pilate's name that of the hierarch. They did not record it. And when the author of the Second Gospel inserted into the traditional account of Jesus' arrest the pericope about the condemnation of Jesus at a nocturnal meeting of the Sanhedrin in the high-priest's residence, he was unable to supply the name of the Jewish high-priest who had been in office when the alleged event was supposed to have taken place.

Nor does the Passion Narrative in the Third Gospel furnish us with the high-priest's name. We find this name, however, in Lc 3, 2 and Acts 4, 6 (probably also in Acts 5, 17). The synchronization in Lc 3, 2 is not based on any tradition emanating from the group of Palestinian messianists who were devoted to the memory of Jesus. It is an editorial note by which the Third Evangelist endeavoured to supply readers with 'historical' information concerning the period in which the βίος of Jesus was set. The present reading in Lc 3, 2 ἐπὶ ἀρχιερέως Ἄννα καὶ Καιαφᾶ is not original; it designates Annas as the high-priest, whilst the words καὶ Καιαφᾶ hang disconnectedly in the air. The Third Evangelist apparently wrote only the first three of the five words in question and assumed that it was Annas who was high-priest in the fifteenth year of Tiberius' reign. Subsequently a corrector wrote the name Καιαφᾶ over Ἄννα, without, however, erasing the latter. Exactly when this interlinear correction was made, it is impossible to say, but it was made at a time when the Gospel according to Matthew already enjoyed sufficient authority in Christian communities to serve as a 'model' for harmonizing or correcting other Gospels. With Καιαφᾶ written over Ἄννα, the manuscript then reached a copyist who was unable or unwilling to de-

---

[1] Mc 15, 1, 2, 4, 5, 9, 12, 14, 15, 43, 44.

cide between the two names. So as to omit neither, he inserted a καί between them and admitted the interlinear correction into the text. In this manner Kaiaphas now makes his appearance in the Third Gospel. It is not clear in what capacity he is there; whereas the functions of all other persons mentioned in Lc 3, 2 are explicitly stated, that of Kaiaphas is not recorded[2]. The case in Acts 4, 6 is similar. Here also only one person is referred to as high-priest, and that person is Annas. After the officiating high-priest's name there appear the names of several members of his entourage or political associates; among them is Kaiaphas. The fact that we here find several names makes it less easy to affirm with certainty how the name of Kaiaphas came to be there. Yet it is propable that the words καὶ Καιαφᾶς were inserted into the text of Acts 4, 6 in the same manner as in Lc 3, 2[3]. At all events, in the Acts as in the Gospel, the high-priest is called 'Annas', while the function of Kaiaphas remains undefined. The reading ἀναστὰς δὲ ὁ ἀρχιερεὺς καὶ πάντες σὺν αὐτῷ ... ἐπλήσθησαν ζήλου in Acts 5, 17 should also be considered. Even if it were assumed that the writer wished to convey the impression that it would have been impolite for members of the Council to give vent to their passionate feelings whilst the high-priest remained *in situ,* the singular form of the participle ἀναστάς is suspect; it is not followed by a finite verb that would also be in the singular. The original would seem to have had Ἄννας[4], possibly written in an abbre-

---

[2] Alfred Loisy, *Les actes des apôtres* (Paris 1920): »... le nom de Caïphe est interpolé« (p. 242; *cf.* p. 275); Kirsopp Lake in *The Beginnings of Christianity,* vol. 4 (London 1933), pp. 41, 42, 56.

[3] Julius Wellhausen, *Das Evangelium Johannis* (Berlin 1908): »In Act. 4, 6 ist καὶ Καιαφας nachgetragen und vermutlich auch in Lc 3, 2, wo der Dual sehr befremdet« (p. 81, note 1); the same, »Kritische Analyse der Apostelgeschichte«, *Abhandlungen der Kgl. Gesellschaft der Wissenschaften zu Göttingen. Philologisch-historische Klasse,* Neue Folge, Band XV, Nr. 2 (Berlin 1914): »Kaiphas ist in [Act.] 4, 6 vielleicht und in Lc 3, 2 sicher nachgetragen. Auch im vierten Evangelium ist ursprünglich Annas der regierende Hohepriester; siehe zu Joa. 18, 12—17. Bei Markus bleibt er anonym, nur bei Matthäus heißt er Kaiphas. Dieser richtige Name ist dann von den Späteren an die Stelle des Annas gesetzt oder wenigstens demselben beigefügt« (p. 8).

[4] Friedrich Wilhelm Blass, *Acta Apostolorum sive Lucae ad Theophilum liber alter* (Leipzig 1896), p. 15, *ad locum.* See also Julius Wellhausen, »Kritische Analyse der Apostelgeschichte«: »'Αναστάς ist sachlich unmöglich. Man erhebt sich um zu reden oder um irgend etwas anderes zu tun, aber nicht um voll Leidenschaft zu werden« (p. 10); Loisy, *o. c.*: »Annas (Hanan) [était] ..., pour le rédacteur, le pontife qui régnait en ce temps-là« (p. 276); Martin Dibelius, »The Text of Acts. An Urgent Critical Task«, *Journal of Religion,* vol. 21, 1941, pp. 421—431, translated by Paul Schubert from the manuscript, also available under the title »Der Text der Apostelgeschichte« in Dibelius' *Aufsätze zur Apostelgeschichte* (Berlin ²1953), pp. 76—83: »Mir scheint [in Apg 5, 17] ... die Lesung Ἄννας an Stelle von ἀναστάς immer noch erwägenswert« (p. 430, resp. 82); English edition (London 1956), p. 91. There actually exists a manuscript belonging to the Spanish recension of the Old Latin Version which reads in Acts 5, 17 *annas autem princeps sacerdotum et*

viated form. The scribal error which resulted in the present confused state of the text occurred at an early date; whether it was an unintentional mistake, or a deliberate alteration, is uncertain. If the substitution of ἀναστάς for Ἄννας antedated the supplementation of Annas' name with that of Kaiaphas in Lc 3, 2, it could have been an involuntary slip made in the process of copying.

In the Third Gospel, then, and in the Acts of the Apostles the high-priest, said to have held office during Jesus' life-time and shortly after his death, is named Anna(s). Whence does this information come? It cannot have as its source a report that would have emanated from any of Jesus' contemporaries or from any of the members of the community that constituted itself after his death. Tradition, though not unadulterated, may lie behind Acts 4, 6; 5, 17, but none appears in Lc 3, 2. Further, at the time to which these passages refer, no high-priest of the name of Annas was in office. The Third Evangelist, when he set out to write his Gospel, collected information in Judaea or adjacent lands; this information made him think that someone named Anna(s) was high-priest in Jerusalem during the life-time of Jesus and in the years following his death. However, the Evangelist did not reproduce the name in his narrative of Jesus' trial. Of whom is the Evangelist thinking when he writes of Annas? We have to fall back on surmises; but it may be said that the Annas referred to can scarcely have been the high-priest who had been appointed under Quirinius and was deposed by Valerius Gratus[5], for Annas' term of office had expired some years before Kaiaphas succeeded him, and long before Jesus started his public activity. The information which led the Evangelist to believe that Annas was the high-priest's name must ultimately have been derived from certain Jewish-Christian circles. Yet which Annas would the Evangelist's informants have had in mind? Perhaps they spoke of Ananus II whom they still remembered for the oppressive measures he had taken against certain members of their sect[6]. His name was חָנָן or חָנִין, transcribed by Josephus with a Greek ending as Ἄνανος. Less literate Judaeo-Christian intermediaries probably rendered the name in a form closer to its Semitic original as Ἄννα. Memories of this Ḥanan, or Ḥanin — who, in fact, only became high-priest a full generation after the death of Jesus

---

omnes ... (the manuscript comes from Perpignan and is at present kept in Paris [Ms lat 321]; it is known under the siglum p or 54). I am indebted to Dom Dr. Bonifatius Fischer, O. S. B., Rector of the Vetus Latina Institut in Beuron, and his assistant Dr. Walter Thiele for the information that besides this manuscript there are others (Paris Ms lat 9380, further a codex kept in the Seminary at Burgos, and the Book of Armagh) which give a conflated reading combining the name *Annas* from the Perpignan Codex with the word *exsurgens* from the received text.

[5] Ananus (Annas) was high-priest from the year 6 CE to 15 CE; Joseph, called Kaiaphas, held office in the years 18 to 36 CE.

[6] Josephus, Ant XX 200.

— might have lingered in the minds of the contemporaries of the Third Evangelist as a person hostile to their beliefs, while the Annas of the years 6—15 CE could hardly have meant anything to them and would long have been forgotten.

The author of the First Gospel gives the name 'Kaiaphas' as that of the high-priest in Mt 26, 3, 57. There is no indication that he derived knowledge of this name from internal Christian tradition; rather it appears that he gathered it from some outside source, possibly of non-Christian Jewish provenance. Unlike the information used by the Third Evangelist, his was historically correct. The First Evangelist recognized the need for mentioning the name of a person who was reputed to have exercised such preponderating influence on Jesus' fate and the final outcome of his trial as did the anonymous Marcan high-priest, and he inserted the name 'Kaiaphas' in his version of the Passion Story.

As far as the synoptic Gospels are concerned, the facts are fairly clear. No apostolic tradition of any sort existed which preserved the name of the Jewish high-priest in Jesus' time. The Third and First Evangelists, independently of each other, found it necessary to supply that name from outside information, and the information on which, respectively, they based their statements, differed. Annas is the high-priest in one Gospel, Kaiaphas in the other. Some uncertainty is possible only with regard to the historical identity of the 'Annas' whom the Third Evangelist and his informants had in mind.

More complex is the situation in the Fourth Gospel. Both names, Annas and Kaiaphas, are mentioned, as in the copyist's conflated reading of Lc 3, 2, but whilst the rank of high-priesthood is in Luke assigned to Annas, and it is left to the imagination of the reader to supply the function of Kaiaphas, the Fourth Gospel as we have it states that Kaiaphas was "the high-priest of that year" (Jn 11, 49, 51, 18, 13 b), whilst Annas was his father-in-law (Jn 18, 13 b). Twice we find Annas' name — Jn 18, 13 a, 24 — and five times that of Kaiaphas: Jn 11, 49, 18, 13 b, 14, 24, 28 a. If our reading in the Fourth Gospel is confined to the verses just enumerated, it might appear that an exact distinction is made between the two persons, and that the high-priest's office is unambiguously assigned to Kaiaphas. But closer examination of the pericope Jn 18, 12—27 shows that the position is far from being as unequivocal as this.

Jesus is said to have been led to Annas (18, 13 a) and to have been interrogated by the high-priest (18, 19, 22) before he was sent from Annas to Kaiaphas (18, 24). Who then is the "high-priest" who conducts the interrogation before Jesus is brought to Kaiaphas? Unmistakably, it is Annas. Although Kaiaphas may be called high-priest (18, 13 b, 24), he himself plays a shadowy rôle in the whole story and takes no part whatever in the questioning of Jesus. The pericope Jn 18, 12—14 (15—18), 19—24 (25—27) in its present form is incoherent; scrutiny reveals retouches superimposed by a second hand, modifications in the orginal text made with less than consummate skill. The subject is sufficiently important to warrant an attempt to restore the text as it stood before it was reshaped.

Jesus is brought to Annas and Peter follows him (Jn 18, 13 a, 15). Jesus is interrogated by a person who is described as high-priest (18, 19, 22 b); this interrogator is Annas, because it is only after the interrogation that Jesus is sent to Kaiaphas (18, 24, cf. 28 a) — who *is* the high-priest (18, 13 b, 14, 24)! Peter is present all the time without moving from one place to the other, both while Jesus is confronted by Annas (18, 15—18) and while he stays in the residence of Kaiaphas (18, 25—27). Apologetic imagination may seek to explain that Annas and Kaiaphas, being relatives, were living in the same building, each occupying a different wing, and that their quarters were divided by a court-yard in which Peter stood near the fire so that it was unnecessary for him to follow Jesus when the latter was transferred from one apartment to another[7]. Such an explanation fails, however, to account for the fact that Jesus, according to vv. 19, 22 b, is interrogated by the high-priest before being sent to Kaiaphas "the high-priest" (18, 13 b, 24).

The solution to the problem of the original wording — a problem that made itself felt from early times[8] — was presented by Julius Wellhausen[9]. The name of Kaiaphas in the Fourth Gospel does not belong to the source behind Jn 18, 12—28 a; vv. 13 b, 14 and 24 intrude upon the text; their insertion is due to a 'correction', after the same manner as the inclusion of Kaiaphas's name in the received text of Luke. Only Annas was originally mentioned in the *Vorlage*. Annas was presumed by the author of the document behind Jn 18, 12—28 a to have been the high-priest in the year of Jesus' crucifixion[10]. The text as we now have it is a careless revision of an earlier wording. The reviser added vv. 13 b, 14, 24 and substituted in v. 28 a the name 'Kaiaphas' for 'Annas'. The *Vorlage* knew of Annas as high-priest, and this view still comes to the

---

[7] A similar disregard for detail is apparent in the Johannine picture of the situation during Jesus' trial before Pilate. Jesus is inside the governor's palace and Pilate privately discusses the case with him, whilst the crowd remains outside. Yet as if endowed with second sight, the crowd senses what is taking place within the praetorium and, still more surprising, what goes on in the absent Pilate's mind; cf. below, pp. 129—130.

[8] The transposition of v. 24 to a place between verses 13 and 14 and of vv. 19—23 to a place between verses 15 and 16, as well as the joining of vv. 25—27 to verse 18, in the Sinaitic Syriac was prompted by a desire to arrange a more logical order by allowing Kaiaphas to conduct the interrogation. Similar transpositions, though less extensive than in the Syriac, were made in the Old Latin text of Jn 18, 12—27.

[9] *Das Evangelium Johannis:* »Kaiphas ist ... überall eingetragen. Die Vorlage kennt ihn nicht, sondern bloss den Annas«, p. 81.

[10] Wellhausen, *Erweiterungen und Änderungen im vierten Evangelium* (Berlin 1907), p. 27.

fore in vv. 13 a, 19, 22 (*cf.* 15—18)[11]. The artificial introduction of Kaiaphas by a second hand is responsible for the incoherence of the account we now find in Jn 18, 12—27. Exact restoration of the original text is impossible, for even if we remove the obvious additions, we cannot be sure whether secondary accretions were limited to the insertion of vv. 13 b, 14, 24 and to the alteration of the high-priest's name in v. 28 a, nor can we be certain whether 'the reviser' omitted something from the original account. Nevertheless, the general outline of the original can be discerned. It would run somewhat as follows: *The detachment of Roman soldiers, under their commander, and the police of the Jews, arrested Jesus, bound him, and brought him to Annas, the high-priest. Jesus was examined by the high-priest about his following and his teaching. He affirmed that he had always openly proclaimed whatever he had taught, and he held no secrets. During the interrogation, a police officer (or an attendant on the high-priest's staff) struck Jesus. In the morning, Jesus was taken from Annas to the governor's palace.*

The story of Peter's denial, Jn 18, 15—18, 25—27, can be accommodated in the same place — Annas's house; it is not necessary for Peter, who had followed him, to move elsewhere.

The result of the foregoing analysis has some significance. As in the original form of the Third Gospel and in the early chapters of Acts, Annas was the high-priest in the Johannine *Vorlage*. Yet the situation is not the same. The Third Evangelist had no literary document at his disposal that gave 'Annas' as the name of the high-priest who officiated in the year of Jesus' death. The text behind Jn 18, 12—27 which mentioned Annas as high-priest was, however, a written document. When

---

[11] »... le premier auteur avait écrit simplement: Et ils l'amenèrent à Annas le grand-prêtre... Pour cet auteur, comme pour le rédacteur des Actes, Annas était le grand-prêtre en exercice. Notre rédacteur introduit Caïphe d'après Matthieu et il s'efforce d'expliquer la comparution de Jésus devant ces deux grands-prêtres«, Alfred Loisy, *Le quatrième évangile* (Paris 1904), p. 458. »Für die Quelle war Hannas der Hohepriester«, Rudolf Bultmann, *Das Evangelium des Johannes* (Göttingen [4]1953), p. 497. »At 18, 19 ›the high priest‹, in view of 18, 24, is apparently Annas«, Robert Henry Lightfoot, *St. John's Gospel. A Commentary*. Edited by C. F. Evans (London 1956), p. 307. »Why should Jesus be sent to Caiaphas... when the high priest (who, John tells us, was Caiaphas) has already questioned him? Why is Jesus first of all brought to Annas, if Caiaphas is to question him? Why do we hear nothing at all of the result of the examination before Caiaphas?«, C. Kingsley Barrett, *The Gospel according to St. John. An Introduction with Commentary and Notes on the Greek text* (London 1955), p. 437. »One notices... the Evangelist's own hand in the parenthetical notes which are attached to Annas (xviii. 13 f.). This parenthesis refers back to Jn xi. 49 ff. and indicates a... Johannine theological theme«, Peder Borgen, »John and the Synoptics in the Passion Narrative«, *NTS* vol. 5, 1959, pp. 246—259, on p. 257. Borgen thinks, however, that the mention of Kaiaphas in the Fourth Gospel represents a traditional element — a view not shared by the present writer.

this document was composed, a tradition had already crystallized assigning the high-priesthood to Annas. The Annas of the Johannine tradition is in all likelihood the same as the Annas of the Lucan 'information' — namely, Ananus II. It was only the reviser of the *Vorlage* of Jn 18, 12—27 who, when he introduced Kaiaphas into the story, made the Annas of his source document the father-in-law of Kaiaphas[12].

Another difference between Luke and John concerns the authentic text of the Evangelists. In that of Luke, we can be sure that Kaiaphas was not mentioned at all. It is not possible to have the same certainty in the case of the Fourth Gospel. The introduction of the lines in which Kaiaphas appears, and is mentioned as high-priest, might be due to a post-evangelical editor — the 'ecclesiastical reviser' who is postulated by many commentators of the Fourth Gospel — or it might have been due to the Fourth Evangelist himself. If it was the Evangelist who inserted the 'Kaiaphas passages', he used an earlier written source; if it was 'the ecclesiastical reviser', the original text of the Gospel would not have contained Kaiaphas' name.

The discussion, so far, has confirmed the view that there is no tradition going back to the generation of Jesus' contemporaries, or to the generation immediately following, which transmitted to posterity the name of the person who occupied the high-priesthood in Jesus' time, be it at the beginning of his preaching career or at its violent termination. The first guesses regarding the identity of the high-priest (Lc 3, 2; Jn 18, 19, 22 b) were erroneous. Only at a late date, when historical interest on the part of individual Christians had already been awakend and had stimulated researches into non-Christian records, was the identity of Kaiaphas as "the high-priest of that year" established. It was the First Evangelist who, probably conversant with Jewish documents, made the identification (Mt 26, 3, 57). Knowledge of Matthew prompted the revision of the account given in John before its final redaction, and the insertion of the name 'Kaiaphas' in the chronological summary in Luke by a copyist after the Third Evangelist had completed his work.

According by, the name of Kaiaphas came into John 18 only through the revision of an earlier account — a revision secondary in its nature, whether it was due to the Evangelist himself who reshaped his *Vorlage*, or to a post-evangelical editor who modified what the Evangelist had written. But we still need to account for the presence of Kaiaphas's name in the other Johannine pericope, 11, 47—53, where it also occurs. In Jn 11, 49, 51 Kaiaphas is introduced by the same unusual phrase ὁ ἀρχιερεὺς τοῦ ἐνιαυτοῦ ἐκείνου as in 18, 13 b. The two passages come from the same hand, the 'reviser' of Jn 18, 12—28 a. It is incumbent on

---

[12] There is no corroboration for the statement in Jn 18, 13 b. It is by no means established whether any family relationship existed between Kaiaphas and any bearer of the name Annas or Ananus.

us to consider whether there are elements in Jn 11, 47—53 which antedate the reviser's time, and if so, to distinguish them from his work.

Apart from the fact that Jn 11, 47—53 also mentions a meeting of
the Sanhedrin before Jesus' arrest — as does Mc 14, 1—2 and its deriva-
tives — there is no synoptic counterpart to the Johannine pericope.
The Second Evangelist, in Mc 14, 10—11, connects the betrayal by Judas
with the Sanhedrin's plot against Jesus' life; the Fourth Evangelist does
not present the story of the betrayal but records merely that "from that
day" the Jewish authorities sought to kill Jesus (Jn 11, 53)[13], and that
they issued orders to the effect that anybody knowing of his whereabouts should denounce him (Jn 11, 57). If the Fourth Gospel reports
nothing which would correspond to Judas's conspiracy with the hierarchy, it contains other interesting features absent from Mark and the
synoptic parallels. There is a speech by the high-priest which supplies
a reason for the Council's decision to have Jesus arrested. The question
arises: does the Johannine description of the Council-Meeting contain
traditional elements or is the entire pericope — parts of which we had
to attribute to a 'secondary hand' — the Evangelist's, or the reviser's
own *creatio ex nihilo*? Investigation seems to show that there is in the
extant narrative a traditional residue. This is more particularly evident
in v. 48 and, to a lesser degree perhaps, also discernible in v. 50. It is
not, of course, suggested that the Evangelist (or whoever wrote these
lines) had access to the minutes of the Council-Meeting and was in a
position to quote the high-priest's speech. Yet there is more in Jn 11,
47—53 than Johannine theology.

In the view of the Evangelist, οἱ 'Ιουδαῖοι are the pre-existent antagonists of the Christ, the dark forces that persist in trying, unsuccessfully,
to overcome the light. No such mythological concept transpires from
the passage under review. The theme of the report of a Council-meeting
at which a decision to arrest Jesus was arrived at, properly belongs to
the Passion Narrative. As it stands, however, it forms no part of the
Johannine Passion Story, being widely separated from the description
of Jesus' arrest and trial as given by the author of the Fourth Gospel.
It has the appearance of an erratic boulder in an alien landscape. Indeed, the mere location suggests that Jn 11, 47—53 once formed part of
a larger context and preserves, however modified, elements of an earlier
tradition. For if the Evangelist was not utilizing traditional material,
but was freely inventing what he wrote, he would have found a place
for the passage in his description of Jesus' arrest and trial. That he did
not do so, indicates that he had before him a 'source' or a 'tradition'
which he did not wish to discard yet which he found unsuitable for inclusion within the framework of his own narrative of the trial. For this

---

[13] A curious statement to be made at this point, since the main pre-occupation of
the Jews in the Fourth Gospel from an early stage is to find means for killing Jesus;
so Jn 5, 18; 7, 1, 19 b, 25, 32; 8, 37 b, 40, 59; 10, 31; 11, 8.

reason he reproduced the tradition, with modifications of his own, in another place, separated from the account proper of Jesus' trial.[14] This rather general deduction from the isolation of Jn 11, 47—53 (—57) is not the only, or the weightiest, argument for maintaining the view that the pericope, in spite of modification, had an independent origin. When we compare the contents of vv. 48, 50 with those of vv. 51, 52, doubts about the existence of a traditional nucleus must disappear. What we read in the latter two verses is manifestly the Evangelist's interpretation. The high-priest's words have a plain, perhaps unpleasant but straightforward, meaning. The fact that the Evangelist — or the 'ecclesiastical editor' if the inclusion of the pericope into the Gospel was due to him — thought it necessary to foist upon the speaker's words a tortuous piece of theological interpretation, indicates that he himself was not the author of vv. 48, 50. The traditional report of the high-priest's speech[15] before the Council caused our evangelist some difficulty; he felt compelled to substitute 'a deeper meaning' of his own for the blunt undissimulating plea of a worldly politician. It may even be that the traditional report was more explicit about the cause of the high-priest's disquiet and his apprehensiveness at the possibility of Roman intervention[16]. Without such interpretation as is produced in vv. 51, 52 the words of the high-priest as recorded in vv. 48, 50 were felt to be too harsh, too realistic, to be reconciled by the author with bis own understanding of the events. Hence the addition of a subtly theological exposition, and the removal of the whole pericope from its germane context of Jesus' arrest and trial.

The contrast between the stark realism in the high-priest's words and the interpretation given to them points to the conclusion that Jn 11, 47a—48 preserves some element of a tradition (or 'source') which was in existence before the author of the Fourth Gospel undertook his work. In vv. 50, 53 and 57 we may discern faint traces of the same tradition, but the editorial contribution is here more in evidence. Verses 51, 52 are plainly editorial. Verse 47 b provides a connection with the σημεῖον

---

[14] »[Jn xi. 47—53] is a complete *pericope*, and might quite well have reached [the Evangelist] in tradition as a separate unit, for which he had to find a ... setting. In any case, he has provided a connecting passage, xi. 45—6, which is clearly designed to bring the report of the Council-meeting into the closest relation with the story of Lazarus«, Charles Harold Dodd, *The Interpretation of the Fourth Gospel* (Cambridge 1953), p. 367.

[15] We do not suggest that the words in Jn 11, 48, 50 are based on a verbatim report of the high-priest's speech, but there manifestly existed a tradition ascribing to the high-priest some such utterance. See note 14 above, and J. Wellhausen, *Das Evangelium Johannis*, pp. 25, 54.

[16] *Cf.* Eduard Schwartz, »Aporien im vierten Evangelium«, *Nachrichten von der Kgl. Gesellschaft der Wissenschaften zu Göttingen. Phil.-Hist. Klasse* 1907, pp. 342—379; 1908, pp. 115—148, 149—188, 497—560 (Berlin 1907—1908), on p. 171.

of Lazarus's resurrection and also belongs to the Evangelist (or 'editor').
Verses 54—56 form no part of the pericope concerning the Sanhedrin's
consultations. Hence we are left with v. 49. It comes from the same
hand as Jn 11, 51 and Jn 18, 13 b, Kaiaphas being introduced by the
phrase "the high-priest of that year".

From the examination of Jn 18, 13 b, 14, 24, 28 a it emerged that the
introduction of Kaiaphas into the account of Jesus' detention in the
high-priest's house was due to a secondary hand, though it was left
open whether it was the Fourth Evangelist who inserted the 'Kaiaphas
passages' into a written source at his disposal, or whether it was an
ecclesiastical redactor who revised and supplemented the Evangelist's
account. The same dilemma exists in regard to Jn 11, 49, 51—52 and
the retouches throughout the remainder of the pericope. However,
though the question may be of considerable interest in an examination
of the process by which the Fourth Gospel came into being in its present form, it is of little relevance in a discussion of the historical background of the trial narratives contained in the Gospels.

From the context of the pericope Jn 11, 47—53 we have been able
to extricate traditional elements of which traces persist in vv. 47 a, 48
and, to a minor degree, in vv. 50, 53. These elements provide no clue
regarding the high-priest's name. As in Mc 14, 1—2 (tradition) and
Mc 14, 53 b 55—64 (editorial accretion), the high-priest remains name-
less.

Although it is not often realized by writers of books about the trial
of Jesus, the reticence of the earliest tradition in respect of the high-
priest's identity is significant. To recapitulate: neither the tradition in
Mc 14, 1—2 nor the Evangelist's description of a night-session in Mc 14,
53 b, 55—64, nor the tradition behind Jn 11, 47—53 (freely reproduced
with embellishments by the writer to whom the present wording owes
its existence) preserves any recollection of the name of the Jewish high-
priest who was in office when Jesus appeared for trial. The Third Evangelist, and apparently the source underlying Jn 18, 12—28 a, knew
Annas as the high-priest. Only in Matthew and in the re-fashioned accounts of Jn 11 and Jn 18 is Kaiaphas introduced. The mention of Kaiaphas' name[17] in this connection is not due to any transmitted early tradition, but to a conscious effort on the part of individual writers who
drew on information that was historically sound, though not derived
from internal communal sources. In the process of the formation of the
New Testament, historical interest became active at a relatively late
stage.

The absence of any early interest in the identity of the high-priest
gives considerable force to the argument that the hierarch's actual part

---

[17] 'Kaiapha' (Hebrew קיף, Aramaic קייפא) is in fact a by-name; the real name
was Joseph. See Joseph., Ant XVIII 35, 95.

in the proceedings against Jesus was far from being as commanding as the evangelists suggest.

Having come to the conclusion that Kaiaphas' name in Jn 11, 49 was due to the adaptation, by a secondary hand, of some traditional account of the Sanhedrin's consultations, it remains for us to look more closely at what were described as 'traditional elements' in the pericope under review. It is especially the high-priest's utterance — anonymous though the speaker now appears — in v. 48 in its literal meaning that deserves attention.

The words ἡμῶν ὁ τόπος are normally understood to denote the Temple. This exegesis may be correct. The possibility exists, however, that another, and more specific, meaning was attached to this expression. The word τόπος can signify 'office', 'position' (the German Stellung) and was used in this sense in particular of the positions filled by holders of priestly offices. Besides several topoi in profane Greek documents, there are passages in the writings of the Apostolic Fathers where the word appears with this meaning. One such passage, at least, occurs even in the New Testament; in Acts 1, 25 we read of the τόπος (= office) "of deaconship and apostleship". It can be argued that the high-priest, when he spoke of "our place", referred to the official status, the position, the rank, which he and other members of the Supreme Council held under the constitution granted by Rome to the representatives of the Jewish nation. The impression that this is the correct meaning is strengthened when we read the complete sentence: ἐλεύσονται οἱ Ῥωμαῖοι καὶ ἀροῦσιν ἡμῶν καὶ τὸν τόπον καὶ τὸ ἔθνος. The Romans could hardly "take away" (αἴρειν) the Temple from where it stood, but they could take away the rights of individual members of the Sanhedrin to sit in an assembly which was authorized to legislate, administer, and judge, in matters of local or internal interest. It is improbable that ἡμῶν τὸ ἔθνος, in the mouth of a Jewish speaker, denotes "our people". The word ἔθνος in this context seems to signify "nationhood", "national status", rather than the population as such. The meaning of the words in Jn 11, 48 is thus: "If these things continue, the Romans will deprive us of our official position (ἡμῶν ὁ τόπος) and of our statehood (ἡμῶν τὸ ἔθνος)". The high-priest shows himself apprehensive for the rights, and status, he and his colleagues enjoyed as members of an autonomous organ of the Jewish community in Judaea. He betrays fears lest the Romans, perturbed by commotions occasioned by Jesus' activities, should deprive the holders of senatorial office of their positions, and perhaps even abolish Jewish autonomy. As a precaution against this eventuality, the high-priest recommends that Jesus be arrested. The motion put to the Council by its chairman can be understood without the gratuitous interpretation offered in vv. 51, 52. The political situation in Judaea under prefectorial rule was tense. Jewish factions of all sorts were stirring the people to defy foreign domination. The more widespread outbreaks of disorder became, the more frequently discontent was voiced, the greater would become the probability that the governor would take counter-measures and, in so doing, encroach upon the authority that had remained in the hands of the Sanhedrin[18]. In all likelihood, therefore, Jn 11, 48 stems from a tradition of which a mere fraction has been preserved by our evangelist, who, moreover, obscured the original meaning by transposing what he retained from that tradition into an alien context.

The word ἔθνος occasionally occurs in the New Testament (as the word גוי in the Old) with the meaning 'the Jewish nation'. It has that meaning in Jn 18, 35 and is used in the same sense in Lc 7, 5 and 23, 2 as well as in half a dozen passages of the Acts of the Apostles. In the context of the pericope here considered the meaning of the word is, however, more abstract; καὶ ἐλεύσονται οἱ Ῥωμαῖοι ἀροῦσιν ἡμῶν καὶ τὸν τόπον καὶ τὸ ἔθνος has to be translated in the following manner: *and the Romans will come and deprive us of our office, and abolish our national autonomy.*

As the Gospel now reports it, the high-priest bases his fears of Roman intervention on the possibility that publicity about Lazarus' resurrection might reach Pilate — a most unconvincing explanation[19]. It is difficult to see why the resurrection of Lazarus should have had such an alarming effect upon Pilate as to induce him to act in the manner contemplated in Jn 11, 48 b. Nor would the other "signs" performed by Jesus have provoked him to such action[20]. On the other hand, an intervention by the occupying power would be comprehensible if it were occasioned by reports such as Jn 6, 15 provides, namely, that it was the intention of certain Jews to make Jesus their king.

The traditional threads that underlie Jn 11, 47—53 are irreparably broken. The effort at rephrasing the original account, and the substitution of profound theology for the high-priest's sober realism, succeeded

---

[18] »... il faut en finir avec l'agitateur, afin de prévenir les conséquences inévitables de l'agitation«; »L'auteur entend que, le soulèvement reprimé, le sanhédrin ne subsistera plus et ses membres perdront le pouvoir qu'ils avaient sur ceux de leur nation, comme il est advenu en effet après la guerre de Judée«, Alfred Loisy, *Le quatrième évangile*, p. 357. »... it must have been apparent... that undue provocations, such as messianic disorders, would result in decisive action by the Romans. There is ... no reason why the Sanhedrin should not have regarded Jesus as in this way a danger to the State«, C. K. Barrett, *The Gospel according to St. John*, p. 338.

[19] »Les membres du sanhédrin ne voient dans les miracles qu'un germe possible de révolution, une menace pour leur crédit et pour la paix de la nation. Cette crainte a, dans les synoptiques, quelque raison d'être; mais elle n'en a aucune dans notre évangile... L'idée d'un soulèvement [politique] ... n'était pas encore trop incroyable ... [mais dans le quatrième évangile] elle déconcerte le lecteur, tant elle est sans rapport avec la doctrine christologique dont [cet] évangile est rempli«, Loisy, *o. c.*, p. 356.

[20] »... die vielen Wunder gehören nicht in die Grundschrift, und der Hohepriester Kaiphas auch nicht«, Julius Wellhausen, *Das Evangelium Johannis*, p. 54.

in almost completely obscuring the import of this passage before it underwent the drastic changes at the hands of the person or persons responsible for its adjustment. All we may say with some degree of certainty is that behind Jn 11, 47—53 there lies a report imparting information to the effect that the activities of Jesus — or the reaction of the people to Jesus' activities — caused the high-priest to express anxiety respecting the governor's possible counter-measures. To the high-priest, as well as to the entire 'upper strata' of the nation, any agitation among the easily aroused masses constituted a threat to public order and especially to their own political privileges. An increase of unrest among the people could easily give a pretext for prefectorial interference with the rights of the Jewish Senate, and lead to diminution of such limited self-rule as the Sanhedrin still enjoyed. The decision to arrest Jesus (Jn 11, 53) and execute him (Jn 11, 57), motivated in Mark by the elders "envy" (15, 10), is in Jn 11, 48 motivated by apprehensiveness regarding Pilate's attitude to the spreading of public agitation. The arrest is counselled to serve as a deterrent to further expressions of popular discontent. Owing to the character of our sources, their late date and their apologetic aim, we do not know of the exact nature of the Council's meeting nor of the reason for its being assembled. A mere glimpse is offered of the course of its deliberations in the words of the high-priest in Jn 11, 48. But that some such meeting did take place before Jesus was brought to trial, may be asserted with confidence. Differ though they do in their descriptions of the course of the proceedings, the reports in Mc 14, 1, 2, (10, 11) and in Jn 11, 47—53 both bear witness to the fact that a meeting took place.

If the Sanhedrin convened with the object of deliberating on the possibility of repercussions arising from Jesus' activities, repercussions likely to affect relations between the Jewish and the Roman authorities, it would point to the fact that the high-priest — and the Sanhedrin as a whole — played a certain part in bringing Jesus to trial. The information that Jesus after his arrest was taken to the high-priest's residence, though doubted by some scholars[21], seems to be historically un-

---

[21] »...nur von [Pilatus] kann die römische Cohorte unter einem römischen Hauptmann beordert sein, welche [Jesu] Verhaftung vornimmt«, Wellhausen, o. c., p. 105. Wellhausen expressed the opinion that the *Grundschrift* of the Fourth Gospel reported that Jesus after his arrest was immediately despatched to Pilate; a later *Bearbeiter* inserted the story of Jesus' examination before the high-priest Annas (o. c., pp. 105, 106). Although assuming that Jesus had, on Pilate's order, been taken before the Sanhedrin, Maurice Goguel took a view similar to Wellhausen's in »Juifs et Romains dans l'histoire de la Passion«, RHR tome 62, 1910, pp. 165—182, 295—322. »...l'auteur du récit johannique a connu une tradition dans laquelle c'étaient les Romains qui prenaient l'initiative de poursuites contre Jésus et qui procédaient à son arrestation« (*l. c.*, p. 303). Goguel believed that there were even in Mark vague traces of this tradition; on Mc 9, 31 he noted: »...on est en droit de penser que notre fragment provient d'une tradition dans laquelle Jésus était livré par Judas

suspect. This piece of information later gave rise to fanciful descriptions of what went on in the high-priest's palace. Yet the unadorned report from Mc 14, 53 a itself provides evidence for supposing that the high-priest acted in concert with Pilate. Either of them might have ordered the arrest; both must have had knowledge that the arrest was impending. We are entitled to deduce from the words in Jn 11, 48 that the high-priest was acting under compulsion. The extent of such compulsion cannot be determined. Pilate was worried by the prevalence of disaffection among the population, and he may have cautioned the high-priest and advised him to take measures calculated to stem the spread of disloyalty, threatening at the same time that he would have to do so himself if the Jewish authorities failed to act. Whether Pilate knew of Jesus, and whether he was of the opinion that his preaching contributed to popular unrest, it is impossible to say. If he did, he might have demanded specifically that the high-priest should take charge of Jesus and put an end to his activities. If, as is more likely, Pilate's information about Jewish affairs was of a less definite character, he would merely have sent a warning to the local authorities instructing them, in general terms, to 'put their house in order'. Was the initiative to act against Jesus taken directly by Pilate? Or did the governor merely express displeasure with conditions in the country and insist that something be done about them? There is no answer to this question. The report underlying Jn 11, 47—53 warrants the contention that the governor demanded of the Sanhedrin proof of its own loyalty to Rome[22]. If Pilate's warning was framed in general terms, the high-priest himself may have been responsible for advocating the expedient of setting an example, with a view to deterring radical demands for political change.

---

entre les mains des Romains« (*l. c.*, p. 172); »... la relation qu'il y a dans le récit actuel entre le procès juif et le procès romain n'est pas primitive, mais provient uniquement du rédacteur« (*l. c.*, p. 175).

Regarding the tradition which comes to the fore in Jn 18, 12, 13 a, the case has been stated with clarity by Eduard Schwartz: »Wenn Iesus von der römischen Cohorte verhaftet wird, dann hat Pilatus sie ausgeschickt«, »Aporien im vierten Evangelium«, p. 352; »Wie Pilatus dazu kam Iesus von sich aus verhaften zu lassen, ist in dem vierten Evangelium jetzt nicht mehr zu erkennen«, *ibidem*, p. 355; »Jetzt ist der wichtigste Zug, daß die Verhaftung Pilatus zugeschoben wurde, unterdrückt ...«, *ibidem*, p. 180; *cf.* pp. 354, 358.

[22] The Slavonic Version of the Jewish War contains the following information: »The Jewish leaders gathered together, with the high-priest, and spoke: We are powerless and too weak to withstand the Romans ... We will go and tell Pilate what we have heard, and we shall be free from anxiety lest he hears it from others and we be deprived of our substance«. The words "we will go and tell Pilate what we have heard" might appear to indicate that the initiative for the arrest of Jesus came from the assembled Jewish dignitaries; the Slavonic text of the War is, however, too doubtful a source of information to serve as a premise for historical deductions concerning the circumstances of Jesus' arrest and trial.

The decision to use Jesus for the purpose of making an example and to let "one man die that the whole nation perish not"[23] could have been due to the hierarch's recommendation.

The description of the Council's meeting before the arrest of Jesus (Mc 14, 1—2; Jn 11, 47—53) is different in the Fourth Gospel from that in the Second. The tradition, however, on which both renderings are ultimately based, was the same. Different channels of transmission, various intermediaries, additions here, omissions there, to or from the original, account for the divergence. Has something been preserved in the Second Gospel that tallies with what we have gleaned from the Fourth? In Mc 14, 2 we read that the Council members decided to arrest Jesus, yet to do so not during the feast "lest there be an uprising of the people". Subsequently, Jesus is arrested — though exactly "during the feast"! It has long been noticed by exegetes and commentators that there is something out of order. If the words "not during the feast" are eliminated, the complexion of the passage is changed and, surprisingly, it tallies with the tradition that lies behind the Fourth Gospel. It could have been that the Council was motivated not so much by fears regarding the correct timing of the arrest as simply by the fear that an uprising of the people would occur (μήποτε ἔσται θόρυβος τοῦ λαοῦ) if Jesus' preaching to the masses was allowed to continue. This piece of Marcan information, granted the deletion of the words "not during the feast", accords with the expression of anxiety by the high-priest in Jn 11, 48 that Roman intervention would ensue if the fame of Jesus' activities should spread. It must be pointed out, however, that these are insufficient grounds for allowing the excision of the four words μὴ ἐν τῇ ἑορτῇ from Mc 14, 2.

The very fact that the evangelists exaggerate the rôle played by the Jewish high-priest and by his associates in the drama of Jesus' trial and death is likely to influence readers who are anxious to distinguish fact from fiction, and induce them to fall into the opposite error of minimizing the Sanhedrin's share in the events. No doubt the high-priest and his camp-followers were anxious lest their vested interests should be adversely affected by complications threatening to arise from unchecked popular propaganda. There is evidence from the first century of other cases in which certain high-priests — Ananus II, for instance, and Jesus, the son of Gamalas[24] — vainly tried to stem popular move-

---

[23] The high-priest recommends the sacrifice of the rights of an individual to the interests of the state or community. If Kaiaphas actually said what he is reported to have said in Jn 11, 50, though not becoming the founder of a religion, he could have boasted of having a greater following among Christians and non-Christians than Jesus ever had.

[24] Jesus, son of Gamalas, and Ananus, son of Ananus, οἱ... δοκιμώτατοι τῶν ἀρχιερέων, hoped to sway the population of Jerusalem and make them reject the Zealotic faction of the revolutionary movement (Josephus, B. J. IV 160). The high-

ments. Their predecessors were faced with a situation essentially the same. Whatever they may have done in order to remain masters of the situation, there is no need to ascribe exceptional wickedness to them on this account. Their decision, and subsequent action, can be understood as having been motivated by legitimate anxiety to prevent the people's affairs from entering upon a course which threatened to engulf the nation in violence and tragedy. Maligned by Christians and maligned by Jews[25], the Sadducaean aristocracy in Judaea from whose midst the high-priest and his advisers were selected acted in accordance with the exigencies of the situation and the duty of statesmanship. Faced on one side by growing popular discontent and on the other side by an overwhelming foreign power, they tried to preserve what they could of the residue of Jewish self-rule. Their fears were real, and were justified. Whether their part in the arrest of Jesus was small or great, they acted from motives they considered to serve the best interests of the nation — and *the best interests,* as so often, happened to coincide with their own.

---

priest Jesus in question is said by Josephus, who was closely connected with him, to have been "next in seniority to Ananus" (B. J. IV 238) whose fate he shared (B. J. IV 316; *cf.* Vita 193).

[25] Christian reproaches are based in the main on the utter disregard which Kaiaphas and his associates showed for the decisions taken by the Councils of Nicaea and Chalcedon. Jews of our present time, spiritual heirs of the Pharisees, not seldom evade a discussion of the historical problem of Jesus' trial by readily conceding that it was an unfair trial and heaping every blame on the Sadducees; *cf.* Samuel Rosenblatt, »The Crucifixion of Jesus from the Standpoint of Pharisaic Law«, *JBL* vol. 75, 1956, pp. 314—321.

## 5. THE CIRCUMSTANCES AND GROUNDS OF JESUS' ARREST

In the preceding sections, when discussing the description of the Sanhedrin's night session in Mark and various traditions concerning the identity of the high-priest in office at the time, we referred in passing to the Gospel accounts of Jesus' arrest. The circumstances and the grounds of his arrest will now be more closely examined.

There are two main streams of tradition. According to the synoptic Gospels Jesus was arrested by an armed crowd sent out by "the chief priests, the scribes and the elders", *i. e.* the Sanhedrin. Against Mark and the evangelical reports based on Mark there stands the testimony of the Fourth Gospel to the effect that the arrest was carried out by a cohort — of Roman troops — in company with "the officers from the chief priests and the Pharisees". There is actually a discrepancy between the statement in Jn 18, 3 (Judas being said to have been in charge of the cohort) and that in Jn 18, 12 (where the command is assigned to a military tribune). This discrepancy will be considered later; we have first to examine the relative claims of the indefinite ὄχλος μετὰ μαχαιρῶν καὶ ξύλων of Mc 14, 43 and the σπεῖρα καὶ ὑπηρέται of Jn 18, 3, 12 as the agents that carried out the arrest.

Since the author of the Fourth Gospel betrays throughout decidedly anti-Jewish feelings, a statement to the effect that Jesus was arrested *by Roman military personnel* calls for attention. The Marcan record, followed in its essentials by the Third and the First Evangelist, makes no mention of Roman participation in the event. Should we assume that the Fourth Evangelist, when he refers to Roman troops in this connection, introduced the item without the support of tradition, or that he reproduced a source which had, for some reason, not been preserved in Mark, Luke and Matthew?

Though separated in the Fourth Gospel as it now stands — by the Evangelist's re-arrangement of his materials[1] — the report underlying Jn 11, 48, 53 on the one hand and that behind Jn 18, 3, 12—13a, 19—23 28a on the other are thematically connected: Roman pressure forces upon the assembled members of the Sanhedrin the necessity of taking action against the spread of disaffection among the populace; Roman

---

[1] »...es gehört zur Eigenheit der johanneischen Komposition, dass der Evangelist... ursprünglich zusammengehörige Stücke auseinanderreisst«, Johannes Schneider, »Zur Komposition von Joh 18, 12—27«, ZNW vol. 48, 1957, pp. 111—119, on p. 113.

military personnel takes part when the decision to arrest Jesus is carried out. The Fourth Gospel does state that the σπεῖρα under its χιλίαρχος was accompanied by a contingent drawn from the Jewish Temple Police, οἱ ὑπηέται τῶν ᾽Ιουδαίων, but theirs is only an auxiliary function; the principal part in Jesus' arrest falls to the Roman troops. A notice of this kind is found nowhere else than in the Fourth Gospel. The information from Jn 18, 3, 12 corresponds to strata of early tradition that are still discernible[2] in the rendering of Jn 11, 47—53[3]. Was it a 'reviser' or the Evangelist who for his own reasons introduced the χιλίαρχος and the σπεῖρα into the narrative of Jesus' arrest[4]? Or does this report arise from a tradition of the same provenance as that in Jn 11, 48, which the synoptists failed to reproduce? In Jn 11, 48 we recognized an element of earlier origin than the date at which the Gospel as such was composed. It is inherently unlikely that the author of the Fourth Gospel whose sympathies lay with the Romans rather than with the Jews[5] would have assigned any part in the arrest of Jesus to the troops of the Emperor if he had not possessed a report bearing out such Roman participation. The leanings of the Fourth Evangelist in the Passion Story are marked by a conciliatory attitude towards Pilate and Rome, whereas his attitude towards the Jews is one of bitterness[6]. Had there been no record, no

---

[2] See above, pp. 51—53.

[3] »[Die Beratung der Hohenpriester und Pharisäer in Joh 11, 47—53] stellt die von den Römern drohende Gefahr in den Vordergrund. Davon findet sich bei den Synoptikern auch nicht die geringste Spur; um so besser harmoniert dieser Zug mit der Verhaftung Iesu durch die Cohorte...«, Eduard Schwartz, »Aporien im vierten Evangelium«, *Nachrichten von der Königlichen Gesellschaft der Wissenschaften zu Göttingen, Phil.-hist. Klasse aus dem Jahre 1907* (Berlin 1907), pp. 342—379, and *aus dem Jahre 1908* (Berlin 1908), pp. 115—188, 497—560, on page 171.

[4] Loisy thought that the mention of Roman troops in the Johannine narrative of Jesus' arrest was due to »un rédacteur préoccupé de symbolisme«, *Le quatrième évangile* (Paris 1904), p. 453, and thus not derived from tradition. It is likely that the editor exaggerated the strength of the detachment and the rank of the officer in command of the troops, but not that he freely invented the report of Jesus' arrest by the Romans.

[5] *Cf.* Jn 19, 11 b.

[6] »... die Darstellung [des Prozesses vor Pilatus im Johannes-Evangelium ist] ganz von dem apologetischen Interesse beherrscht. Das Bild des Prozesses Jesu wird mit Farben gemalt, die Johannes nur zum Teil der evangelischen Überlieferung entnimmt, zum anderen sich von seiner Gegenwart reichen lässt, von der Einsicht in die Nöte der Gemeinden und von dem Wunsch, sie zu erleichtern: Jesus vor Pilatus, das ist zugleich der Christ vor der heidnischen Obrigkeit... Es gilt..., ihn zu verteidigen... Niemand würde etwas gegen [die Christen] haben, wenn nicht das Juden... sie als Übeltäter und Rebellen denunzierten. Waren es die Juden doch, die schon im Falle Jesu nicht ruhten, bevor nicht das Urteil vollstreckt wurde... Der römische Beamte glaubte fest [an Jesu] Unbescholtenheit... und erschöpfte sich in Versuchen, den Gefangenen freizubekommen... Daß eine bei ihrer Entstehung derartigen [apologetischen] Einflüssen ausgesetzte Darstellung Spuren von Ungeschichtlichkeit

earlier tradition, stating that Roman military personnel had apprehended Jesus, the Evangelist of his own accord would scarcely have charged them with the rôle of the arresting party.

The analysis of Jn 18, 12—14, 19—24, 28a yielded the result that retouches from a second hand are to be seen in the picture which we now have of the interrogation of Jesus[7]. The same is true of the pericope Jn 18, 3—11, 12. In v. 3 Judas is described as being in command of the cohort; in v. 12 it is a Roman officer. Although mentioned twice, Judas plays practically no part in the pericope concerning the arrest — as far as the literary composition of the story goes, the mention of the name 'Judas' is secondary. From a historical point of view it is impossible to suppose that Judas was in command of a σπεῖρα or indeed even of a smaller detachment of imperial troops. The name has been *inserted after the primary rendering of what we find in Jn 18, 3—11 had been composed* — in all probability by the same person who inserted the name 'Kaiaphas' into the subsequent report of the interrogation. Originally only a Roman officer was referred to as being in command of the arresting party. The mention of Judas in vv. 3, 5 results from an attempt to harmonize the Johannine with the synoptic account.

Thus there are two accounts, standing over against each other: (1) the Johannine t r a d i t i o n according to which Jesus was arrested by Roman troops, under their own commander, and assisted by a posse of the Temple Police; (2) the synoptic r e p o r t, based on Mark, according to which an ὄχλος apprehended Jesus. Commenting on this observation, Maurice Goguel expressed the opinion that originally there existed two traditions of which the earlier attributed the arrest of Jesus solely to the Romans, the later to the Jewish police force. Goguel maintained that the Fourth Evangelist combined these two traditions, whilst the Second reproduced only the later one[8]. On weighing the arguments

---

aufweist, kann nicht wundernehmen«, Walter Bauer, *Das Johannes-Evangelium* (Tübingen ³1933), p. 221.

[7] See above, pp. 47—50.

[8] Goguel recognized two strata in the extant accounts of Jesus' trial: one with Romans as the initiators of the prosecution, the other with the Jews in that rôle, and observed: »... ce fait donne à penser que les auteurs des évangiles ont corrigé une tradition ancienne où les Romains seuls intervenaient, en la combinant avec une tradition plus récente qui faisait aussi jouer un rôle aux Juifs«, »Juifs et Romains dans l'histoire de la Passion«, *RHR* tome 62, 1910, pp. 165—182, 295—322, on p. 181.

»... la mention des soldats romains dans le récit johannique de l'arrestation nous [détermine à] considérer ici ... la tradition johannique comme primitive. Le récit de Marc est une correction qui trahit la tendance apologétique à réduire au minimum le rôle des Romains dans l'arrestation de Jésus«, Maurice Goguel, *Les sources du récit johannique de la Passion* (Paris 1910), pp. 81, 82; *cf.* p. 74.

»La tendance philoromaine étant, dans le quatrième Évangile, plus accentuée encore que dans les Synoptiques, il est impossible de supposer que la cohorte et le

it seems more likely that the author of the Second Gospel would have refrained from mentioning Roman participation in the arrest than that the writer of the Fourth would have invented it. Mark was written in Rome, it appears, shortly after the year 70 CE, when the memory of the conflict between Jews and Romans was in everyone's mind. The Romans still considered Christianity as nothing else than a Jewish apocalyptic movement, the propagation of which was bound to produce the disruption of the *ordre public* and lead to happenings of the kind recently encountered[9]. By stating that it was the Emperor's troops who

---

centurion ont été introduits dans le récit par Jean. Il faut donc admettre qu'il suit ici une source qui mentionnait une collaboration des Juifs et des Romains ou bien qui ne parlait que des Romains. Les Juifs auraient été ajoutés par l'évangéliste sous l'influence des récits synoptiques«, Maurice Goguel, *La vie de Jésus* (Paris 1932), pp. 453, 454; English edition *The Life of Jesus* (London 1933), pp. 468, 469.

Goguel's view has been accepted by Oscar Cullmann who points out that »from the beginning the entire action [against Jesus] proceeds from the Romans«, *The State in the New Testament*, p. 45. Similarly, Eduard Schwartz in »Aporien im vierten Evangelium«, p. 352 (*cf.* above, p. 57, note 21).

[9] There was a fair amount of justification for the Roman assessment. The Second Gospel preserves traditions which betray an attitude far from one of appeasement with regard to Rome. Anti-Roman animus, despite the efforts of the Evangelist, may be detected in the story of the Gerasene swine (Mc 5, 1—13; *cf.* below, pp. 180 f.). Another indication of anti-Roman sentiment appears in the designation of 'Pharisees and Herodians' as adversaries of Jesus. This latter points to a situation during the great revolt against Rome, when Agrippa II and various representatives of Pharisaism tried to enter into an understanding with the Romans, whose forces were at the time stationed in Galilee.

The very fact that Jesus of Nazareth lives on in history as XPICTOC, *i. e. messiah,* clearly proves that an important group among his adherents pursued political aims, and assigned to the second advent a political significance, for a 'messiah' is the political leader of Israel, a leader whose functions are performed within the social life of the nation. When Josef Pickl, who assumes that messianism was common in Jesus' time, disparages Jews other than those who were followers of Jesus in that »their hope for the Messias... showed a strong tinge of worldliness« (*Messiaskönig Jesus in der Auffassung seiner Zeitgenossen*, Munich [2]1935, English translation *The Messias*, London 1946, on p. 43), he misjudges the meaning of the term 'messiah'. T h e   w o r d   d e n o t e s   a   w o r d l y   r u l e r, a man among men, not a leader of celestial beings. The Gospels leave no doubt as to the fact that a claim to 'kingship' was made on Jesus' behalf by some of his disciples, and that Jesus was tried and executed on such a charge.

*Cf.* my statement in *Die Zeit Jesu,* ed. H. J. Schulz (Stuttgart 1966), p. 49; Engl. trans. *Jesus in his Time* (Philadelphia 1971), p. 55: »As for the Sadducees, it is improbable that they ever shared the belief in an eschatological messiah. We cannot say with absolute certainty whether this is true or not, because our sources are silent about it. But their traditional interpretation of scripture alone would hardly have suggested to the Sadducees any belief in a messiah like that held by the community of Jesus or by the Pharisees. Moreover, they were anxious to work peacefully and without friction with the Ptolemies, Seleucids, and later the Romans;

had seized Jesus, the Evangelist would have invited opprobrium on his cause and would have made it more difficult for himself to achieve what he wished to achieve — to convince his readers of the unpolitical character of the message of salvation through Jesus[10]. An explanation can be found as to why the part of Roman soldiers in the arrest should have been passed over in silence in the Second Gospel; it is more difficult to find a reason explaining why the Fourth Evangelist should have reported it without actually possessing what he considered to be reliable information on the matter.

We are not informed of the identity of the imperial troops stationed in Palestine in Jesus' day. Some ten or fifteen years after his death, the *Cohors Secunda Italica*[11] and auxiliaries recruited from among the inhabitants of Sebaste and Caesarea[12], Greek townships, constituted the Roman garrison stationed in the province, and it is just possible that the same units served in Judaea at the time of Jesus' arrest.

Grounds of principle favour the view that behind the mention of a σπεῖρα and of a χιλίαρχος (Jn 18, 3, 12) there lies an early account of Jesus' arrest. The actual expressions used in the Fourth Gospel may be those of the Evangelist, who specified in exact military language what his source might have conveyed in a terminologically less precise fashion. The element, however, belongs to tradition. It remains to be seen whether or not this tradition also mentioned members of the Temple Police as accompanying the detachment of Roman soldiers on their errand.

--------

political caution would have ruled out for them any fervent and enthusiastic expectation of a messiah in the eschatological sense of the word. For them the word still had the old, temporal sense as in the Old Testament and was the title of the reigning high priest. So the question 'Are you the messiah, the son of the most high?' is quite impossible on the lips of a Sadducean high priest, for the high priest laid claim to the title of messiah for himself.«

[10] »L'évangéliste met d'abord en cause tout le sanhédrin, chefs des prêtres, scribes et anciens, parce qu'il veut faire porter à ce sénat des Juifs la responsabilité principale dans le jugement et la condamnation du Christ. Mais il est peu croyable que l'arrestation de Jésus ait été opérée par décision de cette assemblée«, Alfred Loisy, *L'évangile selon Marc* (Paris 1912), p. 419.

The charge of blasphemy (Mc 14, 64 a), or the charge of threatening the Temple (Mc 14, 58), was introduced into the Passion Narrative by the Second Evangelist when he invented what we now read in Mc 14, 53 b, 55—64. Neither of these charges played any rôle in the arrest of Jesus or in his condemnation to death by crucifixion. »Les poursuites contre Jésus, et cela dès le début, n'ont pas été une affaire purement juive puisque la cohorte a procédé à l'arrestation. Jésus n'a donc pas été arrêté comme blasphémateur, mais comme agitateur ou comme personnage susceptible de devenir le prétexte ou l'occasion d'une agitation«, Maurice Goguel, *La vie de Jésus*, p. 465; Engl. edition, *The Life of Jesus*, p. 481.

[11] Ἡ σπεῖρα καλουμένη Ἰταλική, Acts 10, 1.

[12] Ant XIX 365.

All four Gospels report that Pilate was available in the morning, ready for Jesus' trial. This indicates that he must have had advance information about what was taking place in the night — a fact which accords with the Fourth Evangelist's statement that the arrest was carried out by Roman personnel. Wellhausen considered the pericope Jn 18, 12—27 to be of a secondary nature; according to the earlier account, he maintained, Jesus was despatched to Pilate immediately after his arrest[13]. Dibelius followed Wellhausen to some extent, holding that Jn 18, 19—24 was an invention of the Fourth Evangelist (whilst he considered the Johannine account of Peter's denial to be based on tradition)[14]. If Wellhausen's view on this point is correct, the presence of the Temple Police in addition to Roman troops at the arrest might seem superfluous, and Goguel's opinion that only Roman soldiers appeared in the earliest account would gain in probability. Nevertheless, there are strong arguments against it: if there had been no mention of the Temple Police in the primary tradition, it is not possible to give a reasonable explanation as to how the Marcan way of representing the facts could have been called into existence. The tradition that was available to the Second Evangelist was identical with a less developed form of the tradition underlying Jn 18, 3—11. Let us repeat: the report of Roman participation in the arrest of Jesus cannot be due to an unsupported predilection on the part of the author of the Fourth Gospel; he places the burden of responsibility for the death of Jesus on the shoulders of the Jews and exonerates the governor completely.

---

[13] »Pilatus wird [in dem uns vorliegenden Bericht des Evangelisten] nicht eingeführt und tritt doch als bekannt auf. Er muß ursprünglich schon vorher erwähnt [worden] sein. Nur er konnte die Cohorte beauftragen und zu ihm mußte der Chiliarch zurück, um ihm nach der Ausführung des Auftrags wenigstens Bericht zu erstatten«, Julius Wellhausen, Das Evangelium Johannis (Berlin 1908), p. 83., Wellhausen considered the pericope Jn 18, 12—27 to be an insertion.

See also Eduard Schwartz's study »Aporien im vierten Evangelium«, referred to above, p. 52, note 16: »... der wichtigste Zug, daß die Verhaftung [Iesu dem] Pilatus zugeschoben wurde, [ist in dem uns überlieferten Evangelium jetzt] unterdrückt« (cf. p. 354).

[14] »Daß der vierte Evangelist einem Bericht benutzt, der nicht mit einem der synoptischen identisch ist, erkennt man vor allem an denjenigen nicht-synoptischen Motiven, von denen der Evangelist keinen Gebrauch im Sinne seiner Theologie macht: Todesdatum, Verräterprophezeiung, Verleugnung des Petrus ...«, Martin Dibelius, Die Formgeschichte des Evangeliums, p. 204, note 4. »... die Verleugnungsgeschichte bei Johannes [ist] vom Evangelisten in kleiner Weise für seine besonderen Zwecke theologisch ausgewertet; [sie gehört] zu der Tradition ..., die dem Verfasser vorliegt«, o. c., p. 217. »Die Darstellung [der Verleugnungsgeschichte] wird vom Verfasser durch die Verhörszene 18, 19—24, die ganz sein Gepräge trägt, zersprengt. Irgendeine johanneische Beleuchtung der Verleugnung findet sich nirgends ... Dagegen ist die Darstellung selbst in sich geschlossen und originell«, o. c., p. 217, note 2. Engl. edition, pp. 204, 216.

If, despite the Fourth Evangelist's general assessment of the situation, his work contains a specific statement which assigns the arrest of Jesus to the Romans, the statement in question is doubtless based on tradition. The identical tradition could have been known to the Second Evangelist who, however, decided not to reproduce it[15], preferring to attribute the arrest to an unspecified ὄχλος. The Marcan statement that the ὄχλος had come "from the chief priests and the scribes and the elders" is more easily explicable if the primary account had alluded to the presence of members of the Temple Police. Neither Goguel's view that only Romans figured in the early tradition underlying Jn 18, 3—11, 12, nor Wellhausen's appraisal of the secondary character of Jn 18, 12—27, 28 a allows of a satisfactory explanation of the emergence of the Marcan account. The balance of probabilities is in favour of accepting the report of Jesus' detention in the high-priest's residence as a trustworthy representation of what actually occurred. The earliest tradition reported such a detention; some account agreeing both with Mc 14, 53 a and with Jn 18, 13 a (reading "they led him first to the high-priest") was i n c l u d e d in the primary report of Jesus' arrest and trial. This then would suggest that, besides the Roman cohort, certain officers of the Temple Guard, the ὑπηρέται τῶν Ἰουδαίων, were there when the arrest was made. Their presence would have expedited the despatch of the prisoner to the high-priest for the interrogation necessary in preparing an indictment for the actual trial in the governor's court. The Jewish oligarchy at the time held their positions by imperial favour, and in order to retain these favours, they cooperated with the Emperor's representative. The reference to the presence of the Temple Police at the arrest could have provided the Second Evangelist with an opportunity for omitting all allusion to Roman troops and for substituting the rather indefinite "crowd [armed] with swords and sticks"; apparently those "with swords" correspond to the Johannine "cohort" and those "with sticks" to the Johannine "officers of the Jews".To the author of Mark, who wrote in Rome, it was apparently embarrassing to recall Roman participation in the event.

Complete elucidation of the facts concerning the circumstances under which the arrest of Jesus took place is impossible. The matter soon became a theme for legendary elaborations. However, there are faint indications in the Third Gospel which may support the Fourth Evangelist's mention (Jn 18, 12) of the presence of the Jewish police, οἱ ὑπηρέται τῶν Ἰουδαίων. In Lc 22, 52 we read of "the captains of the Temple Guard", οἱ στρατηγοὶ τοῦ ἱεροῦ, a quasi-military force under Jewish command. The στρατηγοί of v. 52[16] also appear in Lc 22, 4. In

---

[15] See above, pp. 33—34.

[16] »Luc a ... suivi ici une source qui lui paraissait sûre«, Marie-Joseph Lagrange, Évangile selon Saint Luc (Paris 1921), p. 565.

itself this may not warrant the assumption that the information was derived from a special written source, but it suggests that the Third Evangelist was acquainted with non-Marcan traditions. Emphatic as the Third Evangelist is — both by his omission of Marcan statements (Lc 18, 32, 33; 22, 54—65) and by his own affirmation (Acts 13, 27, 28) — that Jesus had not been sentenced to death by the Sanhedrin, he reports that Joseph of Arimathaea (whom apparently he presumed to have been a member of the Sanhedrin) "had not consented to their counsel and deed" (Lc 23, 51). It is difficult to understand the precise significance of the words "their counsel and deed". The words appear to be a gloss, due to the Evangelist (or could they be a later interpolation?), and if they are, the Evangelist would have supposed that some counsel had been taken, and was acted upon, by the members of the Sanhedrin. The account which the Third Evangelist gives of the proceedings by the πρεσβυτέριον τοῦ λαοῦ excludes all possibility of identifying "their counsel and deed" with the condemnation of Jesus; it may therefore — with some hesitation — be understood as referring to an official approval of the charge-sheet and the decision to despatch Jesus to Pilate.

Despite the necessary vagueness of every deduction due to the character of our sources, what emerges from the foregoing discussion is that b o t h Roman soldiers and Temple Police were reported to have taken part in the arrest of Jesus. It is likely that this was set forth in the primary tradition. A similar assessment applies to the evangelists' report that Jesus was conducted to the residence of the high-priest, apparently in compliance with an order that an indictment be prepared for a prefectorial trial.

So much can be said of the circumstances under which the arrest was carried out. We may now try to ascertain whether there still remain in the Gospels any trustworthy indications regarding the grounds for the arrest.

There is a significant statement in Mc 14, 48 h, 49. Jesus remonstrates with the people who have come to apprehend him in the deep of the night, and says: ὡς ἐπὶ λῃστὴν ἐξήλθατε μετὰ μαχαιρῶν καὶ ξύλων συλλαβεῖν με· καθ᾽ ἡμέραν ἤμην πρὸς ὑμᾶς ἐν τῷ ἱερῷ διδάσκων, καὶ οὐκ ἐκρατήσατέ με, which may be translated in the following manner: *As against a rebel, you have come out [armed] with swords and sticks to lay hold of me. I was with you in the day-time teaching in the Temple precincts, and you did not arrest me.* The crucial words are καθ᾽ ἡμέραν. They could mean "day by day (= daily)", *quotidie, täglich* — and so they are usually rendered — but they could also mean "in the hours of daylight", "in the course of day", "by day", *die, tagsüber*[17]. The former interpretation, though generally accepted, does not recommend itself

---

[17] *Cf.* Lc 19, 47 ἦν διδάσκων τὸ καθ᾽ ἡμέραν ἐν τῷ ἱερῷ and Lc 21, 37 ἦν δὲ τὰς ἡμέρας ἐν τῷ ἱερῷ διδάσκων.

in the Marcan context; Jesus is presented in the Second Gospel as having been within the Temple precincts no more than twice, once in Mc 11, 15—18, the next and last time in Mc 11, 27—55; 12, 1—44. The distributive sense of κατὰ ἡμέραν is thus unsupported by the narrative itself. We have a parallel to Mc 14, 48 b, 49 in the defence argument given in Jn 18, 20: "I have spoken openly . . . I have taught in the synagogues and within the Temple precincts where all Jews come together. I have not spoken anything in secret (= I have not spread any clandestine propaganda)". The Johannine παῤῥησίᾳ here corresponds to the Marcan καθ᾽ ἡμέραν. The stress is on the public or open character of Jesus' activity.

The context given to the words in Mc 14, 48 b, 49 supports the view that καθ᾽ ἡμέραν should be read as "during day-time", and not "daily". Jesus reproaches those who h a v e  c o m e  u p o n  h i m  b y  n i g h t — ὡς ἐπὶ λῃστήν — a s  u p o n  a  g u e r i l l a - f i g h t e r[18], although he is not a leader of a secret band who would conduct his affairs under the cover of night; he is a preacher, a religious teacher (διδάσκων) and should not be treated as a political insurgent (λῃστής). The antithetic parallelism between διδάσκων (or διδάσκαλος) and λῃστής requires us to read the words καθ᾽ ἡμέραν as an antithesis to κατὰ νύκτα. A rebel leader may have to be sought out in his haunts by night, but a teacher can be found among his pupils at any time of the day. The temporal setting of the arrest, in the night-time, determines the manner in which the καθ᾽ ἡμέραν is to be understood.

We have in Mc 14, 48 b, 49 a faint trace of an early tradition which implied that the arrest of Jesus was undertaken as a precaution against possible insurrectionist activities.

"And with him they crucified two revolutionaries, one on his right, and one on his left" (Mc 15, 27; cf. Mt 27, 38; Lc 23, 32; Jn 19, 18 b). This is history. It was later taken to be a fulfilment of prophecy, and the next verse — Mc 15, 28 — was added to explain what had happened in this sense. The Gospels do not offer any information on the sentencing to death of the two persons executed simultaneously with Jesus. If their crucifixion took place at the same time as that of Jesus, there is reason for assuming that they were also tried and sentenced at the same time. The ground upon which they were condemned has been left in the dark, except for their designation as λῃσταί, by Mark (and Matthew). We do know, however, the ground, the αἰτία, for the crucifixion of Jesus, which the evangelists h a v e  p l a c e d  o n  r e c o r d :

ΙΗΣΟΥΣ Ο ΝΑΖΩΡΑΙΟΣ Ο ΒΑΣΙΛΕΥΣ ΤΩΝ ΙΟΥΔΑΙΩΝ.

It is implicitly stated in Mc 14, 48 b on what ground Jesus was arrested: ἐπὶ λῃστὴν ἐξήλθατε συλλαβεῖν με. The charge on which he was

---

[18] Codex D does not have the ὡς.

executed is proclaimed explicitly in the *titulus* on the cross. Yet though Mc 14, 48 b gives the correct reason for Jesus' arrest, it also refutes the correctness of the charge. For Jesus of Nazareth was not in any sense of the word a ληστής. He was no revolutionary, prompted by political ambitions for the power of government; he was a teacher who openly proclaimed his teaching. He never announced the coming of his own kingdom[19], but preached the Kingdom of God that comes without observation[20]. Senseless though the arrest, cruel though the sentence was, the oldest of the Gospels preserved the reason for both: Jesus was arrested, accused, condemned, and executed, on a charge of rebellion[21].

---

[19] Jesus was neither a *Jenseitsschwärmer* with his mind fixed on what was to come in a life after death, nor was he a political rebel (ληστής = *partisan, guerilla fighter*) who sought by violent means to transform social conditions on earth. Religion without politics was equally unthinkable to him as politics without religion. The one would have meant "faith that has no works", the other "judgment that is without mercy". In Jesus' thought, as generally in Jewish thought, religion and politics are inseparable. Preoccupation with one to the exclusion of the other has been condemned throughout Jewish history.

[20] On οὐ μετὰ παρατηρήσεως, see August Strobel, »Die Passa-Erwartung als urchristliches Problem in Lc 17, 20 f.«, *ZNW* vol. 49, 1958, pp. 157—196, but compare Hans Conzelmann, *Die Mitte der Zeit* (Tübingen ⁴1962), p. 114, note 1. Engl. ed. *The Theology of St Luke* (London 1960), p. 124, note 1.

[21] »Jesus Christ was condemned for the crime of sedition and tumult«, Orazio Marucchi, »The Crucifixion of Jesus Christ« in *The Catholic Encyclopedia*, vol. 4 (New York 1908), pp. 519—520, on p. 520.

»Jesus was... arrested... as an agitator, or as a person who might... become the occasion of a political agitation«, Maurice Goguel, *La vie de Jésus*, p. 465; Engl. edition *The Life of Jésus*, p. 481.

»Christ was scourged as a rebel, then He was crucified as a traitor to Caesar«, Josef Pickl, *o. c.*, p. 224.

»The Gospels make it quite clear that Jesus was executed on the charge of a political crime. The authorities were afraid of his political power. He had been acclaimed "King of the Jews". This title he never denied, and he bore it nobly to the end. Jesus not only matched the zeal of a Zealot, he was crucified "as a Zealot"«, William Reuben Farmer, *Maccabees, Zealots and Josephus* (New York 1956), p. 197.

»Jesus... was condemned by the Romans and not by the Jews, and in fact, as a Zealot«, Oscar Cullmann, *Der Staat im Neuen Testament*, p. 33; French edition *Dieu et César*, p. 46; Engl. edition *The State in the New Testament*, p. 48.

[*Revisers' addendum: Cf.* S. G. F. Brandon, *The Trial of Jesus of Nazareth* (London 1968), p. 150 (a work reviewed by T. A. Burkill in *The Jewish Chronicle*, London, 27th December 1968, p. 21). For the view that there was no organised political party of revolutionary Zealots before the winter of 67—68 CE, see the article »Zealots and Sicarii, Their Origins and Relation«, *HTR*, vol. 64, 1971, pp. 1—19, by Morton Smith, who writes: »As for the notion (of Brandon) that the presence of a "zealot" among Jesus' disciples proves the existence of the Zealot party in Jesus' time, that is not an argument, but a bad pun« (p. 6). A somewhat similar thesis is defended by Marc Borg, »The Currency of the Term "Zealot"«, *Journal of Theological Studies*, n. s., vol. 22, 1971, pp. 504—512.]

## 6. PILATE IN HISTORY AND IN CHRISTIAN TRADITION

The Gospels are our earliest extant records in which a comprehensive description of the circumstances of Jesus' death is attempted. When investigating the cause and the course of Jesus' trial, the historian must concern himself primarily with these documents. He cannot, however, hope to arrive at an accurate assessment of what actually happened by a mechanical process of harmonizing the divergent and often conflicting accounts of Jesus' trial in the Gospels; he has to pay due regard to the motives that contributed to the coming into existence of the Gospel Narratives of the Passion and Resurrection. It was not the aim of individual evangelists to give in their descriptions an exact account of actual events, as seen in the light of history[1], nor were they in any position to give such an account had it been their intention to do so. What they intended, and what they did, was to present the significance of Jesus' death, as contemplated in the light of religious faith.

Literature, whether sacred or profane, does not germinate in a vacuum. The historical circumstances in which Christians lived before and when the Gospels were composed, external exigencies as well as internal interests and beliefs, were the decisive factors that dictated what came to be recorded of the Passion. Before assessment can be made of the historical value of the different narratives of Jesus' trial in the New Testament, it is necessary to recognize the formative motives behind their composition. The Gospels we now have are the literary creations of individual writers who utilized traditions current in certain communities, and who addressed themselves both to the communities that had produced the traditions and to the world outside. The situation in which any particular community finds itself will be the determining influence in the literary productions of persons belonging to that community. The history of the messianist brotherhood in Palestine — from which Christianity sprang — provides the framework within which the gospel story of the Passion and the Resurrection is set.

---

[1] »Die Passionsgeschichte ist vor allem heilige Geschichte; einzig im stilisierten Gewand dieser heiligen Geschichte konnte das mitgeteilt werden, was darin wirklich ›Geschichte‹ war«, M. Dibelius, »Das historische Problem der Leidensgeschichte«, ZNW vol. 30, 1931, p. 201; also in *Botschaft und Geschichte*, vol. 1 (Tübingen 1953) p. 257. *Cf.* P. Benoit, O. P., who refers to the Gospels as »des œuvres de catéchèse où s'exprime une théologie« (review of Josef Blinzler's *Der Prozeß Jesu* in *Revue biblique*, vol. 60, 1953, on p. 452).

What we read in the four Gospels of the trial, death and resurrection of Jesus varies to a greater degree than other depositions concerning his activities and life. This fact shows that there were compelling reasons, be they of a subjective or objective nature, for constantly amending, restating, supplementing, and annotating, the transmitted presentation of the fundamental event in which the faith in the messiahship of Jesus was grounded. Sometimes the variations in the treatment of certain details in the story, as effected by successive evangelists, will enable us to diagnose the interests by which the writers were prompted.

Foremost was the cultic interest. Jesus' humiliation was seen as the prelude to his triumphant vindication. Early Christian preaching centred around the theme of the Messiah's suffering and exaltation. Hence the necessity of bringing tradition into line with a continuous and ever-deepening religious meditation. Here it may be noted that the more de-tailed, and specific, a particular evangelist's account of the legal pro-ceedings against Jesus becomes, the less the probability that his ren-dering follows the trend presented in early tradition, or corresponds to the actualities of history.

Besides the cultic, were apologetic interests and motives. Before any written Gospels existed, there was the preaching — and it was the aim of the earliest preachers to convince their Jewish compatriots that what appeared to be proof of Jesus' rejection (Deut 21, 23 b) was in reality a reassuring sign of the fulfilment of God's plan and promise[2]. Though it would seem that God had been wroth with *His Anointed,* and had reproached the footsteps of *His Servant* — in truth, *He will not allow His faithfulness to fail nor His Covenant to be broken* (Ps 89). The use of Old Testament prophecy in the elaboration of descriptive details of the crucifixion is d u e  t o  c o n s c i o u s  r e f l e c t i o n : "God fore-showed by the mouth of all the prophets that his Christ should suffer" (Acts 3, 18). Those to whom the preaching was addressed were invited to recognize the fulfilment of prophetic promise in a contemporary event. With regard to some passages in the Gospels it is impossible to determine whether it was prophecy that gave rise to a certain story, or whether there were definite events that invited comparison with prophecy. History was built around a text — and to adapt the narra-tive to the quotation, the story was told from such an angle as to give occasion for pertinent scriptural quotation.

When relations between the apostolic preachers and their compa-triots deteriorated, the tidings spread to the Gentile world. This situa-tion forms the basis from which most of the traditions that are incor-

---

[2] »Das Ärgernis des *gekreuzigten Messias* musste als die göttliche Weisheit be-hauptet werden«, R. Bultmann, »Kirche und Lehre im Neuen Testament«, *Zwischen den Zeiten.* vol. 7, 1929, pp. 9—43, on p. 38; now also in *Glauben und Verstehen,* vol. 1 (Tübingen ³1958), pp. 153—187, on p. 182; *cf.* Wilhelm Brandt, *Die Evange-lische Geschichte und der Ursprung des Christenthums* (Leipzig 1893), pp. 85—87.

porated into the Gospels developed. In the parable of the vineyard, Mc 12, 1—9, the argument is that the vineyard will be given to others. Whilst the Jews normally took pride in proclaiming Israel to be the true vine (Hosea 10, 1, Isaiah 5, 7, Jeremiah 2, 21 a, Psalm 80, 9[8]) that pleased God above other trees (4 Ezra 5, 23; *cf.* Pseudo-Philo's Liber Antiquitatum Biblicarum 12, 8; in the seer's vision in 2 Baruch 36, 3—11 and its intepretation, 2 Baruch 39, 2—8, the vine, originally a symbol of Israel, becomes the symbol of an individual, the Messiah), those amongst whom the preaching involved in Mc 12, 1—9 originated were already sufficiently removed from this line of thought to assert that the vineyard no longer belonged to Israel.

The evangelists, then, as individual authors who availed themselves of collective communal traditions so as to present their own literary propositions, plead not so much with the Jews as with non-Jews — and chiefly with those politically in power: the Romans. In addition to the concern of the early preachers to persuade Jews that the crucifixion proved Jesus to be the Elect of God expected of old, there enters a new motive (yet early enough to have influenced *all* the evangelists in their descriptions of Jesus' trial), namely, the apologetic purpose of convincing Roman officials that the profession of the Christian faith was not subversive of imperial institutions. The manner of Jesus' death, known to have been ordered by the representative of Roman rule, was a serious obstacle to the propagation of Christianity throughout the provinces of the Empire. Hence the peculiar sort of rôle assigned to Pilate in all other person whose name appears in the Gospels. Yet there could not Gospels and in Christian traditions generally.

More is known of Pontius Pilate from outside sources than of any be a greater discrepancy between the Pilate known from history and the feeble figure who plays such a vacillating part in the Passion Drama — the Pilate with whom the reader of the Gospels is made acquainted. We have fairly detailed descriptions of the real Pilate in the writings of Philo and of Josephus.

There are reasons for supposing that Philo's testimony as to Pilate's character is the most trustworthy we possess. In the first place, as a contemporary of Pilate, Philo was in a better position than any of the later writers to come to an accurate assessment; in the second place, Philo's judgment was not in any way influenced by the part Pilate played in the crucifixion — indeed, he does not seem to have been aware of the existence of Jesus. Philo describes Pilate as a man of inflexible disposition, harsh and obdurate[3]. At one point, Philo does afford information which *prima facie* appears to lend some support to a passage in the Fourth Gospel, namely, that Pilate was afraid lest

---

[3] Leg. and Gaium 301, where a letter by Agrippa I is cited; regarding its reliability, see below, p. 89, note 52.

Jewish leaders should complain about his conduct to the emperor[4]. The incident recorded by Philo relates, however, to the setting up of ornamental guilded shields in Jerusalem[5]. Philo is more explicit than the Fourth Evangelist; he states that Pilate feared lest Jewish notables should send a deputation to Tiberius and expose his arbitrary government in Judaea, denouncing his insolence, his rapacity, his high-handed treatment of his subjects, and his disposition to cruelty which led him in numerous cases to order the execution of people without previous trial. Philo's activities during his governorship combines the reproach of arbitrariness with that of responsibility for countless atrocities[6].

---

[4] Cf. Jn 19, 12.

[5] There is some similarity between the incident which Agrippa I mentioned in the letter quoted by Philo (Leg. ad Gaium 299—305), namely the array of votive shields, and the case of which we read in B. J. II 169—174, Ant XVIII 55—59, concerning the setting up of military standards in Jerusalem. The incident which Josephus records appears, however, to have been the earlier one, falling near the beginning of Pilate's governorship in Judaea.

The death of Jesus probably also occurred in the early period of Pilate's rule, perhaps in the year 28 CE. Even a date as early as 27 CE has been suggested, not without serious reasons. See Gustav Hölscher, »Die Hohenpriesterliste bei Josephus und die evangelische Chronologie« Sitzungsberichte der Heidelberger Akademie der Wissenschaften, Phil.-hist. Klasse, Jahrg. 1939—40, 3. Abh., Heidelberg 1940: »Jesu Zug nach Jerusalem und sein Tod hängt wohl mit den Unruhen des ersten Amtsjahres des Pilatus zusammen« (p. 26); »Die durch den Täufer und durch Jesus verursachten religiösen Bewegungen gehören, politisch gesehen, in die Reihe der vielen Unruhen, von denen Josephus zwischen 6 und 66 n. Chr. berichtet. In beiden Fällen ist es die politische Obrigkeit, die eingreift« (p. 30).

The earliest chronological notice concerning the date of Jesus' death occurs — so far as is known to the present writer — in Clement of Alexandria, Stromateis I (chapt. xxi) 145, 5 (GCS Clemens II, p. 90; MPG 8, col. 885). Clement dated the crucifixion 42 years and 3 months before the day on which the Romans destroyed Jerusalem. This would correspond to the year 28 CE. If the reference to three months (μῆνες γ') is understood to indicate exactly three months of the Jewish calendar — of any Jewish calendar — the day of Jesus' crucifixion would be designated as coinciding neither with the 14th nor the 15th Nisan, but with the ninth day of that month. I do not know whence Clement derived his information. It could have been based simply on a comparison of Josephus' report of the capture of Jerusalem with the mention of the 15th year of Tiberius in Lc 3, 1. In general cf. my article »The Trial of Jesus«, Commentary, New York, Sept. 1964, pp. 35—41, on pp. 35, 36.

[6] Leg. ad Gaium 302. Cf. Eduard Norden, »Josephus und Tacitus über Jesus Christus und eine messianische Prophetie«, Neue Jahrbücher für das klassische Altertum, Geschichte und Deutsche Literatur, vol. 16, 1913, pp. 637—666: »Pontius Pilatus — der geschichtliche, nicht der schon in den Evangelien vom Schleier beginnender tendenziöser Legende umwobene — zeigte sich in seiner zehnjährigen Amtstätigkeit als ein reizbarer, brüsker und herrischer Vorgesetzter, ohne jedes Verständnis für die Sonderart seiner Untergebenen, Konflikte eher suchend als ihnen aus dem Wege gehend, aber zielbewußt und durchgreifend wie sein Herr in Rom« (p. 639).

Josephus informs us more fully than Philo on Pilate's rule in Judaea, recording several happenings that occurred during his term of office[7]. They all supply ample illustration of the contemptuous manner in which Pilate dealt with the people of the province. What is of importance in assessing the trustworthiness of these reports is that Josephus also mentions Pilate's cruel behaviour towards Samaritans, a nation for whom Josephus had no particular fondness.

A passage in the New Testament bears out the portrayal of Pilate's character vouchsafed by Philo and Josephus. It does not occur in any of the accounts of Jesus' trial. In Luke 13, 1—2 we read of an act of Pilate's which accords with our secular authors' references to the governor's unbridled cruelty. We do not learn from the Third Evangelist on what occasion the act of "mixing the blood of the Galilaeans with their sacrifices" was committed[8]. In its present context the allusion is

---

[7] B. J. II 169—177, Ant XVIII 55—64, 85—87; Eusebius, Historiae ecclesiasticae II 6, 6, 7 (GCS Eusebius II, 1, p. 122; MPG 20, col. 153); cf. Emil Schürer, Geschichte des jüdischen Volkes..., vol. 1 (Leipzig ³1901), pp. 488—492; English edition revised by G. Vermes and F. Millar, The History of the Jewish People..., vol. 1 (Edinburgh 1973), pp. 383—387.

The details which Josephus gives of what took place in Judaea under Pilate's rule are in all likelihood derived from a written source, some sort of chronicle composed by a contemporary of Pilate.

[8] The information in Lc 13, 1—2 is not sufficient to allow the exact historical localisation of the incident referred to. There have been numerous surmises or attempts to fix the occasion of Pilate's butchery amongst Galilaean pilgrims. Ephrem Syrus thought that it was intended as a punitive action following upon the decapitation of John the Baptist (Evangelii Concordantis Expositio... In Latinum translata a I. B. Aucher, cuius versionem... edidit Georgius Moesinger, Venezia, 1876, p. 165). Modern writers are hardly less ingenious. Joseph Klausner, o. c., assumed that it occurred in Archelaus's time. Robert Eisler, ΙΗΣΟΥΣ ΒΑΣΙΛΕΥΣ ΟΥ ΒΑΣΙΛΕΥΣΑΣ (Heidelberg 1929—1930) placed it in the last days of Jesus' life, connecting it with an uprising during Jesus' sojourn in Jerusalem. Josef Pickl, Messiaskönig Jesus in der Auffassung seiner Zeitgenossen (Munich ²1935), Engl. ed. The Messias (St. Louis and London 1946), tried to make out that the event took place six months before the death of Jesus, combining it with a hypothetical revolt of Barabbas. Albert Olmstead assigned it to the time of popular uproar caused by Pilate's appropriation of money from the Temple Treasury to pay for the building of a new aqueduct. Ethelbert Stauffer places the event in connection with a »messiaspolitische Passahrevolte der galiläischen Festpilger im Frühjahr 31«. Oscar Cullmann, o. c., presumed that the notice in Lc 13, 1 referred to an uprising of Galilaean Zealots. Josef Blinzler, in »Die Niedermetzelung von Galiläern durch Pilatus«, Novum Testamentum vol. 2, 1957, pp. 24—49, dealing in great detail with the incident, assumed that it occurred at a Passover season, one year before the death of Jesus, and that Jesus was informed about it in Galilee since he had not gone to Jerusalem for that particular Passover. Blinzler goes as for as to date the event: it was "Monday the 18th April AD 29" when it occurred (p. 32, n. 3). Blinzler's assumption that Jesus disowned the Galileans (p. 47) is fairly improbable.

dislocated. The passage is evidently derived from a source — or tradition — that has not been preserved in its original completeness nor maintained in its original setting[9]. As it now stands, Lc 13, 1—2 forms part of a conversation between Jesus and some persons of his following. It may or may not reproduce an historical utterance of Jesus — what is significant is the fact that Jesus' followers preserved a memory of the governor's harshness. Whereas all the canonical trial accounts have evidently been refashioned by the evangelists themselves (if not by later, post-evangelical, editors), the brief notice in Lc 13, 1 escaped undue editorial revision[10]; it has reached us in a form in which it had been

---

Christian tradition would scarcely have preserved the memory of persons, otherwise insignificant, with whom the followers of Jesus had not established close relationship, or at least, with whom they had not been in general agreement.

[9] While the incident cannot be dated with exactitude, there is no reason to doubt that Lc 13, 1 refers to an historical fact and that the event took place during Pilate's term of office. It might have occurred before, and even after, the crucifixion. The utterance in Lc 13, 2 could have been attributed to Jesus retrospectively. If Josephus omits to mention the event, this is probably due to the circumstance that it was but one of many incidents of that kind which abounded under Pilate's governorship, and that Josephus considered it to be of less importance than others. The words in Lc 13, 1 "whose blood Pilate had mingled with their sacrifices" are oriental picturesque language; they need not imply that Pilate's soldiers had entered the Court of Priests on the Temple Mount where animal sacrifices were offered. Any desecration of the Temple area in Pilate's time by the invasion of Roman troops would not have passed unnoticed by Josephus.

»Josephus mentions several [acts of brutality by Pilate], and though he does not mention this one — as no one else does — there is not the least reason to doubt that it was a real occurrence. But while a Judaean writer like Josephus might neglect to note it, ... Galilaeans would not forget it...«, Max Radin, The Trial of Jesus (Chicago 1931), p. 103.

[10] »Indem der Vorwurf gegen Pilatus so gefasst ist: er habe das Blut der Galiläer und das der Opfertiere vermischt, kommt das jüdische Empfinden, das die Beflekkung des Temples durch Blut als ... Frevel fürchtet, anschaulich zur Darstellung Nicht nur die Ermordung von Menschen, sondern ebenso die Entweihung des Tempels und Opfers nötigt nach der Meinung der Redenden Jesus, sich gegen eine solche Untat zu erheben. Wenn er nun ... antwortet: "Ihr alle werdet ebenso untergehen", so ist ... damit auf das römische Schwert hingezeigt, durch das das Gericht am Volk vollstreckt werden wird, wie es die Jerusalem beklagenden Worte [Lc 13, 34—35; 19, 43—44 (21, 20—24), 23, 27—31] sagen«, Adolf Schlatter, Die beiden Schwerter, Lukas 22, 35—38. Ein Stück aus der besonderen Quelle des Lukas (Beiträge zur Förderung christlicher Theologie, Jahrg. 20, 1916, Heft 6; Gütersloh 1916), p. 32. The assumption that the incident mentioned in Lc 13, 1 occurred within the Temple precinct is not substantiated (see preceding note).

If there is a connection between the Vorlage which the Third Evangelist followed in Lc 13, 1—2 and the lament for Jerusalem, the Evangelist's source would be of a date not earlier than 70 CE. Yet that need only have affected the wording in Lc 13, 2, whilst v. 1 could still have retained recollections of events that took place during Pilate's prefecture.

transmitted by people who still retained a lively memory of Pontius Pilate's indifference to suffering and of his lordly contempt for the religious susceptibilities of those whom he governed. This representation contrasts remarkably with the "faint-hearted weakling"[11] in the canonical descriptions of Jesus' trial.

The chance, or accident, in history that connected the life of Pilate with that of Jesus at a critical moment ensured that the name of an obscure governor in a minor Roman province should live on whilst others slipped into oblivion. Yet for this very reason it is virtually impossible to do justice to Pilate, and to see him *sine ira et studio* as the man he was. He must have been one of the more able administrators whom Rome sent to Judaea. The relatively long term of his office is in itself proof of his capabilities. Nor was he completely oblivious of the interests of those whom he ruled. Josephus, or the chronicler responsible for Josephus' source, who dislikes him intensely, records that some of the measures which Pilate introduced[12] were intended to benefit the population. The Jews, however, resented his methods. A Roman realist, Pilate had no understanding of the workings of a priest-ridden theocracy nor any patience with his subjects' habits of squabbling about 'names and words'.

Meanness, avarice, cruelty, haughty disdain for the feelings of others, are the charges levelled against Pilate by secular writers. The evangelists describe him in a different light: inspired by the most humane and honourable intentions for those who are subject to his rule, he does his best in trying to persuade them to desist from their folly, and when compelled by necessity to discharge a distasteful duty, he washes his hands before he commits the prisoner — to be executed. In any investigation as to how it happened that such a different picture of the same man is given on the one hand by Philo, Josephus, and the authors of the source in Lc 13, 1, and on the other hand by the evangelists in their descriptions of Pilate's actions at the trial of Jesus, we have to trace the thread of Pilate's changing pattern as it runs through early Christian traditions. We should not confine ourselves to the portrayal of the governor's character and actions in the canonical Gospels if we wish to elucidate the motives behind that pattern; we have also to consider the rôle assigned to Pilate in post-evangelical Christian traditions, for the motives which were operative in the minds of the evangelists continued to influence the communal activities of Christian believers for a long time after the Gospels had been written. It is only by considering later records in conjunction with the Gospels that we can arrive at a clear appreciation of the factors that governed the continually changing representation of Pilate's personality.

---

[11] ἄνανδρος σφόδρα καὶ μαλακός, Chrysostom, In Matthaeum Homilia LXXXVI (LXXXVII); MPG 58, col. 765. *Cf.* Origen, MPG 13, col. 1775.

[12] B. J. II 175, Ant XVIII 60.

There is enough divergence in the four Gospels themselves. In Mark, Pilate is described as a dim-witted, weak-minded, but well-meaning provincial dignitary who lacks the strength of character, when confronted by the clamour of an excited mob, to stand by his convictions and acquit a man whom he considers innocent. Yet we know exactly from Josephus that Pilate had a way of dealing with an unruly crowd that proved unamenable to gentle persuasion[13]. Matthew adds little to the picture. The name of the high-priest is given (Mt 26, 57), and this contains a trustworthy historical reminiscence. The rest of the Matthaean supplementations are legendary accretions[14]. The bitterness against those shouldered with responsibility for the execution of Jesus is, however, more prominent in the First Gospel, whilst the good, if ineffective, intentions of the governor are underlined. The "converted rabbi"[15] who attributed the collective misfortune that befell the Jewish people in the year 70 CE to the individual misfortune that had befallen Jesus of Nazareth more than forty years earlier[16], displays a definite tendency to depict Pontius Pilate in a favourable light as a witness to Jesus' innocence[17]. The supplementation of the Marcan story by the dream of Pilate's wife (Mt 27, 19)[18] and the washing of Pilate's hands

---

[13] Cf. B. J. II 175—177, Ant XVIII 60—62.

[14] Cf. R. Bultmann, *Geschichte der synoptischen Tradition*, (Göttingen ²1931), pp. 304, 305; English edition (Oxford ²1968) pp. 280, 281.

[15] A *sobriquet*, given by Benjamin Wisner Bacon, in the wake of Gustav Volkmar, to the author of the First Gospel. Cf. Ernst von Dobschütz, »Matthäus als Rabbi und Katechet«, ZNW vol. 27, 1928, pp. 338—348.

[16] Mt 27, 25. It was a Jew who thought out, and wrote, these words. A Church Father of Gentile descent, by no means of philojudaic leanings, remarked: ἔστω γάρ, ὑμῖν [ἐ]αυτοῖς ἐπαρᾶσθε· τί καὶ ἐπὶ τὰ τέκνα τὴν ἀρὰν ἕλκετε, Chrysostom, In Matthaeum Homilia LXXXVI (LXXXVII); MPG 58, col. 766.

[17] »Nichts ist deutlicher als dass Matthäus mit allen seinen Aenderungen und Zusätzen nur bezweckt, die Schuld an dem Tod Jesu noch mehr als Marcus es bereits gethan von Pilatus... auf die Juden abzuwälzen«, Wilhelm Brandt, o. c. pp. 97, 98.

»Warum Matthäus die beiden Stücke bringt, ist klar: Er will Jesu Schuldlosigkeit und gleichzeitig die Schuld der Juden unterstreichen«, Josef Blinzler, *Der Prozeß Jesu. Das jüdische und das römische Gerichtsverfahren gegen Christus* (Regensburg ²1955), p. 155. Cf. Martin Dibelius, *Die Formgeschichte des Evangeliums*, p. 197; English edition, p. 196.

[18] »The legendary dream of Pilate's wife... intensifies the guilt of the Jews. The heathen woman seeks to save the righteous Jew«, Claude Goldsmid Montefiore, *The Synoptic Gospels* (London 1909), p. 771. Montefiore noticed: »she had frightening dreams, but these dreams are heaven-sent« *(ibidem)*, and in the second edition of his work (London 1927) he compared the story with the report of the dream which Calpurnia, Caesar's wife, had on the night before her husband's assassination. Wolfgang Trilling, in his book *Das wahre Israel. Studien zur Theologie des Matthäusevangeliums (Erfurter Theologische Studien*, vol. 7; Leipzig 1959), makes the important observation that the First Evangelist, although responsible for the present

(Mt 27, 24; a Jewish, not a Roman, habit to express non-participation in a bloody deed; cf. Deut 21, 6—7; Ps 26, 6 a; 73, 13 b)[19] brings this tendency clearly to the fore[20]. In Luke we have not simply an elaboration of the Marcan rendering of the Passion Narrative. Traces of traditional material are discernible, material which the Third Evangelist interweaves with that derived from Mark. The non-Marcan tradition has been worked over and thoroughly assimilated to the Third Evangelist's style and manner, but some of its elements appear to be of early origin. Although we have reason to assume that the Third Evangelist modified the Marcan account in some measure because of his own knowledge of a non-Marcan tradition, there is nevertheless no mistaking *his editorial intention,* namely, to stress Pilate's friendly disposition towards Jesus; dramatically he repeats three times the protestation of his innocence[21]. Finally, in the Fourth Gospel, Pilate is described as having

---

form of Mt 27, 19 might have used an element from tradition in which the suffering in a dream was indicative of some disaster that was to befall Pilate as a retribution for condemning Jesus to death. »Ursprünglich könnte die kleine Szene so gemeint gewesen sein, daß die Schuld des Pilatus unterstrichen, vielleicht sogar seine Bestrafung angekündigt werden sollte. Trotz der göttlichen Warnung hat er das ungerechte Urteil vollstreckt« (o. c., p. 49). Under the Evangelist's hand the tradition was transformed in such a manner as to exonerate the governor: »Der Evangelist hat die Mahnung... als Vorbereitung für v. 24 f. verwendet und dadurch als Entlastung des Pilatus verstanden. Das könnte gerade das Gegenteil [der] ihm vorliegende[n] Tradition [sein]... [Der Evangelist] verwendet das Wort der Heidin als helle Folie, damit die Schuld der Juden sich um so dunkler abhebe« (o. c., p. 50). Cf. Martin Dibelius, *Die Formgeschichte des Evangeliums,* pp. 113, 114; Engl. ed., p. 117.

[19] »Die Juden, Obrigkeit und Volk, haben die ganze Schuld und übernehmen sie auch ausdrücklich, um Pilatus zu entlasten... Er wird schon bei Marcus milde beurteilt und von den Späteren noch mehr rein gewaschen«, Julius Wellhausen, *Das Evangelium Matthaei* (Berlin 1904), p. 145.

[20] Trilling observes on Mt 27, 24—25: »Wir haben es *formkritisch* nicht mit einem legendären Zug, sondern mit einem dogmatischen Theologumenon zu tun« (o. c., p. 54).

[21] There is a noticeable difference in character between those sections of the Lucan narrative dealing with the arrest and those describing the trial. In Lc 22, 47—66 the narrative is concise and not inherently incredible, whereas in Lc 22, 67—71 and in Lc 23, 13—25 it is overloaded and confused. While Lc 22, 47—66 gives the impression of being 'more logical' than the Marcan parallel passage, this is not so with respect to the trial account proper. In Lc 23, 4 Pilate declares Jesus completely innocent, yet in vv. 14—16 and again in v. 22 he declares that he has found no justifiable reason for inflicting the death penalty and proposes the release of Jesus after scourging. The Evangelist gives no indication of the grounds on which the governor thought scourging to be appropriate.

The motif from Lc 23, 16, 22 b recurs in a more developed form in the Fourth Gospel. In Luke, Pilate *offers* to have Jesus scourged and released; in John, he actually *orders* the scourging before any verdict has been arrived at.

already an awareness, however hazy, of the divine character of the prisoner before him (Jn 19, 8).

Most instructive is a comparison between passages in the Gospels (Mc 15, 15; Mt 27, 26; Lc 23, 24; Jn 19, 16) in which the evangelists refer to Pilate's final decision. All are reluctant *to state plainly that the sentence of death was pronounced by the governor.* It is evident that Jesus could never have been put to death by the manner of crucifixion unless a verdict to this effect had been given by a Roman magistrate. If a capital sentence, passed by a Jewish court of law, required the governor's confirmation to be put into effect, such a sentence would not have resulted in the condemned person's crucifixion, but it would have been carried out in accordance with Jewish penal procedure. The apologetic motive of the authors of the Gospels emerges when we notice how laboriously they seek to get round the plain historical fact. They are at pains to avoid an explicit statement that would put on record the passing of the death sentence by Pilate. Progressively, the language of the evangelists becomes more involved. In Mc 15, 15 and Mt 27, 26 we are told that "Pilate delivered Jesus to be crucified"; in Lc 23, 24 we find that Pilate "decided that their (=the Jews') demand should be granted"; in Jn 19, 16 it says: "he handed him over to them (= the Jews) to be crucified". Comparison shows how the governor's connection with the execution of Jesus is presented in an increasingly indirect way. In Mark and Matthew, though Pilate does not *explicitly* pass sentence, yet *he himself* takes an action which presupposes that the verdict has been pronounced by him. Such is what we must gather from the evangelists' words. In the Third Gospel the language is deliberately ambiguous: Pilate takes action, but it is not his own will that determines the action[22]. The words in Jn 19, 16 finally can only be

---

The statements in Lc 23, 16 and 22 b are more difficult to understand as in Roman Law scourging was integral to the punishment of crucifixion (*cf.* Livy, Historiae XXXIII xxxvi 3; Josephus, B. J. II 306). The flagellation which *de lege* preceded actual crucifixion was often administered with such brutal force that it resulted in mortal wounds; crucifixion itself merely prolonged the condemned man's agony.

Scholars who contend that the concise character of the Third Gospel's narrative up to Lc 23, 3 is due solely to the Evangelist's 'streamlining' of the Marcan account overlook the fact that in the ensuing sections Luke is far less intelligible than Mark.

[22] »Lukas ... scheint mit seinem παρέδωκεν τῷ θελήματι αὐτῶν die Auffassung [zu vertreten], dass Pilatus Jesum den Juden ausliefert. Aber die Meinung des Markus erhellt daraus, dass V. 16 die Soldaten ihn übernehmen«, Johannes Weiss, *Das älteste Evangelium,* p. 329; »Eine Folge [der] Beseitigung der Soldaten ist es — oder zielte Lukas eben darauf ab? — dass die Kreuzigung nun von den Juden auszugehen scheint«, p. 332.

»En disant que Pilate a livré Jésus à ce que voulaient les Juifs, il n'a pas seulement évité de dire en termes crus que Pilate avait envoyé Jésus à la croix, mais il a entendu transférer aux Juifs toute la responsabilité du fait. Pilate compte, et

understood in the sense that Jesus was actually handed over to the Jews for crucifixion.

The statement to the effect that Pilate handed Jesus over for crucifixion to the Jews (παρέδωκεν αὐτὸν αὐτοῖς ἵνα σταυρωθῇ) and that the Jews took hold of him (παρέλαβον τὸν ᾿Ιησοῦν, Jn 19, 16) and led him to a place of execution where *they* crucified him (Jn 19, 18) is immediately contradicted by the ensuing narrative[23]. It is Pilate who orders the

___

beaucoup, mais comme témoin de moralité pour le Christ«, Alfred Loisy, *L'évangile selon Luc* (Paris 1924), p. 551.

Cf. Hans Conzelmann, *Die Mitte der Zeit. Studien zur Theologie des Lukas* (Tübingen ⁴1962): »Pilatus ist [bei Lukas] nur noch passiv beteiligt, indem er den Galiläer den Juden überlässt« (p. 81). »So macht Lukas dem römischen Verfolger seiner eigenen Zeit klar, dass das einstige Vorgehen gegen Jesus (auf dem das heutige gegen die Christen basiert) auf jüdischer Verleumdung beruhte und bis zur Gegenwart falsch dargestellt wird« (p. 78). »Daß Lukas politisch-apologetische Absichten hat, sollte man nicht bestreiten. . . . Die apologetische Tendenz tritt am stärksten in der Passionsgeschichte . . . zutage« (pp. 128, 129); English edition *The Theology of St. Luke* (London 1960), pp. 88, 85, 137, 138.

[23] The passage caused difficulties already in ancient times. Augustine, In Ioannis Evangelium Tractatus CXVI 9, wrote: »*susceperunt autem Iesum, et eduxerunt*, potest ad milites iam referri apparitores praesidis« (Corpus Christianorum series latina 36, p. 650; MPL 35, col. 1944). Augustine read the Gospel more carefully than others apparently did. He found in Mc 15, 16, 20 and Mt 27, 27, 31 that Jesus had been taken to his execution by (Roman) soldiers. In Lc 23, 26 the subject is not explicitly stated. In Jn 19, 16—18 the implication is that it was done by Jews.

From the second to the twentieth century, the chorus of voices reproaching the Jews with the murder of Jesus never becomes silent. Justin clearly was of the opinion that the Jews had laid their own hand on Jesus (Dial XVI 4, CXI 3, CXXXIII 6; further σταυρωθεὶς ὑπὸ τῶν ᾿Ιουδαίων, 1 Ap XXXV 1; see Edgar J. Goodspeed, *Die ältesten Apologeten. Texte mit kurzen Einleitungen* [Göttingen 1914], p. 50; MPG 6, col. 384). Melito of Sardis, in the Homily on the Passion, expatiates as follows:

(74) τὶ ἐποίησας, ὦ ᾿Ισραήλ, . . . ἀπέκτεινας τὸν κύριον

. . . . . .

(80) σὺ μὲν ἦσθα [ἦς] εὐφραινόμενος
    ἐκεῖνος δὲ λιμώττων
  σὺ ἔπινες οἶνον καὶ ἄρτον ἤσθιες
    ἐκεῖνος ὄξος καὶ χολήν
  σὺ ἦσθα [ἦς] φαιδρὸς [ἐφεδρὸς] τῷ προσώπῳ
    ἐκεῖνος δὲ ἐσκυθρώπαζεν
  σὺ ἦσθα [ἦς] ἀγαλλιώμενος
    ἐκεῖνος δὲ ἐθλίβετο
  σὺ ἔψαλλες
    ἐκεῖνος δὲ ἐκρίνετο
  σὺ ἐκέλευες
    ἐκεῖνος προσηλοῦτο
  σὺ ἐχόρευες
    ἐκεῖνος ἐθάπτετο

inscription on the cross (Jn 19, 19; *cf.* Mc. 15, 26; Mt 27, 37; Lc 23, 38). In Jn 19, 23 the Evangelist states explicitly that it was soldiers — Romans — who carried out the crucifixion. Finally there is the account of Joseph of Arimathaea's petitioning for the body of Jesus. The Fourth Evangelist, Jn 19, 38, asserts — as do the others (Mc 15, 43—45; Mt 27, 58; Lc 23, 50—52) — that Joseph asked Pilate's permission to take the body of Jesus down from the cross and bury it. If Pilate, as is implied in Jn 19, 16, had really let "the Jews" have their own way and decide what to do with the accused (if he had "washed his hands of the whole

> σὺ μὲν ἐπὶ στρωμνῆς μαλακῆς [στρωμὴν μαλακὴν] ἦσθα [ἧς] κατακείμενος
> ἐκεῖνος δὲ ἐν τάφῳ καὶ σορῷ
> ......
> (92) ἐφ' ᾧ καὶ ὁ Πιλᾶτος ἀπενίψατο τὰς χεῖρας
> σὺ δὴ τοῦτον ἀπέκτεινας ἐν τῇ μεγάλῃ ἑορτῇ
> ......
> (96) ὁ δεσπότης ὕβρισται [παρύβριστε]
> ὁ θεὸς πεφόνευται
> ὁ βασιλεὺς [τοῦ] Ἰσραὴλ ἀνῄρηται
> ὑπὸ δεξιᾶς Ἰσραηλίτιδος [Ἰσραήλ].
> ὦ φόνου καινοῦ
> ὦ ἀδικίας καινῆς [κενῆς].

Campbell Bonner, *The Homily on the Passion by Melito Bishop of Sardis (Studies and Documents* XII; London and Philadelphia 1940; *cf. Textus Minores* vol. XXIV, Leiden 1958, ed. Bernh. Lohse). In addition to the manuscript from the Chester Beatty Papyri (Frederic G. Kenyon, *The Chester Beatty Papyri,* fasciculus viii, London 1941), another manuscript with Melito's homily Περὶ τοῦ Πάσχα has come to light in Papyrus Bodmer XIII. [*Revisers' addendum:* Méliton de Sardes, *Homélie sur la Pâque,* ed., M. Testuz (Cologny — Geneva 1960). Its variants are represented by the parenthetical readings in the quotation.]

Taking a vast leap from the second to the twentieth century, we find fundamentally the same view expressed in an article by Harold P. Cooke, »Christ Crucified — And By Whom?« *(The Hibbert Journal,* vol. 29, 1930, pp. 61—74). Taking ›the plain sense‹ of Jn 19, 16, Cooke arrives at the conclusion that Pilate »delivered Christ unto the Jews who themselves lead him forth« and put him to death (p. 62). The author then refers to various passages in the Talmud and in the Toledoth Yeshu where he had read that Jesus was stoned. It would hardly be necessary to waste one's time in exploring such opinions were it not for the fact that there are statements in the Talmud which, in conjuction with the deliberate misstatement in Jn 19, 16, are apt to confuse uncritical readers. The fact that the Talmud contains notices to the effect that Jesus was stoned by Jews proves two things. It proves that the transmitters of this information had no independent historical records nor personal recollections of Jesus, and did not even know the New Testament. They based their assumptions on popular allegations such as were voiced abroad in Christian communities with whom Jews came into contact. Having unquestioningly accepted the allegation as a fact, rabbinical authors presumed that Jesus would have been put to death in a manner prescribed in Jewish Law. This also shows that the tradents of rabbinical records were convinced of the Sanhedrin's competence to carry out any sentence of death it had passed.

affair" and "delivered him up to their will"), the right to dispose of the dead body would have been in the hands of the Jews. The Fourth Evangelist, no less than the others, reports that it was necessary to obtain the governor's permission for the burial. Unless sentence and execution had been in Roman hands, permission would have been superfluous[24]. The mode of expression in Jn 19, 16 not only betrays a tortuous effort to avoid any mention of the fact that Pilate had passed sentence, but it is so framed as to suggest that the actors in Jn 19, 16—18 were the Jews. This is the more remarkable seeing that in the Fourth Gospel *no trial of Jesus is being conducted by a Jewish tribunal* and, furthermore, "the Jews" notify the governor Jn 18, 31 b) of their lack of juridical powers.

All four Gospels report — and dramatize — a demonstration by a Jewish crowd demanding that Jesus should be crucified. And it is in the realm of historical possibilities that a mob, incited by opponents of Jesus, might have gathered outside the praetorium and shouted slogans of vindictive bitterness and hate. A display of this kind could be construed as having been staged so as to convince Pilate that the masses made no common cause with a man accused of sedition. Such a demonstration would have been regarded as a declaration of loyalty to the Imperial Government — and perhaps it was a tactical move engineered by the priestly rulers to prove that the population of Judaea was immune against being inveigled into insurrection by political agitation. A report of some such vociferous action seems to have been at the disposal of the evangelists — and they seized upon it in their endeavour

---

[24] Joseph of Arimathaea is an historical person. He was neither a member of the Great Sanhedrin — though the Third Evangelist made him such — nor was he a follower of Jesus. He was a member of a lower Beth Din (there were three Jewish Courts in Jerusalem) whose duty it was to ensure that the bodies of executed persons were given decent burial before nightfall. He fulfilled this duty in accordance with Jewish law, and this act of piety was remembered. Tradition transformed Joseph of Arimathaea into a Christian.

»[Marcus] hat ... [bei den Worten εὐσχήμων βουλευτής] nicht an die Mitgliedschaft des Synedriums, des Hohen Raths der Juden, gedacht ..., [erst die] ihm nachfolgenden Evangelisten haben den Titel darauf gedeutet«, Wilhelm Brandt, *o. c.*, p. 80.

In Acts 13, 29 the burial of Jesus is attributed to 'the inhabitants of Jerusalem and their rulers'.

Josephus, reporting the assassination — by Jewish insurgents — of the former high-priests Ananus II and Jesus the son of Gamala, appears to be as much outraged by the fact that the murdered persons had not been given decent burial as by the murder itself: »... they (= the assassins) went so far in their impiety as to cast out the corpses without burial, although the Jews make careful provision for [the prescribed] obsequies and even ensure that malefactors who have been sentenced to death by crucifixion are taken down [from the cross] and buried before sunset« (B. J. IV 317).

to exonerate the Roman governor. However, although the fact of a demonstration by the street-rabble is historically credible, its influence upon a person of Pilate's domineering disposition belongs to the province of apologetics[25].

The development in the portrayal of Pilate — which started with the canonical Gospels as literary instruments for the spreading of the faith — did not culminate with the completion of the Canon. In non-canonical Christian records the favourable traits in the representation of Pilate's character secure still greater emphasis.

Ignatius of Antioch mentions Pilate in passages of an anti-docetic purport; he stresses the reality of Jesus' suffering[26]. What Ignatius still does not say is stated by Aristides: ['Ιουδαῖοι] αὐτὸν [= 'Ιησοῦν] προ-έδωκαν Πιλάτῳ τῷ ἡγεμόνι .... καὶ σταυρῷ κατεδίκασαν[27]. "He was crucified (pierced) by the Jews"[28]. In the apocryphal Gospel of Peter we are a stage further: *the governor had no part whatever in the condemnation and execution of Jesus.* The moral and legal responsibility rests exclusively with the Jews. The Acts of John can repeat: "the Jews crucified him on the tree". Justin, though he refers in 1 Apol. XIII 3 to 'Ιησοῦς Χριστὸς ὁ σταυρωθεὶς ἐπὶ Ποντίου Πιλάτου τοῦ ... ἐπιτρό-που[29] implies in other places[30] that the crucifixion was the work of Jews. Melito of Sardis speaks of the Jews who not only had sentenced Jesus, but nailed him to the cross with their own hands: "Though Jesus *must needs be crucified,* Israel should have let him suffer at the hand of the Gentiles, by the oppressor's hand, *not by Israel's action*"[31]; rhetorically Melito addresses Israel: "for whom even Pilate washed his hands, you have slain him"[32]. In the Apostles' Creed the name of Pilate is mentioned in a non-committal manner; it is no more than a

---

[25] *Vanae voces populi non sunt audiendae; nec enim vocibus eorum credi opertet, quando qui obnoxium crimine absolvi aut innocentem condemnari desideraverint,* Codex Justinianus IX xlvii 12 (the formulation comes from Diocletian's time).

[26] δοξάζω 'Ιησοῦν Χριστόν... ἀληθῶς ὑπὶ Ποντίου Πιλάτου καὶ 'Ηρῴδου τετράρχου καθηλωμένον, Ad Smyrnaeos I 1—2 (MPG 5, col. 708); *cf.* col. 841); ... ἀληθῶς ἐδιώχθη ἐπὶ Ποντίου Πιλάτου, ἀληθῶς ἐσταυρώθη καὶ ἀπένεν, Ad Trallianos IX 1 (MPG 5, col. 681); *cf.* Ad Magnesios XI (MPG 5, col. 672).

It is of interest to note that in the spurious, interpolated, version of the Epistle to the Trallians the responsibility for having sentenced Jesus is unequivocally stated to have been Pilate's: ἀπόφασιν ἐδέξατο παρὰ τοῦ Πιλάτου... ὑπὸ τῶν ψευδο-Ιου-δαίων καὶ Πιλάτου τοῦ ἡγεμόνος, ὁ κριτὴς ἐκρίθη,... κατεκρίθη, ἐσταυρώθη... (MPG 5, cols. 789, 793).

[27] Apud Historiam Barlaam et Iosaphat, see James Rendel Harris, *The Apology of Aristides on Behalf of the Christians* (Cambridge 1891), p. 110.

[28] J. R. Harris, *o. c.,* p. 37.

[29] E. J. Goodspeed, *o. c.,* p. 34; MPG 6, cols. 345, 348.

[30] See below, p. 108, note 31.

[31] The Homily on the Passion, lines 75, 76; C. Bonner, *o. c.,* p. 137.

[32] The Homily on the Passion, line 92; *cf.* note 23 *supra.*

chronological pointer — "suffered under Pontius Pilate" — without
indication that Pilate had been in any way instrumental in bringing
about this suffering. In the spurious Epistle of Pilate to the Emperor
Claudius, Pilate asserts that Jesus had been executed by Jewish subter-
fuge[33]. In a strange mixture in which features of the Lucan and Johannine accounts can be discerned, Irenaeus relates that Herod [Antipas]
and Pontius Pilate came together and condemned Jesus to be crucified.
"For Herod was frightened lest he be ousted by him (= Jesus) from the
kingship ... while Pilate was constrained by Herod and by the Jews
around him to deliver [Jesus] unwillingly to death on the grounds that
not to do so would be to go against Caesar by liberating a man who
was given the title of king"[34]. Tertullian, referring to current notions
of Jesus amongst his contemporaries, does so by saying: ". . . et vulgus
iam scit Christum, hominem utique aliquem, qualem Iudaei iudica-
verunt"[35]. ". . . interfecerint eum [Iudaei] ut adversarium"[36]; "Omnis
synagoga filiorum Israel eum interfecit"[37]. So far advanced had the
refining process in the portrayal of Pilate become, that by the time of
Tertullian the Church Father could actually refer to the governor

---

[33] »... the chief priests, moved by envy against him, took him and delivered
him unto me, and brought against him one false accusation after another, saying
that he was a sorcerer and did things contrary to their law. But I, believing that
these things were so, having scourged him, delivered him unto their will: and t h e y
c r u c i f i e d   h i m.

And when he was buried, they set guards upon him. But while m y   s o l d i e r s
watched him, he rose again on the third day. Yet so much was the malice of the
Jews kindled that they gave money to the soldiers, saying: Say that his disciples
stole away his body. But [the soldiers], though they took the money, were not able
to keep silence concerning what had happened; for they also have testified that
they saw him arisen and that they received money from the Jews.

And I report these things ... lest anyone lie otherwise (sic!) and you should be
inclined to believe the false tales of the Jews«.

This epistle, written by a dead Pilate to a dead Claudius (who had become
emperor some twelve to fourteen years after the crucifixion), is chiefly interesting
because of the fact that it mentions sorcery as an accusation against Jesus. The
writer seems to have known that sorcery was also punishable by crucifixion in
Roman Law. Regarding another spurious letter of Pilate, this time addressed to
Emperor Tiberius, see below 89, note 52.

[34] Chapter 74. Quoted from St. Irenaeus' Proof of the Apostolic Preaching. Translated and annotated by Joseph P. Smith, S. J. (Ancient Christian Writers, vol. 16,
Westminster, Maryland, 1952), pp. 95, 96.

[35] Apologeticus XXI 3 (Corpus Christianorum, Tertulliani Opera, pars I, p. 123;
CSEL 69, p. 53; MPL 1, col. 392).

[36] Adversus Marcionem, liber tertius, VI 2 (Corpus Christianorum as above,
p. 514; CSEL 47, p. 383; MPL 2, col. 327).

[37] Adversus Judaeos VIII 18 (Corpus Christianorum, Tertulliani Opera, pars II,
p. 1363; MPL 2, col. 616).

as being already convinced of Christian truth: "Pilatus ... iam pro sua conscientia Christianus"[38]. In the third century Didascalia there is a fair summary of the Gospel accounts: "... et a Pilato [Iudaei] occisionem petierunt. Et crucifixerunt eum ... parasceue"; "... nam ille qui gentilis erat et e populo alieno, Pilatus iudex, operibus iniquitatis eorum non consentit"[39].

There is a definite connection between two facts: t h e   m o r e   C h r i s t i a n s   a r e   p e r s e c u t e d   b y   t h e   R o m a n   S t a t e, t h e   m o r e   g e n e r o u s   b e c o m e s   t h e   d e s c r i p t i o n   o f   P o n t i u s   P i l a t e   a s   a   w i t n e s s   t o   J e s u s '   i n n o c e n c e. It is in no way surprising that there should be a correlation of this kind. The stratagem of depicting Pilate as being unwilling to sentence Jesus to death is in line with the general pattern of Jewish, and subsequent Christian, apologetics addressed to the Roman authorities. When Gaius Caligula was about to enforce measures which were offensive to the Jews, or when a Roman proconsul in Alexandria sided with a faction hostile to the Jews in that town, Philo submitted to the Emperor a long list enumerating all the privileges which the Emperor's ancestors and predecessors had bestowed upon Jewish communities. The purpose of this action was to remind Caligula how different from his own had been the attitude of his forbears towards Judaism. Defenders of Christianity, *mutatis mutandis,* resorted to the same device. Suffering for their belief under Roman emperors and officials, they employed the technique of portraying Pilate as Jesus' friend, so as to reproach their present persecutors. None of the Gospels is earlier than the reigns of the Flavian emperors. Under Vespasian, Titus and Domitian, persons believed to be descendants of King David, and their adherents, were put to death in great numbers[40]. Persecutions continued in Trajan's

---

[38] Apologeticus XXI 24 (Corpus Christianorum, Tertulliani Opera, pars I, p. 127; CSEL 69, p. 58; MPL 1, col. 403). Tertullian is also the author of an interesting report that Tiberius had, on Pontius Pilate's submission, suggested to the Roman Senate that Jesus Christ should be included in the Pantheon; see Apologeticus V 2 (Corpus Christianorum, *l. c.,* pp. 94, 95; CSEL 69, p. 14; MPL 1, cols. 290, 291).

[39] Franz X. Funk, *Didascalia et Constitutiones Apostolorum* (Paderborn 1905), numbers the respective passages V 14: 8, 9 and V 19: 4 (pp. 274, 290). In Hugh Connolly's *Didascalia Apostolorum. The Syriac Version translated and accompanied by the Verona Latin Fragments* (Oxford 1929) they are numbered as XXI 14: »they asked him of Pilate to be put to death. And they crucified him ... on Friday« (p. 182) and XXI 19: »He who was a heathen and of a foreign people, Pilate the judge, did not consent to their deeds of wickedness« (pp. 189, 190).

[40] Eusebius, Historiae ecclesiasticae III 12: καὶ ἐπὶ τούτοις Οὐεσπασιανὸ[ς] μετὰ τὴν τῶν Ἱεροσολύμων ἅλωσιν πάντας τοὺς ἀπὸ γένους Δαυίδ, ὡς μὴ περιλειφθείη τις παρὰ Ἰουδαίοις τῶν ἀπὸ τῆς βασιλικῆς φυλῆς, ἀναζητεῖσθαι προσ[έταξεν] (GCS Eusebius II, 1, p. 228; MPG 20, col. 248). Cf. Hist. eccl. III 19 and 20 (GCS Eusebius II, 1, pp. 232—234; MPG 20, cols. 252, 253, 255).

time[41]. The reason for Roman severity was the determination, on the emperors' part, to eradicate apocalyptic trends in Judaism and to nip in the bud any attempt to restore the Davidic dynasty and re-establish its rule over the Jewish people[42]. It was in this period that the Gospels assumed their final form. That Jesus was crucified as "King of the Jews" could scarcely be kept secret. Nor could it be entirely concealed that Pilate had ordered his crucifixion. The evangelists then, in their pleading with Rome, fell upon the expedient of representing Pilate as acting against his own better conviction, and giving way to pressure, when he himself — as they maintained — considered the prosecution unjustified. We possess evidence, though coming from later times, that there were Roman officials who found it revolting to have Christians put to death for no other reason than their profession of faith. Pilate, in fact, was of a different type. Yet the evangelists borrowed the paint for Pilate's portrait from their own later experience of more humane Roman magistrates who might have existed in various places even before the time for which we have evidence of such.

As late as in the time of Tacitus, Romans of the highest rank regarded the Christian movement as a hotbed of political unrest wherever there was a Jewish population within the Empire. The *exitiabilis superstitio* which had sprung up in Judaea and had spread to Rome, was a source of trouble. Tacitus apparently saw Christianity behind the great Jewish revolt of the years 66 to 70 CE. His diagnosis was wrong, but the fact that Tacitus made it — and could make it almost half a century after the outbreak of the revolt — shows that revolutionary stir and apocalyptic speculation were associated with the Christian conviction in influential Roman circles even at a time when Christianity had begun to lose its early apocalyptic character. It has been persuasively argued[43] that Tacitus' words *repressa [per procuratorem*

---

[41] Eusebius, Hist. eccl. III 32 (GCS Eus. II, 1, pp. 266—270; MPG 20, cols. 281, 284); III 36, 3 (GCS Eus. II, 1, p. 274; MPG 20, col. 288).

[42] See Suetonius, Vespasianus iv 5: *Percrebuerat Oriente toto vetus et constans opinio esse in fatis ut eo tempore Iudaea profecti rerum potirentur; cf.* Tacitus, Historiae V xiii 4: *pluribus persuasio inerat... eo ipso tempore fore ut valesceret Oriens profectique Iudaea rerum potirentur;* also Josephus, B. J. VI 312.

[43] See Peter Corssen, »Die Zeugnisse des Tacitus und Pseudo-Josephus über Christus«, ZNW vol. 15, 1914, pp. 114—140: »Was ist mit dem Wiederausbrechen [des unheilvollen Aberglaubens] gemeint? Er brach nicht nur in Judäa, sondern auch in Rom aus. Also ist an zwei gleichzeitige Bewegungen gedacht. 64 ist der neronische Brand, 66 bricht der Krieg in Judäa aus. Was anders kann gemeint sein als dieser? Somit ist der jüdische Krieg als ein Wiederaufleben der von Pilatus unterdrückten Bewegung bezeichnet« (*l. c.,* p. 123).

Cf. Martin Dibelius, »Rom und die Christen im ersten Jahrhundert«, *Sitzungsberichte der Heidelberger Akademie der Wissenschaften,* Phil.-hist. Klasse, 1941/42 Heft 2 (Heidelberg 1942); also in *Botschaft und Geschichte,* vol. 2 (Tübingen 1956) pp. 177—228, esp. on pp. 204—207. Further, see below, p. 89, note 52.

*Pontium Pilatum] in praesens exitiabilis superstitio r u r s u m   e r u m -
p e b a t ,   n o n   m o d o   p e r   I u d a e a m , originem eius mali, s e d
p e r   u r b e m   e t i a m* imply that the obnoxious superstition, tem-
porarily restrained by Pontius Pilate, broke out again in all its destruc-
tiveness — at approximately the same time, so we have to understand
— in Judaea as well as in Rome.

Outside the Gospels there is ample evidence for the expedient of
emphasizing the favours, or benevolence, allegedly displayed by earlier
Roman rulers towards Christian communities — in a plea for contemporary religious toleration. The method can be traced throughout the
first three centuries as is shown by the handing down of the *Rescriptum
Hadriani*[44] and by the invention of the *Rescriptum Marci Aurelii An-
tonini*[45]. The latter instance demonstrates that exponents of Christianity
did not, on occasion, shrink from blatant falsification in their endea-
vours to persuade a hostile ruler that some of his predecessors had been
favourably disposed towards the Church[46].

---

[44] Eusebius, Hist. eccl. IV 9, 1—3 (GCS Eus. II, 1, pp. 318—320; MPG 20,
cols. 325, 328); *cf.* Justin, I Apologia (towards end), Hadrian did not in fact ease
the situation for the church, but he did threaten those who made formal denunciations without proof. Telesphorus, bishop of Rome during Hadrian's reign, suffered martyrdom.

[45] Eusebius, Hist. eccl. IV 13, 1—7 (GCS Eus. II, 1, pp. 326—330; MPG 20,
cols. 333, 336).

[46] »La tradition chrétienne aura senti de très bonne heure la nécessité apologétique de présenter le supplice de Jésus comme uniquement imputable aux Juifs:
il importait à la nouvelle religion que son fondateur ne parût pas avoir été condamné par une juste sentence de l'autorité romaine; d'autre part, il était fort délicat
d'accuser de prévarication Pilate lui-même, et il était impossible de nier que la sentence
de mort eût été rendue par lui; restaient les dénonciateurs et les accusateurs du Christ,
les Juifs, adversaires du christianisme naissant, détestés eux-mêmes dans le monde
païen; rien n'était plus facile que d'élargir leur rôle, da façon à transporter de Pilate
sur eux la responsabilité entière du jugement rendu contre Jésus; à cette fin, l'on
aura imaginé tout le procès devant [le sanhédrin] ... et dans le procès devant Pilate
on aura introduit l'épisode de Barabbas, pour que le magistrat romain ne semblât
pas seulement avoir laissé exécuter une condamnation dont il n'était pas l'auteur,
mais avoir fait tout le possible pour que ce jugement inique fût frustré de son effet.
Ainsi le supplice [de Jésus] n'était pas une action de la justice romaine: ce n'était
que le crime des Juifs. Rien ne sert de dire que les chrétiens n'avaient aucun intérêt
à disculper, au temps de Néron, un fonctionnaire de Tibère, qui était mort en
disgrâce. Il ne s'agit point ici de la personne de Pilate, mais de l'autorité qu'il re-
présentait. C'est pour ce motif que, dans [les évangiles], on chargera de plus en plus les
Juifs, et Pilate, c'est-à-dire l'autorité romaine, apparaîtra de plus en plus favorable
à Jésus«, Alfred Loisy, *L'évangile selon Marc* (Paris 1912), pp. 435, 436.

»Sous l'influence des nécessités de l'apologétique, on a ... tendu à diminuer le
rôle des Romains dans l'histoire de la passion pour aggraver d'autant la responsabilité des Juifs«, Maurice Goguel, *Les sources du récit johannique de la passion*
(Paris 1910), p. 6.

The process by which the governor who had sentenced Jesus to death by crucifixion became in apologetics an instrument for the defence of the Christian faith was a gradual one. The stern Pilate grows more mellow from Gospel to Gospel. In Mark he is greatly astonished and offers to release Jesus in whom he can find no guilt. In Matthew he renounces responsibility for the execution which he nevertheless orders. In Luke he repeats three times his assertion of Jesus' innocence, yet gives in to the will of the Jews. In John he hands Jesus over for execution to the Jews themselves. Post-canonical traditions stress even more Pilate's benevolent disposition. The stature of Pilate grows and increases in favour with God and men. The more removed from history, the more sympathetic a character he becomes[47].

Suddenly, in the fourth century, this development comes to an end. There is still, in the Gospel of Nicodemus, a belated echo of the tendency to accentuate Pilate's friendly disposition towards Jesus[48], and to present him as a witness to the illegality of the latter's execution. But from Eusebius onward the prevailing current takes a sharp turn in the opposite direction, and Pilate's fortunes in Christian tradition enter upon a steep decline[49]. The circle is closed. It only remains to read the portents.

The historical conditions in which the Christian communities lived from the first to the fourth century are the background of Pilate's developing portrait; and it is they that help us to explain why, after such a promising beginning, the governor's reputation subsequently failed to reach yet further heights. Pilate was cheated in his posthumous career by Emperor Constantine. Had it been one generation later, or perhaps two, when Christianity became a *religio licita*[50], Pontius Pilate would

---

[47] »...l'attitude de Pilate est une fiction des évangelistes. Pilate ne s'est pas borné à ratifier une sentence du sanhédrin, il a jugé Jésus pour grief politique, et il l'a condamné au supplice de la croix«, Alfred Loisy, *Les actes des apôtres* (Paris 1920), p. 876.

[48] »Let Jesus be brought hither [but] with gentleness!« Acta Pilati I 2.

[49] Eusebius, Hist. eccl. II 7 (GCS Euseb. II, 1, p. 122; MPG 20, col. 155).

It must not be understood that the swing of opinion set in i m m e d i a t e l y after 312 CE or that it prevailed everywhere at the same time. History does not work in this way. For some time the amicable attitude towards Pilate lingers on in Christian traditions even after the year 312, but the depiction of Pilate as a friend of Jesus comes to a stop under Constantine, and d e v e l o p s  n o  f u r t h e r. The situation t h e n  r e m a i n e d  s t a g n a n t at the point it had reached: the Jews are blamed for the crucifixion (as in Jn 19, 16—18), but Pilate is no longer exonerated.

[50] Roman lawyers did not actually use the words *religio licita* as a technical legal expression. There were, however, in Imperial Rome certain religions that were favoured, or tolerated, by the authorities, and others that were not. Terminological exactitude apart, *religio licita* is a convenient expression for denoting a situation which did obtain.

doubtless have been a saint to-day in Western Christendom as his wife is in the Greek Church. The Edict of Milan (312)[51] made it no longer necessary for the Church to have in Pilate an authorized official who testified that "he found no guilt in this man", implying, as it does, that the profession of Christian beliefs and attendance at Christian cultic practices were nonsubversive from the point of view of the *raison d'état* of the Imperium Romanum.

The process had begun before the Gospels. It ended after the battle at the Milvian Bridge. The upward trend in Pilate's reputation abruptly comes to an end, and this occasions no surprise when we consider that the inducement to represent the governor as a witness to Jesus' innocence was no longer operative. All the restrictions imposed by Rome on Christian worship were now lifted; Constantine eventually became converted — and Pilate missed canonization[52].

---

[51] As popularly used, the words *Edict of Milan* refer here to the decrees of the years 311 *and* 312. See Eusebius, Hist. eccl. VIII 17, 3—11 (GCS Eus. II, 2, pp. 790—794; MPG 20, cols. 792, 793) and X 5, 2—14 (GCS Eus II, 2, pp. 883—887; MPG 20, cols. 880, 881, 884, 885).

[52] For some further observations relevant to the theme of the present chapter, see my articles »A Letter from Pontius Pilate«, *Novum Testamentum* vol. 7, 1964, pp. 37—43 (esp. re the groundlessness of the view that Agrippa I was moved by personal animosity in his assessment of Pilate — on p. 72); and »Tacitus and Pliny: The Early Christians«, *Journal of Historical Studies* vol. 1, Princeton N. J. 1967—68, pp. 31—40 (esp. re the association in the official Roman mind of Christian apocalypticism with social ferment and political disruption — on pp. 34, 35 *et passim*).

# 7. THE PENALTY OF CRUCIFIXION

Basic to the present thesis is the consideration that a sentence of death carried out in Judaea in the first century of our era by the mode of crucifixion was a sentence which had been passed by a Roman authority. There are scholars who hold that Jesus was sentenced to death by the Sanhedrin for blasphemy or some other offence under Jewish Law, but that the Sanhedrin was prevented through a constitutional deficiency from putting its verdict into effect. On this view, the Sanhedrin's verdict required ratification from the representative of the Imperial Government before it could be executed. The obvious objection to such an exegesis is that if a Roman magistrate merely ratified a sentence which had been passed by a local Jewish court, the sentence would not have been carried out by crucifixion, but in a manner specified in the regulations governing Jewish penal procedure.

In an attempt to evade the objection and uphold the historical character of the Marcan and Matthaean presentations of the Sanhedrin's night session at which a capital sentence had been pronounced upon Jesus, the proposition has been put forward that crucifixion was an established manner of inflicting the death penalty among the Jews[1]. The suggestion is made that this form of punishment had been taken over by the Jews in the time of Antiochus Epiphanes whose soldiers inflicted it upon Jews unwilling to renounce their ancestral religion. In his report of the Syrian persecution, Josephus states that Jews "were crucified while they were still alive and breathed" (ζῶντες ἔτι καὶ ἐμπνέοντες ἀνεσταυροῦντο)[2]. The Syrian soldiers also strangled women and their circumcised male children, hanging the little boys around the necks of their mothers who had been fastened to the crosses[3]. The words "while they were still alive and breathed" in Josephus's report are significant. To a pagan Roman reader, this would be scarcely worthy of mention, for such was the ordinary practice in Roman crucifixion. In Jewish law, however, there was no provision for hanging condemned persons on a stake, or a cross, alive — but only the provision that the corpses of executed criminals should be affixed to a stake (apparently

---

[1] Ethelbert Stauffer, *Jerusalem und Rom im Zeitalter Jesu Christi* (Bern 1957), pp. 123—127.

[2] Ant XII 256.

[3] τὰς δὲ γυναῖκας καὶ τοὺς παῖδας αὐτῶν οὓς περιέτεμνον... ἀπῆγχον ἐκ τῶν τραχήλων αὐτοὺς τῶν ἀνεσταυρωμένων γονέων ἀπαρτῶντες. Ant XII 256. The account in 2 Maccabees 6, 10 differs.

as a deterring example) and subsequently taken down and buried before nightfall[4]. The explicit statement by Josephus that those whom the Seleucid soldiery crucified were crucified alive, demonstrates that a procedure of this sort had something unusual about it for the Jewish mind.

To find support for the view that crucifixion was a recognized mode of carrying out a sentence of death in Jewish Law, Ethelbert Stauffer refers to the Assumption of Moses 8, 1, where we read "rex regum terrae ... confitentes circumcisionem in cruce suspendet" *(the king of earthly kings will crucify those who confess to their circumcision)*[5]. Stauffer[6] understands the passage to refer to events in the time of Antiochus Epiphanes, and his argument is that the Jews, having been made familiar with the practice of crucifixion, subsequently adopted it themselves. It is likely that chapters 8 and 9 of the Assumption of Moses are based on a record of older date than the composition of the whole work, and that this record referred to persecutions under the Syrian king Antiochus IV. The composition of the Assumption of Moses as a whole falls, however, roughly in the time of Jesus' life when Jews had come to have much further experience of the practice of crucifixion from Roman activities in Judaea. When the book took the form in which it has been transmitted to later ages, crucifixion was certainly not unknown to the inhabitants of Palestine as an instrument of punishment. Roman officers inflicted this penalty upon Jews *en masse*[7]. Whether the Hebrew expression which lies behind the words "in cruce suspendere" in Ass Mos 8, 1[8] comes from a record more ancient than

---

[4] Deut 21, 22—23. After execution the corpse had to remain exposed to public view for the rest of the day, but it was compulsory in Jewish law that the body should be buried before sunset. An exception — it is not a case of judicial sentence, but of political revenge — is recorded in 2 Samuel 21, 6, 8—14. Even the bodies of dead enemies (*cf.* Joshua 8, 29; 10, 26; 2 Samuel 4, 12) were not to be left without burial. See B. J. IV 317, Ant IV 265.

What the case recorded in 2 Sam 21 involved, is not quite clear. The precise mode of execution cannot be determined from the record. It does not refer to an act resulting from the verdict of a court of law, but to an act of vengeance from political motives. The injunction to bury the dead bodies of executed persons was not observed in this instance, but one ought to bear in mind that the reference goes back to a time prior to the legislation contained in Deuteronomy.

Roman law did not provide for the burial of persons who had been crucified. The bodies of slaves crucified just outside the city of Rome, in the *sessorium,* were interminably left hanging on the crosses — till the corpses became the prey of vultures or animals.

[5] Robert Henry Charles, *The Assumption of Moses* (London 1897), p. 29.

[6] *O. c.,* p. 124.

[7] B. J. II 75, Ant XVII 295 (Quintilius Varus ordered the crucifixion of some 2000 men); further Ant XX 102 (Tiberius Alexander), B. J. II 241, Ant XX 129 (Ummidius Quadratus), B. J. II 253, Ant XX 161 (Antonius Felix), B. J. II 306 (Gessius Florus), B. J. V 449—451 (Titus Flavius).

the composition of the book itself, cannot be said with confidence, nor can it be asserted what the actual Hebrew words were. The compiler of the Assumption could have introduced an expression different from that in his source. Even if we assume that the wording of the source remained unaltered, and that later it was correctly rendered in the course of successive translations into Greek and Latin, it would only prove that the penalty of crucifixion was known to the Jewish writer — not that crucifixion was practised as a mode of execution by the Jews themselves.

According to Stauffer, Antiochus' example was followed by the high-priest Alcimus who officiated in the years 163/62 to 160/59 BCE and who during his term of office allegedly ordered the crucifixion of sixty Assidaeans[9]. No evidence for this statement exists. In 1 Maccabees 7, 16 we read that Alcimus put sixty Assidaeans to death; in Antiquities XII 396 the action is attributed to Bacchides. But whether it was Bacchides or Alcimus who was responsible for the deed, neither the author of 1 Maccabees nor Josephus reports that it was a case of crucifixion.

To supplement his information from 1 Macc 7, 16, Ethelbert Stauffer refers to the fragment from the Nahum Pesher which was discovered in Qumran Cave 4[10]. There occurs the expression תלה אנשים חיים but Alcimus is not mentioned. On this point, later.

Even more arbitrary is the argumentation based on a report in the Mishnah (in itself obscure) which is taken to imply that eighty women — "witches" — were crucified on one day at the order of Shimeon ben Shetaḥ[11]. The story is given in connection with tannaitic regulations concerning the proper method of stoning (Mishnah Sanhedrin vi 4). The entire section explicitly refers to *stoning*, not to *crucifixion*. When a person condemned to death by stoning was actually stoned, and death had occurred, the corpse was to be publicly exhibited by being hanged on a tree or stake. Such was the Law[12]. A dispute eventually arose

---

[8] In the Assumption of Moses 6, 9 there is another mention of crucifixion, apparently referring to Roman times, namely, the execution of Jews at the order of Varus (B. J. II 75, Ant XVII 295).

[9] Stauffer, *o. c.*, p. 124.

[10] *O. c.*, p. 125, note 14; also p. 162. For the Qumran fragment see John Marco Allegro, »Further Light on the History of the Qumran Sect«, *Journal of Biblical Literature,* vol. 75, Philadelphia 1956, pp. 89—95; *Discoveries in the Judaean Desert,* vol. 5 (Oxford 1968), pp. 37—42; *cf.* Frank Moore Cross Jr., *The Ancient Library of Qumrân and Modern Biblical Studies* (London 1958), on pp. 91—94. Why Stauffer connects the reference with Alcimus is unknown. It is generally assumed that the Nahum Pesher refers to Alexander Jannaeus of whom Josephus reports that he ordered 800 Jews to be crucified (B. J. I 97, Ant XIII 380).

[11] Stauffer, *o. c.*, p. 125.

[12] *Cf.* note 4 above. »All who have been stoned must be hanged«, Mishnah Sanhedrin vi 4. »He shall be put to death, and [afterwards] you shall hang him on a tree«, Siphre on Deut 21, 22.

among second-century rabbis as to whether this undecorous procedure should, or should not, be observed in the case of women who had been executed by stoning. The majority of the rabbis maintained that the dead bodies of executed women should never be exhibited in this way. The authority of Shimeon ben Shetah was invoked against making an exemption for women, and it was alleged that the celebrated scholar — whom the rabbis held in high repute — had the corpses of eighty women hanged on one and the same day at Ascalon. When or why Shimeon took this action, and whether he took it at all, are unanswered questions. As the "hanging up" is said to have taken place at Ascalon, it would not have been carried out in pursuance of an order issued by the Sanhedrin of Jerusalem[13]. No doubt at all attaches to the fact that the passage in Mishnah Sanh vi 4 does not refer to putting people to death by crucifixion, but to the public exhibition of the corpses of people who had already been executed by stoning.

To pick out more evidence for his claim that crucifixion was a Jewish mode of execution, and that the Jews were in the habit of nailing the limbs of a crucified person to the cross — not even the synoptic Gospels state that Jesus was nailed to the cross — Stauffer takes recourse to a passage in Mishnah Shabbath vi 10[14] where a mention occurs of "the nails of one [who was] crucified". The passage gives no information as to the identity of the crucified person, nor of the cause of crucifixion, nor of the agency that carried it out. It is not even clear from the words used whether the nails in question refer to the affixture of the body on the cross or to the securing of the crossbeam (patibulum) to the vertical stake (simplex) planted in the ground. The passage does not allow of the definite interpretation which Stauffer has advanced.

The expression תלה אנשים חיים, to hang up men alive, found in the Pesher Nahum[15], is elsewhere attested in later rabbinical records. It indicates crucifixion[16]. The very fact that Jews had no such institution as crucifixion was responsible for their not having a word for it. Hence the necessity to circumscribe it with the phrase "to hang up alive".

---

[13] See Emil Schürer *Geschichte des jüdischen Volkes im Zeitalter Jesu Christi*, vol. 1 (Leipzig ³1901), p. 289. [*Revisers' addendum:* English edition *The History of the Jewish People in the Age of Jesus Christ* (revised and edited by G. Vermes and F. Millar) vol. 1 (Edinburgh 1973), p. 231.]

[14] O. c., pp. 125—126.

[15] See above, note 10.

[16] Naftali Wieder, »Notes on the New Documents from the Fourth Cave of Qumran. The Term תלה חי«, *Journal of Jewish Studies*, vol. 7, London 1956, pp. 71—72. »תלה … does not necessarily mean ‹crucify›, תלה חי certainly does« (*l. c.*, p. 72). [*Revisers' addendum: Cf.* more recently, Y. Yadin, »Pesher Nahum (4Qp Nahum) Reconsidered«, *Israel Exploration Journal*, vol. 21, Jerusalem 1971, pp. 1—12. See also the discussion in Schürer-Vermes-Millar, *o. c.*, vol. 1, pp. 224—225, note 22.]

Even in Greek the verb κρεμάω, to hang up, תָּלָה, could be used by Jewish writers in the sense of σταυρόω. In Lc 23, 39 the words "one who had been hanged" (κρεμασθείς — εἷς τῶν κρεμασθέντων) are applied to one of the men who were crucified at the same time as Jesus. In the active voice the verb occurs in Acts 5, 30; 10, 39 where Peter is said to have blamed the Jews for having "hung up" Jesus from a tree. It is Jewish usage which makes its presence felt in the phrase. Similarly, when reporting the siege of Machaerus and the threat, by Lucilius Bassus, to have Eleazar crucified, Josephus writes: [Βάσσος] ... προσέταξε καταπηγνύναι σταυρὸν ὡς αὐτίκα κρεμῶν τὸν Ἐλεάζαρον[17]. Rabbinical sources, however, usually make a distinction between the punishment of crucifixion ("hanging up a living person", תלה ח׳, σταυροῦν) and the exhibition of the corpses of persons stoned to death or otherwise executed ("hanging up", תלה, κρεμᾶν) by specifying of the former כדרך שהמלכות עושה that is: *as is the way* (the procedure, the custom, *Rechtspflege*) *of the [Roman] government*[18] — in other words: *in conformity with Roman penal practice.* Jewish procedure is thus sharply distinguished from the Roman.

Far from providing proof that crucifixion was an established (or incipient) Jewish custom, dating from the time of Antiochus IV, the writer of the Nahum Commentary refers with abhorrence to the deed of Alexander Jannaeus אשר יתלה אנשים חיים = *who hanged men alive,* as a thing [אשר לא יעשה] בישראל מלפנים = *which was never done in Israel before*[19].

[17] B. J. VII 202.

[18] Siphre on Deut 21, 22; cf. T. B. Sanh 46 b.

[19] Lines 7 and 8 of the Pesher Nahum; cf. Geza Vermes, *The Dead Sea Scrolls in English* (Harmondsworth 1968), pp. 231, 232.

»La Judée ne connaissait pas le supplice romain de la croix«, Joseph Derenbourg, *Essai sur l'historie et la géographie de la Palestine* ... (Paris 1867), p. 203, note 1.

»Aus dem ... Vorgehen des Königs Alexander Jannai ... kann für das Vorhandensein dieser Strafe [*i. e.* der Kreuzigung] im jüdischen Rechte keinerlei Beweis abgeleitet werden«, Adolf Büchler, »Die Todesstrafen der Bibel und der jüdisch-nachbiblischen Zeit«, *Monatsschrift für Geschichte und Wissenschaft des Judentums,* vol. 50, Berlin 1906, pp. 539—562, 664—706, on p. 703.

Modern writers not seldom confuse the issue. So, for instance, Rudolf Pfisterer in »Wie empfindet der Verurteilte seine Strafe«, *Evangelische Theologie,* vol. 17, Munich 1957, pp. 416—423, when he writes: »Die Todesstrafe der Kreuzigung war nur den Römern vorbehalten, während die Todesstrafe durch Steinigen den Juden zugestanden war (vgl. Act 7, 57)« (*l. c.,* p. 420). The author correctly realizes that the Jews had in procuratorial times the right to execute persons whom a Jewish court had sentenced to death. The idea that the Romans made reservations with regard to crucifixion is fanciful; there was no need for any such reservation as crucifixion was not a Jewish mode of judicial execution.

[*Revisers' addendum:* For the present state of the debate concerning crucifixion in Palestine, see Schürer-Vermes-Millar, *o. c.* quoted in note 16. Cf. also E. Bammel,

The history of crucifixion as a mode of legal execution goes back far beyond the time of Jesus[20]. The Romans adopted this institution to inflict the death penalty upon rebellious slaves and seditious provincials. It was deemed to be the most degrading and brutal mode of execution[21]. After sentence had been passed, the condemned person was scourged, the scourging being of such a severe nature that loss of blood and frequently a general weakening in the condition of the doomed man took place. This evidently happened in the case of Jesus, making it necessary for the executioners to compel a man who passed by to assist him in carrying the cross (Mc 15, 21) after his flagellation (Mc 15, 15). A heavy wooden bar *(patibulum)* was placed upon the neck of the condemned man, and his outstretched arms were fastened to the beam. In this position, he was led to the place of execution. There he was lifted up, the beam being secured to a vertical stake *(simplex)*, fixed in the ground, so that his feet hung suspended in the air. The arms of the prisoner were usually tied with ropes to the patibulum, though sometimes nails may have been driven into the prisoner's palms[22]. No nails were used for affixing the feet[23]. They were either left dangling a short distance above the ground, or were fastened to the post by ropes.

---

»Crucifixion as a Punishment in Palestine« in *The Trial of Jesus* (ed. Ernst Bammel; London 1970), pp. 162—165. For archaeological evidence regarding the use of nails in crucifixion, see the ossuary of a certain John found in 1968 at Giv'at ha-Mivtar, north of Jerusalem, with an iron nail still piercing his heel-bones. *Cf.* V. Tzaferis, »Jewish Tombs at and near Giv'at ha-Mivtar, Jerusalem«, *Israel Exploration Journal,* vol. 20 (1970), pp. 18—32; N. Haas, »Anthropological Observations on the Skeletal Remains from Giv'at ha-Mivtar«, *ibidem,* pp. 38—59; Y. Yadin, »Epigraphy and Crucifixion«, *ibidem,* vol. 23 (1973), pp. 18—33.]

[20] See article »Crux« by H. Hitzig in Pauly-Wissowa's *Real-Encyklopädie,* vol. 8 (Stuttgart 1901), cols. 1728—1731; article »Croix« by Orazio Marucchi in *Dictionnaire de la Bible,* tome 2 (Paris 1899), cols. 1127—1131; article »Crucifixion« by Emil G. Hirsch in *The Jewish Encyclopedia,* vol. 4 (New York 1903, [3]1925), pp. 373—374; article »The Cross as an Instrument of Punishment in the Ancient World« by Orazio Marucchi in *The Catholic Encyclopedia,* vol. 4 (New York 1908), pp. 518—519; article »Le supplice de la croix« by H Leclercq in *Dictionnaire d'archéologie chrétienne et de liturgie,* vol. III, 2 (Paris 1914), cols. 3045—3048.

[21] *Supplicium crudelissimum taeterrimumque,* Cicero, In Verrem V 64; *servile supplicium,* Cicero, In Philippum 66, Tacitus, Historiae IV iii 11; *mors turpissima crucis,* Origenes, In Matthaeum CXXIV; *infame genus supplicii, quod etiam homine libero quamvis nocente videatur indignum,* Lactantius, Institutiones I v 26.

[22] *Cf.* Josephus, B. J. V 451.

[23] [*Revisers' addendum:* See, however, note 19 above.] There is no indication in the synoptic Gospels that Jesus was nailed to the cross. From Jn 20, 25 we may draw the inference that the Fourth Evangelist wished to imply that Jesus had been nailed by his hands. The Gospel of Peter 6, describing how Jesus' body was taken down from the cross, also mentions the nails which were drawn from his hands. The Gospels nowhere state that Jesus' feet were nailed to the cross.]

Stripped of his clothes, the condemned was left on his cross till death intervened.

"It represented the acme of the torturer's art: atrocious physical sufferings, length of torment, ignominy, the effect of the crowd gathered to witness the long agony of the crucified. Nothing could be more horrible than the sight of this living body, breathing, seeing, hearing, still able to feel, and yet reduced to the state of a corpse by forced immobility and absolute helplessness. We cannot even say that the crucified person writhed in agony, for it was impossible for him to move. Stripped of his clothing, unable even to brush away the flies which fell upon his wounded flesh, already lacerated by the preliminary scourging, exposed to the insults and curses of people who can always find some sickening pleasure in the sight of the tortures of others, a feeling which is increased and not diminished by the sight of pain — the cross represented miserable humanity reduced to the last degree of impotence, suffering, and degradation. The penalty of crucifixion combined all that the most ardent tormentor could desire: torture, the pillory, degradation, and certain death, distilled slowly drop by drop"[24].

In the wars for Jewish independence from Roman rule during the years 66 to 70 and 132 to 135 CE both armies fought with extreme ferocity. They each treated their opponents, and the civilian population of the affected territory, with a cruelty that knew no bounds. There were occasions when the Romans took Jewish prisoners, and when the Jews captured Roman soldiers. Neither party were wont to treat their captives with leniency. They generally killed them by one means or another. Yet whereas the Romans crucified Jewish prisoners of war by their thousands — "there was not enough room for the crosses, nor enough crosses for the condemned" (Josephus, B. J. V 451) — we know not a single instance in which the Jewish guerillas, pitiless as they were in dealing with the enemy, resorted to the method of crucifixion in disposing of those who had fallen into their hands.

Crucifixion was not a punitive measure that can be shown actually to have been used by Jews during or after the life-time of Jesus[25].

---

[24] Albert Réville, *Jésus de Nazareth* (Paris 1897), tome 2, pp. 405, 406, quoted here in Olive Wyon's translation of Maurice Goguel, *The Life of Jesus* (London 1933), on pp. 535, 536.

[25] [*Revisers' addendum:* See further J. M. Baumgarten, »Does *tlh* in the Temple Scroll refer to Crucifixion?«, *JBL* vol. 91 (1972), pp. 472—481.]

# 8. THE JEWISH DEATH PENALTIES

The Mishnah tractate Sanhedrin includes rules of Jewish judicial procedure that come from various periods. Scholarly scepticism as to whether these rules were ever operative[1] is unjustified. The legal provisions enumerated in the Mishnah were each in force at some given time[2], although they may never have been in force collectively. In the eyes of the compilers statutes and practices from different eras assumed the form of a harmonious whole, and the rabbis made little effort to specify what regulations were operative in any particular period.

As it now stands the Mishnah contains provisions that obviously come from a period when the Great Sanhedrin had ceased to be the governing body of the Jewish nation, and merely exercised the functions of a rabbinical court, a בית דין. There is, for instance, the provision that the Sanhedrin might conduct its business either within or without the Land of Israel[3] — a clause clearly devised when this body of councillors had ceased to represent the Senate of the nation and, though still bearing its time-honoured name, was no more than a magisterial bench of experts on matters of religious law. The Mishnah also stipulates that if a capital case were tried, and any student who happened to be in the audience offered to plead for the accused, he should be given a chance to speak; if by his *plaidoyer* he secured the defendant's acquittal, the successful advocate was permitted, for the day, to retain his seat amongst the members of the court[4] (according to a parallel report he was permanently co-opted on to the tribunal[5]). This may not be just imagination — the report may offer a glimpse of the situation when the

---

[1] George Foot Moore, *Judaism in the First Centuries of the Christian Era. The Age of the Tannaim* (Cambridge Mass. 1927—30): »The rules of procedure impress us as purely academic« (vol. 2, p. 187); »Not less palpably academic are the modes of execution« (vol. 2, p. 187, n. 6).

[2] We should probably here exempt the stipulation stating that a defendant on whose guilt on a capital charge the judges were unanimously agreed should be acquitted (Mishnah Sanh iv 1; *cf.* the statement by Rab Kahana in T. B. Sanh 17 a). Such a provision would be practicable only if there were a corollary provision making it obligatory that at least one of the judges would *ex officio* cast his vote for the accused's acquittal. Without this corollary the stipulation would have had preposterous results.

[3] Mishnah Makkoth i 10.

[4] Mishnah Sanhedrin v 4.

[5] »... if there is substance in his words, they acquit him, and he [the advocate] would never go down from there«, Tosefta Sanhedrin ix 3.

Sanhedrin had exclusively juridical functions — but certainly it does not fit in with the state of affairs when it exercised legislative and administrative responsibilities as the Supreme Council of the nation[6].

It is unlikely that descriptions of penal procedure presented in the tractate Sanhedrin conform to practices that were in force at the time of Jesus' life. Before the present Mishnah was compiled, there existed the Mishnah of rabbi Aqiba, and earlier still there prevailed older regulations embodied in the 'First Mishnah' (possibly connected with rabbi Yishmael ben Elisha)[7]. All the ordinances, however, from the 'First Mishnah' to the one which we possess, were based on principles of rabbinical-pharisaic exegesis. As the Pharisees were not the ruling group within the Senate of the Jewish nation in Jesus' time, the probability is that Jewish judicial procedure was then largely determined by Sadducaean principles. What the particular ordinances were in which those principles found their expression, and whether these ordinances had been handed down orally without being embodied in a written code, or had been incorporated in such a code, are disputed questions. As long as there existed a central authority in the Great Sanhedrin of Jerusalem, and outlying subordinate tribunals could easily contact the central authority, there was no necessity to lay down in writing what regulations should apply in the administration of the Law. Sadducaean administration of justice, probably established in 'common' as against 'statutory' law, could dispense with prescriptions as to the implementation of the basic Law. The Sadducees denied the compulsory character of 'bye-laws' not contained in the Torah; they would thus scarcely have gone to the trouble of codifying such 'bye-laws'. From what we know of Sadducaean tenets[8], we might be right in assuming that the Sadducees would demand rigid observance of Old Testament precepts, whilst Pharisaic instruments of law represented a more flexible interpretation of the Torah, adjusted to contemporary needs and conforming with current ways of thought. Such differences as there were between the

---

[6] Julius Wellhausen, *Die Pharisäer und die Sadducäer*, pp. 31, 40—41.

It is, however, possible that the stipulation in Mishnah Sanhedrin v 4 (concerning the defender of a person who was accused of a capital offence) might have been operative — even before the year 70 CE — in proceedings before a lower court, a sanhedrin of 23 members.

Some of the provisions of the tractate Sanhedrin appear to be borne out by the narrative of Susanna (Greek additions to Daniel). Compare Susanna 49: the convicted person's return from the way to execution upon the offer of new evidence, and retrial of the case (Mishnah Sanh vi 1); Susanna 50: the defender takes his seat amongst the judges (Sanh v 4); Susanna 54, 58: ὑπὸ τί δένδρον ἴδες αὐτούς (Sanh v 1: Rabban Yoḥanan ben Zakkai's method of testing evidence ›even to enquiring about the stalks of figs‹); Susanna 60: ... ἐφίμωσαν αὐτοὺς καὶ ἐξαγαγόντες ἔρριψαν εἰς φάραγγα resembles the Pharisaic form of stoning (Sanh vi 4).

[7] Mishnah Sanhedrin ii 4.

[8] Ant XIII 297.

two main Jewish parties would be reflected in their methods as to how the Law should be applied. We know for certain that the penalty of death by burning was inflicted according to Sadducaean practice in the strict sense[9], quite different from what the Mishnah classified as 'burning'[10]. We may presume that stoning in Sadducaean penal practice was carried out rather in the manner indicated in Acts 7, 58—59 than in Mishnah Sanh vii 4. We have evidence that the Sadducaean interpretation of the law concerning the punishment of false witnesses in capital cases differed from that of the rabbis[11] and their Pharisaic predecessors. Yet all we know of Sadducaean practices in detail, comes from records composed by their opponents. No 'Sadducaean Code' is extant.

Various scholars have based an argument for the existence in the first century of such a code on the Megillath Ta'anith[12] in which the mention of a "Book of Decrees" occurs. The information obtainable from this source is hardly sufficient to warrant a definite opinion. The Aramaic text merely reads: בארבעה עשר בתמוז עדא ספר גזירתא = *on the fourteenth Tammuz the Book of Decrees was abolished* (Meg. Ta'anith 10). A Hebrew scholiast who centuries later added a gloss to this passage explained that it referred to the abrogation of a Sadducaean

---

[9] Compare the description given by rabbi Eleazar ben Ṣadoq (Mishnah Sanh vii 2, Tosefta Sanh ix 11, T. Y. Sanh vii 2 24 b, T. B. Sanh 52 b); see above p. 19, note 23.

Josephus (Ant IV 248) reports that unchastity of betrothed women was normally punished by stoning (καταλευέσθω), but if the offending party was a priest's daughter, her penalty was to be burned alive (καιέσθω ζῶσα). As Josephus does not add any qualification to his statement, we must assume that when he spoke of burning he had in mind the form of execution which rabbi Eleazar ben Ṣadoq described.

Josephus also reports (Ant III 209) that when Aaron's sons Nadab and Abihu were burnt, the flame consumed their bodies and mutilated their faces. A dictum ascribed to rabbi Eleazar in T. B. Sanh 52 a puts the matter differently: the flame entered Nadab's and Abihu's nostrils, »burning up their souls« without injury to their bodies — »the body remained intact«. Although the death of Nadab and Abihu did not result from a judicial sentence passed in a law court, but was the result of an act of God, the difference between the description offered by Josephus and the statement of rabbi Eleazar will assist us in determining the approximate date at which the mishnaic stipulations concerning execution by 'burning' were enacted. When Josephus was writing, the mishnaic form of 'burning' had not yet come into existence. As the method of carrying out death sentences by *burning* in mishnaic terms is virtually identical with that of *strangling*, we may assume that strangulation was not introduced into the Jewish Penal Code before the end of the first century.

[10] Mishnah Sanh vii 2.

[11] Mishnah Makkoth i 6.

[12] Adolf Neubauer, *Mediaeval Jewish Chronicles and Chronological Notes (Anecdota Oxoniensia)*, vol. 2 (Oxford 1895), pp. 3—25; the relevant passage occurs on pp. 8—9).

judicial code. He augmented the scanty information of Meg. Ta'anith by presenting a disputation, imaginary or real, between exegetes who adhered to Pharisaic and to Sadducaean principles, respectively. According to this mediaeval gloss, the Pharisees upbraided their Sadducaean opponents for holding views which had no support in the Pentateuch. The glossator's assignment of rôles to the two religious parties is surprising: the Sadducees could have criticized the Pharisees for adopting new-fangled ideas that had no foundation in the precepts of Written Law, but scarcely vice versa. For it was the Pharisees who by dexterous methods of hermeneutics gave new meanings to the words of the ancient books. Whilst far from being fond of innovations, they frequently felt compelled to enact new rulings which, however, they presented as being based upon ancient authority and as having been revealed to no other than Moses himself. When necessary, they would take a text, forcing their own meaning into the words of the Torah, and interpret it to suit prevailing needs and present circumstances, under the pretext of complying with old law[13]. The stress under which the Jews lived in the second century made it necessary to resort to such expedients. Leaders of the Jewish people, determined to preserve Israel's religious identity, insisted that the connection with the past must not be broken. Yet many of the ordinances of the past had outlived their usefulness and could no longer be literally applied. Hence the endeavour of the rabbis to uphold the Law in its completeness, and where this proved impracticable, to give at least the appearance of continuing in its observance. The rabbis knew what they were doing. From rabbi Eleazar of Modin, a contemporary of Aqiba, comes the saying "He who discloses aspects in the Torah (המגלה פנים בתורה) which are not in accord with rabbinical teaching (שלא כהלכה) has no portion in the world to come"[14]. Rabbis and Pharisees were aware of the fact that their method of forcing the meaning of scriptural passages was sometimes tortuous[15]. Hence it is

---

[13] Abraham Geiger, »Sadducäer und Pharisäer«, *Jüdische Zeitschrift für Wissenschaft und Leben,* vol. 2, Breslau 1863, pp. 11—54 (also published separately, in the same year, with a pagination running from 5 to 48): »... die Pharisäer [verstehen sich] zu einer exegetischen Künstelei, um dem Leben eine Concession zu machen, ohne das Bibelwort verdrängen zu müssen« (p. 28, resp. 22); »... sie gingen ... in die Bedürfnisse des Lebens, der sich ... entwickelnden Verhältnisse ein und waren bemüht, denselben die bestehenden Vorschriften anzupassen« (p. 33, resp. 27); »Sie waren zwar bemüht, das bestehende Gesetz dem Leben anzupassen ... suchten sich [jedoch] mit dem Worte des Gesetzes abzufinden, ja ihre neuen Anordnungen in das alte Wort hineinzulegen« (p. 33, resp. 27).

[14] Mishnah Pirqe Aboth iii 15 (16); *cf.* Aboth de-Rabbi Nathan ch. 26.

[15] The rabbis knew what they were doing — and at times they could be less solemn about it than rabbi Eleazar of Modin was. This is exemplified by an anecdote in the Babylonian Talmud (Menaḥoth 29 b) that tells the following delightful story: When Moses left the earth and ascended to heaven, he found the Almighty scribbling flourishes and ornamental lines upon every letter of the Torah. Moses

surprising to read that a reproach of making innovations to the Law should have been launched by the Pharisees themselves against the Sadducees.

The Hebrew gloss to the Megillath Ta'anith, explaining that the Sadducees possessed a written code in which specific penalties were prescribed for various crimes, yields no historically reliable information[16]. The "decrees" mentioned in the Aramaic document could have been those imposed at some time by a foreign government[17], and the scholiast who added his gloss many centuries later might have erroneously identified the ספר גזרתא with a Sadducaean Code. "It is a critical error", in the words of George Foot Moore, "to take [the glossator's] learned combinations for tradition"[18]. Moore speaks of "uncritical confidence with which scholars have erected imposing historic constructions on this foundation of sand"[19].

---

asked God what he was doing, and God replied: In generations to come there will be a man, Aqiba ben Yosef, who will deduce heaps and heaps of rules from each little stroke of the pen. Moses expressed a wish to see that man. God granted his request; when Aqiba's time came, Moses descended to earth and visited Aqiba's school-house where he took a seat in the back-row among the freshmen. There he listened to learned discussions, overcome and bewildered, because he was unable to follow the scholarly argumentation. When, finally, a difficult problem arose and one of the more advanced students was bold enough to ask rabbi Aqiba whence he derived his authority to lay down a ruling that would settle the matter, Aqiba replied: הלכה למשה מסיני, *it is a ruling given to Moses on Sinai.* Whereupon Moses felt much elated, and his self-confidence was restored.

[16] »Einige Abweichungen im Gebiete des Rechtsverfahrens führt nur der Scholiast zur Fastenchronik als streitig an, aber sicher bloss als eigene Conjectur«, Abraham Geiger, *Urschrift und Übersetzungen der Bibel in ihrer Abhängigkeit von der inneren Entwicklung des Judenthums* (Breslau 1857), p. 148; »[des Glossators] einzelne Angaben haben gar keinen selbständigen Werth, es steht ihm keine wirkliche Überlieferung zu Gebote, sondern er ist auf Combination angewiesen«, Julius Wellhausen, o. c., p. 63 (cf. pp. 61, 62).

Further: »Der Verfasser der Anmerkungen zur Fastenrolle hatte eine vorzügliche Quelle vor sich gehabt, sie behandelte eine Diskussion zwischen Sadduzäern und Pharisäern, er hat sie missverstanden und glaubte sie zur Erklärung eines Festtages verwenden zu dürfen... Der vielgenannte sadduzäische Strafkodex ist... endgültig zu begraben«, Rudolf Leszynsky, *Die Sadduzäer* (Berlin 1912), p. 80.

Compare also Jacob Z. Lauterbach, »The Sadducees and Pharisees. A Study of their Respective Attitudes towards the Law«, *Studies in Jewish Literature issued in Honor of Professor Kaufmann Kohler* (Berlin 1913), pp. 176—198, p. 178, n. 1, p. 186; Jean Juster, o. c., tome I, p. 25; Hans Lichtenstein, »Die Fastenrolle. Eine Untersuchung zur jüdisch-hellenistischen Geschichte«, *Hebrew Union College Annual* vol. VIII—IX (Cincinnati 1931—32), pp. 257—351, p. 295, etc.

[17] *Solomon Zeitlin, Megillat Taanit as a Source for Jewish Chronology and History in the Hellenistic and Roman Periods* (Philadelphia 1922), p. 83; George Foot Moore, o. c., vol. 3, pp. 27, 45, 46.

[18] O. c., vol. 1, p. 160.

[19] O. c., vol. 3, p. 46.

Following the advice of Moore, we need not concern ourselves with the gloss to the Megillath Ta'anith in our quest for the penal procedure valid in the first century. If the Sadducees, as Josephus asserts[20], disputed the binding force of regulations that were not embodied in the Torah, it is not likely that they formulated their ordinances in any written form. We have the Pharisaic code of judicial procedure in the tractate Sanhedrin of the Mishnah; we have no corresponding record of Sadducaean legal practice. However, if the forms of implementing a statute differed in Sadducaean and Pharisaic procedures, the basic penalties for certain offences were the same as those in the Torah.

Mishnah Sanhedrin vii 1 mentions four ways of inflicting the death penalty:

(a) סקילה    stoning,

(b) שריפה    burning,

(c) הרג    slaying,

(d) חנק    strangling.

The first three of these modes of execution are recognized in the Old Testament; the fourth is not.

There is no evidence that a capital sentence passed by a Jewish court was ever carried out by strangling[21] prior to the second century of the present era.

---

[20] See note 8 supra. *Cf.* Morton Scott Enslin, *The Prophet from Nazareth* (New York 1961), p. 105, n. 11: »The Sadducees of necessity had their tradition which amplified and made explicit the written Law, and it was often definitely more austere and rigorous than that of the Pharisees. Unlike the latter, they did not give to it the authority of the Law. It was opinion«.

[21] Josephus mentions cases of strangling that were carried out at the order of Herod the Great. One such instance is the assassination of Hyrcanus II. Josephus states that Herod showed to the Sanhedrin a letter sent to Hyrcanus by Malchus of Arabia (Ant XV 173) purporting to exculpate his arbitrary action on the grounds of necessity of state in the face of conspiracy. Josephus does not say that the Sanhedrin passed sentence upon Hyrcanus. On the contrary, he reports that it was Herod himself who gave the order for strangulation (B. J. I 433, Ant XV 176).

Another instance occurred when Herod decided to do away with his own sons Alexander and Aristobulus. Again Herod brought no formal accusation against his sons before the Sanhedrin, but tried to forestall possible charges of illegality by consulting the Emperor in Rome. Having been authorized by Augustus, he conducted an enquiry before a joint council consisting of members of Herod's own household and of Roman dignitaries. This enquiry took place outside Jewish territory in Beyrouth and was presided over by Roman officers (B. J. I 538). Eventually Alexander and Aristobulus were strangled at their father's command in Sebaste, again a non-Jewish town (B. J. I 551, Ant XVI 394). Herod's arbitrary actions in dealing with opponents and with members of his own family (Ant XV 87, 229, 231, 236, XVI 319, XVII 44, 167, 187) do not permit deductions as to what was Jewish legal procedure. When he accused his wife Mariamne (Ant XV 229), Herod chose to do so

This has important implications. The rabbis who compiled the Mishnah, and their predecessors who enacted the ordinances and regulations it contains were not innovators. They conceived of their task in terms of preserving; the very name 'tannaim' means *repeaters*. Even when their interpretation of the Law moved with the spirit of the times, they were, on principle, anxious to give the appearance of strictly preserving the letter of the Law. Rabbinical devotion to the Torah, embodying the Will of God — once revealed, immutable forever — need not be doubted. So the introduction into the Mishnaic Code of a new method of capital punishment, unheard of in the Old Testament, is a glaring departure from the deductive method which the rabbis professed and to which they normally adhered. There must have been compelling causes which induced them to depart from their principles in this instance and which moved the repeaters to act as innovators.

Before we examine *why* a new mode of administering the death penalty was introduced, the fact *that* it was introduced should be appreciated in its correct perspective. Codifiers of law do not invent new practical measures for enforcing the law unless this law is actually in effective use. The fact that an entirely new species of execution was added to those inherited from earlier times proves incontrovertibly that at the time of the codification of the Mishnah, capital punishments were being inflicted upon persons whom Jewish rabbinical courts had sentenced to death. If it had been merely the intention of the codifiers to give an academic compendium of past legal customs — for purposes of theoretical study without any thought of practical application in the present — they would have been content to enumerate such methods of execution as had been established in the past, but would scarcely have added a new one. The introduction into Jewish penal procedure of strangling (smothering by a towel; a hard cloth, wrapped in a soft one, was twisted around the neck of the condemned person until he or she died of suffocation) makes it clear enough that executions *de facto*

---

not before the Sanhedrin, but before a circle of members of his own household (οἰκειότατοι, B. J. I 443), and he applied a similar procedure against the wife of his brother Pheroras (B. J. I 571, Ant XVII 56).

From his youth Herod was wont to treat legal restrictions with indifference; he put large numbers of people to death in violation of Jewish law (B. J. I 209): καὶ γὰρ Ἡρῴδης ... ἀπέκτεινε ... πολλούς, παραβὰς τὸν ἡμέτερον νόμον ὃς κεκώλυκεν ἄνθρωπον ἀναιρεῖν καὶ πονηρὸν ὄντα, εἰ μὴ πρότερον κατακριθείη τοῦτο παθεῖν ὑπὸ τοῦ συνεδρίου (Ant XIV 167). Though these words are recorded in the form of a speech addressed by Jewish leaders to Hyrcanus II, they describe the situation in Judea which Josephus knew *from his own experience*. His own acquaintance with the legal system of the country, as it existed until the year 70 CE, gave Josephus the words to compose the speech in question.

Besides strangling his victims, which was unknown at the time in Jewish penal procedure, Herod applied Jewish forms of execution, like burning, in cases for which they were not provided (B. J. I 655, Ant XVII 167).

took place in pursuance of instructions issued by Jewish law courts, whatever the situation was *de lege* in relation to the State authorities.

With this in mind, it is now necessary to consider why Jewish lawyers of the second century should have seen fit to institute an additional punitive measure for carrying out sentences of death. We can dismiss the suggestion that execution by strangulation had been instituted as a more humane way of inflicting the extreme penalty. The Mishnah leaves no doubt that strangling was held to be more severe than decapitation[22].

That strangulation was a relatively new instrument in Jewish penal law at the time when the Mishnah was being compiled becomes plain when a comparison is made between the specifying ordinances referring to offences punishable by stoning, by burning, or by beheading (Mishnah Sanhedrin vii 4—11, viii 1—7, 1—6) and those appertaining to strangulation. The former are most detailed and circumstantial; they contain stipulations in the nature of *Durchführungsverordnungen* (provisions whereby a statute may be implemented) which go back to the earlier Mishnah of rabbi Aqiba and the Mishnah before rabbi Aqiba's time. When the Mishnah's survey of expert opinions, given with all minutiae, is compared with the scant specifications concerning crimes punishable by strangulation (Mishnah Sanhedrin xi 1—6)[23], it cannot be doubted that the latter method of execution had been in use for but a relatively short period when the present Mishnah came into existence.

What, then, was of such compelling influence that the rabbis of the second century were induced to add a fourth punitive measure to the three prescribed in the biblical Law?

Sometimes it has been conjectured that the introduction of strangulation into Jewish penal law was due to a pious desire on the part of the executioners to facilitate the task of the Almighty when the bodies of those whom they had executed would be resurrected to stand for judgment in a Higher Court[24]. This argument carries little weight.

---

[22] Mishnah Sanhedrin vii 1: »The order of severity is: burning, stoning, strangling, beheading«; *cf.* T. Y. Sanh vii 2, 24 b, T. B. Sanh 50 b: »strangulation is more severe than decapitation«.

See Adolf Büchler, »Die Todesstrafen der Bibel und der jüdisch-nachbiblischen Zeit«, *Monatsschrift für Geschichte und Wissenschaft des Judentums,* vol. 50 [Neue Folge 14], 1906, pp. 539—562, 664—706. »... die Strafe [der Erdrosselung] ... muß ... zu den schwersten gezählt werden« (p. 683).

[23] The note in Mishnah Sanhedrin ix 6 referring to rabbi Aqiba's opinion on the punishment of persons of non-priestly descent who arrogated to themselves the right to serve in the Temple is purely academic. There was no Temple in Aqiba's time. *Cf.* Büchler, *l. c.,* p. 677.

[24] Büchler, *l. c.:* »Es ist ... möglich, daß die Pharisäer in ihrem Kampfe mit den Sadduzäern betreffs des Auferstehungsglaubens die Erhaltung des Körpers für das Grab anstrebten und dadurch, daß sie auch dem Verbrecher ... den Körper nicht vernichten lassen wollten, den Glauben an die Auferstehung im Volke zu festigen

Established legal practices are frequently defended by philosophical and theological speculation; seldom does such speculation motivate the introduction of new practices into judicial procedure. Men alter their methods of applying the law as a result of objective circumstances — facts with a harder core than cogitation of a theological type.

It may be objected that this is an *a priori* assertion made regardless of the evidence, and as such without validity when seeking to ascertain the causative forces responsible for the rabbinical introduction of strangulation into Jewish penal procedure. In any event, does the opinion that execution by strangling was instituted in deference to the resurrection-faith (it being implied that the executioner wished to preserve his victims' bodies unmutilated) stand up to scrutiny? A belief in resurrection was widely held among Jews at least from the second pre-Christian century onwards. Evidently for some 250 years this belief had no practical results in bringing about any alteration in the methods of administering the death sentence. It might be argued that until the year 70 CE the Sadducees largely determined how the Law of the Old Testament was to be applied in actual cases that were brought before a court. The Sadducees did not share the belief in resurrection. With the elimination of Sadducaean influence Jewish law courts might have been guided to a greater extent by Pharisaic principles. Although this is true, the argument fails to explain the introduction of strangulation into the

---

suchten« (p. 558; Büchler remarked that this theory had first been suggested by N. Brüll in בית תלמוד, vol. 4, pp. 7 ff.); »... das Streben, den Körper des Hinzurichtenden nicht ... zu vernichten« (p. 686) is made to account for the novel method of execution.

Further, Josef Blinzler, »Die Strafe für Ehebruch in Bibel und Halacha. Zur Auslegung von Joh viii 5«, NTS vol. 4, 1957, pp. 32—47: »Es steht fest, dass die Rabbinen ... statt der alten Strafe der Steinigung die Erdrosselung empfohlen haben. ... Hier scheinen ... verschiedene Motive ... wirksam gewesen zu sein. ... Die Pharisäer verlangten, daß der Körper des Verurteilten nach Möglichkeit unversehrt und unverändert bleiben solle, was anscheinend mit ihrem Auferstehungsglauben zusammenhängt« (pp. 38, 39).

*Cf.* also David Daube, »Evangelisten und Rabbinen«, ZNW vol. 48, 1957, pp. 119—126: »Die hergebrachten Hinrichtungsarten ... werden durch die neuen ... ersetz ...; und Erdrosselung wurde zur Normalform der Hinrichtung« (p. 122). »Certain forms of capital punishment dating from the pre-Christian era would involve a disfigurement serious enough to create difficulties for the early believers in resurrection«, idem, *The New Testament and Rabbinic Judaism* (London 1956), p. 304; »... wherever the Bible did not specify the form of execution, the Pharisees insisted on strangling ... in this case no mark whatever will be left on the body« (p. 305). Daube thinks that the reform of the modes of execution was gradually effected between the years 100 BCE and 100 CE. He realizes, however, that political considerations »may well have been an additional motive for substituting strangulation [for other modes of execution because this form of punishment] attract[ed] less notice« (p. 307).

second-century ordinances of Jewish courts, for had the resurrection-faith been the motive for this introduction, would not the earlier procedures of stoning, burning[25] and beheading have been abolished altogether? Each of these methods involved a disfigurement of the bodies of those subjected to such treatment. Yet these methods of inflicting the death penalty were not abolished; they were retained along with the new method of strangulation — the new not superseding the old, but supplementing them[26]. Thus the argument from religious motives fails to elucidate the determining factor behind the innovation.

It was not belief in bodily resurrection that provided the inducement for the introduction of strangulation as a new, non-biblical, mode of administering capital punishment on persons sentenced to death by a rabbinical בית דין. Even those sections of the Jewish people who embraced the resurrection belief were far from being unanimous on the question as to whether all the dead would rise again from their graves or whether such would be the destiny of those only who had lived a good life. In earlier times the prevailing view was that the just alone would be awakened from the sleep of death. This is what Josephus, writing after the year 70 CE, asserts: "To those who observe the laws ... God has granted a renewed existence and ... the gift of a better life"[27]. A belief in a resurrection restricted to persons who had lived in compliance with God's commandments is attested in the literature of the time[28]; not all men would rise from the dead — only the righteous ones will have a part in the world to come. A consi-

---

[25] 'Burning', in mishnaic terms, was admittedly virtually identical with strangulation. *Cf.* above, p. 99, note 10.

[26] There are cases in the Old Testament where apparently the form in which the death penalty was to be carried out remained unspecified. Under Mosaic Law such cases were dealt with by stoning, which was the standard procedure in ancient Israel. In Leviticus ch. 20, for instance, stoning is mentioned at the beginning (v. 2) and the end (v. 27), and this covered such cases where מות יומת occurs without any mention of the particular method of execution, the exception being Lev 20, 14 where burning is explicitly stipulated. This apparent 'gap' in Mosaic legislation provided the rabbis with an opportunity to introduce strangulation; compare the view of rabbi Yonathan: »By every unspecified death in the Torah strangulation is meant« (T. B. Sanh 52 b). *Cf.* Adolf Büchler, *l. c.*, pp. 664—669, 674—676.

[27] Contra Apionem II 218.

[28] Enoch 51, 1—5 (61, 1—5?); 91, 4—11; 92, 3; Qumran Hodayoth col. VI, lines 29—30; Psalms of Solomon 3, 13—14; 9, 9; 13, 10; 2 Maccabees 7, 9—14; 1 Thessalonians 4, 14—17; 1 Corinthians 15, 23, 52; Philippians 3, 11; Luke 14, 14; 20, 35—36; Revelation 20, 4—5; Didache 16, 6; 4 Ezra 8, 1. The belief that only the righteous will be resurrected and inhabit the new earth lingers on for a long time; it is expressed with reference to sinners in the magnificently contemptuous words of rabbi Yehudah ben Bathyra, T. B. Sanh 108 a: »They will neither revive nor be judged«.

derable body of opinion, expressed in writings that come from the inter-testamentary period, in the New Testament, in secular books of Jewish authors, in late Jewish apocalypses, and even in rabbinical records, denied the resurrection of the wicked. Sinners will not be revived. Such a belief clearly excludes individuals who for their criminal actions suffer the death penalty as the result of a verdict by a Jewish Court. Even the Mishnah, in the tenth chapter of the tractate Sanhedrin — the tractate in which strangulation is enumerated among the various modes of administering the death penalty — speaks of p e o p l e  w h o  w i l l  n o t  b e  resurrected and will have no part in a future life.

Facing the problem and taking into account the political conditions under which Jews in Palestine lived in the second century of our era, we shall have little difficulty in eliciting the reason for the innovation. The destruction of Jewish statehood in 70 CE deprived the Jewish judiciary of their powers to deal with capital cases as they had done during the whole of the procuratorial period. No longer could Jewish criminal courts run the risk of operating openly and officially. "The sanhedrin, as a political institution with . . . legislative, executive and judicial powers, came to an end with the fall of Jerusalem . . . The sanhedrin, which succeeded the political body was essentially a rabbinical school, which also came to function as a sort of ecclesiastical court whose powers were derived solely from its moral influence over those who remained loyal to Judaism"[29]. If sentences of death — which still continued to be passed even after the year 70 — were to be carried out by stoning, by burning, or even by beheading, an element of publicity would be involved in each such instance. That had to be avoided. We may safely assume that Roman authorities would not have been particularly disturbed if a few provincials were put to death on the instructions of rabbinical courts, provided the sufferers were of no influence by Roman standards, but Roman propraetors in Syria were reluctant to give official sanction to such action. Rabbinical courts then, though they continued to exercise jurisdiction even in capital cases, were constrained to find a method of carrying out the death penalty more likely to evade detection than the methods formerly in use. There is evidence that in certain cases a death sentence passed by the rabbis remained ineffective and was never carried out. It was no more than an academic pronouncement, the court lacking the power to put its verdict into effect. It was left to God, or fate, to fulfil the court's judgment[30]. In other instances, when executions *were* carried out, it was done *secretly* because of the political danger that would attend a public execution. The methods formerly in use — burning, stoning, beheading — would

---

[29] T. A. Burkill, *Mysterious Revelation* (Ithaca N. Y. 1963), p. 282. Of course this should not be taken to imply that after 70 CE the Roman authorities did not allow the Beth Din some measure of jurisdiction over Jews.

[30] *Cf.* T. B. Soṭah 8 b, Sanh 37 b.

have been a flagrant contravention of Imperial Rule. Strangling and the similar procedure that went under the name of 'burning' provided convenient ways of escaping detection[31]. Such was the reason why the rabbis, otherwise so meticulous in efforts to show that their rulings were deduced from the letter of the Torah, resorted to the expedient of execution by strangling, *thereby bringing into their statute book a new form of inflicting capital punishment of which the Old Testament had known nothing.*

This identification of the causality behind the introduction of strangulation into Jewish penal procedure during the second century is of significance in assessing the Sanhedrin's judicial competence prior to 70 CE. No case is known of any death sentence passed by a Jewish court that was put into effect by strangulation before that year. Executions known to have been ordered by Jewish judicial institutions during

---

[31] Γίνεται δὲ καὶ κριτήρια λ ε λ η θ ό τ ω ς κατὰ τὸν νόμον, καὶ καταδικάζονταί τινες τὴν ἐπὶ τῷ θανάτῳ, οὔτε μετὰ τῆς πάντη εἰς τοῦτο παῤῥησίας, οὔτε μετὰ τοῦ λανθάνειν τὸν βασιλεύοντα. καὶ τοῦτο ἐν τῇ χώρᾳ τοῦ ἔθνους πολὺν διατρί-ψαντες χρόνον μεμαθήκαμεν καὶ πεπληροφορήμεθα. Origen, Epistola ad Africanum 14 (MPG 11, col. 84). *This first-hand testimony from the beginning of the third century provides us with a better assessment of the reasons for the introduction of strangulation into the Mishnaic penal code than modern speculations about the influence of the resurrection-faith.*

It was not unknown in ancient times that the statement in Jn 18, 31 b containing the Jews' reply to Pilate about their lack of competence to carry out death sentences (if such had been passed by a Jewish judicial tribunal) did not accord with fact. Hence various attempts to give to that statement a more restricted meaning. Augustine, in In Ioannis Evangelium Tractatus CXIV 4, tried to get round the difficulty by explaining: *Intelligendum est eos* (= Iudaeos) *dixisse non sibi licere interficere quemquam, propter diei festi sanctitatem, quem celebrare iam coeperant* (Corpus Christianorum series latina 36, p. 641; MPL 35, col. 1937); and Chrysostom, In Ioannem Homilia LXXXIII 4, has the same explanation: εἰ δὲ λέγουσιν »οὐκ ἔξεστιν ἡμῖν ἀποκτεῖναι οὐδένα«, κατὰ τὸν καιρὸν ἐκεῖνόν φασιν. ἐπεὶ ὅτε γε ἀνῄρουν καὶ ἄλλῳ τρόπῳ ἀνῄρουν... (MPG 59, col. 452). Yet in the Fourth Gospel the trial of Jesus takes place b e f o r e the festival, and the words in Jn 18, 31 b contain an absolute denial of authority, not merely a statement to the effect that there were limitations of what might be done on certain specific days.

There are also statements in Justin's Dialogus cum Tryphone Judaeo which may have a bearing on the question; *e. g.* Dial XVI 4: οὐ γὰρ ἐξουσίαν ἔχετε αὐτόχειρες γενέσθαι ἡμῶν διὰ τοὺς νῦν ἐπικρατοῦντας· ὁσάκις δὲ ἂν ἐδυνήθητε, καὶ τοῦτο ἐπράξατε (Edgar J. Goodspeed, *Die ältesten Apologeten. Texte mit kurzen Einleitungen* [Göttingen 1914], p. 109; MPG 6, col. 512). *Cf.* Dial CXXXIII 6: τὸν Χριστὸν ἀποκτείναντες οὐδ' οὕτως μετανοεῖτε, ἀλλὰ καὶ ἡμᾶς . . . . . φονεύετε, ὁσάκις ἂν λάβητε ἐξουσίαν (Goodspeed, *o. c.*, pp. 225, 256; MPG 6, col. 785). It is possible, but by no means certain, that Justin could have referred to the authority of the Sanhedrin. Another possibility is that he had here in mind oppressive measures enacted by the messiah Simeon ben Kosebah against the adherents of another messiah, Jesus.

the procuratorial period[32] were still carried out in the traditional manner as stipulated in the Old Testament, for as yet the situation did not call for the introduction of a method adapted to the requirement of secrecy. The conclusion is inescapable: b e f o r e  t h e  y e a r  70 CE t h e  S a n h e d r i n  h a d  f u l l  j u r i s d i c t i o n  o v e r  J e w s c h a r g e d  w i t h  o f f e n c e s  a g a i n s t  J e w i s h  r e l i g i o u s l a w ,  a n d  h a d  t h e  a u t h o r i t y  o p e n l y  t o  p r o n o u n c e a n d  c a r r y  o u t  s e n t e n c e s  o f  d e a t h  i n  a c c o r d a n c e w i t h  t h e  p r o v i s i o n s  o f  J e w i s h  l e g i s l a t i o n .  Only after the fall of Jerusalem was the Sanhedrin deprived of its right to execute persons whom it had tried and sentenced to death[33].

---

[32] See above, p. 23, note 38.

[33] Statements in the Talmud to the effect that the Sanhedrin had to abandon the Hall of Hewn Stones and moved to the bazaar (חנות) forty years before the Temple was destroyed (T. B. Shabb 15 a, Abodah zarah 8 b, Sanh 12 a 41 a, Rosh hashanah 31 a) were at a later time, when Christianity had become the religion of the Roman State, interpreted in the sense that the Sanhedrin had lost its juridical competence (T. Y. Sanh i 1 18 a, vii 2 24 b). This interpretation was prompted by apologetic aims — it served as a defence in face of Christian reproaches that the Sanhedrin had sentenced Jesus to death. Cf. Jean Juster, o. c., tome 2, p. 133, and David de Sola Pool, Capital Punishment among the Jews (New York 1916), pp 36, 37.

From other statements in the Talmud, e. g. T. B. Sotah 8 h, Keth 30 a, Sanh 37 b 52 b, Ber 58 a (cf. Midrash Rabbah Deut 17, 9), it is evident that no change in the Sanhedrin's competence of jurisdiction occurred before the year 70 CE.

# 9. »IT IS NOT WITHIN OUR AUTHORITY TO EXECUTE ANYONE«

One of the most bewildering descriptions in the accounts of the proceedings against Jesus is given by the Fourth Evangelist in Jn 18, 28—32. The Jewish authorities are represented as demanding Pilate to take legal action against Jesus; actually the persons who make the demand are vaguely referred to as αὐτοί; since the scene follows immediately upon the removal of Jesus from the high-priest's residence to the governor's palace[1], we have to assume that αὐτοί are persons in an official capacity, holding some position on the high-priest's staff, and apparently including the ἀρχιερεῖς, Jn 18, 35, whoever these may be. The culpability of Jesus is announced, and the question of the authority competent to conduct his trial is raised by the official delegation. These issues are dealt with by the Fourth Evangelist in the following manner:

> When they had brought Jesus to Pilate, the governor asked them: »What charge do you prefer against the man?« They replied: »If he were not a criminal, we would not have handed him over to you«. Pilate consequently said to them: »Take him yourselves and judge him in accordance with your law!« The Jews [here the αὐτοί are denoted] rejoined: »We have no authority to carry out a death sentence [literally: »to kill anybody]« — so that the word of Jesus might be bulfilled which he had spoken indicating in what way he would die.

In plain words, Pilate proposes to the Jews that they should take Jesus and try him under Jewish Law (v. 31 a). Later on in the story, Jn 19, 6 b, Pilate is even more explicit and suggests that the Jews should crucify Jesus. As in the end (Jn 19, 16 b—18) Jesus is crucified by the Jews, it must have been sheer obstinacy on their part not to have done so straightaway, thereby saving exegetes the difficulties of having to explain what is reported in Jn 18, 31 b to 19, 16 a.

An examination of these difficulties should begin with the intimation the Evangelist gives to his readers in Jn 18, 32. This is an undisguised piece of his interpretation: the declaration by the Jews to the effect that they possessed no authority for carrying out a death sentence h a d  t o b e  m a d e  i n  o r d e r  t h a t  J e s u s'  p r e d i c t i o n ,  in Jn 12,

---

[1] When in Jerusalem, the governors normally took up residence in Herod's palace (located in the south-western corner of the present-day walled city, near the Jaffa Gate). The palace which Herod the Great built in Caesarea is also called τὸ πραιτώριον in Acts 23, 35. Josephus called the procuratorial residence τὰ βασίλεια (B. J. II 301). See Pierre Benoit, »Prétoire, Lithostroton et Gabbatha«, Revue biblique, tome 59, 1952, pp. 531—550.

32—33, of his "being lifted up", might be fulfilled.
What is related before this avowedly interpretative remark, purports,
however, to be a factual account of the formalities of judicial procedure
that were applied when Jesus was brought before the judge. The extra-
ordinary statement made by the deputation from the high-priest[2] is
strangely reticent about the offence imputed to Jesus, the offence which
forms the basis of the demand that Pilate should try him. It remains
a matter of wonder to the reader by what divinatory power Pilate, with
no other information than that given in v. 30, came to open his subsequently reported interrogation of Jesus with the question "Are you the
king of the Jews?" (18, 33). But first, it is the preliminaries to the interrogation with which we are here concerned.

Without being informed specifically of what Jesus is accused, Pilate
with a grandiose gesture refuses to try the case and refers it to the
Jewish judiciary. He explicitly authorizes the deputation from the high-
priest to apply Jewish law (31 a). Whereupon the governor has to be
told by his subjects that such a procedure is impossible owing to a constitutional limitation of their jurisdiction (31 b). Pilate is not convinced
by this reply; later he again suggests to the Jews that they should take
the matter into their own hands, pass sentence and carry it out themselves (19, 6 b).

The governor's apparent ignorance of the laws which Rome was
supposed to have established in Judaea is not at all surprising when we
recall that Jews were, in fact, tried by Jewish courts for capital offences
during the procuratorial period, and that sentences which the courts
had passed were put into effect by Jewish judicial institutions. The Acts
of the Apostles mentions the trial of Stephen by the Sanhedrin (Acts 6,
12)[3], a trial ending with the defendant's execution. Besides giving some

---

[2] C. K. Barrett, *The Gospel according to St John* (London 1955), refers to Jn 18,
30 with the words »an incredible remark« (p. 438). »No reliance can be placed on
[the Johannine] version of the story« *(ibidem)*.

[3] The wording of Acts 7, 58 makes it quite clear that Stephen was executed by
stoning in consequence of a regular trial and judicial verdict. The story in Acts
6, 12—7, 57 has its setting in the Council-Hall of the Sanhedrin to which the mob
had no access. It is by no means impossible that the passing of a death sentence by
the judges was originally mentioned *expressis verbis* in a place corresponding to
Acts 7, 57, but later omitted by an early copyist who might have wished to avoid
an odious comparison with Jn 18, 31 b.

Even if no such omission took place, the text as it stands warrants the conclusion that Stephen was found guilty by the court. It is totally unjustified to postu-
late a source document which reported no trial, but attributed Stephen's death to
mob violence, and to conjecture that the writer of the Acts presented his readers
with a fictitious account of the proceedings before the Council. The introduction of
Paul into the story of Stephen's death may be unhistorical, but in other respects the
procedural details mentioned in Acts 7, 58 are too much in accordance with Jewish
forensic practice to be an invention by a non-Jewish writer (*cf.* Deut 17, 5—7).

sort of a description of Stephen's trial, the Acts also reports that the Sanhedrin claimed authority in another capital case — that of Paul.

The account in Acts of what Paul experienced from the moment he was seized on the Temple Mount by a hostile mob (Acts 21, 27) to the time of his departure for Rome to appear there in the Emperor's Court (Acts 27, 1) contains descriptions of several scenes of a judicial nature. The narrative of Paul's prosecution is far from being a sober or disinterested report on the progress of a series of legal transactions; if we learn anything of these, it is not because the *raconteur* intended us to gain definite information of the legal issues involved in the Apostle's case, but rather because despite his intention the narrative still yields certain clues as to what was at stake. Overlaid with apologetics that were of grave concern to the author's own generation, namely, regarding the relationship of Christianity to the Roman State[4], and the relationship of Christianity to Judaism, the account given by the writer of Acts tends to lose sight of the concrete juridical circumstances of Paul's case. More interested in making the Apostle deliver long and edifying speeches — whether these have any bearing on his case or not — than in reporting the actualities of the situation, the writer produces in Acts 21 to 27 a curiously garbled presentation of the crucial facts. His description sheds little direct light upon the legal problem of Paul's case: the controversial issue as to whether Paul should be tried by a Roman or a Jewish court. Much that is quite irrelevant to this issue has been introduced into the story, and one can scarcely avoid the impression that the author of Acts wished to obscure rather than illuminate

---

[4] »Hier kommen ... Argumente zur Sprache, die nicht nur für und wider Paulus, sondern für und wider das Christentum zeugen, und zwar vornehmlich zur Zeit des Verfassers; von ihnen ... soll der Leser Kenntnis nehmen, um dadurch ... gestärkt zu werden«, Martin Dibelius, »Die Reden der Apostelgeschichte und die antike Geschichtsschreibung«, *Sitzungsberichte der Heidelberger Akademie der Wissenschaften*, Phil.-hist. Klasse, Heidelberg 1949, p. 16; also available in *Aufsätze zur Apostelgeschichte* (Göttingen ²1953), p. 129; *cf.* p. 49, resp. 115; English edition *Studies in the Acts of the Apostles* (London 1956), p. 149.

»Lukas ist offenbar nicht darauf bedacht, die Leser in die Rechtslage und den Prozeß des Paulus einzuführen ... Es sind vielmehr Gedanken der christlichen Verkündigung, die deutlich und in mehrfacher Wiederholung ausgesprochen werden ... [Es sind] Gedanken, die in der Zeit des Lukas besonderes Gehör beanspruchen, in den Jahrzehnten, da die Kirche sich sichtbarlich vom Judentum scheidet. Lukas will in diesen Kapiteln ... nicht das Gewesene darstellen, sondern das Seiende«, Martin Dibelius, »Der erste christliche Historiker«, *Schriften der Universität Heidelberg*, Heft 3, 1948, pp. 112—125, on p. 122; in *Aufsätze zur Apostelgeschichte*, p. 117; English edition, pp. 133, 134.

»[Für Lukas] ist die Anklage gegen Paulus nicht eine Sache der Vergangenheit, sondern die Gegenwartsfrage des Christentums«, Ernst Haenchen, *Die Apostelgeschichte* (Göttingen 1956), p. 575. Compare Hans Conzelmann, *Die Mitte der Zeit* pp. 132—135; English ed. *The Theology of St Luke*, pp. 141—144.

some of the salient facts[5]. Certain items are alluded to in a veiled manner while others have slipped out altogether[6]. We read nothing of what became of Trophimus, a Gentile from Ephesus, whose alleged entry into an inner area of the Temple was the occasion for Paul's arrest (21, 29). It is stated that the allegation was untrue — and this may be so — but the reader is left without any information regarding Trophimus's fate or his failure to appear in Caesarea in order to bear out the Apostle's defence. Nor does the author of Acts tell us anything of the final outcome of Paul's trial in Rome — tradition has it that Paul was found guilty and beheaded under Nero[7]. There is an obvious effort on the writer's part to divert attention away from the subject by the introduction of irrelevances. Points of law are left aside. Nevertheless, certain historical facts emerge from the tangled account that shed light on the basic issue, and throw into relief the legal-judicial conditions prevailing in the sixth decade of the first century in Judaea. The basic issue concerned a conflict of judicial competence between the Sanhedrin

---

[5] »Man hat bei dem Bericht über die Gefangennahme und den Prozeß des Paulus in Jerusalem und Caesarea den Eindruck, daß da absichtlich gewisse Hauptsachen verdunkelt sind«, Julius Wellhausen, »Kritische Analyse der Apostelgeschichte«, *Abhandlungen der Kgl. Gesellschaft der Wissenschaften zu Göttingen.* Philologisch-historische Klasse, Band XV, Nr. 2 (Berlin 1914), p. 46. »Il semble que le rédacteur ait dramatisé vaguement l'arrestation de l'Apôtre, en supprimant certaines circonstances plus précises et réelles qui étaient indiquées dans la source«, Alfred Loisy, *Les actes des apôtres* (Paris 1920), p. 806; cf. p. 809.

[6] »La position juridique de l'affaire est ici effacée comme dans le procès de Jésus... Mais l'apologétique de notre auteur est plus subtile...«, Loisy, *Les actes des apôtres*, p. 833; »... le rédacteur... veut effacer les lignes principales«, p. 873. »... le caractère tendancieux du récit n'est guère contestable«, Loisy, »Le proconsul Gallion et Saint Paul«, *Revue d'histoire et de philosophie religieuses*, tome 2, 1911, pp. 142—144, on p. 143.

»The narrative... is an untechnical account with apologetic motive«, Henry Joel Cadbury, »Roman Law and the Trial of Paul« in *The Beginnings of Christianity. Part I. The Acts of the Apostles.* Edited by F. J. Foakes-Jackson and Kirsopp Lake, volume 5 (London 1953), pp. 297—338, on p. 298.

»Die Rede- und Verhörsszenen Act 22 bis 26 [sind von] einheitlichen apologetischen Gedanken durchzogen«, Martin Dibelius, »Die Apostelgeschichte als Geschichtsquelle«, *Forschungen und Fortschritte*, vols. 21—23, 1947, pp. 67—69, on p. 68; see also *Aufsätze zur Apostelgeschichte*, p. 92. Having thus briefly and aptly characterized the narrative, Dibelius added: »Das schliesst nicht aus, dass einmal eine wirkliche Intention des Redners verarbeitet worden ist. [Das gilt] auch [von] den Verteidigungsreden des Paulus Kap. 22 bis 26, die zusammen eine sehr wirkungsvolle Apologie der jungen Reliegion ergeben«, *ibidem*, p. 68, resp. 93. »Im Rahmen des Paulus-Prozesses gibt Lukas... eine Darstellung... zu apologetischem Zweck«, Dibelius, »Paulus in der Apostelgeschichte«, *Aufsätze zur Apostelgeschichte*, p. 180; see his *Studies*, pp. 105, 213.

[7] Cf. 1 Clem 5, 7; Eusebius, Hist. eccl. II 25, 5 (GCS Eus. II, 1, p. 176; MPG 20, col. 208).

and the procurator. The whole description of Paul's prolonged detention revolves historically around the question whether his trial should be conducted by a Roman or a Jewish court. It is with reference to this problem that we now examine what the Acts reports.

Certain Jews from Ephesus who were in Jerusalem at the same time as Paul suspect the latter of having brought Trophimus into an inner court of the Temple (21, 27—29). Admission to such an area was limited to Jews, and it was a capital offence for any Gentile to pass beyond the boundary. An imperial decree confirmed the authority of Jewish courts to inflict the death penalty on offenders, even if they were Roman citizens[8]. It appears that Paul was arrested for 'aiding and abetting', as an accessory before the fact[9]. A tumult flares up; visitors from Asia incite the crowd, denouncing Paul for having instructed Jews, outside Judaea, to disobey the Law, and charging him with irreverence for the sanctuary. The mob threatens to lynch Paul. The incident is observed by the commanding officer of the garrison in the adjacent Antonia, who intervenes and takes Paul into custody (21, 33; 22, 24). The nature of the custody cannot be clearly determined; it might initially have been intended as protective custody to save Paul from the fury of the mob; at a later stage it is apparently preventive custody or imprisonment on remand, as Paul is suspected of having committed certain acts for which he may have to account either before a Jewish or before a Roman court. The officer, Claudius Lysias, orders Paul to be brought to the Antonia (21, 34; 22, 24)[10]. Lysias is uncertain of the

---

[8] See above, p. 18, note 22.

[9] We lack specific information as regards the culpability of Jews who assisted Gentiles in committing the offence of trespassing beyond the space »given unto the nations« (Rev 11, 2). It is reasonable to assume that they would be held to account for their action. »... dans [le] cas [de profanation du temple], bien que Paul ne fût pas le profanateur, il aurait été l'auteur responsable de la profanation, et Félix l'aurait tout de suite rendu au sanhédrin, parce que la qualité de citoyen romain n'aurait pas protégé le coupable«, Loisy, Les actes des apôtres, p. 877. It would appear from the account in Acts that the charge of having profaned the Temple, though never dropped, was in the later stages of Paul's trial treated merely as a subsidiary charge, the main accusation being that he had incited Jews to forsake the Law. It is possible that by the time when Festus arrived in Judaea, it had become difficult to call witnesses — visitors from Asia who might have left the country in the meantime. As regards the general charge, i. e. inciting Jews to abandon their ancestral laws, the Sanhedrin's case was weakened by the fact that the offences were committed outside Judaea, hence in a territory not under the jurisdiction of the Jewish authorities in Jerusalem.

[10] Paul's speech in Acts 22, 1—21 need not be considered in an examination of facts. It is a splendid example of the skill which the author of Acts displayed in composing effective speeches that have no relation to the situation. In Acts 21, 5 Paul invokes the testimony of the high-priest (is he present among the crowd?) regarding his earlier commission to go to Damascus (Acts 9, 1—2). The story given

cause which had evoked the crowd's hostility towards Paul (21, 33—34; 22, 24); he suspects that Paul is the Egyptian who had recently incited the population to insurrection against Roman authority (21, 38)[11], and if this suspicion proves correct, Lysias will have reason to detain the prisoner until his delivery for trial before a Roman military court. To find out who Paul is, and what precisely he has done to cause offence, Lysias orders torture to be applied (22, 24—25 a). Paul claims Roman citizenship (22, 25 b—28); the examination by torture is stopped, and Paul informs the officer of his identity (21, 39).

The moment Lysias learns who Paul is, he reports to the Sanhedrin. It appears to him that there is no reason for further detention of the prisoner from the Roman point of view, but he has to inquire whether the Jewish authorities wish to make any charge against him. The commander of the Roman garrison does not summon a representative of the Council to his own office so as to make enquiries about Paul's offence, but conducts Paul to the Sanhedrin's assembly hall (22, 30). How are we to account for Lysias' course of action? The writer tells us that the garrison commander intended to make sure of the accusation against Paul. The pretence is bizarre[12]; to obtain information, a less cumbersome machinery was at Lysias's disposal than that of asking the Sanhedrin to convene. There are two issues that should not be confused: one is the question why Paul was taken before the Jewish Law Court; the other, why Lysias accompanied him. The writer of Acts gives an answer to this second question. Lysias might not have been entirely satisfied by the suspect's deposition, and by attending the Sanhedrin's session he may have hoped to obtain elucidation on matters concerning such activities of Paul as could have brought the Apostle into conflict with Roman law — in which case Lysias would continue to detain him in prison. It is also possible that the officer accompanied Paul to the session of the Sanhedrin simply because of the prisoner's claim to Roman citizenship. However this may be, it does not account for the fact that Paul had to appear before the Jewish Senate. The author of Acts evidently conceals the reason: Paul was conveyed before the Sanhedrin

---

in Acts 9 is a quarter of a century removed from that in Acts 21; during the interval there had been many changes in the person holding office as high-priest.

The high-priest officiating at the time of Paul's arrest is called Ananias (Acts 23, 2; 24, 1). The chronology causes difficulty; Ananias, the son of Nedebaeus, was appointed high-priest during the procuratorship of Tiberius Alexander (Ant XX 103), but seems to have been deposed to give way to the re-instated Jonathan who held the high-priestly office when Antonius Sextilius Felix was procurator (Ant XX 162).

[11] Josephus, B. J. II 261—263; Ant XX 169—172.

[12] »Singulière façon de mener une enquête sur l'incident qui s'est produit dans le temple... Le sanhédrin se réunissant pour que le tribun sache à quoi s'en tenir, est purement ridicule«, Loisy, Les actes des apôtres, p. 824.

because the Jewish authorities had demanded it. Lysias complied with their demand, realizing that Paul, though possibly innocent of any crime against Roman law, nevertheless might have been guilty of an offence against the Jewish legal order, and would thus have to answer for his conduct before Jewish authorities.

The writer of Acts puts it differently. According to him, Lysias brought Paul before the Sanhedrin, because he — Lysias — wanted to learn what accusations the Jews had against the prisoner. The shallow pretext under which the writer attempts to camouflage the legal facts in Paul's case, has been aptly described by Loisy as "enfantillages" which, however, "ne sont pas de simples fantaisies, mais qui ont été inventés délibérément pour cacher la vérité, pour dissimuler au lecteur que Paul n'avait échappé aux autorités juives qu'en sa qualité de Romain, et parce qu'il s'en était lui-même prévalu"[13]. If we read, as we probably should, in Acts 23, 20 with codices Vaticanus, Freerianus, and Alexandrinus ὡς μέλλων τι ἀκριβέστερον πυνθάνεσθαι, we find fiction carried to the point of absurdity. The author makes Paul's nephew say to Lysias: "The Jews" — was not Paul's nephew a Jew himself? — "have agreed to ask you to bring Paul down tomorrow to the council-hall as though you might intend to make some more accurate enquiries about him". This means no less than that the members of the Sanhedrin d e m a n d e d that Paul should be brought again before their assize — to enable Lysias to obtain such information as h e  w a s  d e s i r o u s of collecting[14]!

The session of the Sanhedrin to which Paul is brought is presided over by the high-priest (23, 2) and the Council is clearly determined not merely to act in an examinatory capacity on Lysias's behalf, but to assume jurisdiction in the case on the strength of Jewish legal ordinances. So much emerges from Paul's speech: "You sit to judge me according to the Law" (23, 3). The description of the Senate's session in Acts 23, 1—10 is not what we would expect from a critical historian. The author of Acts reports nothing of the course of the judicial inquiry and does not even list the charges; without a single word of these issues he reports Paul's speech and the ensuing tumult. The information that the Sanhedrin met to deliberate on Paul's case (22, 30) is historically trustworthy; it is borne out by the later report of the Sanhedrin's delegations to Felix (24, 1) and Festus (25, 2—3, 7), requesting that Paul should be

---

[13] O. c., p. 837. »[Le rédacteur des Actes] n'a pas voulu dire que le sanhédrin avait réclamé Paul pour le juger, parce qu'il aurait obligé de dire que Paul avait décliné la compétence de ce tribunal; selon lui, c'est le tribun qui avait réuni le sanhédrin pour s'informer et s'éclairer«, ibidem.

[14] The reading μέλλων is accepted as the original one by Westcott-Hort. Codex ℵ has μέλλων; later manuscripts read μέλλοντες. If either of these is correct, the meaning would be that the Sanhedrin as a body, or its members, wished to have another chance of obtaining information.

handed back to the Council's jurisdiction. The vivid scene in which the two factions represented on the Council come to blows, threatening "to pull Paul to pieces" (23, 19), is hardly an accurate description of the final phase of the proceedings[15]. Whatever lack of good manners the members of the Sanhedrin may have been guilty of, they were mostly elderly persons. It appears that the author's potent imagination carried the scene of Paul's seizure in the open from Acts 21, 30 to the secluded location of the Council's session. What actually seems to have taken place, is that the Council failed to arrive at a decision. Pharisees may have fallen out with Sadducees, the former possibly advocating Paul's acquittal, the latter taking the opposite view (23, 7—10 a). The session is adjourned and Lysias little wiser than he was before, orders Paul to be brought back to the Antonia (23, 10 b). It is futile to speculate what Lysias might have done, had the Council actually reached an adverse verdict. The high-priest directs that the inconclusive session of the Sanhedrin should be resumed, and demands that Lysias hand the prisoner over to the Jewish judiciary (23, 15, 20).

Lysias is in a quandary. He has no precedent to guide him in this perplexing case. In his custody is a Roman citizen who is a Jew and is suspected of a multiplicity of offences, some of which may come under the jurisdiction of a Jewish, others under the jurisdiction of a Roman court. To avoid making a decision for which he may later be held responsible, he leaves the decision to his superior, the procurator in Caesarea[16]. He at once despatches Paul to him (23, 23—25). That Lysias simultaneously forwarded a written report to the procurator is most likely, but whether this report agreed with the letter cited in Acts 23, 26—30 is another matter. Two items mentioned in that letter could have been contained in the officer's report: that Paul claimed Roman citizenship (v. 27) and that the Sanhedrin laid to his charge various offences under Jewish law (v. 29). The report probably included also a reference to the fact that Lysias had informed the Council of Paul's removal from Jerusalem to Caesarea (23, 30).

When the procurator receives his subordinate's report, and Paul is brought before him, the first thing Felix does is to satisfy himself that the prisoner is not a resident of Judaea. He then decides to hear the case when he is informed of the accusers' viewpoint (23, 34—35).

---

[15] »Le romanesque atteint ici au comble de la fantaisie la plus naïve«, Loisy, o. c., p. 825.

[16] The story of Paul's nephew who crops up from nowhere in Acts 23, 16, and is swallowed up into nowhere soon afterwards, and of the unfortunate forty odd conspirators who must have starved to death (Acts 23, 12) is of no interest except as illuminating the descriptive methods of the author in reporting an involved legal case. Cf. the statement in Acts 23, 31 concerning the march-route covered by soldiers on foot in a single night; the journey from Jerusalem to Antipatris would have been across some forty miles of rough terrain.

A few days later, a delegation from the Great Sanhedrin arrives in Caesarea. The procurator arranges for a hearing. The delegation, led personally by the high-priest, consists of an unspecified number of councillors and also includes the lawyer Tertullus who has been briefed to present the Sanhedrin's point of view to the procurator[17]. Tertullus's speech and Paul's counter-plea are the crucial part of the entire account of Paul's 'trial'. These speeches are not a complete invention, but the author of Acts would not have been true to himself if he had simply reproduced whatever information was available to him, or mentioned the facts of the case without embellishments of his own. The historically relevant data have to be extracted from the colourful description he has given of the proceedings and their outcome[18]. Tertullus states the charges. These are: (1) the spreading of seditious propaganda outside and inside Judaea by the proclamation of proscribed Naṣorean views; (2) an attempt at the profanation of the Temple (24, 5—6). The delegation does not at any moment suggest that the procurator should pronounce judgment on Paul for these offences, but demands that the prisoner should be handed back for trial to the Sanhedrin. The Vulgate text gives a fuller, and more explicit, account of the petition submitted by Tertullus than most of the uncial Greek codices. It contains, after Acts 24, 6, the following words: "... quem voluimus secundum legem nostram iudicare. Superveniens autem ... Lysias ... eripuit eum de manibus nostris, iubens accusatores eius ad te venire"[19]. It is easier to understand why the text of most of the Greek uncials should have been mutilated by the omission of these lines – they are in E, Ψ, the Peshitto, the Harclean Syriac, and were known to Chrysostom — than to see any reason for their insertion at a later date in the Vulgate and a number of minuscles. The words quoted are likely to have belonged to the original text of the Acts. There are good reasons *against regarding them as an interpolation*. These words have no self-contained meaning; they make sense only in Tertullus' speech. They explicitly presuppose conditions permitting the Sanhedrin to pass — and presumably carry out

---

[17] Tertullus may have been a non-Jew, as Acts 24, 9 seems to suggest.

[18] »Welche Anklage man eigentlich gegen Paulus erhoben hat, können wir nur erraten; exakt mitgeteilt wird es uns nicht. Es muß sich um einen sehr schwerer Vorwurf gehandelt haben, denn Paulus ist in einen Kapitalprozess verwickelt, ir dem es um Leben und Tod geht. Lukas hat nicht das mindeste Interesse daran, diese Anklage mit aller historischen Genauigkeit aufzufrischen«, Ernst Haenchen, *Die Apostelgeschichte* (Göttingen 1956), p. 563. English edition (Oxford 1970), p. 628

[19] Two relatively late Greek uncial codices preserve the reading we have in the Vulgate. They are Codex Laudianus E (6th cent.) and Codex Laurensis Ψ (8th o 9th cent.). Wellhausen considered this reading unauthentic, whilst Loisy (*Les acte des apôtres*, p. 854), Lake (*The Beginnings of Christianity*, vol. 4, p. 299) and Di belius (»Die Reden der Apostelgeschichte und die antike Geschichtsschreibung« p. 18, note 2; *Aufsätze zur Apostelgeschichte*, p. 130, note 5) thought it was origina

— sentences in judicial proceedings on a capital charge. As the statement attributed to Tertullus in Acts 24, 6 c—7 challenged Christian views on the Sanhedrin's lack of juridical authority in this respect, there might have been some motivation for omitting the passage but none for adding it to a supposedly original text in which it did not appear.

When Tertullus has finished and the members of the deputation from Jerusalem have concurred with his conclusions, Paul answers. He stresses that he has been in Jerusalem barely twelve days (24, 11)[20], with the intention, perhaps, of contending that anything laid to his charge that did not happen within this period was outside the Sanhedrin's jurisdiction. Whilst he was in Jerusalem, he did not stir up any crowd (24, 12), nor can it be proved that he committed the sacrilege of which he is suspected, namely, of taking Trophimus into an inner court of the Temple (24, 13); his reason for being present in the sacred precincts was innocuous and, moreover, commendable from the point of view of observing Jewish customs (24, 17—18 a). In all things, so the Paul of Acts asserts, he has kept the Jewish Law (24, 14). As if the hearing before Felix were not concerned exclusively with the question of competence, but with a decision *in merito,* Paul comments on the absence of "certain Jews from Asia" who have laid unsubstantiated charges against him (24, 18 b—19).

The speech is a clever one, but it is scarcely Paul's.

---

The omission of the passage from the text is easier explained than its insertion. The words in Acts 24, 6 c, 7, 8 a imply that the Sanhedrin possessed jurisdiction in a capital case.

[20] Loisy, *Les actes des apôtres,* p. 856, found fault with the computation of »twelve days«, Acts 24, 11, from the time of Paul's arrival in Jerusalem. The figure is not inconsistent with the description in the Acts, but we have to understand that it does not include the five days Paul is reported to have spent in Caesarea after he had been taken there from Jerusalem. According to Acts 21, 17—18, Paul stayed two days in Jerusalem before he began his »purification«. This ceremonial lasted seven days (Acts 21, 27). On the last day of his purification, *i. e.* the ninth day of his sojourn in Jerusalem, Paul was arrested (Acts 21, 30). On the following day, he stood before the Sanhedrin (Acts 22, 30), and another day elapsed before Lysias decided to send him to Caesarea (Acts 23, 11—12). Taking the report of the forced night-march to Antipatris and of the continuing journey from there to Caesarea (Acts 23, 31—33) at its face value, there is one more day, making twelve altogether. The days between the arrival of Paul in Caesarea and that of the deputation from the Sanhedrin (Acts 24, 1) are apparently not included in the writer's computation of twelve days.

Loisy considered the report in Acts of what happened on the tenth and eleventh days of Paul's sojourn in Jerusalem unhistorical, assuming that Lysias despatched his prisoner to the procurator immediately after he had learned of Paul's claim to Roman citizenship. However, the elimination of the hearing before the Sanhedrin, Acts 23, 1—10, is unjustified, notwithstanding the fact that the account of the proceedings is both farcical and fantastic.

Whoever contrived this speech, he was primarily concerned with the relationship of Christianity to the imperial authorities, and from this angle he touched on Christian relations to Judaism. The actual legal issues of Paul's case are left in the background. Skilful is the differentiation of terms applied to Christianity by the respective speakers. Tertullus calls it a αἵρεσις (24, 5); the Paul of Acts with almost Buddhist terminology refers to it as ἡ ὁδός (24, 14)[21] — and thus avoids committing himself on the question whether Christianity was a new religion or not.

Although the speech in Acts 24, 10 b—21 is far from reproducing anything like the actual text of Paul's plea before the procurator Felix, the manner in which Paul is made to reply to the classified charges proffered by Tertullus is significant. Whatever he may be accused of having done outside Jerusalem — and he stayed only twelve days in that city — was none of the Sanhedrin's business (24, 11). To have "stirred up a crowd" in Jerusalem (24, 12) might have been adjudged as a κίνησις στάσεως and would have been an offence against Roman rather than against Jewish law; to have brought a Gentile into the Inner Temple Court would have been indictable under Jewish law and be subject to Jewish jurisdiction. Here then lies the dilemma; it is not a clear-cut case, and Felix is left pondering the question as to which of the charges might be the weightier or more easily proved. As was the case with Lysias, Felix now does not know what action to take. He is not convinced of Paul's innocence — innocence, or guilt, have not been argued so far; only the problem of judicial competence has been discussed. Had the procurator been convinced of the defendant's guiltlessness, he could have released Paul at once and ordered him to leave the province. The writer of the Acts makes Felix announce that he would defer his decision until Lysias the tribune came down from Jerusalem (24, 22) — yet the letter in Acts 23, 26—30 contains nothing about a proposal on Lysias's part to report personally to Felix, nor is there any subsequent mention of his visiting Caesarea. Paul remains in detention (24, 23, 27). No decision has been arrived at as to whether he should be tried by a Roman authority or a Jewish one. The narrator's impugnment of Felix's character (24, 26) may be soundly based[22], and may even state the historical ground for Felix's dilatory handling of the case. The statement that Felix kept Paul imprisoned so as to gain favour with "the Jews" (24, 27) is palpably misleading — "the Jews" had asked that Paul should not be kept in a Roman prison, but handed over to them for swift trial. In any event, Paul was not released, and it remained undecided by whom he should be tried.

---

[21] It may be that the teaching of *Two Ways* prompted our author to use this terminology. It is not Paul's own language, but the writer of Acts (9, 2; 19, 9, 23; 22, 4) employs it in passages reporting on the apostle's activities.

[22] *Cf.* Tacitus, Annales XII liv 1, Historiae V ix 3; Suetonius, Claudius xxviii 1.

From the point of view of the local Jewish authorities this was an unsatisfactory state of affairs. When Felix is recalled, and a new procurator, Porcius Festus, arrives in Judaea (25, 1), the Sanhedrin at once demands that he should hand the case over for their jurisdiction (25, 2)[23]. Festus arranges a hearing in Caesarea (25, 6), and again the question of competence is discussed. The Acts lacks precision here concerning the composition of the Jewish deputation ("the Jews who had come from Jerusalem", 25, 7) and their contentions ("many and grievous charges which they could not prove", 25, 75). Only from Festus's reaction to their expostulations do we gather that the delegation had again demanded that Paul should be sent back to Jerusalem and transferred to the jurisdiction of the Sanhedrin. From Paul's defence plea which is reported (25, 8) we may gather that the allegations made against him concerned: (1) offences against Jewish law, and (2) against the Temple in particular, (3) offences against Roman law ("against Caesar"). The case is hence the same as it stood two years earlier, save that in addition to the specific charge of having brought a Gentile to the Inner Temple Court there is now a general clause, covering other violations of Jewish statutory prescriptions which are left unspecified. It may be that the Sanhedrin was trying to strengthen the case for its competence, but the passage in Acts is of too summary a character to allow of definite legal-historical deductions. Nevertheless it may be inferred that the classification of various offences in Paul's enumeration implies that offences against Jewish law, including attempted profanation of the Temple, would come under the jurisdiction of the Sanhedrin, whilst offences against Caesar (such as the incitement of the population) would belong to the procurator's competence. Admittedly, we have here definite evidence only of the Sanhedrin's right *to try* capital cases. But why should the delegation have insisted on having Paul brought before their own court if that court lacked the authority to carry out capital sentences?

In the hearings before Felix, and now before Festus, the parties and the arbiters are not concerned with the merits of the case. There is no mention of witnesses being called for either side; only legal arguments are brought forward, and the dispute centres on the question of juridical competence.

Festus is not impressed by Paul's pleading. He suggests — this is how the writer of the Acts puts it — that Paul should submit to the jurisdiction of the Sanhedrin in Jerusalem, whilst promising that he would personally be present at the trial (25, 9) — apparently to safeguard the rights of a Roman citizen and protect Paul from possible abuses by

---

[23] »Le sanhédrin n'a pas présenté à Festus une dénonciation et une supplique; il a présenté une requête motivée, pour que le prisonnier Paul fût remis à ceux qui prétendaient être ses juges légitimes et avoir le droit de le juger à Jérusalem selon la Loi«, Loisy, *o. c.*, p. 872.

vindictive enemies. There is some ambiguity in the words used by our author to express Festus's suggestion: εἰς Ἱεροσόλυμα ἀναβαίνειν ἐκεῖ κριθῆναι ἐπ᾽ ἐμοῦ. If ἐπ᾽ ἐμοῦ should be understood in the sense that the trial in Jerusalem was to be presided over by Festus ("under myself"), it would have been a Roman trial, and there would not be any reason at all why it should be held in Jerusalem (ἐκεῖ). The parties are present in Caesarea, and so is Festus. One could surmise that the newly appointed procurator was anxious to show his courtesy to the local authorities by sparing them the inconvenience of travelling from Jerusalem to Caesarea, but the same can hardly be said if it was only a matter of summoning witnesses to the seat of the procurator's court. The ἐπ᾽ ἐμοῦ indicates Festus's willingness to attend as an observer Paul's trial in Jerusalem by the Sanhedrin. The author of Acts tries to screen the facts. The curious expression χαρίσασθαι (25, 11) in Paul's reply to the procurator's suggestion, employed to denote a judicial decision, betrays the unreality of the description. The procurator could not "grant" Paul to the Jewish authorities in Jerusalem if he had not come to the conclusion that they were competent to try his case. Paul's response to the suggestion (25, 10) definitely excludes the possibility of understanding these words in the sense of "under me as president of the court"[24]: "I am standing before Caesar's tribunal (= before a Roman judge) [and this is] where I ought to be judged. To [the] Jews I have done no wrong". These words make no sense if the preceding sentence merely implied that Festus meant to adjourn the session of his court and to re-open it later in Jerusalem. Had Festus, whose authority Paul could not fail to recognize, suggested nothing else than that he would hold the trial in Jerusalem instead of Caesarea, such a strong protest as that lodged by Paul would not have been called for. The ἐπ᾽ ἐμοῦ thus means "in my presence", "with myself as an observer". Festus would have Paul tried by the Sanhedrin, yet so as to ensure that the accused's right be not prejudiced in proceedings conducted by the Jewish judiciary, he promises to be present at the trial[25].

---

[24] It is again Loisy who correctly understood, despite the pains which the author of Acts took to obscure them, what Festus's words in Acts 25, 9 imply: »Festus s'est déclaré incompétent; la réponse de Paul montre que le procurateur l'avait purement et simplement renvoyé devant le tribunal juif«, Les actes des apôtres, p. 877. Kirsopp Lake, in The Beginnings of Christianity, vol. 4, p. 308, expressed the opposite opinion, whilst Henry J. Cadbury, in the same work, vol. 5, is more circumspect in his assessment: »The book of Acts, in spite of its obscurity, suggests that Paul might conceivably have been tried by the Sanhedrin«, l. c., p. 302, and »... both Lysias and the procurators pay considerable deference to the opinion of the Sanhedrin about Paul, and it [might be understood] that... what Lysias first undertook and what Festus finally proposed was an actual trial of Paul by the Sanhedrin«, p. 303. Ernst Haenchen, o. c., p. 598, reverted to Lake's opinion.

[25] It may be noticed that in Acts 25, 20 where Festus's proposal to let Paul's trial run its course in Jerusalem is referred to, the words ἐπ᾽ ἐμοῦ are absent. This con-

Paul vehemently protests against the procurator's proposal. He objects to "being granted" (= surrendered, handed over) to Jewish jurisdiction: "I appeal to Caesar" (25, 11)[26]. As the defendant is a Roman citizen, and there is a possibility that apart from the charge of having facilitated a Gentile's trespassing into the Inner Temple (Paul's civic status would not have precluded the Sanhedrin from exercising jurisdiction in this instance) other matters might be brought up, matters that could be deemed to be of a political nature (κινεῖν στάσεις), and based on incidents which occurred outside the area under the procurator's jurisdiction, Festus first consults with the συμβούλιον — perhaps those members of the Sanhedrin who are present?[27] — and then announces his decision to send Paul to Rome (25, 12). The author of the Acts gives no details regarding the subject of the procurator's consultation. It would have considerably added to our understanding of the legal situation had this question not been left in the dark.

---

firms the view that Acts 25, 9 contains the procurator's explicit recognition of the Sanhedrin's judicial authority to try Jews, in the present case even a Roman citizen, for capital offences against the Jewish Law.

[26] Paul claimed the right of *provocatio* by which a case pending in a provincial magistrate's court devolved to the Emperor's court in Rome. Festus could not refuse Paul's ›appeal‹ without the risk of committing a serious crime himself: *lege Julia de vi publica damnatur qui aliqua potestate praeditus civem Romanum, antea ad populum, nunc ad imperatorem appellantem, neca[ve]rit, necarive iusserit, torserit, verbaverit, condemnaverit..., Sententiae Pauli, liber V, titulus xxvi (ad legem Juliam de vi publica et privata), 1.

We are not called upon to judge the motives for Paul's desperate decision in making use of his prerogative as a Roman citizen. He had probably good cause to doubt the impartiality of the authorities in Jerusalem which by that time were anxious to suppress messianic enthusiasm and who might also have been hostile to Paul because of his activities in communities of the Jewish Diaspora where he could not be brought before a Jewish court on a capital charge. Neither are we to judge the motives of his adversaries who acted with the objective of upholding the religious, social, and legal order of their country.

»Si Paul n'avait pas été citoyen romain, il est bien probable qu'il aurait été mis à mort à Jérusalem«, Maurice Goguel, »Juifs et Romains dans l'histoire de la Passion«, RHR tome 62, 1910, pp. 165—182, 295—322, on p. 316. »...l'autorité romaine n'aurait pas vu grand inconvénient à livrer ce Juif... au tribunal juif qui le réclamait, si Paul n'avait été citoyen romain et ne s'était prévalu de son droit«, Loisy, Les actes des apôtres, p. 834; »N'ayant que le choix entre la sentence de mort que lui réserve le sanhédrin, et la chance d'absolution que lui offre l'appel à César, il en appelle au tribunal de l'empereur... Se faisait-il beaucoup d'illusion sur la justice du tribunal impérial? On ne saurait le dire«, ibidem, p. 878.

[27] It is possible that the composition of the συμβούλιον is indicated in Acts 25, 23. If so, it consisted of οἱ χιλίαρχοι (apparently Roman officers) and of οἱ κατ' ἐξοχὴν τῆς πόλεως ἄνδρες (apparently Jewish councillors from the City of Jerusalem, i. e. members of the Senate).

Paul evades being handed over for trial to the Jewish authorities by virtue of his Roman citizenship. There is corroborative evidence, though from a later time, for Festus' decision to send the prisoner to Rome; in a letter from Pliny the Younger to the Emperor Trajan we read: *Confitentes ... interrogavi, supplicium minatus; perseverantes duci iussi ... Fuerunt alii ... quos, quia cives Romani erant, adnotavi in Urbem remittendos*[28].

In spite of the effort to obscure the legal issue, one point emerges clearly: the procurator recognizes the judicial competence of the Sanhedrin to try Paul on a capital charge. It would indeed be strange for a Roman procurator to have proposed to Paul to submit to the Sanhedrin's jurisdiction in a case involving the death penalty, if that body had no power to pass death sentences and to ensure that its judgments were carried out (Jn 18, 31 b). Throughout the whole description of Paul's detention[29] the members of the Sanhedrin do not act as if they were devoid of all legal right to exercise their judicatory function. Nor do the representatives of Roman rule consider the Sanhedrin's demand for Paul's extradition to be outrageous. Had it not been doubtful by whom Paul should be tried, Lysias, Felix, and Festus, would have paid little attention to the Sanhedrin's opinion on the matter. Yet the proceedings are held back for two years by a drawn-out legal wrangle about the question of judicial competence. For only this, not the question of guilt, was under discussion. When Lysias had taken Paul from the hands of the mob into Roman custody, he might himself have immediately called for the examination of witnesses, who were on the spot, had he thought that the case was one that came under Roman jurisdiction. But once he learns that the prisoner was not identical with the Egyptian revolutionary, he desists from further action on his own behalf and reports the case to the Sanhedrin. A decision that would settle the case is prevented only through lack of agreement among the Council's members. The course which the meeting took could have startled Lysias and raised his doubts; it may be that matters were brought up during the Sanhedrin's session concerning Paul's activities outside Judaea, and that this occasioned Lysias's indecision. The high-priest demands of Lysias, as a right, that Paul should be brought back to the Sanhedrin. Lysias evades compliance with this demand by despatching the prisoner quickly to Caesarea. A delegation from the Council to the procurator insists on the Council's competence. Felix does not gainsay the Sanhedrin's authority, but procrastinates. Festus explicitly acknowledges the competence of the Sanhedrin to try the case.

---

[28] Letters, X 96, 4.

[29] From Acts 21, 33 to 28, 31 Paul is a prisoner in Roman hands, but from 21, 33 to 25, 12 (or perhaps 26, 32) the narrative evolves around the question whether he might have to be handed over to stand trial before a Jewish court of law.

There may be many questions to which the writer of the Acts failed to provide an answer, but one thing stands out clearly: not only Pilate was unaware that the Sanhedrin lacked authority to pass and carry out sentences upon Jews guilty of capital offences against Jewish law, but Claudius Lysias, Antonius Felix, Porcius Festus, and the rhetor Tertullus, seem to have been equally ignorant of any limitation of the Jewish Senate's rights in this respect[30].

Notwithstanding the writer's effort to disguise them, two facts may be elicited from the Acts' narrative of Paul's detention in Jerusalem and Caesarea: (1) the Sanhedrin demanded that Paul should be tried before a Jewish court; (2) the Roman authorities seriously considered this demand, and at one point were inclined to accede to it. The author of the Acts admits, implicitly, that the Sanhedrin possessed the right to impose and carry out sentences of death — he states in Acts 5, 33 that some members of the Sanhedrin wished to exercise this right, and in Acts 26, 10 he puts into Paul's mouth words to the effect that, by the authority of the chief priests, the Apostle had consented to the execution of many believers in Jesus' messiahship (cf. Acts 8, 3; 22, 4)[31]. Whether or not the statement in Acts 26, 10 represents history, the fact that the writer makes Paul say what he does, indicates an awareness of the Sanhedrin's competence to pass and execute capital sentences.

The writer of Acts is concerned to present Paul's case — which to him is the case of Christianity — as completely innocuous from the viewpoint of Imperial Rome. Hence he strives to conceal from his readers the fact that the Roman authorities were at one stage disposed to hand Paul over for trial to the Jewish court in Jerusalem[32]. The apologetic tendency comes out strongly in Acts 28, 17—19. There, Paul is made to say that the Romans, after having investigated the charges preferred against him, wished to set him free but were hindered from so doing by Jewish opposition. Here the author's concern comes to light: he wished to give the impression that the Roman authorities considered Paul innocent (cf. Acts 25, 25; 26, 31). Unhampered by any source material in Acts 28, 18, he boldly exposes his apologetic concern, whereas in passages where he is making use of traditional information he cannot go so far. He suppresses, and deliberately colours, particular items of the tradition he possessed regarding Paul's arrest and the proceedings before Felix and Festus, but the source does not permit him

---

[30] We may add Titus Flavius. In his speech to the defenders of Jerusalem he asserts: ἡμεῖς (we, the Romans) ... τοὺς ὑπερβάντας ὑμῖν (to you, the Jews) ἀναιρεῖν ἐπετρέψαμεν, καὶ Ῥωμαῖός τις ᾖ (B. J. VI 126).

[31] Before the year 70 CE it fell to the priests to supervise the punishment of people condemned by the court. See Josephus, Contra Apionem II 187, 194.

[32] Far from denying the Jewish authorities the right to execute persons whom their own courts had sentenced to death, the Romans — in exceptional cases — even allowed them to execute their own army officers; see B. J. II 246, Ant XX 136.

the freedom, exemplified in Acts 28, 18, to assert that the tribune or the procurators wished at any stage of the proceedings to liberate Paul. Only in a passage where no source information has been used (28, 18) is our writer quite unimpeded in giving expression to his apologetic bias.

The writer of the Acts undoubtedly had source materials at his disposal for his narrative concerning Paul's custody in Jerusalem and Caesarea and the attendant legal proceedings. He modified such materials, being guided by the intention to show that Christianity was considered harmless by the Roman authorities. Hence Paul is made to say that the Romans desired to set him free, but were thwarted by Jewish opposition. Nowhere from Acts 21, 33 to 25, 12 do we find any suggestion to justify an assertion of this kind. If Felix or Festus had intended to set Paul free, the Jews could not have prevented them from doing so any more than they could have prevented Pilate from liberating Jesus. There existed no legal instrument by which the Sanhedrin could appeal against a verdict of acquittal. The Jewish leaders would not even have been in a position to lodge a complaint of administrative malpractice. Paul was not a Judaean; once he had left the country after having been set free by Felix or by Festus, the Jewish authorities in Jerusalem would have had no further say in the affair. The writer of the Acts did all he could to cover up the facts of the situation[33]. The information to which he had access, perhaps memoirs of witnesses, reported that the procurator Festus explicitly recognized the competence of the Jewish Law Court to conduct Paul's trial. It was only Paul's appeal to the Emperor that prevented the Sanhedrin from actually assuming jurisdiction in the matter.

From a legal point of view, Paul's case was more complicated than that of Jesus. The defendant claimed Roman citizenship. He was not a Palestinian resident, and had been in Judaea only about a fortnight. Some of the offences with which he was charged had been committed outside Judaean territory. Even those allegedly committed in Jerusalem were of a controversial nature: some may have come under Jewish jurisdiction, whilst others were subject to Roman law. The defendant had been in Roman detention since the day of his apprehension and had remained in such detention for a prolonged period of time. Paul was

---

[33] »Rede und Redeszenen sind es, die diese Kapitel beherrschen ... Das ... lässt vermuten, dass hier der Schriftsteller gegenüber der Tradition die Oberhand hat ... Die Reden sind ... für den Leser bestimmt. Was Lukas in diesem Teil seines Buches für Nachrichten gehabt und verwendet hat, können wir nicht erkennen; denn so wie sie uns vorliegen, sind die fraglichen Kapitel seine literarische Leistung«, Martin Dibelius, »Stilkritisches zur Apostelgeschichte« in *Eucharisterion. Studien zur Religion und Literatur des Alten und Neuen Testaments, Hermann Gunkel dargebracht,* edited by Hans Schmidt, vol. 2 (Göttingen 1923), pp. 27—49, on pp. 32, 33; also in *Aufsätze zur Apostelgeschichte,* pp. 9—28, on p. 14; English edition, p. 7.

never under sentence by the Sanhedrin as Mc 14, 64 (Mt 26, 66) makes Jesus out to have been. Paul himself expressed his preference for a trial by a Roman judge. Under these circumstances, after long uncertainty, the question of juridical competence was decided in favour of the stronger party. Paul is sent to Rome, and meets his death in Rome. The long delay of the final decision, the behaviour of Lysias in Jerusalem, of Felix and Festus in Caesarea, all these would be incomprehensible if it had been understood from the start that the Sanhedrin had no authority to judge Jews on a capital charge, and such, among other accusations, was the charge of inducing a Gentile to desecrate the Temple. If a conclusion can be drawn *a maiore ad minus* — the procedure in the case of Paul on the one hand, that against Jesus on the other — there can be no uncertainty in our verdict on the historicity of the statement in Jn 18, 31 b. The complications which rendered it difficult to reach a decision in the case of Paul, were absent in the case of Jesus. Nevertheless, from the fact that the question whether Paul's fate should be decided by the Sanhedrin remained in suspense for so long, we can make the following deduction: If the Jewish High Court had tried and sentenced Jesus to death for an offence against the Torah, there would have been no legal objection on the part of the Roman authorities to the Sanhedrin's carrying out its sentence.

The statement which the Fourth Evangelist attributes to the delegation from the high-priest in Jn 18, 31 b is nullified by the attitude and the actions of Roman officials — in Jerusalem and Caesarea — when the problem arose whether the Apostle Paul should be arraigned for trial before a Jewish court or a Roman one. Yet this statement, so obviously in conflict with all the known facts of history, has until recent times obfuscated the views which historians have held on the trial of Jesus. To understand why this statement should have been made at all by the Jews of the Fourth Gospel, it is necessary to consider it in the perspective in which the Evangelist saw and pictured the events. Not the political or juridical conditions, but the Evangelist's theology is the determining factor in Jn 18, 31 b. "It is difficult", writes Kingsley Barrett, "to assent to the view that the Sanhedrin could not have executed Jesus without reference to Pilate"[34], or, as Robert Henry Lightfoot put it, "there is no decisive evidence, apart from this passage [*viz.* Jn 18, 31 b], that the Jews could not, for religious offences, pronounce and execute the death sentence"[35]. We may go further: Jn 18, 31 b provides no evidence at all of history — the assertion denying the competence of Jewish law courts to

---

[34] *The Gospel according to St. John*, p. 446.
[35] *St. John's Gospel. A Commentary* (Oxford 1956), p. 310.

administer capital punishment has its basis in the theological scheme devised by the Fourth evangelist. "Das ist stilisierte Darstellung, aber nicht irgendwie wägbare historische Relation"[36].

As elsewhere in the Gospels, when examining what the evangelists report of the trial of Jesus, we must ask: What was the aim of the writer in making the particular assertion contained in Jn 18, 31 b? The author himself gives the answer in the next verse. The utterance was made to guarantee the fulfilment of a saying of Jesus (Jn 12, 32, 33): had Jesus not foretold in what manner he would die, the Jews would never have said what they do say in Jn 18, 31 b.

Unlike the Christ in Mark and Luke who predicts his death but not the manner of his dying (Mc 8, 31/Lc 9, 22; Mc 9, 31; Mc 10, 34/Lc 18, 33)[37], the Christ of the Fourth Gospel like the Jesus in Mt 20, 19 foretells specifically that he will die by crucifixion. The statement ascribed to the Jews in Jn 18, 31 b is designed to bring about the fulfilment of Jesus' prediction whilst still enabling the Evangelist to maintain Jewish responsibility for the crucifixion. There was no difficulty in the way of proving that the prophecy contained in Jn 12, 33—34 had been fulfilled; Jesus had died by crucifixion. But crucifixion was a Roman mode of execution. The Jewish penal system knew of no such penalty. Hence the Evangelist had somehow to demonstrate that in spite of the fact that Jesus had died in the manner he did[38], it was not the Romans, but the Jews, who had conspired to bring about a death of this kind. For the Johannine Jews are represented as people predetermined to murder Jesus (Jn 8, 37 b, 40, 42, 43, 44). To hold the Jews responsible and yet explain why Jesus did not die by stoning or any other Jewish form of administering the death penalty, the Fourth Evangelist without the slightest hesitation deprives the Jews of all authority to carry out a judicial sentence of death. Though Jesus was crucified, the Jews can now be shouldered with responsibility for his death — no other form than

---

[36] Hans Lietzmann, »Bemerkungen zum Prozess Jesu. II«, ZNW vol. 31, 1932, pp. 78—84, on p. 83; also available in Kleine Schriften, vol. 2 (Berlin 1958), p. 274.

[37] The saying in Mc 8, 34/Mt 16, 24/Lc 9, 23 (cf. Lc 14, 27) does not belong to this category. The words in Lc 24, 7 (unlike those in Mt 26, 2) are not ascribed to Jesus.

[38] »... the Gospel narrative ... makes the fulfilment of Christ's prophecy about the manner of his death a result of the refusal of the Jews to try Him«, Johann Joseph Ignaz von Döllinger. Christenthum und Kirche in der Zeit der Grundlegung (Regensburg [1]1860), p. 454; ([2]1868), p. 457; English edition, The First Age of Christianity and the Church (London 1866), p. 305.

»Dürfen die Juden nicht töten, dann kann Jesus auch nicht die jüdische Strafe der Steinigung erleiden, sondern nur die Kreuzigung, die römische Strafe für Aufruhr: so kommt es zu einer "Erhöhung" und Jesu Wort wird wahr«, Walter Bauer, Das Johannes-Evangelium (Tübingen [3]1933), p. 216. Cf. H. Lietzmann, l. c., p. 83, resp. 274.

crucifixion was open to them. Powerless to carry out their designs by stoning, they must turn to Pilate; and so it comes about that Jesus is crucified. Two goals are now achieved at once: the prophecy is fulfilled and the malice of the Jews accounts for its realization.

From Jn 18, 29 onward the Fourth Gospel contains nothing of any value for the assessment of historical facts. It may appear inconsistent that for Jn 18, 12—13 a, 19—22, 28 a we have claimed a traditional substratum which merits consideration as embodying an early report of a factual nature. Although worked over by at least two different writers, Jn 18, 3—27, 28 a is in substance not a free creation out of nothing; the story contains a kernel of tradition[39]. The situation is very different with regard to what follows in Jn 18, 29—40; 19, 1—30. In Jn 18, 3—27, 28 a it was the non-Johannine texture of the fabric that determined our view of the relative reliability of the underlying account, whilst from Jn 18, 29 onwards the narrative is of a purely 'Johannine' nature[40]. In contradistinction to the taciturnity of Jesus before Pilate in Mark ("insomuch that Pilate marvelled"), the Johannine Jesus is inclined to be loquacious, but when we examine his dialogue with the governor, it will be noticed that he does not, in fact, answer Pilate's questions. Instead, he treats Pilate to a course in Johannine theology. Pilate does not understand its finer points any more than the Jews in the earlier chapters of the Gospel are capable of grasping the significance of Jesus' discourses. But while the Jews pick up stones and throw them at Jesus, the representative of the pagan world is awestruck by what Jesus has to say, and does all he can to save his life.

The religious importance of the Fourth Gospel is not our present concern; in question is its bearing upon an assessment of the facts of history. Omitting here all reference to what is spoken, and concentrating on the scenery and location, we find in Jn 18, 29 to Jn 19, 18 the following tableaux:

| | |
|---|---|
| Jn 18, 29—32 | Jesus has been taken inside the governor's palace. Pilate negotiates with the Jews outside, |
| 33—38 a | enters the praetorium and converses with Jesus. |
| 38 b | Pilate goes outside; Jesus remains inside. |

---

[39] »Dass der Evangelist die Erzählung selbst gestaltet hat, ist klar; ebenso aber auch, dass er sich dabei auf die Tradition stützt; und zwar hat er offenbar e i n e s c h r i f t l i c h e   Q u e l l e   b e n u t z«,   Walter Bauer, o. c., p. 493.

[40] »Man darf ... behaupten, dass die Passionsgeschichte bei Johannes ... am bewusstesten und konsequentesten in den Dienst theologischer Leitgedanken gestellt wurde«, Josef Blank, »Die Verhandlung vor Pilatus John 18, 28—19, 16 im Lichte johanneischer Theologie«, Biblische Zeitschrift, Neue Folge, vol. 3, 1959, pp. 60—81, on p. 60; [Jesu] Rede ist Offenbarungsrede im streng johanneischen Sinne«, p. 62; »[Bei Johannes geht es um ein wesentlich anderes] als um einen ... historisch berichtigenden oder ergänzenden Passionsbericht. Vielmehr handelt es sich um eine eigenständig johanneische, theologisch hochbedeutsame Konzeption«, p. 65.

|       |       |
|-------|-------|
| 39—40 | Barabbas is set free. |
| 19, 1 | Pilate »took Jesus and scourged him«. |
| 2—3   | Jesus is mocked by the soldiers in the courtyard of the praetorium. |
| 4—8   | Pilate again goes outside, taking Jesus with him, and shows him to the Jews. They are not mollified. |
| 9—12 a | Jesus is inside (!) the praetorium. Pilate follows him there to parley with him; he is confirmed in his decision to release Jesus. |
| 12 b  | The Jews who are outside sense what Pilate, inside, intends to do, and start accusing him of disloyalty to the Emperor. |
| 13    | Pilate now comes out, bringing Jesus with him from the interior of the palace, |
| 14—15 | makes his last bid to save his life and, |
| 16 a  | failing in this, hands Jesus over to the Jews |
| 16 b—18 | who take him away and crucify him. |

Such a series of happenings can hardly be accommodated among the realities of space and time.

# 10. PRIVILEGIUM PASCHALE AND BARABBAS

Most enigmatical of all the parts of the Gospel Story of Jesus' trial is the description of Pilate's offer to release Jesus and the rejection of this offer by the Jews who prefer to have another prisoner freed. The following discussion does not pretend to solve the riddle. It is no more than an attempt to indicate the problematical character of the Gospel narratives on the subject, with the intention of showing up the difficulties that stand in the way of arriving at a satisfactory solution.

There are several reasons for the obscurity of the accounts. Chief among them is the fact that not one of the four Gospels is consistent within itself in the matter of Barabbas's release. As if this were not problem enough, each of the four presents the alleged event in a different form. Finally, there is no external evidence of a custom, Jewish or Roman, of granting pardon to a prisoner on the eve of, or during, the feast of Passover. Attempts to uphold the historical veracity of the Gospel accounts have been numerous; Roman and Jewish records have been ransacked in the search for supporting evidence, but the results of these efforts have been negative. There is evidence that a Roman official in Egypt, in deference to a popular request, desisted from inflicting the penalty of scourging on a certain suspect[1], but we do not know whether legal proceedings had already been instituted when the presumed culprit's release was ordered. In any case, the person in question had not been accused of a capital offence. There is also evidence that Jews in Jerusalem who were discharged from prison on the eve of the Passover celebration were permitted to take part in the eating of the paschal lamb[2]. But this regulation has not the slightest bearing on the case reported in the Gospels. It refers to persons — unspecified in number — who were let out from jail too late to be present at the slaughtering of the lamb, yet in time to attend the evening meal. The stipulation provides for the admission of such people to the festive table on the night of the fifteenth Nisan. The synoptic Gospels report that Barabbas was released after that night. Also, in all four canonical narratives it is a

---

[1] Papyrus Florentinus 61, reproduced in *Supplementi Filologico-Storici ai Monumenti Antichi Papiri Greco-Egizii pubblicati della Reale Accademia dei Lincei,* vol. 1, Milan 1906; fascimile on Plate IX.

[2] Mishnah Pesahim viii 6: »... one who has received a promise to be released from prison, and an invalid, and an aged person who can eat as much as an olive — one slaughters on their behalf«; see also T. B. Pesahim 91 a. *Cf.* Johannes Merkel, »Die Begnadigung am Passafeste«, ZNW vol. 6, 1905, pp. 293—316, on pp. 306, 307.

question of liberating just *one* prisonet. Mishnah Pesahim specifes no
number, but it is clear that the ordinance refers to any quantity of persons who happened to be discharged from prison in time to participate
in the meal.

Differences between the various Gospels in relating the Barabbas
incident — that is to say, the departure of the Matthaean, Lucan and
Johannine accounts from that given in Mark — do not present insur-
mountable difficulties; none of the later evangelists had any independent
tradition at his disposal with which to supplement, or correct, the
report from Mark. The modifications in the later Gospels are of a
purely editorial character. Yet Mark itself contains a compound made
up of tradition and editorial accretions. Whatever the traditional basis
of Mc 15, 6—15 may have been, it has reached us in a form which
makes it difficult to extricate tradition from the present text and free
it from the amplifications it had undergone at the hands of the Evangelist. We lack the means that would enable us to distinguish the tradition from its adaptation, the form it assumed in its furtherance of the
aims which the Second Evangelist pursued in his rendering of the story.
Whilst in the case of the report of Jesus' detention in the high-priest's
house (Mc 14, 53—72) we were able to separate the Evangelist's additions from the traditional residue by comparing the Marcan narration
with the accounts in Luke and John, there is no such aid available in
connection with the story of Barabbas and his release.

The examination which follows is divided into two parts; first we
shall discuss the so-called *privilegium paschale,* then its alleged application by Pilate at Jesus' trial.

The supposed custom of setting a prisoner free at the feast of the
Passover is referred to in a different manner by the Second and First
Evangelists on the one hand, and by the Fourth on the other. The Third
Evangelist nowhere mentions such a custom — Lc 23, 17 is a very
late interpolation made at a time when the belief had come to prevail
that a legal obligation compelled Pilate to comply with an established
usage. Evidently there is some significance in the fact that the Third
Evangelist refrained from mentioning a custom, or a habit on Pilate's
part, of granting pardon to a prisoner at the Passover festival. This
shows that, though he knew the Marcan trial account and made use of
it in his own Gospel, the author of Luke was also in possession of other
information which induced him to question the trustworthiness of certain items in the Marcan account. Matthew, however, follows Mark:

| Mark 15, 6, 8 | Matthew 27, 15, 21 a |
|---|---|
| At the feast [Pilate] used to release for them one prisoner whom they asked of him. ... And the multitude went up and asked him to do as he was wont to. | At the feast the governor was wont to release to the multitude one prisoner whom they chose ... The governor said to them: Which one of the two will you that I release for you? |

In neither of these accounts is there any mention of a Jewish custom, or a Roman concession, that would make it binding on the governor to set a prisoner free. What the Second Evangelist reports, and the First repeats, is that Pilate was in the habit of ingratiating himself with the provincial population by granting them at the time of the festival the release of a prisoner of their own choice[3]. How, in fact, a Roman governor, duty-bound to respect Roman Law, could have adopted such a 'habit', the evangelists do not say.

Although there is no external evidence in support of the Marco-Matthaean report, this in itself would not make the story appear incredible. If what the evangelists report was not a general custom but merely a habit which Pontius Pilate had taken up, we may not expect to find corroborative evidence for it except in Pilate's memoirs or biography. Nothing of the kind exists.

The description in the Fourth Gospel is different. So strong was the influence of suggestive imagination that by the time this Gospel was composed, Christians at large had become convinced of the existence of an established custom with which the governor, his habits apart, had to comply[4]. In the Fourth Gospel, Pilate and addresses the Jews:

You have a custom that I should release one man for you at the Passover. Will you then that I release for you the King of the Jews? (Jn 18, 39).

Whilst in Mark and Matthew the release of a prisoner is presented as the governor's habitual favour, in John it is a Jewish custom — one, however, with which Pilate appears to have been better acquainted than the Jews themselves; it needed his prompting to remind the people of its existence[5]. The Jews, usually meticulous about recording the details of national observances, have failed to preserve any trace of, or reference to, this 'custom'.

The three Gospels so far mentioned, as well as Luke, are in accord on one thing: t h a t  t h e  J e w i s h  p o p u l a t i o n  w e r e  e n t i - r e l y  f r e e  t o  c h o o s e  f o r  t h e m s e l v e s  w h o m  t h e y

---

[3] At the time when Lc 23, 17 was inserted into the trial account of the Third Gospel, the conviction that such a custom existed had gained ground.

[4] This development was the easier as Christian authors from the end of the first century onwards were only slightly conversant with Jewish legal usages. Origen, In Mattaeum CXX, compared the alleged custom with the report in 1 Sam 14, 24—45 of the sparing of Jonathan's life (GCS Origenes XI, 2, p. 254; MPG 13, col. 1771) and surmised: »Pilatus ... Iudaico usus est more ... non secundum aliquam consuetudinem Romanorum«, In Matthaeum CXXIV (GCS Origenes XI, 2, p. 259; MPG 13, col. 1774).

[5] »Es ist ungereimt, dass Pilatus selbst die Juden an einen jüdischen Brauch erinnert«, Eduard Schwartz, »Aporien im vierten Evangelium«, Nachrichten von der Kgl. Gesellschaft der Wissenschaften zu Göttingen, Phil.-hist. Klasse 1907, pp. 342—379; 1908, pp. 115—148, 149—188, 497—560, on p. 356.

w i s h e d   t o   b e   r e l e a s e d   (Mc 15, 6 ὃν παρῃτοῦντο *quemcumque petissent;* Mt 27, 15 ὃν ἤθελον *quem voluissent;* Lc 23, 25 ὃν ᾐτοῦντο *quem petebant;* Jn 18, 39 βούλεσθε *vultis*). It is the only item in the Barabbas episode on which there is unanimity. In view of this, it is surprising to find that P i l a t e   s h o u l d   h a v e   l i m i t e d   t h e   p e o p l e ' s   c h o i c e   t o   t w o   p o s s i b i l i t i e s :   the release of Jesus or of Barabbas (Mc 15, 9, 11, 12, 15; Mt 27, 17; Lc 23, 18—20; Jn 18, 39—40). We later read in the Gospel Story that there were at the time at least two other prisoners in Pilate's hands, awaiting justice to run its course, two men who were eventually crucified with Jesus: ἤγοντο δὲ καὶ ἕτεροι κακοῦργοι δύο σὺν αὐτῷ ἀναιρεθῆναι (Lc 23, 32; *cf.* Mc 15, 27; Mt 27, 38; Lc 23, 33 b; Jn 19, 18 b). Whilst the evangelists state explicitly that the crowd was *free to demand* from Pilate *the pardon of any prisoner,* yet at the same time *they imply that the choice was limited* to two individuals. The offer to choose between two persons only in fact denies the free exercise of the prerogative of the people's will. On this point the Gospels are self-contradictory in their reports.

The *privilegium paschale* is nothing but a figment of the imagination. No such custom existed[6].

We cannot be equally sure about Barabbas, and the rôle he plays in the narratives of Jesus' trial. No doubt the episode in Mc 15, 7—15 is coloured by apologetic interest. The Evangelist throws the responsibility for the death of Jesus onto the Jews, making Pilate appear to have acted merely as an instrument of their heinous intention. The tendency is unmistakable — from the start in Mark, and it grows with the advance of time after the composition of the Second Gospel[7]. Never-

---

[6] Johannes Merkel, *l. c.:* »[Es darf] festgestellt werden, dass weder ein jüdisches Gewohnheitsrecht der Gefangenenfreilassung an hohen Festen ... erweislich ist, noch eine dahin gehende Übung der prokuratorischen Regierung«, p. 311. Alfred Loisy, *L'évangile selon Marc* (Paris 1912): »... ce que dit Marc a bien plutôt l'apparence d'une légende populaire que d'une coutume véritable«, (p. 446). Claude Goldsmid Montefiore, *The Synoptic Gospels* (London 1909): »The custom alluded to is wholly unknown« (p. 363). Richard Wellington Husband, »The Pardoning of Prisoners by Pilate«, *American Journal of Theology,* vol. 21, 1917, pp. 110—116: »There is absolutely no evidence that the pardoning or release of a prisoner had ever occurred, even once, before the time of Pilate« (p. 111); »There seems to be no instance on record, either from Rome or from the provinces, in which a Roman officer pardoned any person who had been convicted of a crime« (p. 112). Hermann L. Strack and Paul Billerbeck, *Kommentar zum Neuen Testament aus Talmud und Midrasch.* Erster Band: *Das Evangelium nach Matthäus* (Munich 1922): »Belege für diese Sitte gibt es nicht« (p. 1031).

[7] An interesting side-light in this connection is provided by the Curetonian Text of the Old Syriac Version. It states that Barabbas had been arrested for heresy. But neither in Jewish nor in Roman Law was heresy a criminal offence in Jesus' time; it became a crime — the most nefarious offence — only after Christianity had attained the rank of the State religion. The copyist of the Curetonian was, of course, not

theless, it does not look as if the whole story were invented[8]. The author of the Second Gospel utilized some tradition, a tradition no longer recoverable in its primal form; but however freely the Evangelist may have handled this tradition, Barabbas was certainly mentioned in it. Scholars have questioned whether the tradition which the Evangelist used actually connected Barabbas with the trial of Jesus, or whether this connection had first come about in the Marcan narrative[9]. Categorical denial seems as inadvisable as categorical assertion. The obscurity of the whole account might be conducive to an attempt at solving the problem in such a radical fashion as to eleminate Barabbas altogether from any connection with events at the trial of Jesus[10] — yet it may be doubted whether it is necessary to go so far.

---

concerned about the person of Barabbas, long dead, but rather about the Jews of his age. By making Barabbas a »heretic«, he yields to the temptation to blacken the reputation of the Jews who preferred a heretic to the bringer of truth. In his »Geschichte und Existenz des Gottesvolkes des Alten Bundes als Aufgabe religiöser Unterweisung«, *Freiburger Rundbrief,* vol. 13 (1960—61), pp. 12—18, Karl Thieme calls Barabbas »eine Antichristgestalt, wie sie im Buche steht« — to which one might make the retort: Yes, but in which book?

[8] »Die Erzählung scheint irgend ein Factum zum Anlass gehabt zu haben: die Person des Barabbas ist zu concret, als dass man sie für völlig aus der Luft gegriffen halten dürfte«, Wilhelm Brandt, *Die Evangelische Geschichte und der Ursprung des Christenthums* (Leipzig 1893), p. 102. »The statements about Barabbas seem very precise, and suggest that some historical reminiscence is at the bottom of the tale«, Claude Goldsmid Montefiore, *The Synoptic Gospels* (London 1909), p. 363.

[9] »Ein solcher Fall, *auch wenn er erst viel später sich ereignete* (italics supplied), rief in der christlichen Gemeinde die Reflexion hervor: der Sohn des Rabbân wird freigegeben..., auch wenn er ein Mörder ist, unseren Jesus aber haben sie in den Tod getrieben«, Wilhelm Brandt, *o. c.,* p. 105; *cf.* Johannes Weiss, *Das älteste Evangelium,* (Göttingen 1903), p. 327.
»...the story of Barabbas is a fragment of a tradition which was originally independent of the story of Jesus«, Maurice Goguel, *La vie de Jésus* (Paris 1932), p. 503; Engl. translation *The Life of Jesus* (London 1933), p. 516.
»That at the feast of the Passover the Roman procurators regularly released one prisoner, and that the crowds named the individual no matter what his offence had been, is... contrary to what we know of the spirit and manner of the Roman rule over Palestine... The Barabbas story is certainly not sheer invention... It seems... that a story of how the populace saved by its entreaties a prisoner named Jesus Barabbas was well known... [and that the] fact invited Christian midrashic developments. The Barabbas story has coalesced in Christian tradition with the story of the trial of Jesus«, Bennett Harvie Branscomb, *The Gospel of Mark* (London 1937), pp. 288—290.

[10] »Die Darstellung des Marcus... [kann] auf Geschichtlichkeit keinen Anspruch machen,,, Die Voraussetzung, mit der die ganze Geschichte steht und fällt, ist... unhaltbar. Ein römischer Verwalter, ein Procurator [der]... sich erbietet, einen von denen, die im Gewahrsam ihres Urtheils oder schon der Execution harren, freizulassen und die Wahl des Individuums dem Volke selber — einem lärmenden Haufen

There are several questions we must ask. The first is whether Barabbas was an historical person or not. If this is answered in the affirmative, we have then to enquire how Barabbas came to be held in prison at the time of Jesus' trial. Thirdly, we should ask how far the legal proceedings against Barabbas had progressed before he was released. Only a tentative answer is possible to each of these questions.

From Philo we learn that during a visit at the Passover season by Agrippa I to Alexandria the mob of that city dressed up a lout as a king, mockingly paid homage to him, and in the end beat him up. The actor in this Alexandrian mummery was called Καραβᾶς[11]. Loisy, drawing attention to Philo's report[12], suggested that Καραβᾶς or Βαραββᾶς may not have been the name of a real person, but the title of a rôle in a masquerading prank. In Loisy's view, Pilate "delivered Jesus instead of (= as) Barabbas" to his soldiers to have their rough play with him (Mc 15, 16—20) before they flogged him and took him to the place of execution. Had there not been a prisoner at hand whose crucifixion was impending, the soldiers would have selected somebody else for the rôle of "Barabbas"[13]. Thus it was the extreme improbability of the episode, as it is recorded in the Gospels, coupled with the similarity of the names "Barabbas" and "Karabas", that induced Loisy to deny the existence of such a person and explain the name as due to a rôle in a piece of theatre. But it is unlikely that Loisy's explanation is correct. Some foundation in fact does seem to lie behind the story, and it is arguable that Barabbas was an historical person.

Yet who was he? And how did he come to be cast into prison? The evangelists are remarkably reticent about his antecedents.

"Barabbas" is, of course, not the complete name but just a patronym. Our suspicion that Barabbas was historical is chiefly based on the readings in certain Gospel Codices (such as the Sinaitic Syriac, the Harclean Syriac, the Armenian Version, Codex Koridethi with most of the minuscles belonging to the Lake group such as 1, 118, 131, 209, 872 — but *not* 205, 1192, 1210 — further the minuscles 22, 241, 299, 1582, 2193 and 2992) which render the complete name in the form Ἰησοῦς Βαραββᾶς or Ἰησοῦς Βαῤῥαββᾶς. If the spelling with one ϱ is

---

oder einer geordneten Vertretung gleichviel — anheimgiebt: solch ein römischer Statthalter ist einfach eine Unmöglichkeit. Die Vorstellung aber, dass Pilatus gewohnt gewesen sei, dies alljährlich in der Hauptstadt zu tun, und sogar zur Festzeit, wenn ... Unruhen in der Stadt zu gewärtigen waren, ist ... vollendete[r] Widersinn«, Wilhelm Brandt, *o. c.*, pp. 98—99.

»Die Barabbasepisode mit ihrer novellistischen Erzählungsart ... ist ... für unhistorisch erklärt worden«, Erich Klostermann, *Das Markusevangelium* (Tübingen ⁴1950), p. 159.

[11] In Flaccum 36—38.
[12] *L'évangile selon Marc* (Paris 1912), p. 454.
[13] *O. c.*, pp. 454—455.

preferred, the complete name would be "Jesus, son of Abba"; if ϱϱ is read, it would be "Jesus, the son of the teacher" (*or* "of our teacher"). The scribe of Codex Koridethi (Θ or 038) evidently wished to point out that the proper spelling was BAP PABBAN. Not only did he distinctly write two letters ϱ, but he left some space between βάϱ and the following ϱαββᾶν. The number of manuscripts with ᾽Ιησοῦς written before the patronym "Barabbas" or "Barrabban" may have been greater in ancient times than it is to-day. In the third century this reading, no longer common, is nevertheless attested by Origen: *in multis exemplaribus non continetur quod Barabbas etiam Iesus dicebatur, et forsitan recte, ut ne nomen Iesu conveniat alicui iniquorum. In tanta enim multitudine scripturarum neminem scimus Iesum peccatorem, sicut in aliis nominibus invenimus iustorum, ut eiusdem nominis inveniantur esse etiam iniqui*[14]. As late as in the tenth century old codices with the text of the First Gospel were circulating in which the name was written ᾽Ιησοῦς ὁ Βαραββᾶς, as a scholion to Codex Vaticanus Graecus 354 (S or 028) confirms. None of the manuscripts which the author of this annotation could have seen exists to-day. The scholion reads: παλαιοῖς... ἀντιγράφοις ἐντυχὼν εὗρον καὶ αὐτὸν τὸν Βαραββᾶν ᾽Ιησοῦν λεγόμενον. οὕτως γοῦν εἶχεν ἡ τοῦ Πιλάτου πεῦσις ἐκεῖ· »τίνα θέλετε τῶν δύο ἀπολύσω ὑμῖν, ᾽Ιησοῦν τὸν Βαραββᾶν ἢ ᾽Ιησοῦν τὸν λεγόμενον Χριστόν«.

All traces we can find of the *complete name* "Jesus bar (R)Abba(n)" occur with reference to the text of the First Gospel. We have no such traces in Marcan texts. There is a gap in our evidence which we cannot hope to bridge. As the First Evangelist copied his Trial Narrative from Mark, he must have found in his copy of the Second Gospel something more, or something else, than we possess in Mc 15, 6—15[15]. It may be

---

[14] Origenes, In Matthaeum CXXII (GCS Origenes XI, 2, pp. 255—256; MPG 13, col. 1772).

[15] »Das ᾽Ιησοῦν wäre kaum später zugesetzt worden..., ist also echt... Man kann nur zweifeln, ob nicht auch Mc [15] 7 ἦν δὲ (᾽Ιησοῦς) ὁ λεγόμενος Βαραββᾶς das Älteste ist«, Erich Klostermann, *Die Evangelien (Handbuch zum Neuen Testament,* Tübingen 1919), p. 345. »The phrase ›the person called Barabbas‹ suggests that Mk knew that Barabbas was not his primary name: it may be that he knew that the full name was *Jesus* Barabbas«, A. E. J. Rawlinson, *St. Mark* (London 1925), p. 228. »It is altogether unthinkable that the addition *Jesus* should have been subsequently made to a text which only had *Barabbas*«, Adolf Deissmann, »The Name ›Jesus‹«, in *Mysterium Christi. Christological Studies by British and German Theologians* (London 1930), pp. 3—27, on p. 20; »If the original text of Matthew had *Jesus Barabbas,* then the double name was used also in Mark« (*ibidem,* p. 22). »Jesus Barabbas was probably the form of the name in Mark's text also«, B. H. Branscomb, *o. c.,* p. 289. »It is probable that Mark originally had ᾽Ιησοῦς ὁ λεγόμενος Βαρ(ϱ)αββᾶς, and that ᾽Ιησοῦς was omitted for the sake of reverence«, Charles Ernest Burland Cranfield, *The Gospel according to Saint Mark* (London 1959), p. 450.

that this accounts for the fact that the First Evangelist refrained from connecting Barabbas with any στασιασταί.

Whether the reading should be *bar Rabban* or *bar Abba,* the actual 'first name' is missing except in a minority of codices which supply the name "Jesus". This is the original reading[16]. When Origen affirms his distrust in its correctness because he knew of no sinful man who ever had been named "Jesus", the Church Father not only forgets the high-priest Ἰάσων = Ἰησοῦς, "that ungodly man" (2 Macc 4, 13), and other bearers of the name whom Josephus mentioned in his writings[17], but he provides us with an explanation of the cause why later copyists discarded Ἰησοῦν before Βαραββᾶν. They considered it offensive that any-one as detestable as Barabbas should have borne the same name as the Son of God. While it can be understood why the name might have been omitted, it is impossible to account for its appearance by arbitrary in-sertion in certain manuscripts. It is, in fact, the few manuscripts which contain the complete name Ἰησοῦς Βαρ(ρ)αββᾶ(ν) that furnish t h e s t r o n g e s t   e v i d e n c e   f o r   B a r a b b a s ' s   h i s t o r i c a l   e x i-s t e n c e.

We are nowhere told who Barabbas was. From Mc 15, 7 we learn that he was "bound with the revolutionaries (or "rioters"), men who

---

[16] Tischendorf explained the occurrence of the name Ἰησοῦν before Βαραββᾶν as due to a scribal error; a copyist — so Tischendorf thought — wrote in Mt 27, 17 by mistake YMININ instead of YMIN, and the last two letters were understood to be an abbreviation (IN) for IHΣOYN. But this would not account of the occur-rence of the name Ἰησοῦς in Mt 27, 16. Further, Tischendorf's explanation was given before the discovery of the Sinaitic palimpsest of the Old Syriac Version of the Gospels in which the name »Jesus« is also to be found before »Barrabban«. An inner-Greek corruption is therefore most unlikely.

»Il est difficile d'expliquer l'insertion, tandis que la suppression aurait été in-spirée par la piété«, Marie-Joseph Lagrange, *Évangile selon Saint Matthieu* (Paris 1923), p. 520. ». . . die Namensform ›Jesus Barabbas‹... ist so auffallend, dass sie sowohl ursprünglicher Matthäus-Text als auch echte historische Überlieferung sein muss«, Nils Alstrup Dahl, »Die Passionsgeschichte bei Matthäus«, *NTS* vol. 2, 1955, pp. 17—32, on p. 23.

[17] We find in these writings a fair number of persons whose name was Jesus, and among them several whose conduct does not appear to have been guided by the highest of motives. In Ant XI 298—299a we read of one Jesus, the son of Jodas, who attempted to oust his brother from the office of high-priest; in Vita 66, 105, 108 we read of a Jesus, the son of Sapphia, who was the leader of nautical brigands; there was a Galilaean Jesus in command of revolutionaries in Jerusalem, who is mentioned in Vita 200, 246, possibly identical with the person referred to in B. J. III 450, 457; a priest Jesus, son of Sapphia, is mentioned in B. J. II 566 as commander of Jewish forces who dislodged the Romans from Idumaea in the early stage of the revolt of the year 66 CE; another chief priest Jesus, son of Tebuthi, is reported in B. J. VI 387—391 to have handed over to the Romans the sacred priestly vestments and some of the Temple treasures so as to save his own skin.

had committed murder in the insurrection". The Second Evangelist does n o t state that Barabbas himself had taken part in "the insurrection", nor that he had been imprisoned because he himself had committed murder[18]. The phrase μετὰ τῶν στασιαστῶν δεδεμένος lacks precision. It may imply that Barabbas happened by chance to be held in jail with a number of prisoners who had been arrested on account of a riot in which somebody had been killed, without actually belonging to their company. Or it may imply that Barabbas was one of these rebels. It would certainly provide us with a plausible explanation for Barabbas's release if we could be sure that the first of these two possibilities is the correct one. The successors of the Second Evangelist as well as mediaeval copyists of his Gospel noted the lack of precision. Numerous copyists altered στασιασταί to συστασιασταί, making Barabbas a partner in their crime. The lack of clarity in the original could be due merely to carelessness in expression; if so, the Second Evangelist included Barabbas among the rebels. We have no assurance of this. Did the Evangelist wish to say that Barabbas was accidentally held in the same place of detention as οἱ στασιασταί were, or did he refer to Barabbas as one who belonged to their number? There remains the distinct possibility that the phrase "bound with the insurgents, those who had committed a murder in the insurrection" i m p l i e s  n o  m o r e  t h a n  i t  e x - p r e s s e s : Barabbas was in prison along with certain persons who had been charged with insurrection and murder. The words give no indication that Barabbas himself had taken part in such seditious activity. It should be noted that the Evangelist uses the definite article twice; he speaks of ἡ στάσις and of οἱ στασιασταί. If then it was his intention to assert that Barabbas was included among the rioters, or revolutionaries, who had committed an act of murder, the natural way of doing so would have been by using the expression εἷς ἐκ τῶν στασιαστῶν. To say the least, Mark is indefinite about the point — and as Mark is the only Gospel capable of clarifying the issue, we are unable to come to an unequivocal conclusion.

The authors of later Gospels had no access to independent information[19]. In Mt 27, 16 Barabbas is called a δέσμιος ἐπίσημος, a notable prisoner[20]. Not a single word as to why Barabbas was held in prison. The Third Gospel states that Barabbas was cast into jail for his participa-

---

[18] Johannes Weiss thought that Mc 15, 7 with its unmotivated introduction of *the* insurgents who had committed a murder in *the* insurrection, might have been added by an editor to the primary account *(o. c.,* p. 383), and remarked: »[Der Markusevangelist] begnügt sich mit dem dünnen Faden eines unanschaulichen Berichtes, dem er nur etliche Unglaublichkeiten hinzufügt« *(o. c.,* p. 384).

[19] »... sämtliche Redactionen führen auf den Marcustext zurück. Nur aus e i n e r Quelle sind sie geflossen«, Wilhelm Brandt, *o. c.,* p. 101.

[20] More ›notable‹ is perhaps the unexpected plural εἶχον in Mt 26, 16 = *they had*. Whose prisoner was Barabbas?

tion in "some" insurrection and for a murder he had committed (Lc 23, 19) — but the Evangelist merely rephrases Mc 15, 7 in an endeavour to give a precise formulation in place of the ambiguous Marcan wording. His rephrasing, like the substitution of συστασιασταί by mediaeval copyists for στασιασταί, is made without his being in possession of additional evidence, and does not therefore allow of historical deductions[21]. In John, finally, Barabbas is abruptly called a λῃστής, a revolutionary (Jn 18, 40 b).

The Gospels supply no trustworthy information concerning the cause of Barabbas's imprisonment, and none of its duration. The nearest we can get to the facts — and that only by pressing the meaning of the words μετὰ τῶν στασιαστῶν in Mc 15, 7 — is that Barabbas was suspected of participation in a revolutionary act in which murder had been committed.

Equally unhelpful are the Gospel accounts in respect of the problem whether Barabbas was in detention awaiting trial, or whether his case had already been heard. If Barabbas was suspected of having committed a crime for which he had not yet been sentenced, the governor had no right to stop the proceedings. If he had been sentenced for a crime, his release without reference to the Emperor in Rome would have been even more incredible[22].

---

Josef Pickl, *Messiaskönig Jesus in der Auffassung seiner Zeitgenossen* (Munich ²1935) maintained that ἐπίσημος meant ›leader‹; λῃστὴς ἐπίσημος would imply ›ringleader‹, and δέσμιος ἐπίσημος would denote ›captive rebel leader‹ (Engl. translation *The Messias,* St. Louis and London 1946, p. 96). This explanation is without substance.

[21] The Arabic Diatessaron 50, 25, reproducing Lc 23, 19, speaks of »the« insurrection, as Mc 15, 7; this may be an inner-Arabic textual modification. The uncertain στάσις τις appears to be the Third Evangelist's own formulation when he looked in vain for elucidation in Mark as to the event to which ἡ στάσις referred. Whilst Mark is definite about the στάσις and indefinite about Barabbas' part in it, Luke tries to be definite about Barabbas yet leaves the στάσις undefined.

[22] The right to stop judicial proceedings before sentence (*abolitio*) was reserved to the Emperor; the right of appeal to a higher court when the judgment was unfavourable (*appellatio*) was open (at a later period) to Roman litigants; the right to revoke the findings of a lower court in a criminal case belonged in Republican times to the *populus,* later to the Senate, and was after the establishment of the principate assumed by the emperors (who decided upon *provocatio ad imperatorem*). Provincial magistrates were not free to reverse their decisions without reference to higher authority.

*Ad bestias damnatos favore populi praeses dimittere non debet, sed ... principem consulere debet,* Digesta XLVIII xix 31 (Modestinus; third century CE).

»L'épisode de Barabbas fait pendant au jugement par Caïphe; il s'intercale dans la relation du procès devant Pilate pour faire entendre, contrairement à la vérité, que le procurateur n'a pas condamné Jésus, mais qu'il l'a laissé mettre à mort, se conformant à la sentence du sanhédrin, après avoir essayé vainement de le soustraire à ses ennemies par voie de grâce«, A. Loisy, *L'évangile selon Marc,* p. 445; »... ce

The difficulty is as follows: the evangelists fail to give information about Barabbas's origin and personal status; their account of the reason for his arrest is ambiguous — Lc 23, 19 is spun out of Mc 15, 7, and Jn 18, 40 b is secondary — and they tell us nothing of the state of the proceedings, if any, which had been taken in the case. Reticent regarding issues of this kind, the writers of the Gospels have much to tell of the crowd's clamour for Barabbas's release; their descriptions, however, by no means tally with one other. The Second Gospel reports that the crowd spontaneously asked Pilate "to do as he was wont to do" — that is, release a prisoner. When Pilate suggests releasing Jesus, the King of the Jews, the crowd, stirred up by the priests, chooses Barabbas instead (Mc 15, 8—11). According to the First Evangelist, Pilate, without the crowd's prompting, offers to release either "Jesus who is called Christ or Jesus the son of (R)Abba(n)" and, again under the influence of the priests, the crowd demands that Barabbas be set free (Mt 27, 17—20). In Luke the incident occurs at a later stage; without reference to any custom, or habit, Pilate offers to liberate Jesus, but the crowd rejects his offer and requests — without priestly intrigues this time — that he should free Barabbas rather than Jesus (Lc 23, 13—16, 18)[23]. In the Fourth Gospel, the Jews who have so far been well-behaved and have not demanded anything of Pilate are reminded by the governor of their custom; when Pilate asks them whether they wish that he should free Jesus, they "again" cry out: "not this one, but Barabbas!" (Jn 18, 39—40). Here we can see that the Barabbas episode was originally alien to the Fourth Gospel. The Jews cry again, but there is no mention of any previous cry. The πάλιν in Jn 18, 40 is copied from Mc 15, 13. A reviser of the Fourth Gospel inserted the Barabbas incident into the Johannine story, making cursory and injudicious borrowings.

From these confused and conflicting statements it is impossible to gain information about actual events or to make historical deductions. The apologetic aim of the narratives stands out in every detail. The

---

que dit Marc a bien plutôt l'apparence d'une légende populaire que d'une coutume véritable« (p. 446); »[L'Évangéliste] veut faire entendre que Pilate a été constraint par les Juifs ... de laisser exécuter l'arrêt de mort qu' avait rendu le sanhédrin. Perspective essentiellement fausse, puisque Jésus a été exécuté par des soldats romains, en vertu d'une sentence édictée par Pilate, après examen de la cause par le même. De quelque manière qu'on explique la fiction, l'histoire de Barabbas est inconsistante comme fait« (p. 450).

[23] Jesus' opponents are in Lc 23, 13 named as »the chief priests and the rulers and the people«. It is possible that this reading is due to a copyist's slip who wrote τοὺς ἄρχοντας καὶ τὸν λαόν instead of τοὺς ἄρχοντας τοῦ λαοῦ. The subject intended in v. 18 (»they cried out all together«) appears to be identical with the persons indicated in v. 13. As the Third Evangelist elsewhere blames the ἀρχιερεῖς and the ἄρχοντες for Jesus' execution, but refrains from blaming the people as a whole (cf. Lc 23, 27, 48), the suggested emendation in Lc 23, 13 is not without warrant.

evangelists make it their concern to demonstrate that the decision to sentence Jesus was entirely due to the ill-will of the Jews, not to the governor's judgment. They tell their readers little of Barabbas, but much about the shouting Jews. Strangely, in spite of the efforts displayed by the authors, the stories fail to carry conviction. Pilate had, of course, no authority whatever to grant pardon to a condemned prisoner or stop proceedings against an accused one. But if a custom, such as is hinted at, did exist, and the crowd's choice fell on Barabbas, nothing could have prevented the governor, if he had wished to do so, from releasing Jesus in addition to Barabbas. This would have been an easy thing for him to do if he had pronounced Jesus not guilty. Custom or no custom, the sentencing of Jesus did not depend on the acquittal of Barabbas. The writers of the Gospels are anxious to show that Pilate's good efforts were in vain. Thoughtful readers must come to the conclusion that all the efforts of the evangelists were no less futile.

Whatever differences there are in the Gospel narratives in relation to Barabbas, the evangelists agree that the crowd exerted pressure on Pilate insisting that he should sentence Jesus to crucifixion[24]. In Mc 15, 13 the multitude cries out σταύρωσον αὐτόν, and in v. 14 loudly addresses the same demand to Pilate. In Mt 27, 22 the cry is σταυρωθήτω — as if Pilate were not there at all, and the crowd itself pronounced a verdict.

The Barabbas episode remains an enigma. The tendency in reporting the episode is clear[25]; the facts are far from clear. The following is put forward tentatively in an attempt to explain what *might* have taken place; it cannot be claimed to represent established facts.

There were two persons named Jesus who were at the same time Pilate's captives: Jesus of Nazareth and Jesus the son of (R)Abba(n). Pilate had ordered the arrest of one of them[26] — Jesus the son of Joseph. This Jesus was apprehended by a detachment of Roman soldiers, the Temple Police assisting, on the Mount of Olives. He was thereupon conducted for interrogation to the high-priest (Jn 18, 12—13 a) who had been instructed to have an indictment prepared for a morning session in the prefect's court. The other Jesus, the son of (R)Abba(n), may have been arrested at approximately the same time, and immediately taken into Roman custody. When the first Jesus — Jesus of Nazareth — was brought before him from the Assembly Hall of the Sanhedrin, Pilate

---

[24] »La captivité [de Jésus] pouvait nuire à son crédit, mais non ameuter le peuple contre lui. Que la population ait subitement passé de l'admiration à la haine, et qu'... elle ait demandé avec rage que [Jésus] fût crucifié... c'est [un] trait qui [convient] mieux à la fiction légendaire qu'à l'histoire, et qui ressemblerait plutôt à un effet de théâtre, dans un mélodrame ou une pièce enfantine, qu'à une scène de la vie réelle«, Loisy, *o. c.,* p. 448.

[25] »Die Barabbasepisode dient dazu, die Römer zu entschuldigen und die Juden zu belasten«, Erich Klostermann, *Das Markusevangelium,* p. 159.

[26] See above, p. 65.

might have been unaware of the identity of the two prisoners now in Roman custody, both of whom were called Jesus. The governor's know-ledge of the inner workings of Jewish affairs could not have been pro-found and his circle of acquaintances would not generally have included men of Jesus' status. If informed that two men, both with the name of 'Jesus', had been arrested instead of one, he would have been uncertain of the identity of the person he wished to prosecute. Hence he could have put the question "Which one of the two?" to people outside his palace or to the escorts who had brought one prisoner to him. The dramatic scene in the Gospels describing the mob's clamour for the release of Barabbas and the crucifixion of Jesus of Nazareth may thus in historical fact have amounted to nothing more than a declaration concerning the identity of the two arested Jesuses. From such a decla-ration Pilate would have learned that Yeshu bar (R)Abba(n) was not the person whose arrest had been decreed. He therefore set him free, and proceeded with the trial of Jesus "the King of the Jews".

It cannot be asserted that such a view represents anything more than a conjecture. The jumbled accounts in the Gospels of the Barabbas epi-sode, taken in conjunction with the complete absence of any corrobo-rative evidence of a custom making it obligatory on the governor to free a prisoner, may justify certain surmises, but preclude anything in the nature of firm historical deductions.

Yeshu bar (R)Abba(n) seems to have been a person who actually lived, and who was detained in a Roman prison in Jerusalem at the time when Jesus was brought before Pilate. Who precisely he was, what led to his arrest, what he did after his release — we cannot say[27].

---

[27] Quite unacceptable are the theories of writers who argue that Barabbas was an insurrectionist leader and had spent six to twelve months in prison, awaiting exe-cution, before he was set free on the day of Jesus' trial. Ethelbert Stauffer places the hypothetical revolt under Barabbas a full year before Jesus' arrest; Josef Pickl made out that it occurred at the Feast of Tabernacles, six months before the trial of Jesus. But had Barabbas been arrested and found guilty of a revolutionary act, he would have been executed forthwith. For a development of this conjecture, see H. Z. Maccoby, »Jesus and Barabbas«, NTS vol. 16 (1969—70), pp. 55—60.

# 11. THE MOCKERY

In our examination of the Marcan pericope about the Sanhedrin's nocturnal session in the high-priest's palace, immediately after the arrest of Jesus, we arrived at the conclusion that Mc 14, 53 b, 55—64 is an elaboration which the Second Evangelist introduced into the Passion Narrative without relying on traditional support. One of the considerations that led to this conclusion was the difference of the Lucan and Marcan renderings, and the impossibility of accounting for the Lucan version in any other way than by postulating the existence of a pre-Marcan record which the Third Evangelist knew and followed. Significant in this respect was the divergence of the Lucan rendering of the scene in which Jesus is mocked from the Marcan presentation: in Luke he is derided by the ἄνδρες οἱ συνέχοντες αὐτόν — the police picket guarding Jesus — whereas in Mark it is members of the Supreme Court who indulge in this sort of horse-play. The Third Gospel does not mention a nocturnal session, yet Lc 22, 63—65 presents a scene of brutal ridicule during the night-hours as does Mc 14, 65 (Mt 26, 67—68). It follows therefore that Mc 14, 65 is not a free creation of the Second Evangelist but was based on some tradition at his disposal, however much he may have adapted the motif to his own story of the nocturnal session. Thus the assignment of the theme of Jesus' mockery to its present position in Mc 14, 65 and Lc 22, 63—65 is not the work of an individual writer, the scene having already had this timing in an earlier tradition[1].

Mc 14, 65 and Lc 22, 63—65, respectively, are not the only descriptions of the maltreatment, or mockery, to which Jesus was subjected after his arrest; Lc 23, 11 mentions a mockery at the hands of Herod Antipas and his entourage; in Jn 19, 2—3 the scene is placed in the praetorium before Pilate's final sentence; in Mc 15, 16—20 and Mt 27, 27—31 it comes after Pilate has pronounced sentence. Thus no fewer

---

[1] There are differences of detail; in Luke, Jesus is maltreated *before*, in John *during*, and in Mark after his examination by the high-priest. These differences are due to the varied use which the evangelists have made of a traditional motif. The description in Luke is the least improbable. *Cf.* Willem Cornelis van Unnik, »Jesu Verhöhnung vor dem Synderium (Mc 14, 65 par.)«, ZNW vol. 29, 1930, pp. 310—311. »... die Leute, die Jesus verhafteten, müssen die Zeit mit ihm verbringen ehe er vor das Synedrium geführt werden kann« (p. 311); »[bei Mk] an besonders unglücklicher Stelle einrangiert« Rudolf Bultmann, *Geschichte der synoptischen Tradition*, p. 293; English edition, p. 271.

than five descriptions of a scene containing basically the same motif
are to be found in the Gospels, namely, a maltreatment and mockery
of Jesus in the course of the events preceding his crucifixion, though
placed by the evangelists at different stages of the proceedings. It is
inherently unlikely that the same scene was enacted five times with only
slight differences, by the police, by members of the High Court, by
Herod and his soldiers, and finally by the Roman legionaries before, as
well as after, the governor had passed sentence. The oldest report
manifestly recorded one instance of Jesus' mockery. In the handing down
of the tradition, the description of this incident was shifted to various
places and thereby became attached to different situations. The same
sort of thing occurred in the transmission of the trial account proper;
being circulated by several intermediaries, none of whom had any first-
hand evidence of the facts concerning the judicial proceedings or of the
infliction of maltreatment upon Jesus, the motif of the mockery suffered
displacement from its original context, was multiplied in precisely the
same manner as the trial account itself, and became embedded in diverse traditions. Eventually, the motif reached the authors of the
Gospels in a variety of forms. Desirous of recording the Passion in as
detailed a manner as possible, the evangelists retained the motif in
whatever context those responsible for handing tradition down had
placed it. The scene of which we now have five differing versions had
a basis in historical fact. The oldest narrative concerning the trial of
Jesus gave the scene once only.

It is our concern to establish the original setting of Jesus' mockery.
In order to do this, we have to distinguish in the first place between
editorial modification and underlying tradition, in the second place between the primary and the secondary traditions that resulted in a multiplication of the motif.

In Lc 22, 63—65 / Mc 14, 65 (Mt 26, 67—68) and Jn 18, 22 we have
an event alleged to have taken place *before* Jesus had been handed over
to Pilate; Lc 23, 11, Jn 19, 2—3 and Mc 15, 16—20 (Mt 27, 27—31)
depict one occurring *after* the prisoner's appearance before the governor. This difference may be used to guide us in our analysis, dividing
the discussion into two main stages.

The report of the mockery in Jn 19, 2—3 — the latest to be written
— is a mere modification of that contained in Mc 15, 16—20. The only
difference consists in the timing of the scene. In the Fourth Gospel the
mockery precedes Pilate's final pronouncement of the fate of Jesus,
whilst in the Second it results from the prefect's verdict. The transposition in John to an earlier stage is scarcely based on any independent tradition; it can be accounted for by the Evangelist's aim to make
Pilate appear to have exhausted all means of satisfying the vindictiveness of the Jews; the governor orders Jesus to be scourged (19, 1)
and allows his soldiery to have their rough game with the accused man
(19, 2—3) in the vain hope of placating thereby the insatiable fury

of the Jews and of saving Jesus from suffering a worse fate[2]. The only
argument which might be adduced in support of the contention that the
Fourth Evangelist followed in his rendering some fairly late tradition
could be derived from the circumstance that John reports as a fact what
Luke presents as a suggestion. In the Third Gospel (Lc 23, 16—22) Pilate offers to have Jesus scourged, and then to set him free. The version
of the Third Evangelist is obviously editorial. The repetition of the offer
is an indication of the fact that the writer wished to drive home his
point; it betrays the Evangelist's eagerness to convince the reader that
the governor was anxious to avoid a death sentence. The Lucan version
of this incident is not based on tradition. Without entering into the
question whether a relation exists between Lc 23, 16, 22 and Jn 19,
1—5, it suffices to state that neither of them is more primitive than
Mc 15, 16—20. Both are merely editorial reconstructions of the tradition which has been better preserved in the Second Gospel.

Less direct is the connection between the Marcan account and Lc 23,
11. The scene which is described in the latter passage bears a certain
resemblance to that known from Mc 15, 17a–18, yet the place of Pilate's legionaries is taken by members of Herod's retinue; the robe in
which Jesus is clad is "splendid" (or white? λαμπρά)[3]; omitted are the
mock-crowning and the mock-homage and the divestment of the prisoner (Mc 15, 17b—20a) after the soldiers had finished with their theatrical raillery. An assessment of the character of the Lucan account will
be conditioned by one's views on the derivation of the Herod episode
in Lc 23, 6—7, 8—12. If the whole section is considered to be an invention of the Third Evangelist, such an appraisement would include the
account of the mockery. On the other hand, if it is correct that Lc 23,
6—7 presents the Evangelist's connecting link between Mc 15, 2 (= Lc

---

[2] See Paul Wendland, »Jesus als Saturnalien-König«, *Hermes* vol. 33, 1898,
pp. 175—179. »Der Rettungsversuch des Pilatus, den Joh 19, 7—12 auf die Geise-
lung und Verspottung folgen lässt, ist... historisch unmöglich und auch innerlich
unwahrscheinlich, weil Pilatus damit die Ungerechtigkeit seines Urtheilspruches offen
dokumentiert hätte« (p. 178). There is a strong verbal resemblance between Jn 19,
2a and Mt 27, 29 aα which is the more striking as coincidences of phraseology are
generally rare in the First and Fourth Gospels. The transposition of the account of
Jesus' mockery by Roman soldiers to the place which it now occupies in John could
possibly be due to a 'reviser' who knew the First Gospel and modelled his report
on the wording, if not the setting, of the description found in Matthew.

The attempt by the later evangelists to detach the description of the scourging
from the governor's pronouncement of the sentence is clearly due to apologetic
motives; scourging was an essential part of inflicting the penalty of crucifixion —
see Livy, Historiae XXXIII xxxvi 3; Josephus, B. J. II 306.

[3] There is a faint resemblance in the description of the splendid robe, in which
Jesus, according to the Third Gospel, was dressed when he stood before Herod An-
tipas, and that of the robe worn by Herod Agrippa shortly before his death (Ant
XIX 344).

23, 3) — Lc 23, 2 being perhaps an elaboration of Mc 15, 3 — and some tradition which reported a trial of Jesus before Herod Antipas[4] it would be reasonable to hold that the description of the mockery in Lc 23, 11 comes from a tradition, though a secondary one, which had been shaped before the Third Evangelist collected his materials[5]. In this case, tradition would already have shifted the mockery from the place it occupies in Mc 15, 16—20 to an earlier stage in the proceedings. The ultimate source from which such a tradition had developed, would be the same as that of Mc 15, 16—20[6]. Accordingly Lc 23, 11 has no more any valid claim than has Jn 19, 2—3 to be regarded as antedating the tradition which is embodied in Mc 15. We now must turn our attention to the latter.

It has frequently been noticed that the soldiers, in assembling the whole garrison (Mc 15, 16 b) and proceeding with their burlesque (Mc 15, 17—20 a), act as if they were somehow following a predetermined plan; they do not require any bidding from superiors or outsiders, but strike spontaneously as if rehearsing well-known lines from a conventional play. In particular it has been observed[7] that the buf-

---

[4] The statement that the tradition underlying Lc 23, 8—11 had come into existence by the time when the Third Gospel was composed, requires qualification. It is correct only on the assumption that the Herod episode in Lc 23, 6—12 formed part of the Third Gospel from the start. But the episode is of doubtful origin. Although it is apparently based on some sort of a tradition, we cannot say with any assurance whether the story was introduced into the Third Gospel by the Evangelist himself or by a post-Lucan editor of the Gospel. There are traces of quite a number of post-evangelical adjustments in the Trial Narrative of the Third Gospel. There is a hiatus between Lc 23, 3 and 23, 4; also, Lc 22, 67—71 and 23; 4—25 show signs of having been retouched by a later hand than that of the Third Evangelist. However, the wording of Acts 4, 27 presupposes the existence of the same tradition as that incorporated in Lc 23, 8—12. Cf. below, p. 191, note 1.

[5] In the Gospel of Peter, vv. 6—9, Jesus is mocked by the multitude of the people after Herod has passed sentence.

[6] A different view has been expressed by Richard Delbrueck in »Antiquarisches zu den Verspottungen Jesu«, ZNW vol. 41, 1942, pp. 124—145, who thinks that Lc 23, 11 cannot have evolved from the tradition recorded in Mc 15, 16—20.

[7] Hugo Grotius, *Annotationes in libros evangeliorum* (Amsterdam 1641), *ad Matthaeum 27 29*, seems to have been the first to have noticed the similarity. For more modern literature, see Wendland as above; further, Hermann Reich, »Der König mit der Dornenkrone«, *Neue Jahrbücher für das klassische Altertum, Geschichte und Deutsche Literatur*, vol. 7, 1904, pp. 705—773: »Man sieht die biblische Verspottungsszene und diese alexandrinische Spott- und Mimusszene sind identisch« (p. 728); »Oft genug haben die römischen Soldaten, denen Christus als Judenkönig übergeben wird, den Juden im Mimus verspotten sehen und über die Figur des burlesken Königs im Mimus gelacht. Gerade im Orient blühte... der Mimus« (p. 730). Cf. H. Vollmer, »Der König mit der Dornenkrone«, ZNW vol. 6, 1905, pp. 194—198.

Wendland assumed a connection with the Saturnalia: »Wenn die römischen Legionäre Christus zu einem Saturnalien-Könige ausstaffierten, so lag ihnen jeden-

foonery in which Pilate's soldiery engage for their diversion has a parallel in a sequence of theatrical street-performances enacted by the Alexandrian mob that ridiculed Agrippa I when he visited their town in 38 CE. Philo's *In Flaccum* preserves a fairly detailed account of the manner in which the mob of Alexandria took pleasure in making fun of the king of the Jews, Agrippa. On the occasion of his visit, the rabble collected and proceeded to enact a sort of mime: they dressed a well-known street-lout named Καραβᾶς, decked him out in royal style, putting a papyrus shrub on his head as if it were a diadem, hanging a doormat around his shoulders in place of the χλάμυς, and placing in his hand a papyrus stick for a sceptre. Thus adorned like a carnival-king, Karabas was led by the mob through the streets of the city receiving mock-homages from the merry-making crowds. The Alexandrians' intention was to hold Agrippa up as an object of ridicule. Philo, describing their behaviour, makes explicit mention of the fact that they imitated the composers of vulgar farces and pantomimes: πῇ δὲ καὶ ποιηταῖς μίμων καὶ γελοίων διδασκάλοις χρώμενοι τὴν ἐν τοῖς αἰσχροῖς εὐφυίαν ἐπεδείκνυντο[8] and notes the theatrical fashion of the whole affair: ὡς ἐν θεατρικοῖς μίμοις[9]. Similar accounts of coarse popular plays, *mimicae ineptiae,* are to be found elsewhere in ancient writings. The jocular amusement could on occasion be more cruel than was the case with Karabas, though even here the frolic developed into a pogrom[10]. We read in Martial's *On the Spectacles* of a performance in the amphitheatre in Rome of a play, in which a convict was actually crucified on the stage and, hanging defenceless on the cross, was torn to pieces by a wild bear. "His mangled limbs lived, though the parts dripped gore, and in all his body was nowhere a body's shape":

> *Qualiter in Scythica religatus rupe Prometheus*
> *Adsiduam nimio pectore pavit avem,*
> *Nuda Caledonio sic viscera praebuit urso*
> *Non falsa pendens in cruce Laureolus.*
> *Vivebant laceri membris stillantibus artus*
> *Inque omni nusquam corpore corpus erat*[11].

With such practices customary in the world of *circenses,* it is not strange that the mockery of Jesus, reported in Mc 15, 16—20, displays

---

falls auch der Gedanke nahe, dass er das Schicksal dieses Königs theilte; denn nach der Maskerade wird er sofort zur Kreuzigung abgeführt« (l. c., p. 178).

[8] In Flaccum 34: they displayed their disgraceful inclination *by employing the composers of farces and producers of puppet shows.*

[9] In Flaccum 38: *like actors in theatrical spectacles.*

[10] In Flaccum 54 b—72.

[11] Marci Valerii Martialis De spectaculis Liber VII. Martial describes an actual event which may have taken place during the reign of Gaius Caligula (37—41 CE). Cf. Suetonius, *Caligula* lvii 4: . . . *in Laureolo mimo . . . cruore scaena abundavit.*

some 'typical' features, adumbrating a dramatic pattern, which would account for the apparent spontaneity of the legionaries actions[12]. The soldiers have their fun in the αὐλή of the πραιτώριον with the "King of the Jews" without any bidding either from Pilate or from the Jewish crowd that is assembled ouside. They are not spurred by anybody. Evidently, they re-enact a popular mimic play or burlesque which they had seen performed by street-actors or players in some other place, and which they now imitate at the expense of the convicted "King", without requiring any prompting, or cue, in their performance. The quite un-motivated behaviour of the soldiers towards the convicted prisoner can be understood as representing the parody of a parody — they are doing of their own accord what they have seen done in vulgar dramatic per-formances they had witnessed. They groom and dress Jesus more or less after the fashion in which the street-rabble of Alexandria dressed up the lout Karabas for their coarse amusement.

In view of the external evidence for the prevalence of popular mimes, features of which to a large extent agree with the details given in Mc 15, 16—20, it is hard to avoid the conclusion that the primary setting of the motif of Jesus' mockery must have been at that point of the pro-ceedings to which Mark assigns it. The soldiers indulged in their dra-matic horse-play with Jesus only after the governor had pronounced sentence. Tradition later multiplied the scene. It may be that the Third Evangelist found the motif already associated by secondary tradition with a report of an appearance of Jesus before Herod Antipas. To avoid what he rightly considered to be a doublet, he omitted the mockery after Pilate's final decision. But he must have known the Marcan ac-count, and he assigns to the mockery by Pilate's soldiers a place in his description of the crucifixion, Lc 23, 36—37.

Having dealt with the descriptions in Lc 23, 11 and Jn 19, 2—3, and having determined their secondary character — the one being based on a derivative offshoot from the primary tradition, the other representing merely an editorial modification of this tradition — we are now left with the description of Jesus' maltreatment *before* he was handed over to Pilate, that is, during his detention in the high-priest's residence. The scene, like that in the αὐλή (Mc 15, 16), takes place within enclosing walls, and, in fact, in surroundings less accessible to the public than the barrack-ground of the legionaries. Eye-witnesses' reports are not to be assumed. The description of what Lc 22, 63—65 and Mc 14, 65 allege to have happened differs considerably from that of Jesus' mock-ery at the hands of the Roman soldiers. It is indeed most likely that a report of some sort of the maltreatment of Jesus during his detention

---

[12] It is perhaps incorrect to refer to the imperial troops stationed in Jerusalem in the year of Jesus' death as 'legionaries'. Most Roman troops serving in Judaea in peace time were auxiliaries, locally recruited from among the pagan population of Palestine. See above, p. 64.

in the high-priest's house formed part of a tradition which was available
to the Third Evangelist and was not identical with the extant text of
Mark. The question is now: How did this item come to be contained in
an account of Jesus' custody *before* his being despatched to Pilate?

As testimony from eye-witnesses of what happened during the nocturnal detention of Jesus in the high-priest's residence is to be dis-
counted[13], the most probable source of the accounts in Mc 14, 65 and
Lc 22, 63—65 will be testimony from scriptural prophecy. Isa 50, 6
possibly provides the clue[14]. The similarity of the vocabulary (ῥαπίσματα,
πρόσωπον, ἐμπτύσματα/ἐμπτύειν) to that of the verse of Isaiah is especially
noticeable in the Greek Text of the Prophets, and this may suggest
that the tradition which underlies Lc 22, 63—65 and Mc 14, 65 originated in a Greek-speaking community. A report of Jesus' mockery and
maltreatment had been handed down from earliest days; in the process
of retelling the story, the report underwent variation and multiplication
at the hands of intermediaries; the motif of the mockery became separated from its original setting, Jesus' condemnation. It came to be attached to the narration of events connected with his arrest. Jesus was
arrested by Roman soldiers (Jn 18, 3, 12). It is Roman soldiers who are
the actors in Mc 15, 16—20. The transposition of the motif of Jesus'
mockery — at some stage in the course of oral tradition — to a place
in the Passion Narrative corresponding to Lc 22, 63—65 may have been
facilitated by the tradition preserved in Jn 18, 12, concerning the identity of the escorts. The description of the incident in Lc 22, 63—65/
Mc 14, 65 is sufficiently different from that of the mockery after Pilate's
sentence to prevent us from supposing that any evangelist would have
derived it directly from Mc 15, 16—20 or from its source. O r a l  t r a -
d i t i o n  i n t e r v e n e d. *The report of the mockery in the high-*

---

[13] »Die ganze Szene ist unwahrscheinlich«, Hans Lietzmann, »Der Prozess Jesu«,
*Sitzungsberichte . . .*, p. 317; also in his *Kleine Schriften* vol. 2, p. 257.

[14] Wilhelm Brandt, *Die Evangelische Geschichte und der Ursprung des Christenthums* (Leipzig 1893): ». . . die Darstellung [folgt] genau dem Text von Jesaja 50, 6«
(p. 70). Alfred Loisy, *L'évangile selon Marc* (Paris 1912): »Le détail du voile jeté sur
le visage du Christ pourrait être en rapport avec le passage d'Isaïe (L, 6)«, (p. 437).
»On est . . . fondé à supposer . . . un dédoublement de la dérision dans le prétoire«
(p. 436). On Mc 15, 16—20 Loisy observed: »[La] scène est parallèle à elle qui . . .
suit le procès devant [le sanhédrin]. Mais la scène du prétoire a plus de traits
originaux, sinon authentiques« (p. 452). ». . . aus dem Propheten Jes 50, 6 . . . her-
ausgelesen«, Martin Dibelius, »Die alttestamentlichen Motive in der Leidensgeschichte
des Petrus- und des Johannes-Evangeliums«, *Abhandlungen zur semitischen Religionskunde und Sprachwissenschaft. Wolfgang Wilhelm Grafen v. Baudissin überreicht* (Giessen 1918), p. 131; also in *Botschaft und Geschichte*, vol. 2, p. 227; *cf.* the
same author's *Formgeschichte des Evangeliums*: ». . . die Misshandlung [ist] aus Jesaja
erschlossen [worden]« (p. 293; *cf.* p. 187). Rudolf Bultmann, *Die Geschichte der
synoptischen Tradition* (Göttingen ²1931): »Auf die Verspottungsszene scheint Jes
50, 6 eingewirkt zu haben« (p. 304; English edition, Oxford ²1968, p. 281).

*priest's house is based on a secondary tradition that had taken shape after that reproduced in Mc 15, 16—20 had been formed.* This secondary tradition placed the mockery in the report of Jesus' detention before his despatch to Pilate.

Earliest tradition, based on historical fact even if not on a report from eye-witnesses, knew of only one mockery whilst our Gospels now report five. The original setting of the scene is after Pilate's judgment, as in Mc 15, 16—20 and Mt 27, 27—31. The actors are the legionaries. Meditation on the Passion of Jesus, and its association with prophecy, caused the details of the scene to be amplified and the versions of the account to be multiplied. The motif became attached to scenes other than that in which the original had placed it; both its locale and its temporal setting were shifted. In this way traditions arose which underlie the narratives of Lc 22, 63—65 and Lc 23, 11, respectively. It is traditional elements that are interwoven in these narratives, though the traditions to which they belonged are secondary. At a still later stage, the Second Evangelist modified the secondary tradition which comes to the fore in Lc 22, 63—65, combining it with his presentation of a night session of the Sanhedrin and thus bringing Mc 14, 65 into existence. Similarly, the Fourth Evangelist modified the account of Mc 15, 16—20 by advancing the mockery to the position it now occupies in Jn 19, 2—3[15].

In the Fourth Gospel, which reveals the most pro-Roman and most anti-Jewish attitude of the four, there is only one description of Jesus' mockery, and that takes place at the hands of Roman soldiers — not at the hands either of the Sanhedrin members, as in Mark and Matthew, or of the Jewish police as in Luke. In the account underlying Jn 18, 12—13a, 19—23, the counterpart of these synoptic descriptions of the maltreatment which Jesus underwent before his despatch to the procurator became stripped of any element of 'proof from prophecy'; the account is here rationalized, and the event (v. 22) presented in condensed form as a third-degree interrogation.

It is possible to substantiate the claim that no more than one account of Jesus' mockery was part of the earliest tradition. Decisive evidence may be adduced from Mc 10, 34: the primary tradition of the Passion reported the actions of "mocking", "spitting" and "scourging" i n c o n j u n c t i o n  w i t h  t h a t  o f  "k i l l i n g", and all these actions were attributed to ἔθνη, *i. e.* pagans (Mc 10, 33[16]). T h e  c o m b i n a - t i o n of the four types of action enumerated in Mc 10, 34 f i t s  n o o t h e r  d e s c r i p t i o n  o f  t h e  m o c k e r y  o f  J e s u s  t h a n t h a t  g i v e n  i n  Mc 15, 16—20 (Mt 27, 27—31). Here then is 'the

---

[15] On the possibility that the Fourth Evangelist or a later editor might have drawn from the First Gospel rather than from the Second, for verbal borrowings used in composing Jn 19, 2 a, see p. 146, note 2 above.

[16] *Cf.* above, p. 30, note 6.

original seat' of the mockery in tradition. The account of the mocking scene located in the high-priest's palace whilst Jesus was detained there comes from an offshoot of the primary tradition. Under the influence of the desire to present proof from prophecy — already in the course of oral transmission — the motif came to be connected with a report of what was assumed to have taken place before Jesus was brought into the council-chamber (συνέδριον) of the Sanhedrin (πρεσβυτέριον τοῦ λαοῦ).

# 12. THE INSCRIPTION ON THE CROSS

In all four Gospels we read of an inscription on Jesus' cross though there are variants in its reported wording (Mc 15, 26; Mt 27, 37; Lc 23, 38; Jn 19, 19). The simplest form is that given in Mark: "The King of the Jews". The Second Gospel contains no information regarding the language, or languages, in which this inscription was made, but as Aramaic was the language spoken in Judaea, Aramaic would have been the obvious choice. The actual words of the inscription could have been: מלכא דיהודאיא or מלכא דיהודיא[1].

While the Second Evangelist treats the inscription on the cross as »un détail légal de l'execution«[2], a bare factual statement indicating the ground for Jesus' execution — the offence of which he had been found guilty[3] — later evangelists enlarge upon the simple Marcan report, adding to the words of the inscription itself and emphasizing its multilingual character. The word αἰτία disappears, however, from the Lucan and Johannine renderings of the "détail", being not in accord with the reverence due to Jesus of Nazareth. The change is complete in the Fourth Gospel where the words of the *titulus* — this technical term actually occurs in Jn 19, 19 — instead of being an indication of the cause of pronouncing a judicial verdict are understood to have a prophetic significance. As Kaiaphas, against his own intention, is forced to announce the working out of a providential plan (Jn 11, 51), so Pilate

---

[1] *Cf.* Wilhelm Brandt, *Die Evangelische Geschichte und der Ursprung des Christenthums* (Leipzig 1893), pp. 201—203.

[2] Alfred Loisy, *L'évangile selon Marc*, p. 461. »Jésus a été crucifié; il a subi ce genre de supplice parce qu'il avait été condamné par l'autorité romaine, dans un procès régulier où le thème de l'accusation n'était pas un blasphème contre Dieu..., mais la prétention messianique à la royauté d'Israël. Le procès devant Pilate n'a été en aucune façon la ratification du procès que l'évangéliste a supposé devant le sanhédrin«, *ibidem*, p. 434.

[3] The word αἰτία is euphemistically rendered in translations by »accusation«. In the present context it implies »cause of condemnation« or »guilt«.
»Pour le procurateur romain, l'aveu de Jésus [Mc 15, 2, Mt 27, 11, Lc 23, 3, et Jn 18, 37] établissait le crime de rébellion contre l' Empire... Plusieurs passages de l'Évangile montrent l'importance qu'a joué ce prétendu titre de roi dans la condemnation. Les quatre Évangélistes sont unanimes à rapporter la question précise de Pilate et la réponse de Jésus....... Pilate... ne pouvait pas... ne pas tenir compte... de l'aveu«, Raymond Schmittlein, *Circonstances et cause de la mort du Christ* (Baden-Baden 1950), p. 63.

when ordering that an inscription should be attached to the cross
(Jn 19, 19) does not state the αἰτία for the death of Jesus, but proclaims
his βασιλεία. It is consonant with the general character of the Johannine
account of Jesus' crucifixion. The *titulus* no longer contains a statement
of a condemned man's mortal crime; it is a prophetic confession of
Jesus' kingship over the peoples of all tongues which Pilate — un-
wittingly? — orders to be set on the cross, and to remain there in spite
of Jewish opposition. The stake, no longer associated with man's deep-
est humiliation, has become a symbol of the exaltation of Jesus; far
from being understood in the sense of ταπεινοῦσθαι, the Passion is referred to by the expression ὑψωθῆναι[4]. In spite of such utterances as
"I thirst", the description of Jesus' death in the Fourth Gospel lacks
realism. Death is here but a transient phase in the glorification of the
eternal Λόγος on his way home to the Father who had sent him. Jesus
does not say "I thirst" because he actually felt thirsty, but he makes
this utterance that the scripture might be fulfilled (Jn 19, 28).

It is probably the Johannine interpretation of the words inscribed on
the cross, which has induced certain modern writers to doubt the historicity of the whole report found in Mc 15, 26[5]. This scepticism is without warrant. In his monograph on the Marcan Gospel T. A. Burkill
discusses the inscription and comes to accept Mc 15, 26 as belonging to
the earliest stratum of the Passion Narrative[6], faithfully reproduced in
this instance by the Second Evangelist. Such appears to be the correct
conclusion. Indeed, there are good reasons, besides those which Burkill
has considered, for dismissing any doubt concerning the historical fact
that an inscription like that quoted in Mc 15, 26 was affixed to, or
suspended from, the cross when Jesus of Nazareth was put to death.
If anything that is recorded of his Passion in the four Gospels accords
with history, it is the report that he was crucified and that the cross
that bore his tortured body also bore a summary statement of the cause
for which he had been sentenced to the *servile supplicium*[7].

---

[4] Jn 3, 13—15; 6, 62; 8, 28; 12, 32—33; *cf.* 12, 23; 13, 1. *Cf.* Pseudo-Cyprian, De
montibus Sina et Sion ix: »Pontius Pilatus, impulsita mente a Deo, accepit tabulam
et titulum et scripsit tribus linguis... »Iesus Nazarenus rex Iudaeorum«, et in capite
ligni clavis tabulam cum nomine regis Iudaeorum confixit« (CSEL 3, p. 113; MPL 4,
col. 915).

».. . die Passion ist kaum noch Passion. Der Tod ist vollständig in den Sieg ver-
schlungen und beinahe nur eine Rückkehr zum Vater«; ».. . die Kreuzigung wird
ὑψωθῆναι genannt in einem Sinn, der dem δοξασθῆναι gleichkommt«, Julius Wellhausen, *Das Evangelium Johannis* (Berlin 1908), p. 113.

[5] *E. g.,* Rudolf Bultmann, *Die Geschichte der synoptischen Tradition,* p. 293;
English edition, p. 272.

[6] *Mysterious Revelation,* pp. 295, 296.

[7] Dibelius was prepared to doubt the historical reliability of Mark's account of
the proceedings before Pilate, but not the fact of the *titulus:* »Die Pilatusszene ...

As already suggested, there is no valid reason for regarding the ἐπι-
γραφὴ τῆς αἰτίας αὐτοῦ (Mc 15, 26) as being anything else than bare
historical fact. The words of the inscription contain no Old Testament
allusion, and could thus not have been prompted by a desire to bring
the record of Jesus' last hours into accord with divine prediction. In
some way, the words of Pilate's *titulus* were even offensive to the Christian appreciation of Jesus' person[8]. Far from being prompted by an
inclination to find the fulfilment of prophecy in the words of Mc 15, 26,
i t  w a s  t h i s  v e r s e  t h a t  i n d u c e d  C h r i s t i a n s  t o  a l t e r
t h e  w o r d i n g  o f  P s a l m  95 (96) so as to make the Old Testament bear out what the New recorded; 'the story', here, is  o l d e r
than 'the prophecy'. The words κύριος ἐβασίλευσεν in Ps 95, 10 Gk (96,
10 in the M. T.) were altered in assimilation to the Gospel report of an
inscription on Jesus' cross so as to read ὁ κύριος ἐβασίλευσεν ἀπὸ ξύλου.
It was an early Christian adjustment. The Epistle of Barnabas 8, 5 refers
to it in the words ἡ βασιλεία Ἰησοῦ ἐπὶ ξύλου, and Justin made the most
of it in the Dialogue with Trypho[9]. The reading gained almost common acceptance in the Western Christian World. Tertullian, in Adversus Marcionem, was convinced of its correctness: »si legisti penes David
*Dominus regnavit a ligno,* expecto quid intellegas, nisi forte lignarium
aliquem regem significari Iudaeorum, et non Christum, qui exinde
a passione ligni superata morte regnavit«[10]. Significant is the substitution of "Deus" for "Dominus" and of the future tense "regnabit" for
the perfect in the parallel passage of Tertullian's Against the Jews: »si
legistis penes prophetam in Psalmis *Deus regnabit a ligno,* expecto quid
intellegatis, ne forte lignarium aliquem regem significari putetis, et non
Christum, qui exinde a passione ligni [Christi] superata morte regnavit«[11]. The reference recurs in Pseudo-Cyprian's De montibus Sina et
Sion: »annuntiate regnum Dei in gentibus, quia Dominus regnavit
a ligno et transivit in gentibus«[12], and is repeated by Ambrose, Augustine, Leo the Great, Gregory the Great, Cassiodorus, Peter Damian,
Bernard of Clairvaux and others. In recent Greek recensions of the

---

[Mc] 15, 2—4 [scheint] durch Rückschluß aus der überlieferten αἰτία am Kreuz ge-
wonnen zu sein«, »Das historische Problem der Leidensgeschichte«, ZNW vol. 30,
1931, p. 200 *(Botschaft und Geschichte,* vol. 1, p. 256).

[8] ὡς ψευδόχριστον αὐτὸν [ἐφόνευσαν] (ὡς λέγοντα ἑαυτὸν θεόν) οὐδὲ πλέον
ἔχοντα τῶν λοιπῶν ἀνθρώπων κατὰ τὴν σάρκα, Cyril of Alexandria, Commentarium
in Matthaeum ad XXVI 67 (MPG 72, col. 460).

[9] Dialogus cum Tryphone Iudaeo LXXIII 1 (Edgar J. Goodspeed, *o. c.,* p. 182;
MPG 6, col. 645).

[10] Adversus Marcionem, liber tertius, XIX 1 (Corpus Christianorum, Tertulliani
opera, pars prima, p. 533; CSEL 47, p. 408; MPL 2, col. 347).

[11] Adversus Iudaeos X 11 (Corpus Christianorum, Tertulliani opera, pars secunda, p. 1378; MPL 2, col. 628).

[12] Caput ix (CSEL 3, p. 113; MPL 4, col. 915).

12*

Psalter, the reading has discreetly been banished from the text to the footnotes. It is, however, still to be found in the Psalterium Veronense.

A further consideration against assuming that theology and apologetics were at work in the formulation of the inscription, is even more weighty: the authors of the Gospels compiled traditions which they restated and adapted so as to bring them into line with the notions of a public that was used to reading Greek, and was steeped in ideas current in the ancient Mediterranean world — to them, the significance of Jesus lay not in the fact that he was ὁ βασιλεὺς τῶν Ἰουδαίων, but that he was ὁ σωτὴρ τοῦ κόσμου. Thus the words in Mc 15, 26 cannot be held to have been suggested by the Second Evangelist's theology. Finally, the custom of affixing a *titulus* to the body of a man who had been executed by crucifixion has attestation elsewhere as a feature in Roman penal procedure[13]. The complete absence of any ulterior considerations — *i. e.* apologetic aims on the part of early κηρύσσοντες or theological motives on the part of the Second Evangelist — and at the same time the presence of objective corroborative evidence, permit no doubt as to the historicity of the statement[14].

That Jesus died by crucifixion, and that his cross bore an inscription stating the cause for which he had been sentenced, is the one solid and stable fact that should be made the starting point of any historical investigation dealing with the Gospel accounts of his trial.

As this point some comments may be made concerning 'the last words' which the various evangelists attribute to the dying Jesus. There are three utterances passing as such: Mc 15, 34 (Mt 27, 46), Lc 23, 46 and Jn 19, 30. The Lucan and Johannine presentations of the last words of Jesus have no valid claim to historical trustworthiness; the authors of Luke and John were offended with the thought that Jesus could have given up his spirit while voicing words which might be understood as a cry of despair and dereliction. The very fact that it is possible to read such a meaning into the words "My God, my God, why have you forsaken me"? has been taken by many scholars as proof of the historicity of the exclamation. The argument lacks cogency. The Second Gospel contains a report of Jesus' last words which is already a conflation of two distinct versions of the tradition. According to Mc 15, 37 Jesus died with a loud inarticulate cry; Mc 15, 34 replaces the wordless cry with a quotation from Psalm 22, 2 (in the Greek 21, 2). Those among whom

---

[13] »... titulus qui causam poenae [indicat]«, Suetonius, Domitianus x 1 (*cf.* Caligula xxxii 2).

[14] *Cf.* »Als geschichtlich gesichert können ... gelten: die Datierung nach Mc 14, 2, die Tatsache des letzten Mahles, die nächtliche Verhaftung mit Hilfe des Judas, die Verurteilung durch Pilatus zum Kreuzestod, der Zug zum Kreuz und die tatsache der Kreuzigung«, Dibelius, *l. c.,* p. 201 (pp. 256, 257). It might be said that it is as important to notice what items are omitted from this list as to consider those which are included.

the tradition incorporated in Mc 15, 34 took its rise felt it appropriate that the last words of Jesus should have a scriptural allusion[15]. The Second Evangelist apparently found two traditions, both of which he reproduced side by side, in v. 34 and v. 37. It is the second of these two which evidently corresponds to the primary tradition. Whereas the authors of Luke and John might have been moved by the sentiment that Jesus should not be represented as dying with despairing words on his lips, such a psychologizing attitude can scarcely be ascribed to the Christian-Jewish milieu in which the tradition expressed in Mc 15, 34 came to be formulated. People in this milieu lived, moved, and had their being, in the Bible. Hence any quotation from the Old Testament for them would have been more suitable in the representation of the dying Jesus than a cry without words[16].

---

[15] Cf. Burkill, o. c., pp. 239, 240; Bultmann, o. c., p. 342 (Engl. ed., p. 313).

[16] »Le psaume XXII domine... les récits évangéliques de la passion. Rien de plus natural que d'en mettre les premiers mots dans la bouche du Christ expirant. C'était consacrer l'interprétation messianique du psaume tout entier... Ceux qui ont fait prononcer à Jésus les prermiers mots du psaume songeaient au caractère messianique de cette prière où David était censé parler au nom du Messie. Ce que le psalmiste avait dit pour lui, Jésus avait bien pu, il avait dû le répéter«, Loisy, L'évangile selon Marc, pp. 467, 468. Compare Johannes Weiss, Das älteste Evangelium, p. 337, and Dibelius, Die Formgeschichte des Evangeliums, pp. 194, 195 (English edition, pp. 193, 194).

# 13. JESUS AND HIS COMPATRIOTS

When the earliest of the evangelists began to collect traditions about Jesus and eventually put them together to form a book, he worked according to a preconceived plan which governed his arrangement and grouping of the materials gathered and selected. While the various items were for the most part traditional, the literary framework, the outline of the Gospel, was of the writer's own design. There was only one limitation to his freedom in the treatment of the subject: the contents had to be lined up in such a manner that the crucifixion of Jesus could be recounted towards the end of the work. Whatever came before could be arranged in any order the evangelist pleased to choose; the end was predetermined. Clearly, the evangelist grouped the materials he utilized for describing 'the earlier stages in the life of Jesus' in a sequence concordant with his own theological concept and with the pragmatic purpose of his work.

It is of crucial importance for a correct appreciation of *the facts of history* that we should recognize *the nature of the purpose behind evangelical presentations of the order of various events* in Jesus' life. *The setting forth of earlier stages of this life was controlled by the notion of them as phases in the development of a literary plan which finds its culmination in the crucifixion.* The end was there before the beginning had been thought of, and it was the climax that gave significance to the whole. Traditional elements of the story concerning 'earlier events' are so arranged as to supply the reader with a reasonable explanation of the Passion. No biographical and no historical considerations affected the writers' governing principle: everything is seen from the high-point of Golgotha. Hence no historical or biographical information can be gleaned from the order of the items used concerning the chronological sequence of events in the life of Jesus. Not a historical assessment of factual situations, but a theological purpose was responsible for the framework that holds the diverse parts of Mark, our oldest Gospel, together.

In Mark, almost from the beginning, we read of disputes between Jesus and his contemporaries, and of their hostile attitude towards him. Such statements may not be used in an attempt to elucidate the actual course of historical events. The representation of 'earlier' conflicts between Jesus and his Jewish adversaries, disputes he holds with various opponents — Pharisees, scribes, and others — are there to prepare the reader for the outcome of the whole story. The death of Jesus on the cross, following upon a trial, was the given fact; the Passion overshadows all that goes before it. The ultimate disclosure — suffering, death, and return from death as the Judge of the Aeon — governs the Evangelist's representation throughout. In *the Evangelist's plan,* acts of hostility on the part of Jews, set in the earlier passages of the story, explain, in some measure, the end on the cross; for *our understanding,* the death of Jesus explains the Evangelist's accounts of earlier conflicts. Once the writer had conceived of the plan to ascribe the responsibility for Jesus' death to the ill-will of the Jewish leaders rather than to a clash with Roman authority, he felt it necessary to show how animosity of certain groups had been aroused. He therefore had to introduce certain features into his story from its very beginning, features designed to prepare the reader for what was to come and to evince how Jewish antagonism against Jesus originated and grew.

It is demonstrable that some of the disputes recounted cannot refer to events which actually took place in the life of Jesus. It is very doubtful whether the lustrations mentioned in Mc 7, 3—4 were compulsory for Jews other than priests at that period[1]. Similar suspicions attach to

---

[1] *Cf.* Adolf Büchler, *Der galiläische Am-ha-Areṣ des zweiten Jahrhunderts* (Vienna 1906): »Der Nichtpriester brauchte... weder levitische Waschungen und Reinigungen noch Besprengungen vorzunehmen, ebensowenig seine Gefässe und Geräte levitisch zu reinigen« (p. 126). Wilhelm Brandt, *Die jüdischen Baptismen oder das religiöse Waschen und Baden im Judentum mit Einschluss des Judenchristentums* (Beiheft 18 zur ZAW, Giessen 1910): »Wenn der Evangelist Marcus... behauptet, die Juden ›alle‹ hielten diese Bräuche ein, so ist das höchstens... für seine eigene spätere Zeit ... richtig« (p. 37); »Der Überlieferung, dass die *ṭbilat yadayim* alte Sitte war, möchte ich nicht widersprechen. Aber sie wird nur von den Priestern im Tempel geübt worden sein« (p. 140). The same, *Jüdische Reinheitslehre und ihre Beschreibung in den Evangelien* (Beiheft 19 zur ZAW, Giessen 1910): »Der Autor im Evangelium des Marcus bezeugt als religiösen Brauch, nach Marktbesuch zu baden, bevor man Speise zu sich nimmt, für s e i n e Zeit« (p. 41); »Jene... Rede, was einen Menschen nicht und was ihn wohl verunreinige, ist kaum für eine echte Rede Jesu zu erklären« (p. 62).    One will agree with this judgment if one recalls that the question of permissible foods and sitting at table with uncircumcised persons caused bitter disputes in the apostolic community (Gal 2, 12—13; Acts 10, 14—16; 15, 20, 29; 21, 25). Had the question been settled by an authoritative statement of Jesus himself, his decision — and not that of the πνεῦμα ἅγιον (Acts 15, 28) — would have been invoked by the leaders of the apostles.    See also Claude Goldsmid Montefiore, *The Synoptic Gospels* (London ²1927): »Ritual purity in the age of Jesus seems to have been mainly a matter for priests... When was it made a rule that *all* Jews must ritually wash their hands before meals?... Only some thirty or forty years after the fall of the temple was the rule of washing hands before meals made obligatory... upon laymen« (pp. 132—135).

[*Revisers' addendum:* See also in this connection J. Neusner, »The Fellowship (Ḥaburah) in the Second Jewish Commonwealth«, HTR vol. 53, 1960, pp. 125—142; *cf.* T. A. Burkill, *New Light on the Earliest Gospel* (Ithaca N. Y. 1972), p. 104, note 11; Geza Vermes, *Jesus the Jew* (London 1973), pp. 28—29.]

the exactness of the report in Mc 10, 2—9. This is not a controversy
story in the proper sense, yet it presents the controversial issue of the
permissibility of divorce in the form of a discussion between Jesus and
the Pharisees[2]. As related in the Second Gospel, the discussion is manifestly unhistorical; no Pharisee would have questioned that it was
permitted in Jewish Law to dissolve the ties of marriage[3]. It would seem
that the Evangelist, though with traditional material at his disposal[4], so
shaped the story as to give it the appearance of a controversy between
Pharisees and Jesus.

Another case in point, showing how a 'controversy story' was
adapted and introduced to its present place in the Gospel Narrative, is
Mc 12, 1—12. Verses 1 b—9 had an origin of their own; they contain
a compact story understandable without the tail-piece that ensues. Composed as a reproach against Jews and their unwillingness to embrace
the apostolic preaching, the story was an allegory on the fate of Jesus,
not a parable spoken by Jesus himself. Either the Second Evangelist or
possibly a preacher who preceded him combined the story with the
scriptural passage from Psalm 118, 22—23 (Mc 12, 10—11) to give
greater force to its intended meaning. Originally, the story was not
framed to depict a setting in the life of Jesus. The Evangelist, however,
by adding Mc 12, 1 a and v. 12, gave it a place in the life of Jesus and
transformed it into an account of an alleged controversy between Jesus
and his opponents. It is here seen how traditional material could be
used and so elaborated as to be brought into line with the Evangelist's
purpose[5].

There are cases in which the reference to some argument or other
could go back to an actual occurrence in the life of Jesus, yet the Marcan form of presentation does not allow of any historical deduction
as to the cause, or setting, of the dispute concerned. The problem is
made all the more difficult by the fact that the Second Evangelist,
though he might have been the first to write a connected interpretation

---

[2] Cf. my »Sadoqite Fragments IV 20, 21 and the Exegesis of Genesis 1, 27«, ZAW
vol. 68, 1956, pp. 71—84, 264; Gerhard Delling, »Das Logion Mark x 11 (und seine
Abwandlungen) im Neuen Testament«, Novum Testamentum, vol. 1, 1956, pp. 263—
274; my »Genesis 1, 27 and Jesus' Saying on Divorce«, ZAW vol. 70, 1958, pp. 260,
261; Frans Neirynck, »Het evangelisch echtscheidingsverbod«, Collationes Brugenses
et Gandavenses, vol. 4, Brugge 1958, pp. 25—46.

[3] The First Evangelist, perceiving the improbability of the question as it is formulated in Mc 10, 2, altered the text by adding the words κατὰ πᾶσαν αἰτίαν (Mt 19, 3).

[4] An injunction by which the marriage-bond was declared unique, was known
to Paul who attributes authorship of this injunction to Jesus. Hence the saying in
Mc 10, 6—9 is part of tradition. Yet the setting which the Second Evangelist gave to
the saying in Mc 10, 2—5 — making it part and parcel of a discussion with certain
Pharisees — is neither traditional nor historical.

[5] Similarly, the other items in Mc 12 (as well as the discourse in Mc 13, 3—36)
owe their present positions in the Gospel to the Second Evangelist.

of the story of Jesus' life, was not the first to narrate particular events from that life. "The Gospel grew backwards"[6]. A report of the Passion was formulated before any other occurrence in the career of Jesus had been considered significant enough to be recalled. As we have it, the Second Gospel is in fact an extended Passion Narrative — extended, that is, through the prefixing of a disproportionately prolonged introduction. The 'introduction' does contain traditional elements, but while traditions expanded, the story as a whole remained firmly anchored in the fact of the cross. The earliest exponents of the gospel preached "Christ — and him crucified". When, in the course of early preaching, this or that moment from the life of Jesus was brought to mind, these moments were treated in the light of his death on the cross. When we now read, in Mark and later Gospels, of various conflicts between Jesus and his contemporaries, we are bound to pay attention to this formative motive in the shaping of evangelical tradition.

The writers of the Gospels repeatedly refer to Jewish groups which harboured feelings of hostility towards Jesus. The opponents appear as members of a group, or party, without being named individually. They are not really persons, but representatives of certain classes. This clearly indicates that *gospel traditions concerning controversies* between Jesus and various sections of the Jewish people *presuppose a certain situation in which a 'group-policy' had already crystallized*. It is not individual enmities which come to light here, but antagonisms of group against group. No doubt, there were Jews who opposed Jesus in his life-time. Yet the fact that the evangelists refer to his adversaries by group-designations makes it questionable whether we possess anywhere except in Mc 14, 1 b and its parallels a representation of the occasions on which hostility to Jesus came to expression, or of the causes that produced it.

Between the narratives of the different Gospels we find a complex interrelationship. Sometimes one evangelist is dependent upon the work of another. Besides such literary dependence of one Gospel upon another there exists an interrelationship of traditional elements — even before the time when tradition came to be gathered and shaped in literary form. Stories circulating orally were told and retold in diverse

---

[6] »... [man könnte] die Evangelien Passionsgeschichten mit ausführlicher Einleitung nennen«, Martin Kähler, *Der sogenannte historische Jesus und der geschichtliche, biblische Christus* (Leipzig ²1896), p. 80, note 1. »Die Passionsgeschichte stellt ... den ersten schriftlich fixierten Text der Überlieferung von Jesus dar. Diese ist dann nach rückwärts gewachsen. Das gilt mindestens für das Markusevangelium. ... Markus setzt ... vor die Passionsgeschichte die Überlieferung von Jesus, davor die vom Täufer«, Willi Marxsen, *Der Evangelist Markus. Studien zur Redaktionsgeschichte des Evangeliums* (Göttingen 1956), p. 17. »[In] the first thirteen chapters [the Evangelist] set[s] forth certain regulative ideas in the light of which, ... the reader may be enabled to interpret the passion«, T. A. Burkill, *Mysterious Revelation* (Ithaca N. Y. 1963), p. 218.

manners giving rise to different versions, while still retaining their essential sameness. Sometimes an evangelist, without noticing that he had before him two versions of the same traditional element, incorporated both into his Gospel. In other instances, one evangelist chose this version, another that. We would now expect that all the evangelists when dealing with particular conflicts, or disputes, between Jesus and his compatriots, of which they tell us, would follow the same line in their respective designations of those whom they describe as being adversely inclined towards Jesus. This is not the case. Individual evangelists severally designate the opponents of Jesus by different group-labels. This fact emerges most clearly from an examination of the Matthaean and Lucan treatment of Marcan sections. The differences — conscious alterations — in the designation of Jesus' opponents by authors writing subsequently to that of the Second Gospel demonstrate that these evangelists were moved by interests which had come to the fore only after the Marcan Gospel had been composed. The differences in the designations of Jesus' enemies, in respective Gospels, provide a valuable aid when considering the motives by which the post-Marcan evangelists were guided. Indirectly, they also allow of certain inferences concerning the motives and the method of the writer of Mark.

Before we base deductions on, or draw conclusions from, what in the Gospels appears to be a plain statement of fact, we must review the situation in which the statement was formulated.

The gospel grew in the shadow of the Cross. Before any evangelist had begun to collect traditions about Jesus, before any preacher had proclaimed "Jesus the Messiah, the Son of God", Calvary was a reality. The manner of Jesus' death was known before details of his life had come to be remembered, collected, and recorded. Mark, though the earliest record of Jesus' life in existence, presents already a well-developed form of the gospel: *He died for us — he is gone before us — his second coming is at hand!* The nucleus around which gospel materials accumulated consisted of a bare report of Jesus' arrest and trial, of his crucifixion, together with an announcement of his resurrection and his imminent second coming to assume the government of Israel and the world. It would seem that the old report contained a reference to the decision by the Jewish authorities to hand Jesus over to Pilate. Hence there was a report of a clash between Jesus and the Jewish authorities, a conflict that was set in the story of his arrest. The preaching grew, and the gospel expanded. When it came to include recollections of happenings before Jesus' arrest, when the starting-point of 'the gospel' was set back to the time of his baptism, or his birth, the motif of Jewish enmity was also retrojected. When, still later, the story expanded even more and now took as its point of departure the creation of the world, the theme of Jewish hostility was shifted back yet more: the Jews of the Fourth Gospel are by nature the enemies of the World Saviour, determined to destroy him.

Before they were individually born, their mind was fixed — fixed immovably — on extinguishing the Light of the World, on killing Jesus, for they are ἐκ τοῦ πατρὸς αὐτῶν τοῦ διαβόλου who was a murderer ἀπ' ἀρχῆς[7]. In this respect, the Fourth Gospel only gives a bizarre exaggeration to a notion that is already present in the Marcan outline: *the Jews are a b i n i t i o the enemies of Jesus.*

When the writer of the Second Gospel — more a compiler than an author, but nonetheless a writer with a plan and scheme of his own — started to collect such items of communal tradition as were accessible to him and as he thought suitable for inclusion in his book, he purposely arranged his various materials in accordance with his predetermined literary project; if not by deliberate design, the materials spontaneously so grouped themselves in the Evangelist's mind as to point in one direction, the death of Jesus governing the representation of his life. The successors of the writer of the Second Gospel worked on the same principle.

This guiding motif comes more obviously to the fore in Mark and John than in Luke and Matthew. The greater amount of sayings-material and of parables, incorporated into these Gospels, makes the current flow less rapidly towards its predetermined inevitable end than is the case with the others. But as the writers of Matthew and Luke in the narrative sections of their respective Gospels largely follow the Marcan thematic arrangement, their accounts bespeak fundamentally the same situation. In the Fourth Gospel, the cross as such has lost all of its poignant reality. The death of Jesus of Nazareth is no longer a punishment — it is surrounded by an aureola of glory; instead of being crucified, Jesus is "lifted up" (Jn 3, 13—15; 6, 62; 8, 28; 12, 32—33; *cf.* 12, 23; 13, 1); instead of indicating the cause of condemnation, the inscription on the cross contains a prophecy of Jesus' reign (Jn 19, 19–22; *cf.* above, p. 154). Death and ascension fall, as it were, together. Jesus has gone back whence he had come. His kingdom is not of this world, and allusions to his imminent return to earth are dimmed. In Mark, composed some decades before the emergence of Johannine theology, the cross is still an undisguised reality. Death remains death; there is a perceptible *caesura* between the crucifixion of Jesus and his entrance into glory.

Whatever the difference between Mark and John in the evangelists' presentation of the crucifixion, in each Gospel the Cross is the goal to which all that precedes it leads. The arrangement of particular items, used to describe stages in the life of Jesus, is the literary work of the evangelists. It would be throwing all historical caution to the winds if we were to draw any inference from statements in the Gospels concerning Jesus' disputes with various Jewish groups, without hav-

---

[7] Jn 8, 44.

ing first considered the literary and theological designs of the Gospel
writers, and without having regard to the actual historical conditions in
which the relevant Christian communities lived when any particular
Gospel was compiled. Each of the evangelists lived in a given historical
situation, and historical circumstances influenced their representations
of Jesus' life and death. To these circumstances belonged the hostility
of leading Jewish circles towards the 'Apostolic Church' and Roman
suspicion of Christianity as a disruptive Jewish movement with apocalyptic tendencies. After the death of Jesus, his followers constituted
themselves as a distinctive group within Jewry. This group, which
preached the impending dissolution of the natural and social order and
its replacement by a divinely ordained new order, aroused the antagonism of Rome and Jerusalem alike. The Romans, unable as yet to
distinguish between the 'Apostolic Church' and other Jewish sects, enforced restrictive measures upon all Jews, whether affected by messianic
aspirations or not. Such measures as the Imperial Government took,
were the result of Christian agitation. Hence, induced by the Roman
attitude towards messianic propaganda, the Jewish authorities responsible for the administration of communal affairs saw fit to restrict the
preaching of the coming enthronement of Jesus of Nazareth as Christ,
the King who was to replace all other kings and principalities.

This was the general historical context in which the writers of
the Gospels lived and wrote. To be historically understood, the Gospels
have to be read against this temporal background. The evangelists attempted in their presentation or description of Jesus' trial to allay such
suspicions and to combat such hostility as Christians encountered in
the world around them.

Before the earliest Gospel was written, the struggle for the sympathies of the Jews as a whole had already been decided. It had become
clear that large sections of the Jewish people were not attracted by the
preaching of the Messiah who had been crucified and had risen from
the dead, who after his resurrection had been unaccountably removed
from the earth but would presently return to Jerusalem, or Galilee,
and assume his rightful government over the nation. On the other hand,
Christian preaching of imminent salvation — with the employment of
a somewhat different symbolism — had won sympathy, in town and
country, among the suppressed masses of the Greek-speaking populations in the Roman Empire. The actual historical situation thus again
decided what turn preaching and teaching should take: *the content of
the message announced was itself determined by the mode of reception
it obtained.*

Even before undertaking his task of composing a Gospel, from traditions handed down by way of preaching, the author of Mark knew his
own Jewish contemporaries as people who held themselves aloof from
the faith which he had embraced. It is integral to his own controversy
— with the Jews of *his* time — that he describes the Jews of Jesus'

time as people who had rejected him from the beginning and who brought about his death. Arguments and counter-arguments current in the communal life of the early Christian community were naively retrojected and attributed to Jesus and those of his compatriots who were coeval with him. Quarrels and dissensions, of which the Second Evangelist had knowledge from *his* surroundings, are described as if they had taken place in the life-time of Jesus. As the evangelists more and more abandoned the hope of persuading Jews in considerable numbers to accept the faith in the providential plan of Israel's deliverance through "one Jesus who was dead, whom they affirmed to be alive"[8], the more uninhibited became the disputation with the Jews and, in consequence, the more vicious the denunciations of the Jews that were attributed to Jesus[9]. The experience of the first and second generations of Christians, their arguments, dissensions and controversies with various Jewish groups in the era of the 'Apostolic Church', exercised a decisive influence upon the formation of tradition, as well as upon the evangelists in their presentations of Jesus' life.

Whilst following his own devices in marshalling the materials he used, the writer of the Second Gospel, when selecting his materials, relied largely on traditional elements. The motif of enmity between Jesus and various Jewish groups occurs already in tradition. The Marcan controversy stories, though some may have been made up, are for the most part no mere invention of the Evangelist; only their assignment to particular situations in his work. Once we realise that the assignment of a certain conflict to a particular section of the Gospel is part of the Evangelist's literary plan, we are aware that the present contexts of Jesus' disputations with his compatriots — including his denunciations of the attitude of various Jewish groups — allow of no historical deduction concerning the actual course of events. Reports of conflict, prior to the account of a decision taken by the Sanhedrin to apprehend Jesus and hand him over to the Romans, reveal the Evangelist's intention to prepare his readers for the ultimate *dénouement*. The linking-up and the dovetailing of controversy stories are, in principle, of the same order as the occasional hints regarding the unavoidable necessity of suffering and death. The pen is guided by a literary scheme. The distribution of controversy stories in Mark 2 to 10 and in Mark 12 is of the Evangelist's contriving, with little foundation in early tradition and none in history. The character of the arrangement is most obvious

---

[8] Acts 25, 19.

[9] An example of the way in which hostility grew and feelings of enmity were intensified in the process of time, may be found by comparing Mt 23, 1—36 with the older record in Mc 12, 38—40. »Each Gospel reflects its own period and environment«, Benjamin Wisner Bacon, *Is Mark a Roman Gospel?* (*Harvard Theological Studies* VII, Cambridge, Mass., 1919), p. 73. »...the invective is elaborated and extended both quantitatively and qualitatively«, *ibidem*.

in the concatenation of Mark 12 (forming the main section of the so-called 'Jerusalem Ministry') where the Evangelist heaps controversy upon controversy[10] with the prospect of the impending climax before him[11]. Where they now stand, the controversy stories were meant to present Jesus' final conflict with the authorities as the outcome of "envy" or "jealousy" on the part of holders of high office among the Jews[12]. The 'Galilaean Ministry' and 'Jerusalem Ministry' in Mark are

---

[10] In direct connection with Mc 11, 27—33 (which reports a controversy) there is in Mc 12, 1—12, 13—17, 18—27, 35—37 and 38—40 an agglomeration of disputes and arguments. This arrangement is evidently editorial.

[11] This observation applies equally to some sections in Mc 11 and to most of the contents of Mc 13.

Mark 11, 22—24 displays a Galilaean setting. »This mountain«, to be cast into the sea, would presuppose its proximity to a stretch of water. The allocation of the pericope to the ›Jerusalem Ministry‹ is editorial (cf. J. Wellhausen, Das Evangelium Marci, Berlin 1903, p. 97). Also Mc 12, 28—34 had in antecedent tradition a different setting from that which it now possesses, as is shown by the more primitive parallel in Lc 10, 25—28.

The eschatological discourse in Mc 13, set between the preceding controversy-stories and the following passion narrative, is meant to explain the delay of the parousia while still holding out hopes for its not too distant realisation.

[12] »It is part of St. Mark's *doctrinal purpose* (italics supplied) to make it plain to his readers that the ill-will of [the Jews] was the determining factor behind the crucifixion«, Burkill, o. c., p. 122. The Second Evangelist's intimation in Mc 15, 10 is open to a variety of explanations. If, besides the theological meaning which the Evangelist may have wished to impart, it has any historical significance, it may be understood in the sense that members of the hierarchy were jealous (and, we may add, apprehensive) because of the influence exercised by Jesus upon the masses. The Evangelist's own interpretation of the »envy« probably issued from the belief that the hierarchs envied Jesus for his superior rank in the divine economy.

The account of a consultation on the part of members of the Supreme Council, of which we possess the two different versions in Mc 14, 1—2 and in Jn 11, 47 b, 48, 50, 53, is not without foundation in history. But reports by the evangelists of happenings anterior to the moment of the Council's session, and implying any intention to kill Jesus, are due to the literary schemes of the evangelists, reinforced by communal antagonism between messianist and non-messianist Jewish groups. The elaboration of scenes evincing Jewish hostility has been retrospectively set into the biographical framework of Jesus' career.

The failure to attach primary importance to the varying doctrinal purposes and literary designs of the evangelists, writing amid differing environmental pressures, is a major weakness in such investigations as A. N. Sherwin-White, »The Trial of Christ in the Synoptic Gospels«, Roman Society and Roman Law in the New Testament (Oxford 1963), pp. 24—47; James C. McRuer, The Trial of Jesus (Toronto 1964); and Haim H. Cohn, »Reflections on the Trial and Death of Jesus«, Israel Law Review, vol. 2, 1967, pp. 332—379. On the first of these, cf. T. A. Burkill, »The Condemnation of Jesus: A Critique of Sherwin-White's Thesis«, Novum Testamentum, vol. 12, 1970, pp. 321—342; on the second, cf. my brief assessment in The Anglican Theological Review, vol. 47, 1965, pp. 120—121. [Revisers' adden-

no less due to editorial arrangement than is the 'Journey through Samaria' in Luke[13].

The foregoing considerations apply to the Marcan contexts of reports of conflict between Jesus and Jews — not, however, or in most cases not, to the origin of such reports. The earliest preaching of Jesus' messiahship had already contemplated the events in Jesus' life in some relation to the dramatic happenings in which this life came to its end. When actual recollections were lacking, communal experience filled the gap. Preachers and apostles who themselves encountered hostility from those to whom they addressed their preaching, assumed that the same must have taken place while Jesus was alive[14]. Disputes were frequent in the years 30 to 70 when the formation of gospel traditions took place. Those disputes were now 'antedated', being represented as episodes in Jesus' life[15]. We have thus to consider, besides the literary scheme in Mark, the process by which traditions incorporated into Mark had grown. The medium by which tradition came to expression was different from that of literary production, but the formative motives were fundamentally of the same sort. As the author of the Second

---

*dum:* Cohn's article is superseded by his book *The Trial and Death of Jesus* (London 1971).]

[13] The Second Evangelist would make it appear that Jesus had been in Jerusalem not more than once (though Mc 11, 2 and Mc 14, 13 imply that he had been there before!). There are writers who have recognized that this presentation is based exclusively on the literary scheme of the Evangelist, and who maintain that the Marcan account combines into one two distinct visits of Jesus to Jerusalem, separated by an interval of half a year. Yet in all probability Jesus visited the city at various times. There is no means of determining how often he was there, or at what points in his life, or how long a particular sojourn lasted. The Marcan ›Jerusalem Ministry‹ is an artificial literary construction — and the arrangement of the Fourth Gospel, which reports several visits to Jerusalem, is even more artificial.

[14] »Von Anfeindungen Jesu mag die Gemeinde oft gesprochen haben, weil sie selbst diese erfuhr«, Eduard Schweizer, »Der Menschensohn«, ZNW vol. 50, 1959, pp. 185—209, on p. 199.

[15] »We [can] point to . . . places in the Gospels where the coloration of the time of the Apostles, and . . . even of the post-Apostolic time, has penetrated . . . the Cross and Christ's Resurrection. And yet they are placed in the ›time‹ of Jesus«, Jindřich Mánek, »The Biblical Concept of Time and Our Gospels«, NTS vol. 6, 1959, pp. 45 —51, on p. 46. »[Their] concept of time enabled [the authors of] Mark, Matthew and John to record an event from the life of Jesus of Nazareth and an event from the life of the Primitive Church in one written document. Even though, chronologically . . ., the Primitive Church lives after the death of Jesus, it is his companion« (p. 47). »In . . . our Gospels we find . . . not only the path of the historical Jesus, but also Christ's path with the Apostolic Church . . . The subject of . . . our Evangelists is not just the days of Jesus' life . . . They are not concerned with the ›historical‹ Jesus, but with the living Lord of the Church . . . The figure of Christ in the . . . Gospels belongs not only to the time of the history of Jesus of Nazareth« (pp. 47—48).

Gospel was concerned to promote the communal interests of the group
to which he belonged, so were his predecessors. In the case of the
Evangelist this consideration affected his 'policy' in recording, enlarging,
and arranging what he had collected; with earlier tradents it affected
the very contents of the tradition. The community's involvement in
theological controversy with other Jewish groups, and its vulnerable
openness to suspicion from the side of the imperial authorities, deci-
sively influenced the manner in which traditional elements took their
form. Conditions of tension which obtained between those Jews who
proclaimed the messiahship of Jesus, and other Jews who did not,
deeply affected the presentation of events reputed to have taken place
in the life of Jesus. As the gospel grew, and was traced back from the
crucifixion to the baptism of Jesus, then to his birth, and eventually
to the primal Word of God, so the rivalries which prevailed in the 'apostolic age' between Jesus' followers and others, were thrown back into
the period of Jesus' life. The evangelists had to have precedents.

There are instances in which it clearly emerges from the actual wording of Marcan controversy stories that the conflict which constitutes
the subject of dispute actually arose only after Jesus' death. Representatives of certain Jewish sections castigate the practices of "the disciples" — in Mc 2, 18, 23—24[16]; 7, 2—5; 9, 14 — without having occasion
to find fault with the behaviour of Jesus himself. "The disciples" commit, or omit, a certain act which provides an occasion for controversy.
Manifestly the disputes describe occurrences in the communal life of
"the disciples", i. e. 'the Apostolic Church'[17]. It is not Jesus' own con-

---

[16] In Mc 2, 24 »the Pharisees«, criticizing the conduct of the disciples, address
Jesus himself. In the parallel passage Lc 6, 2—3 the Pharisees reproach the disciples
directly, but nevertheless receive a reply from Jesus. The Lucan version in this instance is not ›better history‹. The Third Evangelist perceived that it was illogical to
blame Jesus for an action which he is not reported to have performed. The Evangelist modified the Marcan report by making the Pharisees address the disciples instead of Jesus; he made no use of an independent source in this place, as can be
seen from v. 3 where Jesus, not one of the disciples, replies to the reproach.

[17] [Es] läßt sich . . . feststellen, dass die Formung des Stoffes überwiegend in der
palästinensischen Urgemeinde erfolgt ist«, Rudolf Bultmann, Die
Geschichte der synoptischen Tradition (Göttingen ²1931), p. 49. »Dass es . . . die
Gemeinde war, die diese Geschichten formte, und dass sie — auch wo einheitliche Konzeptionen vorliegen — nicht ohne weiteres geschichtliche Begebenheiten
wiedergeben, zeigt sehr deutlich die Tatsache, dass mehrfach das Verhalten der Jünger verteidigt wird . . . Die Jünger sind die Angegriffenen, d. h. die Gemeinde ist es,
und sie wehrt sich mit der Berufung auf ihren Meister«, ibidem, p. 50; Engl. edition,
p. 48.

See also Francis Wright Beare, »The Sabbath Was Made for Man?«, JBL vol. 79,
1960, pp. 130—136: »Critical analysis . . . indicates several stages in the formation
of the pericope. It is doubtful if the saying, or pair of sayings (Mark 2, 27—28),
from which it all began, can be regarded as authentic . . . the saying originated not

duct, but that of his disciples which attracts unfavourable comment. Jesus himself is merely introduced into the story to lay down a *halakha* which regularizes the action of "the disciples" and gives sanction to their particularist, or sectarian, interpretation of the Torah. The controversy is seen from the angle of a group differing in its interpretation of legal observances from the interpretation of other groups. It is the *halakha* of the community of Jesus-messianists, but the Evangelist presents it as if reporting an event that took place in Jesus' life. In a similar manner, the rabbis, anxious to back up injunctions which they themselves had introduced, ascribed such injunctions to Moses, who was supposed to have announced them orally. In one case Moses, in the other Jesus, is invoked as the author of certain rulings promulgated by a later generation. The conflict of which we read was a real conflict; but it originated between "the disciples" and other Jewish groups, not between Jesus and his own contemporaries.

The motif of enmity between Jesus and the Jews of his time owes its presence in the Gospels in some measure to the literary framework within which the Second Evangelist chose to arrange his various materials; its presence in tradition is due to the apologetic endeavour to justify the position of those who ascribed messiahship to Jesus. Literary considerations and ecclesiastical policy account for the presentation we now have in the Gospels. This is not to be taken to imply that Jesus never met or made enemies in his life. He doubtless had his own disagreements with some of his compatriots, his own reasons for dissenting from his social environment, his own strictures of the practices and ideas that were current among Jews of his era. Yet there is no warrant for the supposition that there existed among his contemporaries a concerted plan to have Jesus put out of the way.

We read in Mc 3, 6 of "the Pharisees who sought counsel with the Herodians to destroy Jesus". References to disputes and conflicts multiply, and it is part of the Gospel scheme to demonstrate how hostility developed until finally it culminated in the arraignment of Jesus for

---

with Jesus, but with the apostolic church of Palestine, in controversy with the Pharisees, who took exception to the failure of Christian Jews to keep the sabbath. The Christian reply to the accusation (Jesus, the Son of man, the Messiah, is lord of the sabbath) has then come to be regarded as a saying of Jesus himself, and the little story of the disciples in the grainfields has been created as a frame for the saying. The successive supplements — first the appeal to the example of David; then the appeal to the exercise of duties by the priests — enlarge the area of the claim. Not only the law of the sabbath, but the whole system of Jewish observance is subordinate to the authority of Jesus... The followers of Jesus are in the train of ›great David's greater Son‹, and are occupied in the priestly service of the kingdom of God. We look upon this pericope, then, as based indeed upon some reminiscence of the action and attitudes of Jesus, but as owing its present form and most of its substance to complex adaptations in the course of ist transmission, in the service of Christian apologetics against Jewish (Pharisaic) criticism« (p. 135).

trial before the Sanhedrin and his condemnation to death. To argue
that the hostility of Jewish authorities already showed itself at a stage
in Jesus' life *as early as Mark 3, 6* would be to see the passage in
a wrong perspective. For in reality *Mc 3, 6 is not 'earlier' than Mc 14,
64;* both belong to the purview of the Evangelist. Affected by experience
of his own time — quarrels and contention between messianist and
non-messianist groups of Jews — and applying the literary principle of
representing the crucifixion as the necessary outcome of a conflict between Jesus and the leaders of his nation, the author of Mark sets forth
for his readers a relationship of Jesus to the Jews already at an early
stage of his preaching activity as one of conflict. In actual fact, the
conflict is not between Jesus and "the Pharisees and the Herodians",
but between 'the early Church' and certain groups, or classes, from
among the Jewish body politic in the years in which the formation of
Christianity as a distinctive faith took place. Enemies of 'the Church'
are depicted as enemies of Jesus. Such a way of looking at the matter
has historical value only insofar as it makes us aware of the relationship existing between Christians and Jews *when the Gospel was composed,* but it is without any historical or biographical value for assessing the conditions which obtained *during the life of Jesus.* It sheds light
on trends and divisions of thought in the age in which the author of
Mark lived and wrote. It tells us nothing of the conditions in which
Jesus lived.

The tendency to describe conflicts between the Church and various
contemporaneous Jewish groups as if they had arisen within the life-
span of Jesus can be seen not only from such instances as those already
cited, where certain disputes are occasioned by the actions or the behaviour of the disciples, but still more clearly in the designations of
Jesus' enemies such as we find in the various Gospels. *The actual opponents of Christianity, coeval with a particular evangelist, are cited
as adversaries of Jesus.* This is perhaps most evident in the Fourth
Gospel. The Jewish faction which had wielded authority in the time
of Jesus was that of the Sadducees. The Fourth Evangelist completely
omits the Sadducees from his enumeration of Jesus' opponents. When
he was writing, the Sadducees no longer played any significant part in
Jewish politics. The Evangelist is not interested in history as such, but
is concerned about the fortunes of the Christian communities of his
own age. This accounts for his failure to mention the Sadducees among
Jesus' enemies and for his concentrating upon the Pharisees as his official target for attack[18]. The reason is plain: controversies between Christians and Jews of the Fourth Evangelist's time were aimed chiefly at

---

[18] Jn 1, 24; 4, 1; 7, 32—36, 45—49; 8, 13; 9, 13—17, 40; 11, 46—47, 57; 12, 19,
42; 18, 3. The writer of the Fourth Gospel singled out the Pharisees for reproof,
attributing to them responsibility for the adversities of Jesus. In Matthew, the heated
argument derives from disillusion; in John, there is only cold hostility.

the Pharisees who then were the representative Jewish group. In order
to attack them, the Evangelist presents them as the chief foes of Jesus.
Actually, Pharisees had as late as the year 62 CE shown sympathy with
leaders of the apostolic community[19], and Jesus himself in his teaching
stood closer to early Pharisaism than to any other school of thought.

The phenomenon observed — the presentation of contemporary opponents of Christianity as having been adversaries of Jesus — is not
confined to the Fourth Gospel. Its presence at an earlier date may be
detected by comparing the designations of Jesus' enemies in the three
Synoptic Gospels. The following table lists chiefly Marcan material in
an endeavour to trace the development of the very earliest communal
traditions that are accessible to us. Conformity with the Marcan designations of Jesus' opponents by the later synoptists does not call for
attention. We might expect such conformity throughout, for the writers
of Luke and Matthew derived their information from the Second Gospel. The remarkable fact is that even in rendering 'Marcan matter' the
later evangelists often enough unhesitatingly altered the designations in
question for the sake of casting in a hostile rôle such Jewish groups as
were prominent at the time when the evangelists were engaged in their
work.

| | | |
|---|---|---|
| Mc | 2, 6 | some of the scribes |
| Lc | 5, 17, 21 | the scribes and the Pharisees |
| Mt | 9, 3 | some of the scribes |
| | | |
| Mc | 2, 16 | the scribes of the Pharisees |
| Lc | 5, 30 | the Pharisees and their scribes |
| Mt | 9, 11 | the Pharisees |
| | | |
| Mc | 2, 18 | the disciples of John and (of) the Pharisees |
| Lc | 5, 33 | the disciples of John and of the Pharisees |
| Mt | 9, 14 | the disciples of John and the Pharisees |
| | | |
| Mc | 2, 23—24 | the Pharisees |
| Lc | 6, 2 | some of the Pharisees |
| Mt | 12, 2 | the Pharisees |
| | | |
| Mc | 3, 6 | the Pharisees with the Herodians |
| Lc | 6, 7 | the scribes and the Pharisees |
| Mt | 12, 14 | the Pharisees |
| | | |
| Mc | 3, 22 | the scribes from Jerusalem |
| Lc | 11, 15 | some of the multitude |
| Mt | 9, 34; 12, 24 | the Pharisees |
| | | |
| Mc | 7, 1 | the Pharisees and some of the scribes from Jerusalem |
| Mt | 15, 1 | Pharisees and scribes |
| | | |
| Mc | 8, 11 | the Pharisees |
| Mt | 16, 1 | the Pharisees |

---

[19] Ant XX 201—203; Eusebius, Historiae ecclesiasticae II 23, 23—24 (GCS Eusebius II, 1, p. 174; MPG 20, col. 205).

| | |
|---|---|
| Lc 11, 16 | others |
| Mt 12, 38 | the scribes and the Pharisees |
| | |
| Mc 8, 15 | the Pharisees and Herod |
| Lc 12, 1 | the Pharisees |
| Mt 16, 6, 11—12 | Pharisees and Sadducees |
| | |
| Mc 8, 31 | the elders and the chief priests and the scribes |
| Lc 9, 22 | the elders and chief priests and scribes |
| Mt 16, 21 | the elders and chief priests and scribes |
| | |
| Mc 9, 14 | scribes |
| | |
| Mc 10, 2 | Pharisees |
| Mt 19, 3 | Pharisees |
| | |
| Mc 10, 33 | the chief priests and the scribes |
| Mt 20, 18 | the chief priests and scribes |
| | |
| Mc 11, 18 | the chief priests and the scribes |
| Lc 19, 47 | the chief priests and the scribes and the principal leaders of the people |
| Mt 21, 15 | the chief priests and the scribes |
| | |
| Mc 11, 27 | the chief priests and the scribes and the elders |
| Lc 20, 1 | the (chief) priests and the scribes with the elders |
| Mt 21, 23 | the chief priests and the elders of the people |
| | |
| Lc 20, 19 | the scribes and the chief priests |
| Mt 21, 45 | the chief priests and the Pharisees |
| | |
| Mc 12, 13 | some of the Pharisees and of the Herodians |
| Lc 20, (19) 20 | (the scribes and chief priests) spies |
| Mt 22, 15—16 | disciples of the Pharisees with the Herodians |
| | |
| Mc 12, 18 | Sadducees |
| Lc 20, 27 | some of the Sadducees |
| Mt 22, 23 | Sadducees |
| | |
| Mc 12, 28 | one of the scribes |
| Lc 10, 25 | a certain scribe |
| Mt 22, 34—35 | a Pharisee scribe |
| | |
| Mc 12, 35 | the scribes |
| Lc 20, 41 | they (= the scribes) |
| Mt 22, 41 | the Pharisees |
| | |
| Mc 12, 38 | the scribes |
| Lc 20, 46 | the scribes |
| Lc 11, 42—43 | Pharisees |
| Mt 23, 2 | the scribes and the Pharisees |
| Mt 23, 23 | scribes and Pharisees |
| | |
| Lc 11, 39 | Pharisees |
| Mt 23, 25 | scribes and Pharisees |
| | |
| Lc 11, 52 | scribes |
| Mt 23, 13 | scribes and Pharisees |

| | |
|---|---|
| Mc 14, 1 | the chief priests and the scribes |
| Lc 22, 2 | the chief priests and the scribes |
| Mt 26, 3 | the chief priests and the elders of the people |
| Jn 11, 47, 57 | the chief priests and the Pharisees |
| Mc 14, 10 | the chief priests |
| Lc 22, 4 | the chief priests and captains |
| Mt 26, 14 | the chief priests |
| Mc 14, 43 | a multitude from the chief priests and the scribes and the elders |
| Lc 22, 47, 52 | a multitude (including) the chief priests and the captains of the Temple Guard and the elders |
| Mt 26, 47 | a great multitude from the chief priests and elders of the people |
| Jn 18, 3 | the servants of the chief priests and of the Pharisees |
| Mc 14, 53 | all the chief priests and the elders and the scribes |
| Lc 22, 66 | chief priests and scribes |
| Mt 26, 57 | the scribes and the elders |
| Mc 14, 55 | the chief priests and the whole Council |
| Mt 26, 59 | the chief priests and the whole Council |
| Mc 15, 1 | the chief priests with the elders and the scribes and the whole Council |
| Mt 27, 1 | all the chief priests and the elders of the people |
| Mc 15, 3 | the chief priests |
| Lc 23, 4 | the chief priests and the multitudes |
| Mt 27, 12 | the chief priests and elders |
| Lc 23, 10 | the chief priests and the scribes |
| Mc 15, 11 | the chief priests |
| Lc 23, 13 | the chief priests and the rulers and the people |
| Mt 27, 20 | the chief priests and the elders |
| Mc 15, 31 | the chief priests with the scribes |
| Lc 23, 35 | the rulers |
| Mt 27, 41 | the chief priests with the scribes and elders |
| Mt 27, 62 | the chief priests and the Pharisees |

Two striking points emerge from an examination of this table[20]. The first concerns the difference in the Marcan designations of Jesus' enemies in chapters 2 to 12 on the one hand, and in chapters 14 and 15 on the other. The second concerns the differences between the designations in Mark and those in the parallel passages of the later Gospels.

---

[20] In general, *cf.* Bultmann, *o. c.*, pp. 54—56; Engl. ed., pp. 52—54.    Several months after having compiled this contabulation, I came across an article »Scribes, Pharisees, High-Priests and Elders« by A. F. J. Klijn, published in *Novum Testamentum*, vol. 3, 1959, on pp. 259—267. In some respects his findings agree with my own. »We are forced to draw a line between the passion narratives and the rest of

With regard to the first point, except for isolated references in Mc 11 (and of course the prediction of the passion at 8, 31; *cf.* 10, 33), chief priests and elders are not named as Jesus' antagonists in the earlier chapters, whilst only they, together with "the scribes", appear as his enemies in Mc 14—15. The traditions which underlie the last-mentioned two Marcan chapters were formed at a much earlier date than the traditions incorporated in Mc 2—13. *The oldest synoptic tradition* (however re-styled it may have become in the process of literary formulation) *does not include the Pharisees among the enemies of Jesus at all;* there is not a single instance in which Pharisaic hostility towards Jesus finds mention. The pericope Mt 27, 62—66 (the setting of guards at the tomb of Jesus) is only an apparent exception. It does not belong to the synoptic tradition proper, and is commonly recognized as a legendary accretion of late origin[21]. As they do in Mt 27, 62, so the Pharisees appear in Jn 11, 47, 57; 18, 3. These passages, though they go back to an earlier tradition, underwent drastic editorial refashioning before they assumed their present form. It is exclusively in the very latest development that the Pharisees appear, incongruously, alongside their most hated antagonists, the priestly rulers of Sadducaean descent.

There is *no traditional link* between the narratives incorporated into Mark in which hostility towards Jesus is ascribed to *the chief priests* and their associates, and those narratives in which *the Pharisees* are assigned an antagonistic rôle. The two categories belong to entirely different situations, and come from periods in the history of the early Church that are divided from each other by several decades. The traditional cycle in which the "the chief priests" function as the adversaries of Jesus is of relatively early origin; various traditions depicting "the Pharisees" engaged in a campaign of opposing Jesus belong to a much later date.

The principal conclusion to be drawn from our tabulation of the designations of Jesus' enemies *in Mark* is that the controversy stories of which most of chapters 2, 3 and 12 consists have not the same background, and do not bespeak the same situation or the same *milieu,* as the report of Jesus' arrest in Mark 14 and of his execution in Mark 15. These quite distinct segments of tradition were first connected by the Evangelist. Doubts may be entertained with regard to Mc 11, 15—

---

the gospels«, states Klijn (p. 259). The line cannot, however, be drawn as rigidly as he suggests, namely, exactly between chapters 13 and 14 of the Second Gospel (and the corresponding chapters in the other synoptic Gospels). The designations of Jesus' opponents in Mc 11, 18 and 11, 27 indicate that the stories in which they occur have traditional links with the Passion Narrative.

[21] Bultmann calls Mt 27, 62—66 »eine apologetisch motivierte Legende« (*o. c.,* p. 297). The story has no counterpart in either Mark or Luke. It belongs to the very latest strata of the Gospel traditions. Its character is purely legendary, and its purport apologetic.

18, 27—28. If not from the time of its original formulation, then at least at some date before the Second Gospel as such was compiled, a connection between the story of the Cleansing of the Temple and Mc 14, 1 was established. Such connection is indicated by the homogeneity in the designations of the opponents of Jesus. Chapters 12 and 13, however, were put together by the Second Evangelist who introduced them to their present place in the narrative.

We may go further, and express the following view: those passages in Mark in which the chief priests *and* the elders and scribes appear as Jesus' foes correspond to the earliest stratum of tradition, earlier than those in which "the scribes" appear alone. Such passages again are of earlier origin than any passage mentioning the Pharisees. There is some historical foundation in references to the hostility of the priests towards Jesus; there is none in citations of Pharisaic antagonism. *All the Marcan 'controversy stories', without exception, reflect disputes between the 'Apostolic Church' and its social environment, and are devoid of roots in the circumstances of the life of Jesus.* Some of the controversy stories have simply been constructed by the Second Evangelist himself[22], who presented certain traditional items by framing them as a disputation.

When considering the 'hostility' displayed by the high-priest and his *côterie* against Jesus, we should beware of getting things out of focus: the high-priest and his staff played only a minor part in bringing Jesus to trial before Pilate. One might think of a contemporary analogy and compare Kaiaphas's part with that of a native prosecutor who charges a native defendant for an offence under Emergency Regulations imposed by a colonial power, in a trial conducted before a Magistrate who bears the nationality of the sovereign country. To sum up the situation, Kaiaphas and his associates stood less for heroics than for reasonableness in their dealings with the Emperor's representative. Their attitude was one of political pliancy rather than of resistance. It has to be remembered that the high-priest owed his appointment to the governor, and was in fact little more than a tool in his hands. The governor could depose him at any time if he thought that the high-priest did not readily enough fall in with his wishes. As in the analogous case from our own time outraged national feelings are in the first place directed against the indigenous policeman, or indigenous assessor, who has allowed himself to become an instrument of imperial rule, so also Christian tradition turned against priests, scribes and elders with more vindictiveness than against Pilate, the alien[23].

---

[22] As to Mc 10, 2—9 and 12, 1—12, see above, p. 160.

[23] It would be wrong to make generalizing statements concerning the respective attitudes of Sadducees and Pharisees towards Rome. To label the former as ›collaborators‹ and the latter as ›patriots‹ is equally incorrect. Under Hyrcanus II and Aristobulus II — in Pompey's time — the Sadducees were the party that stood for

It is of first importance to recognize that the tradition which underlies Mc 14 and 15 — the earliest Christian tradition — knows of no
hostility whatsoever between Jesus and the Pharisees. There only priests,
elders and scribes figure as Jesus' opponents.

The break between Mc 11 and Mc 14 in the employment of the word
"priests" to denote Jesus' enemies indicates that the materials in chapter
11 are actually more closely related to those in chapter 14 than the
contents of the intervening chapters. The Second Evangelist collected
traditional records or reports originally unconnected with an account
of Jesus' last days, and put them together to achieve a greater dramatic
effect in preparing for the climax of his story. The artificiality of the
composition is demonstrable in special cases.

The second point that is illustrated by the above table concerns the
differences between designations of Jesus' enemies in parallel synoptic
passages. Confining the present survey now to Mc 2 to 12 and parallels,
we observe a tendency to name the Pharisees as Jesus' enemies even in
passages where they are not so mentioned in the Second Gospel. Although the alterations are not numerous, it can nevertheless be seen
that conformity in designating the enemies is not maintained. The later evangelists are prone to add "the Pharisees" in places where they
do not appear in Mark (so Lc 5, 21; Mt 12, 24; 22, 34—35, 41; 23, 2, 13
as against Mark; Mt 21, 45; 23, 13 as against Luke). This confirms the
assertion that the evangelists inclined to identify opponents of Christianity of their own day and generation with the opponents of Jesus.
Not mentioned in a single instance in Mc 14 and 15 as having acted in
a hostile manner towards Jesus, with the advance of time the Pharisees
become in later strata of gospel tradition Jesus' enemies *par excellence*.
The casting of the Pharisees in the rôle of Jesus' implacable opponents
has its historic explanation in the situation which arose when those
persons who professed the belief in Jesus' messianic status were excluded from the synagogues[24].

---

national independence, whilst the Pharisees acquiesced in Roman overlordship. Their
numbers decimated and their power broken, the Sadducees retained nevertheless the
highest offices within the theocratic administration, though the occupants of the
high-priesthood were now hardly more than puppets. Only those prepared to colla-
borate were placed in office by Herod the Great, and they were liable to arbitrary
dismissal. The same situation prevailed in the procuratorial period. Seldom were the
priestly leaders willing to risk a conflict with the Emperor's representative. But in
the year 66 CE it was the scion of a Sadducaean family who sparked off the flame
of revolt (B. J. II 409). Although they disapproved of the extremism of the Zealots,
Sadducees fought in the war against Rome, whereas the Pharisees were indifferent
to political liberty and prepared to submit, provided that religious freedom was
granted. Josephus's account of events during the revolt, and his own conduct,
provide evidence of occasional collusion, on the part of Pharisees, with the Romans.

[24] Hence evangelical polemic with the Pharisees. This polemic coloured even the
Matthaean account of the activites of John the Baptist, as is seen when we compare

More significant even than the occasional addition of the label "Pharisees", whether in passages referring to people hostile to Jesus or in passages containing Jesus' denunciation of others, is the elaboration of traditional material in other directions. Where Mark presents a soberly worded warning against the hypocrisy of officialdom[25], the First Evangelist inserts a prolonged and violent diatribe against the Pharisees[26] for which there is little or no foundation in the Second Gospel.

If any Jews exercised effective influence in the circumstances which led to the death of Jesus, it would have been prominent members of the priestly aristocracy, persons of the Sadducaean persuasion. Yet there is practically no polemic with, or attack upon, the Sadducees as such in the New Testament. Apologetic and polemic are addressed to the

---

Mt 3, 7 with Lc 3, 7. In the Third Gospel the Baptist rebukes the multitudes (οἱ ὄχλοι) in general, calling them »offspring of vipers«. The First Evangelist retains the phrase — he even puts it in the mouth of Jesus, Mt 12, 34; 23, 33 — but substitutes »Pharisees and Sadducees« for the »multitudes« of Luke as the recipients of the address. The Evangelist dislikes the Pharisees, and attributes similar feelings to Jesus, and even to John.

[25] It is one of the commonest fallacies in New Testament exegesis to identify 'scribes' with Pharisees. A scribe, γραμματεύς or νομικός, is an 'official'; in modern parlance we would use the title 'civil servant'. In the ancient Jewish pattern of society this title was given to persons qualified to expound and interpret the Law. There was no difference between Jewish religious law and Jewish State law. Among the scribes were persons of other than Pharisaic persuasion. The erroneous identification is largely due to the author of the First Gospel who ostensibly used the terms as synonyms. The First Evangelist, himself a Pharisee by education, developed a pet aversion for that Jewish group from which he had come.

In the era of the Chronicler, the Levites occupied a position that was later to be taken by the 'scribes'. Originally a lay element, the scribes owed their influence not to birth or privilege as was the case with the priests and elders, but to their superior learning. In the time of Jesus, the γραμματεῖς still occupied only lower positions in the Jewish administration; the higher grades were reserved for the priestly aristocracy. Where 'scribes' are mentioned in the New Testament alongside priests and elders (or 'rulers') as being members of the Great Sanhedrin, their position is analogus to that of officially nominated members of a Legislative Council in contradistinction to the elected members of such an Assembly. This does not mean that the Sanhedrin, besides having 'scribes' among its members, consisted of democratically elected representatives; it means that priests and elders held their position in virtue of a birthright, whereas the scribes held theirs in virtue of education and training.

After the year 70 CE, with the high-priesthood abolished, the rabbis — in virtue of the same qualifications as those possessed by the scribes — attained the spiritual leadership of the nation. Levites, scribes, and rabbis, in succession, played in their relations to the higher class of priests a similar rôle in Jewish history as did the representatives of the plebs in their relations to patricii and optimates in Roman society.

[26] See p. 165, note 9 above.

followers of John the Baptist and to the Pharisees. This is no accident. During his life, Jesus had stood in closest relation to these groups, and after his death it was these groups that were most akin to those followers of Jesus who had formed themselves into a distinct community after the crucifixion. There would have been no point in arguing with the Sadducees; they were too far removed from the Christian position and could not have been converted either by pleading or by abuse. On the other hand, it must have been widely felt among exponents of the gospel that Baptists and Pharisees could perhaps be won over to their side. Propaganda was therefore directed towards these sections of the Jewish population, and for a time it met with some success. Part of the Baptist's following coalesced with the messianist movement, merging with the erstwhile disciples into one apostolic community. Similarly certain Pharisees — not only Paul! — joined forces with the messianist brotherhood of the apostles. In the Acts, we find references to "the Pharisees who have believed" (Acts 15, 5; cf. 21, 20), that is, Jews of the Pharisaic persuasion who embraced the belief in Jesus as the coming messianic ruler. But very soon Pharisaic resistance hardened. Progressively, as Christianity developed, relations between members of its fold and other Jews deteriorated. The disappointments which the preachers encountered among Pharisees whom they had addressed in the hope of winning them over to their cause, turned into hostility. This was the historical situation which resulted from the proclamation of Jesus' messiahship, a situation entirely different from that obtaining during the life of Jesus himself. Early preachers and subsequently the evangelists read back current rivalries between Pharisees and Jesus-messianists (i. e. the apostolic community) into the period of Jesus' own preaching activity. Hostile intentions of the opponents of the Christian movement — aroused at a time when the overt promotion of this movement was liable to cause Roman reprisals — were accommodated among reminiscences from the Master's life. Hence *the addition* of "the Pharisees" in passages mentioning various adversaries of Jesus, and, still more conspicuous, *the substitution* of "Pharisees" for "scribes" *(officials, civil servants)* in the only context for which a definite historical foundation can be reasonably claimed (Jn 11, 47 as compared with Mc 14, 1; Mt 26, 3; Lc 22, 2). In Mark already, the writer's perspective is not historical, but theological — yet there are historical reminiscences. In John and Matthew, history is completely overlaid with apologetic and ideological motifs.

In our demonstration so far we have confined ourselves to the comparison of such sources as are still accessible. As Mark is our earliest extant source, it might seem that we are unable to provide evidence from which we could trace back behind the Second Gospel the propensity to depict contemporary adversaries of the Christian communities as the actual enemies of Jesus. Yet the tendency to do so certainly did not become operative only after Mark had been composed. We are justified in holding that the Second Evangelist himself — and even his predecessors, the tradents of early preaching — were subject to its influence. To succumb to it was even easier for them than it was for the later evangelists, for the original preaching was passed on orally, and alterations in orally transmitted materials are more liable to escape the recorder's attention. We have a pointer to the fact that the propensity in question was at work before the Second Evangelist wrote. We find in Mc 3, 6; 12, 13 references to "the Herodians" and in Mc 8, 15 to "Herod". These references are not reproduced in the later Gospels, save in Mt 22, 16, "the Herodians" having ceased to be meaningful so far as the enemies of Christianity were concerned. The Pharisees were not in alliance with Herod Antipas, the tetrarch of Galilee and Peraea. No Jewish faction that might have been called "Herodians" was involved in the religious or political controversies rampant in Judaea during the life-time of Jesus. No such party existed at the time. The Marcan reference to an inimical attitude on the part of Herodians, or the rebuke administered to the latter, either points to the period of the reign of Agrippa I (41—44 CE) who took oppressive measures against some leaders of the messianist community (Acts 12, 1—5, 12, 16—17)[27] or — as indeed is more likely — to the efforts of Agrippa II and moderate Pharisaic leadership to dissuade the people, in the years 66 and 67, from entering upon a political course of action liable to result in an irreparable conflict with Roman authority[28]. When such a conflict did break out, supporters of the Herodian king and various Pharisees denounced Jewish revolutionaries to Roman officers. Messianists (= Jewish Christians) counted as apocalyptic enthusiasts and were suspected of har-

---

[27] Cf. Benjamin Wisner Bacon, »Pharisees and Herodians in Mark«, JBL vol. 39, 1920, pp. 102—112, especially pp. 107, 110, 112; the same, The Gospel of Mark: Its Composition and Date (New Haven, Conn., 1925), p. 75; for comparison see Elias J. Bi[c]kerman[n], »Les Hérodiens«, Revue biblique, tome 47, 1938, pp. 184—197, and Paul Joüon, »Les Hérodiens de l'Évangile«, Recherches de science religieuse, tome 28, 1938, pp. 585—588; also Ernst Lohmeyer, Das Evangelium des Markus (Göttingen ³1951), p. 67, note 2.

The Latinized form Ἡρῳδιανοί should be noticed. It indicates that in the mind of people among whom the tradition originated, the 'Herodians' were associated with the Romans — they sided with the legionary forces against the Zealot revolutionaries during 66—70 CE. The Latinized form of the word may also be a reflection of the fact that the Marcan Gospel was written in Rome.

[28] The sentiments, if not the ipsissima verba, of Agrippa II are reported by Josephus in the speech recorded in B. J. II 345—404. Many leading representatives of the Pharisees were treated by the victorious Romans not merely with leniency, but with consideration. An apt illustration is provided by the account of Yoḥanan ben Zakkai's escape from beleaguered Jerusalem and his reception by Vespasian who gave him permission to open an academy in Yabhneh (Jamnia); see T. B. Gittin 56 a, b. It can scarcely be doubted that the Romans looked upon the Pharisees as their potential, if not actual, allies.

bouring anti-Roman tendencies. In a Jewish setting, apocalyptic 'other-worldliness' and social-revolutionary 'idealism' were not mutually ex-clusive. The Jewish nationalism of the Zealots and their allies had a strong 'apocalyptic' tinge — and in earliest Christianity both strains, the apocalyptic and the national-revolutionary, were present. The sym-pathies of Jewish Christians were with those Jewish parties that op-posed Rome, and fought the Romans. Their own literary production — Revelation — as well as the fact that they preserved and treasured the Apocalypses of Ezra and Baruch prove their fellow-feeling for the re-bels. It might have been the case that in the early years of the revolt Pharisees and partisans of Aprippa II, possibly both, denounced some Jewish messianists (= Christians) to the Romans, which would explain both the alignment of "Pharisees and Herodians" in Mc 3, 6; 12, 13 and the caveat to "beware of the leaven of the Pharisees and the leaven of Herod" in Mc 8, 15.

In Lc 20, 20 — the passage corresponds to Mc 12, 13 — we read of "spies", sent out by the scribes and the chief priests to catch Jesus, instead of the Marcan dubbing "some of the Pharisees and of the Hero-dians". The Third Evangelist at this point scarcely used a written source other than Mark, yet it is possible that his rendering was prompted by information derived from Jewish Christians. He may have learned that "Pharisees and Herodians" were people who had spied on messianist gatherings, and who had perhaps denounced participants in such ga-therings during the occupation of Galilee, some time in the years 67 or 68 CE.

The opprobrious twin designation "Pharisees and Herodians" (doubt-less taken over by the Second Evangelist from his sources) appears to betray a 'revolutionary' and, by implication, an anti-Roman attitude. An anti-Roman attitude definitely comes to the fore in another place, namely, the pericope about the Gerasene (or Gergesene) swine in Mc 5, 1—13. The Second Evangelist himself shows a pro-Roman tendency — he lived in Rome and wrote there; but the sources from which he drew occasionally betray an anti-Roman sentiment. Whether the story origi-nally circulated as a popular *Schwank*[29] or as a *Novelle*[30], or whatever function it fulfilled when first formulated, need not be discussed here. As it is reproduced in the Second Gospel, an anti-Roman bias at some time affected the character of the narrative. This is discernible in the use of the word Λεγιών as the name of the demonic agency. To the modern reader the word simply denotes 'multitude', but then the mo-

---

[29] Rudolf Bultmann, *Geschichte der synoptischen Tradition*, pp. 224, 225; English edition, pp. 210, 211.

[30] Martin Dibelius, *Die Formgeschichte des Evangeliums* (Tübingen ³1959), pp. 84—87; Engl. ed., pp. 87—89. For a more recent treatment of the story, see Burkill, *Mysterious Revelation*, pp. 86—95.

dern reader is acquainted with the Marcan story. What is remarkable
is that a Latin expression is employed. In Aramaic as well as Greek
there are indigenous words which convey the meaning 'troop' or 'great
horde'[31]. The use of the Latin word constitutes a direct verbal thrust at
the occupation-forces in Jewish lands. The point of the tale lies in the
report that the demons went into the swine, and were drowned with
them. During the years of the great revolt against Rome, the *Legio
Decima Fretensis* was stationed in Galilee, near the place where the
story in Mc 5, 1—13 has ist *locale*[32]. The emblem of the Tenth Roman
Legion was a boar. Though it would be absurd to make definite asser-
tions, it is quite possible that the story of the Gerasene swine assumed
its present form during the years of the Jewish-Roman war. Could it
have been occasioned by an incident in which some Roman legionaries
took a swim in the Lake of Tiberias and were drowned? Although a
definite answer cannot be given to this question, a note of malicious
joy over the unfortunate fate of *Legion* is unmistakable. The Latin
name was not chosen by accident.

There were many divisions among the Jewish people in the time of
Jesus, but no religious party denied another party the right to propagate
their teachings. Concepts such as 'orthodoxy' or 'heresy' did not exist.
Heresy in its modern sense is an achievement of Christian history. The
most accurate, most punctilious kind of Jewish religious observance
is in Acts 26, 5 referred to by the words ἡ ἀκριβεστάτη αἵρεσις τῆς
ἡμετέρας θρησκείας. When Josephus speaks of various *divisions*, αἱρέσεις,
*among the Jewish people*, he includes the group to which he himself
professes to belong. The word αἵρεσις meant 'section', 'party', without
any aspersion of deviation from correct opinion, or any implication of
exclusiveness. It is not used *in malam partem*, for all sections, all Jewish
groups, whatever their theological doctrines, are so called. The idea
that a belief was wrong in the sense that its protagonists were to be
considered as being outside the pale — an entailment of 'orthodoxy' —
— is un-Jewish" it derives from Hellenized Christianity.

Whatever the precise character of Jesus' teaching, it could hardly
have been the ground for his condemnation to death. Apostasy from
Judaism, and blasphemy, would have carried such a sentence, but the
New Testament records no case of blasphemy by Jesus and makes it
abundantly clear that he never preached apostasy. The grounds for his
condemnation were of a political character.

The contention that in the first century Jews did not persecute other
Jews for purely religious reasons, may appear to conflict with certain

---

[31] The fact that the term λεγιών later became a loan-word in Greek and in
Aramaic is irrelevant so far as the question of the story's origin is concerned.
[32] *Cf.* B. J. III 233, 289. The commander of this legion, Trajan — the father
the later emperor — is also mentioned as being in Galilee in the passages B. J. III
8, 485.

evidence we derive from a study of the history of Christian beginnings. Stephen, James and John the sons of Zebedee, Paul of Tarsus, James the brother of Jesus, and apparently others, were persecuted in their time and prosecuted by Jewish judicial authorities. But the ground for such action was political expediency, not dogmatic intolerance. Christianity, in its earliest form, was one of the many apocalyptic Jewish movements that denied the permanence and validity of the existing political order. The early Christians were deeply convinced of their citizenship-rights in Heaven (Phil 3, 20), and it required a certain adjustment before they learned that besides loyalty to their heavenly home they owed obedience to terrestrial rulers. Their attitude towards the State was, to say the least, ambiguous. It is all very well to say "Render unto Caesar what belongs to Caesar" — but what belongs to Caesar at a time when the Kingdom of God is expected to break in any day, any hour? When Paul gave his readers instruction concerning "the powers that be" and impressed upon them that they are "ordained of God" (Rom 13, 1), the bare fact that such an admonition was required proves that it was felt necessary at times to restrain the eschatological fervour of church members by exhorting them to recognize the validity, and respect the existence, of the civil authority. Jews without distinction of their αἵρεσις, regardless of their party affiliation, were most seriously affected by the repercussions of messianist agitation. "Those who have turned the world upside down" (Acts 17, 6) brought great discomfiture upon all the Alexandrian Jews, to whom the Emperor Claudius addressed the warning not to shelter agitators from Syria[33]. Similarly, the entire Jewish community in Rome was expelled from the city because

---

[33] Papyrus Brit. Mus. 1912, lines 96—98: ʽ μὴ ἐπάγεσθαι ἢ προσείεσθαι ἀπ Συρίας ἢ Αἰγύπτου καταπλέοντας 'Ιουδαίους ἐξ οὗ μείζονας ὑπονοίας ἀναγκασ[ ἥσομ[αι] λαμβάνειν: see Harold Idris Bell, Jews and Christians in Egypt. Th Jewish Troubles in Alexandria and the Athanasian Controversy (London 1924), p. 2:

Admittedly, the interpretation here offered is not established beyond doub The words may simply express a prohibition to admit within the Jewish πολιτεία ( Alexandria immigrant Jews from abroad. The decree mentions besides Syria — Ant ochia was the headquarters of messianist missionary propaganda — also Egypt a an area from which undesirable influx might be expected. But would Claudius have used such strong language if it was merely a case of ordinary movements of Jew from one place of residence to another? This in itself could hardly account for th Emperor's »greater suspicions« to which he refers in his decree.

Claudius was not imbued with anti-Jewish prejudice. The fact that he restore Judaea to a Jewish king, making Agrippa ruler over the whole of Palestine, suf ciently proves that he was not in principle hostile towards Jews as such. If he, in h decree to the Alexandrians, blames the Jews for having brought an epidemic upc the whole world (κοινή τις τῆς οἰκουμένης νόσος), he was referring to the ferme which apocalyptic and messianist stirring had caused among the Jewish inhabitan of the entire Empire. Cf. my article »Tacitus and Pliny: The Early Christians Journal of Historical Studies (Princeton), vol. 1, 1967—68, pp. 31—36.

of messianist commotions[34]. The Romans judged the proclamation of
"another king" (Acts 17, 7) to be an act of disloyalty to the Emperor.
In their efforts to eradicate "the pernicious superstition" (Tacitus),
Roman officials also persecuted Jews who had not been affected by
messianic-apocalyptic fervour. Neither able nor willing to distinguish
between the various Jewish sects, they made the whole nation suffer
because of agitation which had been brought about by the missionary
zeal of the apostles. This accounts for the fact that prior to the year
70 CE Jewish leaders, the Sadducaean high-priests and King Agrippa I,
thought it incumbent upon them to take action against the spreading of
messianism, and that after the year 70 CE the Pharisees — who were
moderates politically even though they shared messianic beliefs —
excluded the adherents of Jesus from the synagogues so as to draw a
line and make Roman authorities aware that they themselves took no
part in apocalyptic propaganda. The expulsion of the 'Christians' was
not an isolated event. In later times, other Jewish groups who adhered
to various messiahs, or who persisted in apocalyptic enthusiasm, were
not treated differently. From the middle of the second century, after
the unsuccessful revolt of Ben Kosebah, we have a saying of Rabbi
Yonathan (reported by Rabbi Samuel ben Naḥmani) that at least equals
the resentment accorded to Christianity by some rabbis: תפח רוחם של
מחשבי קצין = *may breath fail those who calculate the times*[35], that is,
who speculate about the end of the existing world and the impending
inauguration of the messianic reign. Such animosity as was displayed
against the Apostolic Church by responsible political leaders of the
Jews in the period between Jesus' death and the outbreak of the great
revolt against Rome has to be considered in the light of Roman reac-
tions to messianism.

The picture which the New Testament gives of Jesus' relationship to
his compatriots is one of over-simplification; they are either presented
as his followers (bearing witness, by the way, to all the christological
claims made on behalf of Jesus by the evangelists) or as his implacable
opponents. Historical facts were, of course, quite different. The Talmud
does not preserve any contemporary evidence of the impression Jesus
made on his co-nationals. Just as the evangelists identified their coeval
Jewish adversaries with the opponents of Jesus, so the rabbis identified
third-century — and later — Christian teaching with that of the
historical Jesus, and attempted to refute it. The attitudes of contemporary Jews towards the preacher from Nazareth were not of the black-
white pattern such as we find in the Gospels or the Talmud.

---

[34] Suetonius, Claudius xxv 4 (*cf.* Acts 18, 2).

[35] T. B. Sanhedrin 97 b. Some manuscripts read עצמן (*their essence*) instead
of רוחם (*their spirit, their breath*). I am indebted to Leon Roth, formerly Rector of
the Hebrew University in Jerusalem, for drawing my attention to this passage and
for suggestions concerning its, admittedly somewhat tentative, interpretation.

Shahrastâni (1076—1153) has preserved information on the existence
of a Jewish sect, the Ananites, who — while rejecting any christological
claim on behalf of Jesus — respected him as a teacher[36]. We cannot say
from where Shahrastâni derived his information. The name "Ananites"
could have been due to some confusion with a group of the Qaraites,
but even if the name were inexact, this would not invalidate the assumption that the writer had heard of Jews who held Jesus in esteem, although they were neither members of the Christian Church nor of
a heretical Judaeo-Christian sect. Presumably, their assessment of Jesus
was such that they considered him to be a vehicle of God's message to
mankind, his teaching being derived from divine inspiration. Some centuries before Shahrastâni wrote, there were of course Jews in Medina,
in the Hedjaz, who venerated the memory of Jesus without accepting
any christological dogmas of the Church. Their religious views had
points of contact with those of the Ebionites of whom something is
known from the Pseudo-Clementines, and about whom Jerome and
Epiphanius have left accounts of rather doubtful value. Those in Medina, however, appear to have remained closer to 'normative' Judaism
than the sectarian Judaeo-Christians, who were exposed to influences
from a Greek speaking Christian milieu. It is inherently improbable
that a section of the Jewish nation with such a 'positive neutralistic'
attitude as that of Shahrastâni's Ananites should have survived and
continued in an unbroken line from the time of Jesus to the eleventh
century. There is a possibility that the "Ananites" were Jews who had
come under the influence of Islam and who had appropriated the Moslem view of Jesus' rôle as a prophet[37]. Even so, the example cited shows

---

[36] *Abu-'l-Fath, Muhammad asch-Schahrastâni's Religionspartheien und Philo-
sophen-Schulen. Übersetzt und mit Anmerkungen versehen* von Dr. Theodor Haar-
brücker. Erster Theil (Halle 1850): »... sie erklären 'Îsa (= Jesus) in seinen Ermah-
nungen und Anweisungen für wahrhaftig, und behaupten, er habe der Thorâ
nicht im Geringsten widersprochen... nur dass sie seine Prophetie und Sendung
nicht anerkennen. Einige von ihnen sind der Ansicht, 'Îsa selbst habe nicht den Anspruch gemacht, dass er ein gesendeter Prophet und der Stifter eines Gesetzes sei
... Sie sagen ferner: die Jahûd (= Juden) haben Unrecht begangen, da sie ihn zuerst
für einen Lügner erklärten, dann seine Berufung nicht anerkannten und ihn zuletzt
tödteten, und dann seine Stellung und Absicht verkannten«, p. 253; in William Cureton's original edition of Shahrastâni's *Book of Religious and Philosophical Sects*
(London 1842), p. 167.

Ash-Shahrastâni may have been informed of the existence of the Ananites by
Al-Birûni. To some extent, his account of their beliefs may be based on combination.
The important fact remains that there were in the Middle Ages Jews who retained
such a clear-headed, impartial and dispassionate conception of the activities of
Jesus.

[37] The Moslem attitude to Jesus is itself a heritage from certain Jews — Jews of
a kind that could hardly be termed 'Jewish-Christian' since they had virtually
no christology.

that Jewish attitudes to Jesus were more diversified than would appear from evangelical descriptions.

The New Testament tells us little, and the Talmud nothing, of the actual relationship between Jesus and Jews outside the circle of discipleship. The relations were much more varied than foes on one side, followers on the other.

The ethical teaching of Jesus is Pharisaic. As for his eschatology, we are unable to point to exact Pharisaic parallels. This could be accidental; except for the Assumption of Moses and, of course, early strata of the New Testament, no Palestinian records have been preserved which supply direct evidence of the beliefs entertained by that generation of Palestinian Jews to which Jesus belonged. Indeed, it may be that the eschatological outlook of Jesus accords with the general mode of an early form of Pharisaic thought. Pharisaism survived the events of the year 70, but did not remain unchanged. Rabbinical sources, coming from a later date, do not furnish precise information regarding the tenets of early Pharisaism. Living under political conditions vastly different from those prevailing before the year 70 CE, the rabbis were desirous of adjusting the profession of Jewish faith to the exigencies of their day. They were consciously striving to arrive at a *modus vivendi* with the Roman authority, and hence their anxiety to suppress what might lead to any conflict with that authority. The exposition of ideas of an eschatological character could stimulate apocalyptic speculation, and this in turn could all too easily renew agitation such as that which had led to armed rebellion, thereby impairing Jewish relations with the State. Prudentialism of this kind promoted the deliberate toning down of those elements in Judaism liable to give rise to apocalyptic excitation.

It is hence possible that rabbi Yeshu mi-Naṣrath — Jesus of Nazareth, that is — might have been representative of pre-rabbinical Pharisaism not only in his ethical teaching, but also in his eschatology[38]. Of course, this is not to be taken to imply that Jesus did not formulate his views in his own individual fashion. It is its general tenor which corresponds with the Pharisaic pattern; on the ethical side quite obviously, and on the eschatological conceivably.

In Christian tradition the word 'Pharisee' has become synonymous with 'hypocrite', or it is applied to one who splits hairs over *minutiae* whilst overlooking really important matters. "To strain out the gnat and swallow the camel" has been accepted as the mental picture of

---

[38] Rudolf Bultmann, *o. c.*: »Die spezifisch eschatologische Stimmung [bildet] das Charakteristikum der Verkündigung Jesu«, p. 222; Engl. ed., p. 205. *Cf.* Amos N. Wilder: »The character and form of Jesus' utterance is uniquely determined by his eschatological conscience and calling«, the Cullmann Freundesgabe *Neotestamentica et Patristica,* ed. W. C. van Unnik (Leiden 1962), p. 8.

Pharisaic attitudes[39]. *Yet in historical reality, Jesus was a Pharisee*. His teaching was Pharisaic teaching, Pharisaic from the period before the conflagration with Roman military might, when an eschatological emphasis may yet have pervaded Pharisaic thought more strongly than in the tannaitic age. What we know of the Pharisees from Jewish records written for Jews comes from a period after the destruction of the Temple. It was formulated under conditions that had undergone a drastic change. Eschatology, together with apocalyptic, was deliberately pushed into the background and a demand for punctilious observance of the legal injunctions took its place. The aim was to preserve the cohesion of the Jews who now had to live everywhere as minorities amidst non-Jewish populations to whose social and political order they were subject.

In the whole of the New Testament we are unable to find a single historically reliable instance of religious differences between Jesus and members of the Pharisaic guilds, let alone evidence of a mortal conflict. A full generation after the death of Jesus, when differences had already developed between upholders of the belief in Jesus' messianic status and 'normative' Pharisaism, representatives of the latter still found it possible to side with the former in a case in which a Sadducaean high-priest used his position to suppress activities of the Jewish-Christian movement[40]. At that time the theological claims advanced by the Jewish-Christian preachers were already well differentiated from the aspirations of the more moderate wing of Pharisaic Jews, yet the differences were less pronounced than those that divided either of the two factions from the Sadducees. In the time of Jesus, differences which obtained around the year 62 CE had not yet arisen. If the evangelists portray Jesus as being in violent opposition to the Pharisees, they depict a state of affairs that had come about only some decades after the crucifixion.

To assist our understanding of the psychological situation in which the community of Jesus-messianists lived, and their deep disappoint-

---

[39] The same reproofs as those which Jesus makes in the synoptic Gospels against the Pharisees in general, are made in the Talmud by various Jewish rabbis against certain classes of Pharisees. In both cases the background is Palestinian. Gospels and Talmud express disapproval of practices that were adjudged by religious leaders to be defective. Jesus could have voiced such views without excluding himself from the 'Pharisaic school', as long as his criticisms were confined to concrete and specific cases. By criticizing individuals, Jesus might have displeased and offended some people in his neighbourhood, but animosity thus provoked would not have constituted a ground for accusing him of a political offence. There was a strong reluctance in Jewish circles to bring internal disputes before a non-Jewish magistrate. Cf. my article »Şadoqite Fragments IX, 1«, *Revue de Qumran* Tome 6, 1967, pp. 131—136.

[40] Ant XX 199—201; Eusebius, Historiae ecclesiasticae II 23, 21—24 (GCS Eusebius II, 1, pp. 172—174; MPG 20, cols. 204, 205).

ment with Pharisees at large, the passage in Lc 19, 39 should be read with great care. We have here a description of how "some of the Pharisees", favourably disposed towards Jesus, were trying to exercise a moderating influence upon the messianist fervour of a crowd of Jesus' followers. Whether historical or not in the sense that the scene depicted actually belongs to the situation in which it is set by the Third Evangelist[41], the narration is historical in another sense: the Pharisees, unsuccessfully, endeavoured to curb the messianic enthusiasm of the primitive *ecclesia,* but their efforts were resented in apostolic circles. Hence, Pharisees and Herodians — to wit, parties opposed to committing the nation to an irrevocable break with Rome — figure in Mark together as antagonists of Jesus, or as persons against whom Jesus warned his followers.

Reports of Jesus' conflicts with various Jews, or rather Jewish groups, are not wholly the creation of the Second Evangelist; such reports are often derived from tradition. What had slowly started in tradition was brought to completion by the efforts of the writers who composed the Gospels. For the most part, the underlying traditions adumbrated communal conflicts which had arisen between early Jesus-messianists and other Jewish groups. In some instances tradition may go back to the recollection of an actual event in Jesus' life, but we cannot say so with any degree of assurance except as regards the final conflict. Statements in the Gospels describing a situation before that referred to in Mc 14,

---

[41] The Third Evangelist undoubtedly used a source for his supplementation of Mc 11, 1—10. What we read in Lc 19, 39—44 is derived from such a source, a source characterized by a favourable attitude towards Pharisaism. The Pharisees are represented in Lc 19, 39 as concerned for the safety of Jesus. There are other passages that come from the 'Special Source' of Luke in which a similar mode of representing the Pharisees is to be found, *e. g.* Lc 13, 31 (the Herod of this passage appears to be Herod Antipas). *Cf.* below, p. 198, note 14.

If, as Schlatter seems to have thought (see above, p. 75, note 10), the pericope Lc 23, 27—31 originated in the same kind of milieu as Lc 19, 39—44, there existed a Christian-Jewish group which maintained amicable relations with Pharisees after the disaster of the years 66—70 CE. For the note of despair, struck in Lc 23, 27—31 (observe the contrast between Lc 23, 29 and Lc 11, 27 b), suggests that the pericope originated only after the fall of Jerusalem (there is a parallel to Lc 23, 29 in 2 Baruch 10, 13—16). The pericope would then preserve a strand of Judaeo-Christian tradition of relatively late date, which betrays sympathy for the Jewish cause; those among whom the tradition arose, felt as Jews in the national disaster. This group appears to have tried to avoid a break with the Pharisees. Traditions from the Lucan 'Special Source' have, generally speaking, preserved their Palestinian *timbre,* whilst 'Marcan tradition' underwent a process of editorial redrafting in Rome. It is perhaps worthy of notice here that the sayings of Lc 11, 27 and 23, 29 are combined in The Gospel of Thomas, Logion 79, the juxtaposition having apparently been made in the interest of an Encratite interpretation.

1—2 (Jn 11, 47—48) and implying that "the Jews" or "the Pharisees" or
"the scribes" or "the priests", or whatever other designation may be
used, "planned to kill Jesus" or "tried to catch Jesus" contain no information of historical or biographical value. Such statements are to be
taken as expressions of the viewpoints of the various evangelists who
themselves were affected by the conditions of their own time, and who
retrojected their experience of Jewish hostility into the time of Jesus.
The employment of the motif of mortal hostility between Jesus and any
of his contemporaries is directly due to the editorial scheme — in Mark
no less than in John.

Jesus was a Jew. He lived among Jews, he learned from Jews, he
taught Jews. The successes he enjoyed and the adversities he suffered
throughout his life were shared with other Jews. Those of whom he
approved and those of whom he disapproved were likewise Jews. It is
only natural therefore that the persons with whom he sometimes disa-
greed were also Jews. In the course of his life, he made friends and
made enemies among the members of the nation to which he belonged.
He came into conflict with the authorities in Jerusalem towards the
end of his life. A decision that he should stand trial on a charge of
seditious activities was arrived at with the connivance or concurrence
of the holders of highest Jewish office. As for earlier conflicts that may
have arisen between Jesus and other Jews before the former's last visit
to Jerusalem, we are unable to make trustworthy historical deductions.
The arrangement of the reports of such conflicts is due to the literary
designs of the respective evangelists. The author of Mark had at his
disposal reports of earlier conflicts, but the order he gave to the
reported incidents is the Evangelist's own work. Though rooted in tradition, the controversy stories bespeak a situation in the period which
followed the crucifixion, illustrating a state of antagonism between the
'Apostolic Church' and certain Jewish groups. Jesus is mentioned in
these stories merely as the mouthpiece of the community. The controversy stories afford no clue to the actual subject of contention — if any
— between Jesus of Nazareth and his contemporaries; they reflect situations in the life of the Christian communities, not in the life of Jesus. As
far as the controversy stories are concerned, the extant records do not
allow us to penetrate beyond communal traditions. Doubtless, not only
the early Church, but Jesus himself had disagreements with Jews and
himself passed strictures upon Jews, but we are unable to determine
the precise circumstances of any such differences.

In stating that Jesus stood close to Pharisaism and that the traditions
underlying Mc 14—15 are in no way indicative of Pharisaic hostility towards him, it is not asserted that Jesus never in his life had any alter-
cation with persons of the Pharisaic persuasion. He apparently came
into conflict with individuals of his immediate environment (Mc 3, 21,

31—35; 6, 4; Jn 7, 5)[42], and it is probable that he also on occasion had disputes with persons who had a religious orientation similar to his own. But controversies of Jewish provenance in which Jesus might have been involved before his last visit to Jerusalem had no determining influence upon his ultimate fate. The grounds for his arrest had nothing to do with personal or religious differences between Jesus and any of his compatriots. Rather than the content of his teaching, it was primarily the effect which his teaching exercised on certain sections of the populace that induced the authorities to take action against him.

---

[42] Even the indications in Mark and John of disagreement between Jesus and his family circle may well be coloured by conditions prevailing in the 'apostolic church', namely, the rivalry between adherents of James the brother of the Lord and those of Peter the leader of the Twelve. *Cf.* my article »I Corinthians XV 3 b—7«, *Novum Testamentum* vol. 2, 1957, pp. 142—150.

# 14. BEHIND THE PREACHING

In the preceding chapters we conducted an analysis of individual items in the Passion Narratives of the canonical Gospels in a sustained attempt to identify apologetic motives introduced by the particular evangelists into the traditional material at their disposal. We also considered the traditional residue, which remained after the exclusion of editorial features, in an endeavour to disentangle theological interpretation from narratives of a factual nature. Consequently, we may roughly classify the contents of the accounts of Jesus' trial into three categories:

(a) primary tradition,
(b) secondary tradition,
(c) editorial accretion.

Although no single part of any of the extant Passion Narratives is entirely free from what may be termed 'editorial accretion', and the primary tradition, in one and the same pericope of a particular Gospel, is frequently mingled with elements from secondary traditions, there is warrant for the employment of the classificatory schema indicated; and in the interests of clarification we may recapitulate the main results of the foregoing investigations as follows:

1. The Arrest of Jesus on the Mount of Olives (Mc 14, 46—52; Lc 22, 49—53; Jn 18, 3, 10—11): based on primary tradition.

2. The Transfer of the Prisoner to the High-Priest's Residence (Mc 14, 53 a; Lc 22, 54; Jn 18, 12—13 a): primary tradition.

3. A Preliminary Investigation by Annas (Jn 18, 19—24): an editorial introduction, in default of tradition, due to the Fourth Evangelist.

4. A Night-Session of the Sanhedrin in the Palace of the High-Priest, including an examination of witnesses and the trial of Jesus, ending in his condemnation to death for blasphemy (Mc 14, 53 b, 55—64): an editorial accretion due to the Second Evangelist.

5. The Mockery of Jesus in the High-Priest's Residence (Lc 22, 63—65; Mc 14, 65): a secondary development founded on proof from prophecy.

6. A brief Deliberation in the Sanhedrin's Council-Hall, early in the morning after Jesus' arrest, resulting in the despatch of Jesus to Pilate (Lc 22, 66; 23, 1; Mc 15, 1): based on primary tradition.

7. A Morning Session of the Sanhedrin for the examination but not the trial of Jesus, without the passing of a death sentence (Lc 22, 67—71): an importation from Matthew with pronounced editorial alterations, possibly due to a post-Lucan adapter.

8. The Examination and Trial of Jesus before Pilate (Mc 15, 2—5; Lc 23, 2—3; Jn 18, 28, 33 b): based on primary tradition.

9. An Examination of Jesus by Herod Antipas (Lc 23, 6—10, 12): a secondary tradition[1], reproduced with clear marks of editorial retouching, by the Third Evangelist or a post-Lucan adapter.

10. The Mockery of Jesus before Herod Antipas (Lc 23, 11): a secondary tradition.

11 a. The Barabbas Episode (Mc 15, 5—15 a): an editorial adaptation of an element from the primary tradition (the parallel non-Marcan reports being without exception derived from the Second Gospel).

11 b. Pilate's Endeavour to spare Jesus' Life (Mc 15, 5 b, 9—11 a, 12—15 a; Mt 27, 18—20, 22—25; Lc 23—4, 13—16, 20—24; Jn 18, 31, 38 b; 19, 5 b, 6 b—12, 15 b): editorial embellishments, becoming progressively more prominent.

12. The Scourging of Jesus by Pilate's Soldiers before the passing of the death sentence (Jn 19, 1—3): an editorial supplementation, arrived at by dislocating the item from its traditional (Marcan) setting.

---

[1] The story is not primitive. Neither is it a creation of the Evangelist or a post-Lucan editor. The account of Jesus' interrogation by Herod is based on a tradition that had grown up later than that underlying the Second Gospel. This tradition, secondary though it is, might in some form also have been known to the author of the Gospel of Peter, but we cannot be certain about this. The author of the Gospel of Peter perhaps based his account on oral traditions which could have developed from the literary basis provided by Luke and Matthew.

Martin Dibelius doubted whether the writer of the Third Gospel was in a position to make use of any non-Marcan traditions, or sources, for his own account of the Passion. Dibelius considered Lc 23, 6—12 to have been constructed by the Evangelist from inferences without recourse to non-Marcan sources: »Lukas besass ... keine konkrete Überlieferung von den Vorgängen bei Herodes«, Martin Dibelius, »Herodes und Pilatus«, ZNW vol. 16, 1915, pp. 113—126, on p. 122; now also *Botschaft und Geschichte, Gesammelte Aufsätze,* Band 1: *Zur Evangelienforschung* (Tübingen 1953), pp. 278—292, on p. 288. »Lukas ... hat ... gehört, dass Herodes und Pilatus im Prozesse Jesu gemeinsame Sache gemacht haben. Diese Nachricht veranlasste ihn, seiner Leidensgeschichte eine Herodesszene einzuverleiben, die des konkreten Inhalts ermangelt und lediglich aus bekannten Motiven aufgebaut ist«, *ibidem,* p. 123, resp. 289.

Though I concur with Dibelius's view that Lc 23, 6—12 is not based on historical reminiscences, I nevertheless do not think that the story was patched up by the Third Evangelist himself in the manner of repeating isolated Marcan items and placing them into a new and different context. It seems more likely that the modification of primitive traditional items had come about in the process of growing tradition, and that the Evangelist — or perhaps a post-Lucan editor of the Third Gospel — having come across a story concerning the involvement of Herod (Antipas) in the proceedings at Jesus' trial, inserted the episode Lc 23, 6—12 into the account of Jesus' examination by Pilate. The wording of Acts 4, 27 indicates that some such tale was in circulation, and doubtless the story had been developed from Ps 2, 1—2 to provide yet further proof from prophecy. *Cf.* above, p. 147, note 4, and W. Koch, ed. *Zum Prozess Jesu,* p. 32.

13. The Death Sentence by Pilate and the Administration of Scourging preliminary to the execution by crucifixion (Mc 15, 15 b): based on primary tradition, but toned down so far as the explicit pronouncement of the governor's death sentence is concerned.

14. The Mockery by Pilate's Soldiers (Mc 15, 16—20): based on primary tradition.

15. Jesus' Removal from the Prefect's Court to the Place of Execution, the Crucifixion, the Inscription on the Cross (Mc 15, 21—26): based on primary tradition.

16. The Lament for Jesus (Lc 23, 27—30): a secondary tradition.

17. The Last Words (Mc 15, 34): a secondary tradition; Lc 23, 46 and Jn 19, 30 are editorial.

18. The Death-Cry (Mc 15, 37): based on primary tradition.

By demonstrating the derivation of constituent parts of the evangelical Passion Narratives we have in a limited way effected a clarification of their literary character — that is to say, we have endeavoured to determine the origin of the various accounts. The results of this investigation afford some assistance in our attempt to shed light on t h e a c t u a l  h i s t o r i c a l  i s s u e s involved, though obscurity may still surround some of these.

With regard to the historical as distinct from the literary problem, we may also employ a threefold classification. There are matters on which certainty prevails; there are such on which a reasonable degree of probability allows of modest inferences; finally there are such on which the available sources offer no clue for the making of historical deductions.

It can be affirmed with assurance that Jesus was arrested by Roman military personnel (Jn 18, 12) for political reasons (Mc 14, 48) and then conducted to a local Jewish administrative official (Mc 14, 53 a; Lc 22, 54; Jn 18, 13 a) during the same night. The following morning, after a brief deliberation by the Jewish authorities (Mc 15, 1 a; Lc 22, 66), he was handed back to the Romans for trial (Mc 15, 1 b; Lc 23, 1; Jn 18, 28 a). The governor sentenced Jesus to death by crucifixion (Tacitus; Mc 15, 15 b, 26), the sentence being carried out in accordance with Roman penal procedure (Mc 15, 15 b, 24 a, 27).

A reasonable degree of probability attaches to the inference that on the night of his arrest — during the interval between his despatch to a local Jewish official and the matutinal deliberation in the Council-Hall — Jesus was interrogated by a member of the high-priest's staff who also questioned witnesses and drew up a charge-sheet which was approved by Jewish magistrates in the morning following the arrest (Josephus; Mc 15, 1 a; Lc 22, 66). After having been sentenced by Pilate, the prisoner was subjected to derision on the part of soldiers from the execution squad (Mc 15, 16—20).

No certain answers can be given to the following questions:

Firstly, what was the immediate cause inducing the authorities to take official action against Jesus?

Secondly, who took the initiative in ordering the apprehension of Jesus?

Thirdly, what precisely did Jesus do to provoke police action against himself?

Not unnaturally, these are questions which many people will deem to be the most important.

It is the non-biographical character of the Gospels that makes it almost impossible to ascertain the immediate cause of the arrest of Jesus. The movement he initiated doubtless possessed political implications. The very fact that his followers saw Jesus' significance in *messianic* terms indicates the presence of political aspirations. Earliest Christianity was an apocalyptic Jewish movement with revolutionary tendencies. Such sayings as are recorded in Acts 1, 6; Mt 19, 28 (Lc 22, 30 b) or Lc 19, 27 exemplify the political concern of the disciples. Yet they do not prove anything about Jesus himself, the aims he entertained and the hopes he cherished. The fact that Jesus was crucified as "King of the Jews" is sufficient to demonstrate that rebellious potentialities were associated with the movement already during the life-time of Jesus. But the evidence for the existence of political motives in the minds of the adherents of Jesus is stronger for the post- than for the pre-crucifixion period. All the same, as Jesus was crucified on the ground of a charge of tumult or sedition, his activities must have had a political aspect for some people even before his death had taken place. But this does not in any way mean that he himself put forward political claims, or asserted his messiahship, *i. e.* his vocation to become Israel's ruler. It would have sufficed as a ground for the condemnation of Jesus if only a small section of his following had understood his preaching in a political sense, and if such a circumstance had come to the knowledge of Pilate.

The sayings in Acts 1, 6; Mt 19, 28 and Lc 19, 27 are evidently 'Gemeindebildungen' though the New Testament reports them as pronouncements made by Jesus. They definitely indicate that the apostolic preachers combined political with religious expectations. But they in no wise afford information concerning Jesus himself. The Gospels contain other sayings attributed to Jesus, in which a chauvinistic flavour is perceptible. Such is the case with Mc 7, 27. The Marcan framework of this saying appears to be unhistorical[2],

---

[2] See above, p. 4; and T. A. Burkill »The Historical Development of the Story of the Syrophoenician Woman (Mark vii: 24—31)«, *NovT* vol. 9, 1967, pp. 161—177; also available in his *New Light on the Earliest Gospel*, pp. 94—120.

while the saying itself might conceivably go back to Jesus. If made by Jesus, the utterance would betray immoderate national pride on his part and a disdainfully exclusive attitude towards everyone and everything non-Jewish; for it should be borne in mind that in the near-Eastern parlance of the time such a use of the term 'dog' would be offensive in the highest degree. In Mt 10, 5 and 15, 24 there are further sayings of a 'nationalistic' connotation, which have an early ring about them. Matthew 18, 17 might also be cited — the height of contempt for a worthless fellow being expressed by equating him with a pagan (ἐθνικός). Persons who do not submit to the authority of "the church" (ἐκκλησία, עדה), and hence are liable to excommunication, have the same status as tax-gatherers and pagans[3]. This saying reveals pronounced nationalistic feeling. The general impression is nevertheless not without ambiguity: the tax-gatherers, considered to be outside the pale by Jesus in Mt 18, 17 b, are in other passages (Mc 2, 15; Mt 11, 19; Lc 7, 34 and 18, 9—14) represented as persons with whom he entertained cordial relations — and these passages would seem to have more claim to historical trustworthiness than Mt 18, 17[4]. We are here provided with evidence that Jesus adopted a friendly attitude towards a class of people whom 'nationalistically-minded' Jews despised. Nevertheless, it would be rash to assume that Jesus was totally free from patriotic sentiments. He shared with other Jews of his time that inordinate pride which stems from a sense of belonging to the people whom God has chosen as his partners, a people bound by an everlasting covenant to be God's servants and witnesses. Jesus was imbued with such self-appreciation, and prided himself on being a Jew. Even so, nationalistic feelings as such constitute no proof of active advocacy of rebellion.

The New Testament contains evidence of the existence of seditious tendencies among the followers of Jesus (e. g. Jn 6, 15), and it is plain that Jesus did not dissociate himself from people who belonged to revolutionary sections of the population. The list, or lists, of his immediate followers contains at least one "Zealot". That Jesus enjoyed friendly personal relations with people adhering to anti-Roman factions is generally recognized: »... [the apostles] had never entertained any other thought, since they had been with Jesus, than that they would

---

[3] The Matthaean setting of the saying militates against the view that we have here an authentic pronouncement of Jesus; Mt 18, 15—17 a is an adaptation of an old, pre-Christian, disciplinary statute. The words in v. 17 b are an addition which does not necessarily derive from Jesus.

[4] The tax-gatherers of the synoptic Gospels are probably not the contractors themselves, but their servants who were responsible for collecting outstanding dues from the rural population. Cf. Joachim Jeremias, »Zöllner und Sünder«, ZNW vol. 30, 1931, pp. 293—300.

fight side by side with Him in the unavoidable war with the Romans«[5]. »Mochte... [die] persönliche Religion [Jesu] noch so sehr an die Innerlichkeit der alten Propheten anknüpfen, die Seinen konnten ihn nicht anders als mit den Augen ihrer Zeit und ihres Volkes betrachten. War er der erwartete Messias, ... so musste er als Davidide den Thron seines Ahnherrn wiederaufrichten, musste die Römer unterwerfen, ja vernichten, und die paradiesische Friedenszeit für Israel bringen. Er starb am Kreuz...«[6] As the different versions of the list of "The Twelve" amply show, the evangelists no longer knew the names of the Twelve. The Simon ὁ κανανσῖος (קַנְאָנָא) of Mc 3, 18 is apparently identical with the Simon ὁ ζηλωτής of Lc 6, 15 and Acts 1, 13. He might be a doubling of Simon the leader of the Twelve who is styled Σίμων βαριωνά in Mt 16, 17[7] — compare also Jn 6, 71 and 13, 26 where not Judas, but Simon, is called ἰσκαριώτης (sicarius?)[8].

---

[5] Josef Pickl, *Messiaskönig Jesus in der Auffassung seiner Zeitgenossen* (Munich ²1935), Engl. ed. *The Messias* (St. Louis and London 1946), p. 146. *Cf.* the chapter »Jesus and the Zealots« in Oscar Cullmann's *The State in the New Testament,* pp. 8—23, and Otto Betz, »Jesu Heiliger Krieg«, *Novum Testamentum,* vol. 2, 1957, pp. 116—137, especially on pp. 133—137: »Das Ende Jesu ist stark von der deutenden Kraft der ersten Glaubenszeugen gestaltet worden. Dabei hat man wohl die zum heiligen Krieg gehörenden Züge nicht etwa verstärkt, sondern eher abgeschwächt. Angesichts der römischen Kontrolle erscheint das durchaus verständlich, denn es war gefährlich, Anhänger eines heiligen Krieges zu sein« (*l. c.,* pp. 135, 136).

[6] Hans Lietzmann, *Der Weltheiland* (Bonn 1909), pp. 30, 31; also in *Kleine Schriften,* vol. 1 (*Texte und Untersuchungen,* vol. 67, Berlin 1958), p. 44.

[7] בַּרְיוֹנָא is an Aramaic word (Hebrew בַּרְיוֹן ), occurring in various passages with the meaning *outcast, outlaw;* so T. B. Berakhot 10 a, Taʿanith 23 b (only in some Mss), 24 a, Sanhedrin 37 a and Exodus Rabba 127 a, 128 c. Jacob Levy, in *Neuhebräisches und chaldäisches Wörterbuch,* vol. 1 (Leipzig 1876), p. 266, gives the meaning of the vocable as *ein roher, zügelloser, ausgelassener Mensch (agrestis, externus; jemand, der sich ausserhalb der menschlichen Kultur befindet), Wüstling.* Marcus Jastrow, in *A Dictionary of the Targumim...,* vol. 1 (London 1903), p. 193, translates *rebel, outlaw, highwayman.* We read in T. B. Gittin 56 a of one אַבָּא סִיקְרָא רֵישׁ בַּרְיוֹנֵי = *the boss [of the] sicarii, headman [of the] baryonê. This* »ringleader of terrorists« was a nephew of the pious and pacifist Yoḥanan ben Zakkai.

In view of the occurrence in the New Testament of various patronyms with *bar* (Bartholomaeus, Bartimaeus, Barabbas, Barsabbas, Barnabas, Barjesus) we cannot exclude the possiblity that βαριωνά in Mt 16, 17 is used in the sense »son of Yonah«. Against this view, however, are the following considerations: (1) the word is spelled without a Greek ending, whereas the other Semitic names, when transcribed, usually, if not always (see Καϊαφᾶ in Mt 26, 3), attract a ς at the ending; (2) there appears to be an antithesis between כיפא and בריונא : the »outcast« has become the »foundation stone« (*cf.* Ps 118, 22).

Even if Σίμων βαριωνά were nothing but a Greek transliteration of שמעון בריונא, we cannot be certain that the word *baryona* is to be understood as »insurgent, bandit, gangster«. Assuming that the passage came to be formulated when Jewish

If the followers of Jesus had aspired to instal their leader as messiah, and if aspirations of this kind had come to the governor's knowledge, Pilate would not have been the man to tolerate such machinations[9]. He would have tried to crush the movement at once by doing away with the leader. The little group that gathered around Jesus clearly had political-revolutionary tendencies, but it appears that these tendencies had not yet gained such an impetus as they had in certain other contemporary Jewish movements. Leading members of the Sanhedrin could have been quicker than Pilate in discerning the possibility of political implications in the movement promoted by Jesus; wary of the repercussions it could have, they perhaps informed Pilate of the latent danger. If so, Pilate would not have been slow in deciding upon what action to take[10].

The Gospel according to Mark contains reports of certain events which might conceivably have occasioned preventative action on the part of the authorities. The reports in question are: Mc 8, 27—30 (cf. 33), Mc 11 (1—7) 8—11 a and Mc 11, 15—17.

There is no need for our present purpose to enter upon a discussion of the problem as to whether the complex narrative in Mc 8, 27—9, 13 refers to an actual occurrence in Jesus' life or whether it is a reflection of discussions that took place some time after his death. Even if Mc 8,

---

Christians were cast out from the synagogues — and the First Gospel was written at that time (85—95 CE) — the meaning of Mt 16, 17—18 could be: the outcast from the Synagogue is made the foundation stone of the new Ecclesia.

[8] Jn 13, 2 probably contained the same reading originally. It would, of course, be possible to derive the name ἰσκαριώτης etymologically from the root שקר (implying *falsehood, betrayal*); see Charles Cutler Torrey, »The Name Iscariot«, *HTR* vol. 36, 1943, pp. 51—62, on p. 59.

[9] »Se trouvant en face d'une agitation populaire dont l'étiquette, pour le moins, était inquiétante, et dont le terme prévu, sinon le but avoué, était le renversement de l'ordre établi, Pilate, quand même il aurait attaché plus d'importance qu'il n'en attachait à la vie d'un homme et à la vie d'un juif, ne dut pas avoir l'ombre d'un doute sur la légitimité de son arrêt. Au surplus, les circonstances ne lui permettaient guère d'apprécier la grandeur morale de Jésus et il était incapable de la comprendre... Pilate n'a pu songer un seul instant à mettre en liberté "le roi des Juifs". Il aurait dû l'arrêter le lendemain«, Alfred Loisy, *L'évangile selon Marc*, pp. 451—452.

[10] Whether or not Jesus definitely made claim to messiahship, would have been more or less irrelevant in the eyes of the governor if it had come to his notice that messianic excitation had been stirred by Jesus' appearances in public: »... [Pilate] ne devait voir en [Jésus] qu'un de ces rêveurs insignifiants et indifférents en eux-mêmes, mais qui peuvent devenir dangereux quand ils provoquent l'enthousiasme populaire«, Maurice Goguel »Juifs et Romains dans l'histoire de la Passion«, *RHR* tome 62, 1910, pp. 165—182, 295—322, on p. 317; »... il ne devait voir en lui qu'un individu à surveilleir parce qu'il fallait se tenir prêt à intervenir pour éviter un mouvement populaire toujours possible avec les Juifs prompts à s'enthousiasmer pour tout ce qui leur paraissait susceptible de favoriser leurs espérances messianiques« (p. 318).

27—30 were taken to be a piece of biography, it would be no more than a messianic declaration on Jesus' behalf by his followers, and by no means a profession of messianic claims by the leader himself. An assertion of his messiahship by Jesus would in fact have been tantamount to raising the flag of revolt. It was not a matter of what Jesus might have understood by the word 'messiah', but how others understood it — and were bound to understand it. Johannes Weiss, who held that the story of Peter's profession at Caesarea Philippi had a historical nucleus, made the following comment: »eher eine Ablehnung als eine Zustimmung, im Ganzen eine . . . Dämpfung [der] Begeisterung [der Jünger] . . . Alles, was sich damals [bei den Jüngern] an ehrgeizigem, stolzem Hoffen regte, wurde mit harten Worten Jesu niedergeschlagen«[11].

Whether expressing a belief formulated by the apostolic community and merely retrojected into the story of Jesus' own life, or whether based on an occurrence in the life of Jesus, the story of the profession at Caesarea Philippi was certainly not the immediate cause for the arrest of Jesus[12].

The second of the three reports is that of the so-called "Triumphal Entry into Jerusalem". As recounted in the Gospels, the event has the appearance of an unmistakable messianic demonstration. As such it would have been open defiance of imperial authority — a proclamation of the will to national liberation from Roman rule — provided, however, that it happened in the manner set forth in the Gospels. But it is quite impossible to deduce anything of historical value from these descriptions. For one thing, there is difficulty in deciding whether the

---

[11] Johannes Weiss, o. c., p. 357; cf. p. 361. See also Erich Dinkler, »Petrusbekenntnis und Satanswort: »Das Problem der Messianität Jesu« in Zeit und Geschichte (ed. Dinkler; Tübingen 1964), pp. 127—153, on p. 152: »Die Caesarea-Perikope ist in ihrer bei Markus vorliegenden Form die nachösterliche Bearbeitung einer ins Leben Jesu zurückweisenden Tradition . . . Die ursprüngliche Tradition bezeugt die Verbindung des Petrusbekenntnisses von Jesus als dem künftigen Messias mit einer expliziten Antwort Jesu, nämlich dem Satanswort. Demnach hat Jesus die Rolle eines Messias abgelehnt . . .«

[12] While holding that the events recounted in Mc 8, 27 b—30 did not antedate the crucifixion, we disagree with Bultmann when he suggests that the report is an Easter story reflecting Peter's resurrection experience as the source of the church's messianic faith (Die Geschichte der synoptischen Tradition, pp. 227—228; English edition, p. 259). The scene depicted presupposes a time-lapse after the emergence of the so-called Easter faith, a period in which exponents of the apostolic gospel assigned different rôles to the risen Jesus in the awaited eschatological drama; such rôles would inevitably be compared and discussed, and it is this kind of situation that finds adumbration in Mc 8, 27 b—30 — as is also the case with the messianic confession in Mc 14, 62; cf. my papers »The Marcan Account of Jesus' Trial by the Sanhedrin«, JTS n. s. vol. 14 (1964), pp. 94—102, on pp. 99—100; and »The Trial of Jesus«, Commentary (New York, Sept. 1964), pp. 35—41, on p. 41.

event that gave rise to these reports actually took place on the occasion of *Jesus' last visit to Jerusalem* or *at some earlier date* and passed unnoticed by the authorities. Tradition may have embellished the account, and the evangelists may have been responsible for assigning it to its present setting. The whole story is strangely unconnected with what follows. After the temendous welcome given by the crowd (in Mark the crowd apparently consists of pilgrims who accompanied Jesus on his journey to Jerusalem; in John the crowd seems to be composed of certain inhabitants of the city itself), Jesus, having made a cursory sight-seeing tour ("having looked upon all things"), is reported to have left Jerusalem again for the obscurity of Bethany (Mc 11, 11)[13]. The story peters out; and the reader is left with the impression that it can hardly belong chronologically to the place it now occupies in the Gospels.

Even if it were in its proper place in the narratives, the importance of the messianic demonstration was magnified by successive evangelists. They obviously redrafted what they had received in the light of their post-resurrection experience and expectations. The Fourth Evangelist, in Jn 12, 16 ( *cf*. 2, 22), goes so far as to state explicitly that the followers of Jesus did not, in the first instance, understand the significance of the event. "They remembered these things when Jesus was glorified". And, indeed, a comparison of the respective reports in the four Gospels even suggests that the evangelists' memory actually improved the further they were from the event they described!

The description in each of the four Gospels has the features of a political demonstration[14]. It is obvious that tradition saw Jesus' entry

---

[13] The words in Mt 21, 10 »all the city was stirred« which have no foundation in Mark are an editorial addition.

[14] Of interest is the supplementation of the Marcan account of the Triumphal Entry in the Third Gospel: Lc 19, 39—44. The Third Evangelist at this point manifestly drew on a written 'special source' of Palestinian provenance. In vv. 39—40 some Pharisees — representing a politically moderate element of the population — are said to have tried to persuade Jesus to constrain the fervour of the masses who acclaimed him as king. The Pharisees are here represented as acting with a friendly concern in their endeavour to curb the crowd's enthusiasm; Jesus is reported to have resigned himself to the emotional demonstration of his followers.

It is difficult to assess the historical value of this information. If the record which lies behind vv. 41—44 was connected in the source with that behind the two preceding verses, the source might have emanated after the year 70 CE from a Judaeo-Christian milieu that was still strongly Jewish in its feeling. The same provenance would be indicated for Lc 23, 27—31. In certain Jewish-Christian circles the separation from 'official' Judaism, even after the year 70 CE, was not as yet so definite as would appear to have been the case in the milieu from which the Second Gospel emerged.

There are in Luke non-Marcan elements that are of a more primitive character than the Marcan rendering of the same topics (*e. g.* Lc 10, 25—28 as against Mc 12,

| Mark 11, 8—10 | Matthew 21, 8—9 | Luke 19, 38 | John 12, 13 |
|---|---|---|---|
| having cut reeds (στιβάδες) | they ... cut branches (κλάδοι) | | a great multitude took palm branches (βάϊα) |
| from the fields they spread them upon the way ... | from the trees and spread them in the way ... | | from the palm trees and went forth to meet him ... |
| Deliver us! | Hosanna to the Son of David! | | Deliver us! |
| Blessed he who comes in the name of YHWH! | Blessed he who comes in the name of the Lord! | Blessed the Coming One, | Blessed he who comes in the name of YHWH — |
| Blessed [be] the Kingdom of our father David! | | the king in the name of the Lord! | yes, the king of Israel! |
| Deliver us, [Thou Who Art] on high! | Hosanna on high! | Peace in heaven and glory on high! | |

into the capital city of Judaea as a symbolical seizure of the reins of government. He is hailed by the masses as king. The Fourth Evangelist who usually suppresses, or dislocates, factors with a political aspect, brings this out most clearly. In Jn 12, 13 the Marcan στιβάδες have become τὰ βάϊα τῶν φοινίκων, "branches of palm trees". At the relatively high altitude of Jerusalem no palms grow. If used in the welcome of Jesus, palm branches would have had to be imported specially for that particular purpose. In modern times a symbol of peace, the branches of a palm tree were in ancient times employed as a symbol of triumph, and were presented to honour victorious conquerors. The branches thrown under the feet of Jesus, and particularly palm branches, would signify the celebration of victory over the pagan oppressor[15]. The comparative table of the evangelical accounts of Jesus' entry into Jerusalem serves to indicate that the messianic colouring of the tradition became

---

28—34, or Lc 22, 24—27 as against Mc 10, 35—37, 42—45), but Lc 19, 39—44 cannot be regarded as primitive in comparison with the Marcan version; cf. above, p. 187, note 41.

[15] The victorious Judith is said, in Judith 15, 12, to have taken branches in her hand and distributed them among her suite. The victory of Judas Maccabaeus and the rededication of the sanctuary after its desecration were observed by festivities and rejoicing, with wreaths of leaves, fair boughs and palm branches, for »a great enemy had been vanquished« (2 Maccabees 10, 7). The conquest of the Acra by Simon the Hasmonaean was celebrated with palm branches (1 Maccabees 13, 51).

increasingly pronounced as we pass from the earlier to the later evangelists. The author of the Fourth Gospel, or the author of the source from
which his account is derived, deliberately introduced the feature of
"palm branches" so as to underline the significance of the event. Some
actual happening probably lies behind the narratives, but we cannot
definitely say at what point in Jesus' life it occurred or what exactly
its nature was[16].

The last of the three reports with which we are concerned is that of
the incident commonly designated with the words "The Cleansing
of the Temple". The air of awe-inspiring authority which the report
communicates is due in a large measure to the fact that New Testament
translators are in the habit of rendering the Greek word τὸ ἱερόν as
'Temple'. In reality it denotes the precincts of the sanctuary, the Temple
Mount, הר הבית, an extensive area comprising a vast complex of administrative buildings, offices, quarters for the accommodation of atten-
dants, cages and pens for sacrificial birds and animals, besides several
great courts. Around the sanctuary (ὁ ναός, היכל or מקדש ) lay the Court
of Priests which even Jewish men of other than priestly descent were
normally not allowed to enter; on the Court of Priests bordered the
Court of (Jewish) Men; beyond that lay the Court of (Jewish) Women.
This was separated by a wall from the Court of Gentiles, these not
being admitted beyond the wall of partition. In the south-eastern corner
of the Court of the Gentiles, on the outskirts of the Temple Mount, in
a place not considered hallowed ground, were the tables of the money-
changers who converted foreign coins carried by pilgrims from distant
lands into Tyrian coinage, and the booths of vendors of sacrificial birds
and animals. The spot was a public market-place, and the incident
known as "The Cleansing of the Temple" could have amounted to
little more than a brawl in an Eastern bazaar. Located at a considerable
distance from the sanctuary, and even from the courts in which Jewish
men and women assembled for worship, the booths of the money-
changers were not sacred objects — except, perhaps, to their owners.
On the other hand, the right to sell doves *etc.* and exchange foreign
coins for locally valid currency was reserved to relatives of the high-
priests and other persons drawn from the ranks of hierarchic families.
Hence a violent and unauthorized interference with the conduct of the
legitimate business of the licensed vendors and bankers, possibly involving damage to their property, would outrage their sense of propriety,
and if angry owners reported the incident to their influential kinsmen,
the report would have contributed to incense the hierarchs against Jesus.

---

[16] Already the Second Evangelist wished to stress the messianic character of
the story; see Heinz-Wolfgang Kuhn, »Das Reittier Jesu in der Einzugsgeschichte
des Markusevangeliums«, ZNW vol. 50, 1959, pp. 82—91. Nevertheless, in the Marcan presentation Jesus receives no *explicit* royal or messianic ovation; *cf.* Burkill,
*Mysterious Revelation,* pp. 193—196.

The record in Mc 11, 15—17 has occasionally been taken to imply an assertion of messianic claims on the part of Jesus, the care and maintenance of the sanctuary being in ancient Davidic times the duty and prerogative of the king. But when divested of the misleading title "The Cleansing of the Temple", the incident is reduced to the category of what a magistrate to-day would call a disturbance of the peace. It was neither sacrilege nor sedition, possibly a hubbub, and certainly an attack on vested interests. As such it would irritate the priests, and arouse their animosity. Other occasions on which Jesus was the centre of public commotion might have been called to mind, in which case they would have been more readily disposed to hostility. So much might be inferred from Mc 11, 27—28[17].

In this connection it would be pertinent to consider a *baraita* in the Babylonian Talmud, Sanhedrin 43 a, which states:

»On the eve of the Passover they hanged Yeshu, and the herald went before him for forty days saying: he is to be stoned because he practised magic and induced Israel to revolt«.

The sources of this tradition — if tradition it is — are not difficult to assess. The fact that it is recorded as a *baraita* must not lead us to think that we have here an unmodified record from tannaitic times. The apologetic tendency is obvious. That the herald prevenes Jesus for

---

[17] [*Revisers' addendum:* Winter came to feel that he had underestimated the significance of the »Cleansing« when calling it a mere brawl; see *Commentary* (New York, March 1965), pp. 27, 28. And there is no doubt that, had he prepared this second edition, he would have revised and expanded the above account of the incident, and that *inter alia* the new presentation would have taken into consideration N. Q. Hamilton's article »Temple Cleansing and Temple Bank«, *JBL* vol. 83 (1964), pp. 365—372. — Apropos of Mc 11, 16 (»and he would not allow that any one should carry a vessel through [the outer court of] the temple«), Winter left a few notes, the gist of which might be briefly rendered as follows: The statement signifies that Jesus objected to the use of the outer court as a thoroughfare (presumably, because it was a short cut), and perhaps those who drew water from the Kidron were the chief offenders. But did he merely voice his objection or did he take measures to obstruct the traffic? The evidence scarcely allows of a definite historical deduction either way. Admittedly, verse 16 immediately follows the report of Jesus' action against the stallholders and the bankers, but can it be inferred from this close association that he actually prevented certain people from passing through the court? Behaviour of this kind could easily have been construed as that of a λῃστής or revolutionary, and as such would it not have directly resulted in a clash with the police responsible for the maintenance of law and order within the sanctuary precincts? Yet, as is expressly asserted in Mc 14, 48, Jesus was freely allowed to teach in the Temple during the daytime. Certainly it requires a great deal of non-biblical inspiration to conclude from the wording of Mc 11, 16 (as some scholars do) that Jesus and his followers held a segment of the Temple area under forcible occupation.]

forty days'vainly seeking witnesses who would come forward to testify
to his innocence, demonstrates that the story had no independent basis,
but was thought out as a rejoinder to Christian reproaches, addressed
to Jews, for the death of Jesus. The *baraita* presupposes Christian
traditions, canonical and non-canonical, and merely gives a negative
appraisal of what is positively appraised in the Gospels. The interval of
forty days between sentence and execution makes clear the report's
unhistorical character. As regards stoning as the mode by which Jesus
is said to have been executed, the story betrays its source: meant as an
apology for the execution of Jesus, the *baraita* was composed by
someone who believed that if the Jewish authorities had executed Jesus,
they must have done so in accordance with Jewish penal law.

We are left with what the *baraita* informs us of the grounds for the
execution: the practice of magic and the seduction of Israel to rebellion.
The charge of magic is legendary and developed during the second
century among Jews who had heard from Christians something of what
the Gospels report of Jesus' miracles. Not disposed to deny the veracity
of miracle-stories, Jews attributed Jesus' marvellous deeds to magical
arts; a second-century letter to the Emperor Claudius includes sorcery
among the Jewish accusations against Jesus. As for the charge of
"inducing Israel to revolt", this could have stemmed from Lc 23, 2 —
not directly, because the author of the *baraita* scarcely knew the New
Testament, but by way of indirect influences — if it referred to Jesus'
relations towards the Roman State authority. If it referred to Jesus'
relations with Jews who interpreted Jewish religious law, it would be
pure inference. The evidential value of the *baraita* for historical purposes is nil.

Pagan testimonies from the second to the fourth centuries, frag-
mentarily preserved by Christian writers who disputed their evidential
value, mention that Jesus was a rebel, a political seducer. Statements
of this kind are based on inferences. Jesus was sentenced by Pilate on
a charge of sedition, and this fact would suffice to justify pagan authors
in their positing that Jesus was a revolutionary.

In the light of the foregoing discussion it can be seen that though
the New Testament contains indications of political aspirations for
national independence, harboured among early followers of Jesus, and
there is reason for thinking that some expression of such aspirations
occurred already in the life of Jesus, we cannot determine with certainty what precisely gave occasion for the ordering of his arrest. We
can safely say that it was not the alleged profession of Jesus' messiahship by his disciples, and there is little likelihood that Jesus' entry into
Jerusalem — which the evangelists wish to set forth as a public proclamation of his royal dignity — had in actual fact the character
which the writers ascribe to it. As for the incident in the Court of the
Gentiles, occurring as perhaps it did towards the end of Jesus' life, we

may assume that it aroused the anger and intensified the anxiety of the Jewish hierarchy.

The Passover season was notoriously a time of political agitation. The great mass of pilgrims who streamed into Jerusalem to celebrate the feast commemorating Israel's liberation from Egyptian bondage were prone to excitement. Among them were politically disgruntled elements. The governors, being aware of this, were on their guard. Normally residing in Caesarea, they came to Jerusalem for the Passover, accompanied by military reinforcements[18].

Though disguised by theological argument, Jn 11, 48 affords evidence of the fact that the Jewish Senate, the Great Sanhedrin, had received an intimation that Pilate might reduce their ethnical autonomy if public order were not more satisfactorily maintained. Since the reign of Herod the Great, the high-priests had ceased to be genuinely independent representatives of the people; they owed their appointment to the favour of a foreign ruler, and were more often than not content to play the servile rôle of an instrument in his hands. Nevertheless, they endeavoured to preserve as much as they could not only of their own privileges, but also of the residue of Jewish national autonomy. The pressure of circumstances compelled them to pursue a policy of moderation with regard to Rome, and to restrain movements directed towards emancipation. When finally, in 66 CE, the priestly aristocracy themselves gave the signal to revolt against procuratorial misgovernment, they were unable to stem the tide of the rebellious forces they had unleashed, and were swept away by passions beyond their control. But during the life-time of Jesus, over a generation earlier, the priestly aristocracy still strove to maintain a peaceable *modus vivendi* with the Romans. If they did receive a warning from Pilate, whether in specific or in general terms[19], they could scarcely have disregarded it.

It would be a mistake to assume that the hierarchy were moved purely by motives of self-interest. Doubtless, such were not absent, and yet, by taking action against Jesus the priests may well have hoped to prevent Roman intervention on a larger scale on the pretext of unrest occasioned by the public activities of Jesus. If disorders occurred, the members of the Great Sanhedrin would be held responsible by the governor and would have risked losing their position of authority (ἡμῶν ὁ τόπος, Jn 11, 48). The existence of a similar situation, though

---

[18] »... the principal feasts ..., for which always a vast and often restive mass of people gathered in Jerusalem, were dangerous and critical days for the Roman conquerors«, Josef Pickl, *o. c.*, p. 218. *Cf.* Josef Blinzler, »Die Niedermetzelung von Galiläern durch Pilatus«, *Novum Testamentum* vol. 2, 1957, pp. 24—49, especially pp. 39, 40; further August Friedrich Strobel, »Die Passa-Erwartung als urchristliches Problem«, ZNW vol. 49, 1958, pp. 157—196, espec. on pp. 165, 183 195; the same, »Passa-Symbolik und Passa-Wunder in Act xiii 3 ff.«, NTS vol. 4, 1958, pp. 210—215.

[19] See above, p. 57.

from a time later than that of Jesus, is attested. One of Pilate's successors in Judaea of whose activities we are better informed — he was a contemporary of Josephus — Gessius Florus, demanded of the chief priests and other prominent citizens of Jerusalem that they should apprehend and hand over certain individuals by whose action he was offended, threatening at the same time to bring his vengeance to bear upon the Jewish leaders if they failed to comply with his demand and to produce the individuals concerned[20]. The peremptory order which Gessius Florus gave to the Jewish authorities issued from a public disturbance in Jerusalem. Nothing as definite is known of the events which preceded and caused the arrest of Jesus. But there are in Mc 15, 7 allusions to a στάσις that had taken place, and Josephus reported the crucifixion in connection with some θόρυβος.

Did the high-priest act at Pilate's prompting, or did he of his own accord inform the governor of an insurrection threatened by commotion among the adherents of Jesus? Neither the Gospels nor other extant sources provide an answer. There were occasions, under Gessius Florus, when leading Jews sent messengers to the Roman governor (and to King Agrippa II) begging him to come speedily to Jerusalem to put down an imminent rebellion before it was too late[21]. However, Pilate would in any case have gone to Jerusalem for the Passover season.

Who issued the order for Jesus' arrest?

If we accept the authenticity of the tradition in Jn 18 (3), 12 that Jesus was arrested by a detachment of Roman soldiers under their own officer, the likelihood is that the order for the arrest was given by a responsible Roman official — perhaps Pilate himself. An inference of this sort is only in apparent contradiction with Jn 11, 57 where the Jewish authorities issue an order demanding that anyone who knew of Jesus' whereabouts should disclose them so that his apprehension might be expedited. Though now separated from the story of the arrest in our Fourth Gospel, the tradition underlying Jn 11, 47—57 must at one time have been closely linked with the source upon which Jn 18, 3 b, 10—13a is based[22]. Inferring from Jn 11, 48 that the Jewish authorities were induced by a warning to take police action against Jesus, we have to read Jn 11, 57 in conjunction therewith. Possibly the Sanhedrin issued a warrant, or rather ordered the Jewish police (οἱ στρατηγοὶ τοῦ ἱεροῦ, Lc 22, 52; οἱ ὑπηρέται τῶν Ἰουδαίων, Jn 18, 12) to assist the imperial military forces (ἡ σπεῖρα, Jn 18, 3, 12) in the task of searching for and seizing Jesus. This would not exclude the possibility that the actual order had in the first instance been given by Pilate. Even if the arrest had taken place without the active participation of any Roman military

[20] B. J. II 301—302.
[21] B. J. II 418—419.
[22] See above, p. 60—69.

personnel, the order could still have come from the governor who could have demanded that the Sanhedrin take this course of action. On the other hand the high-priest, whilst not in a position to tell Pilate what he had to do, could have suggested that he might arrest Jesus as a precautionary measure to prevent further disturbances. On the whole it seems reasonable to suppose that the order was issued by Pilate. The presence of Roman troops at the arrest, of which we read in Jn 18, 3, 12, makes this view more than feasible.

But even if it is allowed that the order for Jesus' arrest was issued by the governor, we still have to consider the question as to who took the initiative. Pilate may have acted of his own accord, provided he had heard of Jesus, or he may have been influenced by suggestions made to him by repreesentative Jewish leaders. That Pilate had threatened intervention if agitation among the populace continued can — in the light of our discussion of Jn 11, 48 — scarcely be doubted. But popular agitation was by no means due solely to Jesus and his associates. Possibly the high-priest, confronted with the governor's warning, decided upon placating Pilate by proposing that Jesus should be arraigned for trial (Jn 11, 50; Mc 14, 1). The arrest of a Galilaean preacher who had no support among influential people and who had become troublesome to the authorities would not, we may assume, have displeased the hierarchy, especially after the incident in the Temple.

It was particularly Goguel[23] who argued that the initiative for the arrest of Jesus was taken by Pilate. Some qualification is called for in this connection. That the general responsibility for the execution of Jesus, like that for the execution of other persons condemned with or without trial for political crimes during Pilate's term of office, belonged to the governor, is undeniable — and yet it is not unlikely that in Jesus' case members of the hierarchy had a hand in the affair as well.

The last and most difficult question with which we are confronted is: What did Jesus himself intend? Did he deliberately put forward claims that brought his sufferings upon him? We have no means of direct access to the mind of Jesus. The disciples, after their Easter experience, saw in him the Messiah, the predestined ruler of Israel. This was what they believed and proclaimed, and their preaching lies

---

[23] »L'initiative du procès ne devait... pas être attribuée aux autorités juives, mais à l'autorité romaine«, Maurice Goguel, »Juifs et Romains dans l'histoire de la Passion«, RHR vol. 62, 1910, pp. 165—182, 295—322, on p. 177; »... il y a dans les évangiles synoptiques un certain nombre de détails qui supposent l'existence d'une tradition d'après laquelle c'était Pilate et non le sanhédrin qui prenait l'initiative des poursuites contre Jésus« (p. 180); »... l'auteur du récit johannique a connu une tradition dans laquelle c'étaient les Romains qui prenaient l'initiative de poursuites contre Jésus et qui procédaient à son arrestation« (p. 303); »L'initiative des poursuites contre Jésus n'a pas été prise par les Juifs, le procès a été un procès romain, non pas un procès juif« (p. 321).

at the heart of the gospel traditions. If, as all the evangelists (Mc 15, 2; Mt 27, 11; Lc 23, 3 and Jn 18, 37) imply, Jesus actually avowed a claim to royal dignity during his examination by Pilate, such an avowal would have constituted *crimen diminutae maiestatis,* and for the governor the case would have been closed forthwith[24]. Yet we have no trustworthy report of Jesus' actual words during the interrogation. The words σὺ λέγεις are ambiguous in themselves, and whilst perhaps not indicating an evasive answer to a direct question on Jesus' part, they may have been evasively formulated by the early tradents who knew that they were not in a position to give an exact account of what took place during the proceedings[25].

Ὁ χριστὸς τέλος νόμου — *the crowning of the revelation contained in the Torah lies in the appearance of the Messiah.* A conception of this kind governs the whole New Testament interpretation of the Old. But there is no evidence that such an interpretation goes back to Jesus himself, nor that he equated or identified himself with a messiah, or with the Messiah, or the Son of Man, or the Suffering Servant, or with a combination of all three figures. And the conclusion seems inevitable: *Jesus was not a crank.* On the contrary, he was a normal person — he was the norm of normality — and he neither identified nor equated himself with anyone except Jesus of Nazareth.

An element of contradiction may seem to be involved in our general argumentation. It is maintained that the gospel records, when critically examined, furnish clear evidence of the fact that Jesus was executed on a charge of sedition at the order of the Emperor's representative. At the same time the contention is made that Jesus was devoid of revolutionary ambitions. The evidence, fragmentary though it is, affords no solid basis for the view that he was engaged in any political activities of a subversive character. T h a t   h e   w a s   e x e c u t e d   a s   a   r e - b e l ,   t o g e t h e r   w i t h   o t h e r s   w h o   w e r e   e x e c u t e d   o n t h e   s a m e   c h a r g e ,   b y   n o   m e a n s   p r o v e s   t h a t   h e   d i d w o r k   f o r   t h e   o v e r t h r o w   o f   t h e   e x i s t i n g   p o l i t i c a l s y s t e m [26]. So far as the governor was concerned, he would have

---

[24] »[Die]... Darstellung des Markus... bietet eine... Verwertung der Nachricht, dass Pilatus wegen des Königsanspruchs Jesu die Hinrichtung beschlossen habe. Das... war die einzige Kunde, die ein Erzähler, der nicht über Augenzeugenberichte verfügte, von der Verurteilung Jesu haben konnte«, Martin Dibelius, »Herodes und Pilatus«, *l. c.,* pp. 116, 117 (resp. p. 282).

»... the essential and specific matter of this trial and execution is the Messianic kingship of Jesus«, Josef Pickl, *o. c.,* p. 174.

[25] [*Revisers' addendum:* On the meaning of Jesus' alleged reply, see G. Vermes, *Jesus the Jew* (London 1973), pp. 147—149.]

[26] »The people's dreams of freedom... and the surging waves of insurrection throughout the land beat in upon the life of Jesus from His childhood to His death«, Josef Pickl, *o. c.,* p. 3.

seen sufficient reason for ordering the crucifixion if he had come to feel that Jesus' itinerant preaching tended to excite the masses to expect the end of the existing order.

A hurried trial over, events moved swiftly on from the fateful moment when Jesus was taken away from Pilate to a place called *The Skull,* to the moment when he inclined his head — and it was finished.

# EPILOGUE

כל עוד בלבב פנימה . . . .

*It is not over . . .*

*Not Pilate's sentence, not the jostling of the soldiers who divided his garments, not even the cry from the cross was the last word.*

*The accusers of old are dead. The witnesses have gone home. The judge has left the court. The trial of Jesus goes on. His is a trial that is never finished, and one in which the rôles of judge and accused are strangely reversed.*

*Tribunals assemble. Tribunals disband. The bailiffs, the informers, the accusers, the witnesses, the governors, the executioners are still with us.*

*Many have come in his name, and have joined the accusers; and there arose new false witnesses among them — yet even so, their testimony agrees not. Never spoken when Jesus was tried, the words "His blood upon us and upon our childern!" have come true — a thousand times. But no valid answer has yet been given to the question "What will you that I do with the King of the Jews?"; only the cry "Crucify him! Crucify him!" echoes throughout the centuries.*

*Rabbi Eliezer ben Hyrcanus, Eliezer the Great, said of Jesus: He owns his share in the Age That Is Coming . . .*

*It was not finished. Sentence was passed, and he was led away. Crucified, dead, and buried, he yet rose in the hearts of his disciples who had loved him and felt he was near.*

*Tried by the world, condemned by authority, buried by the Churches that profess his name, he is rising again, today and tomorrow, in the hearts of men who love him and feel he is near.*

נפש יהודי הומיה . . . .

# SELECT BIBLIOGRAPHY

The present list is largely confined to works mentioned in the footnotes

Abrahams, I., *Studies in Pharisaism and the Gospels.* 2 vols. Cambridge, 1917—1924.

Allegro, J. M., »Further Light on the History of the Qumran Sect«, *JBL*, vol. 75, 1956, pp. 87—95.

—, *Discoveries in the Judaean Desert.* Vol. V. Oxford, 1968.

Bacon, B. W., *The Beginnings of the Gospel Story.* Newhaven, Conn., 1909.

—, *Is Mark a Roman Gospel? (Harvard Theological Studies VII).* Cambridge, Mass., 1919.

—, »Pharisees and Herodians in Mark«, *JBL*, vol. 39, 1920, pp. 102—112.

—, *The Gospel of Mark: Its Composition and Date.* Newhaven, Conn., 1925.

—, *The Story of Jesus and the Beginnings of the Church.* London, 1928.

Bammel, E., ed. *The Trial of Jesus: Cambridge Studies in Honour of C. F. D. Moule.* London, 1970.

Barrett, C. K., *The Gospel According to St. John: An Introduction with Commentary and Notes on the Greek Text.* London, 1955.

—, *Yesterday, Today and For Ever: The New Testament Problem.* Durham, 1959.

Bauer, W., *Das Johannes-Evangelium.* 3rd ed. Tübingen, 1933.

Baumgarten, J. M., »Does *tlh* in the Temple Scroll refer to Crucifixion?«, *JBL*, vol. 91, 1972, pp. 472—481.

Beare, F. W., »The Sabbath was Made for Man?«, *JBL*, vol. 79, 1960, pp. 130—136.

Bell, H. I., *Jews and Christians in Egypt: The Jewish Troubles in Alexandria and the Athanasian Controversy.* London, 1924.

Benoit, P., »Jesus devant le Sanhédrin«, *Angelicum,* vol. 20, Rome, 1943, pp. 143—165.

—, »Prétoire, Lithostroton et Gabbatha«, *Revue biblique,* vol. 59, 1952, pp. 531—550.

—, Review of J. Blinzler's *Der Prozess Jesu* in *Revue biblique,* vol. 60, 1953, pp. 452—453.

Bertram, G., *Die Leidengeschichte Jesu und der Christuskult.* Giessen, 1922.

Betz, O., »Jesu Heiliger Krieg«, *NovT,* vol. 2, 1957, pp. 116—137.

Bickermann, E. J., »*Utilitas crucis:* Observations sur les récits du procès de Jésus dans les Évangiles canoniques«, *RHR,* vol. 112, 1935, pp. 169—241.

—, »Les Hérodiens«, *Revue biblique,* vol. 47, 1938, pp. 184—197.

Black, M., *An Aramaic Approach to the Gospels and Acts.* Oxford, 1954; 3rd ed., 1967.

—, »The Arrest and Trial of Jesus«, *New Testament Essays. Studies in Memory of Thomas Walter Manson,* ed. A. J. B. Higgins. Manchester, 1959, pp. 19—33.

—, *The Scrolls and Christian Origins.* London, 1961.

Blank, J., »Die Verhandlung vor Pilatus Joh. 18, 28—19, 16 im Lichte johannischer Theologie«, *Biblische Zeitschrift,* neue Folge, vol. 3, 1959, pp. 60—81.

Blass, F. W., *Acta Apostolorum sive Lucae ad Theophilum liber alter.* Leipzig, 1896.

Blinzler, J., *Der Prozess Jesu: Das jüdische und das römische Gerichtsverfahren gegen Christus.* 2nd ed. Regensburg, 1955. Engl. trans. *The Trial of Jesus.* Westminster, Md., 1959.

—, »Die Strafe für Ehebruch in Bibel und Halacha: Zur Auslegung von Joh. viii 5«, *NTS,* vol. 4, 1957, pp. 32—47.

—, »Die Niedermetzelung von Galiläern durch Pilatus«, *NovT,* vol. 2, 1957, pp. 24—49.

Bonner, C., ed. *The Homily on the Passion by Melito Bishop of Sardis (Studies and Documents* XII). London and Philadelphia, 1940.

Borg, M., »The Currency of the Term 'Zealot'«, *Journal of Theological Studies,* n. s., vol. 22, 1971, pp. 504—512.

Borgen, P., »John and the Synoptics in the Passion Narrative«, *NTS,* vol. 5, 1959, pp. 246—259.

Bornkamm, G., *Jesus of Nazareth.* New York, 1960.

Bousset, W., *Die Religion des Judentums im späthellenistischen Zeitalter.* 3rd ed., rev. H. Gressmann. Tübingen, 1926.

—, *Kyrios Christos.* Göttingen, 1928; Engl. trans., Nashville, Tenn., 1971.

Brandon, S. G. F., *The Fall of Jerusalem and the Christian Church.* London, 1951.

—, *Jesus and the Zealots.* Manchester, 1967.

—, *The Trial of Jesus of Nazareth.* London, 1968.

Brandt, W., *Die Evangelische Geschichte und der Ursprung des Christenthums.* Leipzig, 1893.

—, *Die jüdischen Baptismen oder das religiöse Waschen und Baden im Judentum mit Einschluss des Judenchristums* (Beiheft 18 zur ZAW). Giessen, 1910.

—, *Jüdische Reinheitslehre und ihre Beschreibung in den Evangelien* (Beiheft 19 zur ZAW). Giessen, 1910.

Branscomb, B. H., *The Gospel of Mark (Moffatt New Testament Commentary).* London, 1937.

Büchler, A., *Das Synedrion in Jerusalem und das grosse Beth-Din in der Quaderkammer des jerusalemischen Tempels (IXes Jahresbericht der israelitisch-theologischen Lehranstalt in Wien).* Vienna, 1902.

—, »Die Todesstrafen der Bibel und der jüdisch-nachbiblischen Zeit«, *Monatsschrift für Geschichte und Wissenschaft des Judentums,* vol. 50, Berlin, 1906, pp. 539—562, 664—706.

—, *Der galiläische 'Am-ha-'Areṣ des zweiten Jahrhunderts.* Vienna, 1906.

Bultmann, R., *Jesus.* Berlin, 1926.

—, »Kirche und Lehre im Neuen Testament«, *Zwischen den Zeiten,* vol. 7, Tübingen, 1929, pp. 9—43.

—, *Die Geschichte der synoptischen Tradition.* 2nd ed. Göttingen, 1931. Engl. trans. *The History of the Synoptic Tradition.* 2nd ed. Oxford, 1968.

—, *Das Evangelium des Johannes.* 4th ed. Göttingen, 1963; Engl. trans. *The Gospel of John: A Commentary.* Oxford, 1971.

—, *Glauben und Verstehen.* 4 vols. Tübingen, I 1933, ⁶1966; II 1952, ⁴1965; III 1960, ³1965; IV 1965, ²1967. Engl. trans. *Faith and Understanding: Collected Essays,* vol. 1, London, 1969.

Bundy, W. E., *Jesus and the First Three Gospels: An Introduction to the Synoptic Tradition.* Cambridge, Mass., 1955.

Burkill, T. A., »The Competence of the Sanhedrin«, *Vigiliae Christianae,* vol. 10, 1956, pp. 80—96.

—, »The Trial of Jesus«, *Vigiliae Christianae,* vol. 12, 1958, pp. 1—18.

Burkill, T. A., »L'antisémitisme dans l'évangile selon saint Marc«, *RHR*, vol. 154, 1958, pp. 10—31.

—, »Sanhedrin«, *Interpreter's Dictionary of the Bible*, ed. G. A. Buttrick. Nashville, Tenn., 1962, vol. 4, pp. 214 ff.

—, *Mysterious Revelation: An Examination of the Philosophy of St. Mark's Gospel.* Ithaca. N. Y., 1963.

—, »The Historical Development of the Story of the Syrophoenician Woman (Mark vii: 24—31)«, *NovT,* vol. 9, 1967, pp. 161—177.

—, »The Condemnation of Jesus: A Critique of Sherwin-White's Thesis«, *NovT,* vol. 12, 1970, pp. 321—342.

—, *New Light on the Earliest Gospel.* Ithaca, N. Y., 1972.

Burkitt, F. C., *The Earliest Sources for the Life of Jesus.* London, 1910.

Bussmann, W., *Synoptische Studien.* 3 vols. Halle, 1925—1931.

Cadbury, H. J., »Roman Law and the Trial of Paul«, *The Beginnings of Christianity,* eds. F. J. Foakes-Jackson and K. Lake, vol. 5, London, 1933, pp. 297—338.

—, *Jesus — What Manner of Man?* New York, 1947.

Carrington, P., *According to Mark: A Running Commentary on the Oldest Gospel.* Cambridge, 1960.

Catchpole, D. R., *The Trial of Jesus (Studia Post-Biblica* XVIII). Leiden, 1971.

Causse, A., *L'évolution de l'espérance messianique dans le Christianisme primitif.* Paris, 1908.

Charles, R. H., ed. *The Assumption of Moses.* London, 1897.

—, ed. *Apocrypha and Pseudepigrapha of the Old Testament.* 2 vols. Oxford, 1913.

Chwolson, D., *Das letzte Passahmahl Christi und der Tag seines Todes.* Leipzig, 1908.

Clermont-Ganneau, C., »Une stèle du Temple de Jérusalem«, *Revue archéologique ou Recueil de documents et de mémoires relatifs à l'étude des monuments, à la numismatique et la philologie de l'antiquité et du moyen âge,* nouvelle série, 13e année, 23e tome, Paris, 1872.

Cohn, H., *The Trial and Death of Jesus.* New York, 1971; London, 1972.

Connolly, H., ed. *Didascalia Apostolorum: The Syriac Version Translated and Accompanied by the Verona Latin Fragments.* Oxford, 1929.

Conzelmann, H., *Die Mitte der Zeit: Studien zur Theologie des Lukas.* 4th ed. Tübingen, 1962; Engl. trans. *The Theology of St. Luke,* London. 1960.

Corssen, P., »Die Zeugnisse des Tacitus und Pseudo-Josephus über Christus«, *ZNW,* vol. 15, 1914, pp. 114—140.

Cranfield, C. E. B., *The Gospel according to Saint Mark.* Cambridge, 1959.

Cross, F. M., Jr., *The Ancient Library of Qumran and Modern Biblical Studies.* London, 1958.

Cullmann, O., *Urchristentum und Gottesdienst.* Basel, 1944.

—, *Der Staat im Neuen Testament.* Tübingen, 1956; French trans. *Dieu et César.* Neuchâtel, 1956; Engl. trans. *The State in the New Testament.* London, 1957.

—, *The Christology of the New Testament.* London, 1959.

Cureton, W., *Book of Religious and Philosophical Sects.* London, 1842.

Dahl, N., »Die Passionsgeschichte bei Matthäus«, *NTS,* vol. 2, 1955, pp. 17—32.

Dalman, G., *The Words of Jesus.* Edinburgh, 1902.

—, *Orte und Wege Jesu.* Gütersloh, 1919; Engl. trans. *Sacred Sites and Ways.* London, 1935.

Dalman, G., *Jesus-Jeschua. Die drei Sprachen Jesu. Jesus i der Synagoge, auf dem Berge, beim Passahmahl am Kreuz.* Leipzig, 1922; Engl. trans. *Jesus-Jeschua: Studies in the Aramaic Gospels.* London, 1929.

—, *Jerusalem und sein Gelände.* Gütersloh, 1930.

Danby, H., ed. *The Mishnah.* Oxford, 1933.

Daube, D., *The New Testament and Rabbinic Judaism.* London, 1956.

—, »Evangelisten und Rabbinen«, ZNW, vol. 48, 1957, pp. 119—126.

Deissmann, A., »The Name 'Jesus'«, *Mysterium Christi: Christological Studies by British and German Theologians.* London, 1930.

Delbrueck, R., »Antiquarisches zu den Verspottungen Jesu«, ZNW, vol. 41, 1942, pp. 124—145.

Delling, G., »Das Logion Mark x 11 (und seine Abwandlungen) im Neuen Testament«, NovT, vol. 1, 1956, pp. 263—274.

Derenbourg, J., *Essai sur l'histoire et la géographie de la Palestine d'après les Thalmuds et les autres sources rabbiniques.* Paris, 1867.

Dibelius, M., »Herodes und Pilatus«, ZNW, vol. 16, 1915, pp. 113—126.

—, »Die alttestamentlichen Motive in der Leidensgeschichte des Petrus- und des Johannes-Evangeliums«, *Abhandlungen zur semitischen Religionskunde und Sprachwissenschaft, Wolfgang Wilhelm Grafen v. Baudissin überreicht,* Giessen, 1918, pp. 125 ff.

—, »Stilkritisches zur Apostelgeschichte«, *Eucharisterion: Studien zur Religion und Literatur des Alten und Neuen Testaments, Hermann Gunkel dargebracht,* ed. Schmidt, H., vol. 2, Göttingen, 1923, pp. 27—49.

—, »Das historische Problem der Leidensgeschichte«, ZNW, vol. 30, 1931, pp. 193—201.

—, »The Text of Acts, An Urgent Critical Task«, *Journal of Religion,* vol. 21, Chicago, 1941, pp. 421—431.

—, »Rom und die Christen im ersten Jahrhundert«, *Sitzungsberichte der Heidelberger Akademie der Wissenschaften,* phil.-hist. Klasse 1941—42, Heft 2, Heidelberg, 1942.

—, »Die Apostelgeschichte als Geschichtsquelle«, *Forschungen und Fortschritte,* vols. 21—23, 1947, pp. 67—69.

—, »Der erste Christliche Historiker«, *Schriften der Universität Heidelberg,* Heft 3, 1948, pp. 112—125.

—, »Die Reden der Apostelgeschichte und die antike Geschichtschreibung«, *Sitzungberichte der Heidelberger Akademie der Wissenschaften,* phil.-hist. Klasse, Heidelberg, 1949, pp. 1 ff.

—, *Botschaft und Geschichte: Gesammelte Aufsätze.* 2 vols. Tübingen, 1953—56.

—, *Aufsätze zur Apostelgeschichte.* Göttingen, 1951; Engl. trans. *Studies in the Acts of the Apostles.* London, 1956.

—, *Die Formgeschichte des Evangeliums.* 3rd ed. Tübingen, 1959; Engl. trans. *From Tradition to Gospel.* London, 1934.

Dobschütz, E., v. »Matthäus als Rabbi und Katechet«, ZNW, vol. 27, 1928, pp. 338—348.

Dodd, C. H., *The Interpretation of the Fourth Gospel.* Cambridge, 1953.

Döllinger, J. J. I., v. *Heidenthum und Judenthum,* Regensburg, 1857.

—, *Christentum und Kirche in der Zeit der Grundlegung.* Regensburg, 1860; 2nd ed. 1868; Engl. trans. *The First Age of Christianity and the Church.* London, 1866.

Eisler, R., ΙΗΣΟΥΣ ΒΑΣΙΛΕΥΣ ΟΥ ΒΑΣΙΛΕΥΣΑΣ. 2 vols. Heidelberg, 1929—30.

Enslin, M. S., *The Prophet from Nazareth.* New York, 1961.

Farmer, W. R., *Maccabees, Zealots and Josephus*. New York, 1956.

Finegan, J., *Die Überlieferung der Leidens- und Auferstehungsgeschichte Jesu* (Beiheft 15 zur ZNW). Giessen, 1934.

Foakes-Jackson, F. J. and K. Lake, eds. *The Beginnings of Christianity*. 5 vols. London, 1920—33.

Funk, F. X., *Didascalia et Constitutiones Apostolorum*. Paderborn, 1905.

Geiger, A., *Urschrift und Übersetzungen der Bibel in ihrer Abhängigkeit von der innern Entwicklung des Judenthums*. Breslau, 1857.

—, »Sadducäer und Pharisäer«, *Jüdische Zeitschrift für Wissenschaft und Leben*, vol. 2, Breslau, 1863, pp. 11—54.

Goguel, M., *Les chrétiens et l'empire romain à l'époque du Nouveau Testament*. Paris, 1908.

—, *Les sources du récit johannique de la passion*. Paris, 1910.

—, »Juifs et Romains dans l'histoire de la passion«, *RHR*, vol. 62, 1910, pp. 165—182, 295—322.

—, *Introduction au Nouveau Testament*. 2 vols. (uncompleted) Paris, 1923—26.

—, *La vie de Jésus*. Paris, 1932; Engl. trans. *The Life of Jesus*. London, 1933; 2nd ed. *Jésus: histoire des vies de Jésus*. Paris, 1950.

Goodspeed, E. J., *Die ältesten Apologeten: Texte mit kurzen Einleitungen*. Göttingen, 1914.

Grotius, H., *Annotationes in libros evangeliorum*. Amsterdam, 1641.

Gutschmidt, A., v. »Vorlesungen über Josephos' Bücher gegen Apion«, *Kleine Schriften*, ed. F. Rühl, Leipzig, 1893, pp. 336—589.

Haas, N., »Anthropological Observations on the Skeletal Remains from Giv'at ha-Mivtar«, *Israel Exploration Journal*, vol. 20, 1970, pp. 38—59.

Haenchen, E., *Die Apostelgeschichte*. Göttingen, 1956; Engl. trans. *The Acts of the Apostles: A Commentary*. Oxford, Philadelphia, 1971.

Hamilton, N. Q., »Temple Cleansing and Temple Bank«, *JBL*, vol. 83, 1964, pp. 365—372.

Harris, J. R., *The Apology of Aristides on Behalf of the Christians*. Cambridge, 1891.

Hirsch, E. G., »Crucifixion«, *Jewish Encyclopedia*, vol. 4, New York, 1903; 3rd ed. 1925, pp. 373—374.

Hitzig, H., »Crux«, Pauly-Wissowa's *Real-Enzyklopädie*, vol. 8, Stuttgart, 1901, cols. 1728—1731.

Hoenig, S. B., *The Great Sanhedrin*. Philadelphia, 1953.

Hölscher, G., »Die Hohenpriesterliste bei Josephus und die evangelische Chronologie«, *Sitzungsberichte der Heidelberger Akademie der Wissenschaften*, phil.-hist. Klasse, 1939—40, 3, Heidelberg, 1940.

Huber, J., *De lingua antiquissimorum Graeciae incolarum (Commentationes Aenipontanae, IX)*. Vienna, 1921.

Husband, R. W., »The Pardoning of Prisoners by Pilate«, *American Journal of Theology*, vol. 21, 1917, pp. 110—116.

Jeremias, J., »Zöllner und Sünder«, ZNW, vol. 30, 1931, pp. 293—300.

—, *Jerusalem zur Zeit Jesu*. 2 vols. 3rd ed. Göttingen, 1962. Engl. trans. *Jerusalem in the Time of Jesus*. London, 1969.

Joüon, P., »Les hérodiens de l'évangile«, *Recherches de science religieuse*, vol. 28, 1938, pp. 585—588.

Juster, J., *Les juifs dans l'empire romain: leur condition juridique, économique et sociale*. 2 vols. Paris, 1914.

Kähler, M., *Der sogenannte historische Jesus und der geschichtliche, biblische Christus.* 2nd ed. Leipzig, 1896.

Klausner, J., *Jesus of Nazareth: His Life, Times and Teaching.* London, 1925.

Klijn, A. F. J., »Scribes, Pharisees, High Priests and Elders«, *NovT,* vol. 3, 1959, pp. 259—267.

Klostermann, E., *Die Evangelien (Handbuch zum Neuen Testament).* Tübingen, 1919.

—, *Das Markusevangelium (Handbuch zum Neuen Testament).* 3rd ed. Tübingen, 1958.

Kuhn, H. W., »Das Reittier Jesu in der Einzugsgeschichte des Markusevangeliums«, *ZNW,* vol. 50, 1959, pp. 82—91.

Lagrange, M.-J., *Évangile selon Saint Luc.* Paris, 1921.

—, *Évangile selon Saint Matthieu.* Paris, 1923.

Lauterbach, J. Z., »The Sadducees and Pharisees: A Study of their Respective Attitudes towards the Law«, *Studies in Jewish Literature issued in Honor of Professor Kaufmann Kohler,* Berlin, 1913, pp. 176—198.

Leclercq, H., »Le supplice de la croix«, *Dictionnaire d'archéologie chrétienne et de liturgie,* vol. III 2, Paris, 1914, cols. 3045—3048.

Leszynsky, R., *Die Sadduzäer.* Berlin, 1912.

Lichtenstein, H., »Die Fastenrolle: Eine Untersuchung zur jüdisch-hellenistischen Geschichte«, *Hebrew Union College Annual,* vols. 8—9, Cincinnati, 1931—32, pp. 257—351.

Lietzmann, H., *Der Weltheiland.* Bonn, 1909.

—, »Der Prozess Jesu«, *Sitzungsberichte der Preussichen Akademie der Wissenschaften,* phil.-hist. Klasse, 14, Berlin, 1931, pp. 313—322.

—, »Bemerkungen zum Prozess Jesu«, *ZNW,* vol. 30, 1931, pp. 211—215; vol. 31, 1932, pp. 78—84.

—, *Kleine Schriften. (Texte und Untersuchungen,* 67—68, 74), 3 vols. Berlin, 1958—62.

Lightfoot, R. H., *St. John's Gospel: A Commentary,* ed. C. F. Evans, Oxford, 1956.

Lohmeyer, E., *Das Evangelium des Markus.* 3rd ed. Göttingen, 1951.

Loisy, A., *Le quatrième évangile.* Paris, 1903; 2nd ed. 1921.

—, *Les évangiles synoptiques.* 2 vols. Paris, 1907—08.

—, »Le proconsul Gallion et Saint Paul«, *Revue d'histoire et de philosophie religieuses,* vol. 2, 1911, pp. 142—144.

—, *L'évangile selon Marc.* Paris, 1912.

—, *Les actes des apôtres.* Paris, 1920.

—, *L'évangile selon Luc.* Paris, 1924.

Maccoby, H. Z., »Jesus and Barabbas«, *NTS,* vol. 16, 1969—70, pp. 55—60.

Mánek, J., »The Biblical Conception of Time and our Gospels«, *NTS,* vol. 6, 1959, pp. 45—51.

Mantel, H., *Studies in the History of the Sanhedrin.* Cambridge, Mass., 1961.

Marucchi, O., »Croix«, *Dictionnaire de la Bible,* vol. 2, Paris, 1899, cols. 1127—1131.

—, »The Cross as an Instrument of Punishment in the Ancient World«, *The Catholic Encyclopedia,* vol. 4, New York, 1908, pp. 518—519.

—, »The Crucifixion of Jesus Christ«, *ibid.,* pp. 519—520.

Marxsen, W., *Der Evangelist Markus: Studien zur Redaktionsgeschichte des Evangeliums.* 2nd ed. Göttingen, 1959; Engl. trans. *Mark the Evangelist: Studies on the Redaction History of the Gospel.* Nashville, Tenn., 1969.

McRuer, J. C., *The Trial of Jesus.* Toronto, 1964.

Merkel, J., »Die Begnadigung am Passafeste«, ZNW, vol. 6, 1905, pp. 293—316.

Montefiore, C. G., The Synoptic Gospels. 2nd ed. London, 1927.

Moore, G. F., Judaism in the First Centuries of the Christian Era. 3 vols. Cambridge, Mass., 1927—30.

Neirynck, F., »Het evangelisch echtscheidingsverbod«, Collationes Brugenses et Gandavenses, vol. 4, Bruges, 1958, pp. 25—46.

Neubauer, A., Mediaeval Jewish Chronicles and Chronological Notes (Annecdota Oxoniensia). Oxford, 1895.

Neusner, J., »The Fellowship (Haburah) in the Second Jewish Commonwealth«, HTR, vol. 53, 1960, pp. 125—142.

Norden, E., »Josephus und Tacitus über Jesus Christus und eine messianische Prophetie«, Neue Jahrbücher für das klassische Altertum, Geschichte und Deutsche Literatur, vol. 16, 1913, pp. 637—666.

Olmstead, A. E., Jesus in the Light of History. New York, 1942.

Pfisterer, R., »Wie empfindet der Verurteilte seine Strafe«, Evangelische Theologie, vol. 17, 1957, pp. 416—423.

Pickl, J., Messiaskönig Jesus in der Auffassung seiner Zeitgenossen, 2nd ed. Munich, 1935; Engl. trans. The Messias, St. Louis and London, 1946.

Pool, D. de S., Capital Punishment among the Jews. New York, 1916.

Radin M., The Trial of Jesus. Chicago, 1931.

Rawlinson, A. E. J., The Gospel according to St. Mark (Westminster Commentaries). London, 1925.

Reich, H., »Der König mit der Dornenkrone«, Neue Jahrbücher für das klassische Altertum, Geschichte und Deutsche Literatur, vol. 7, 1904, pp. 705—733.

Réville, A., Jésus de Nazareth. Paris, 1897.

Rosenblatt, S., »The Crucifixion of Jesus from the Standpoint of Pharisaic Law«, JBL, vol. 75, 1956, pp. 314—321.

Schlatter, A., Die beiden Schwerter, Lukas 22, 35—38: Ein Stück aus der besonderen Quelle des Lukas (Beiträge zur Förderung christlicher Theologie), vol. 20, 1916, Heft 6, Gütersloh, 1916.

Schmittlein, R., Circonstances et cause de la mort du Christ. Baden-Baden, 1950.

Schneider, J., »Zur Komposition von Joh 18, 22—27«, ZNW, vol. 48, 1957, pp. 111—119.

Schürer, E., »Der Versammlungsort des grossen Synedriums: Ein Beitrag zur Topographie des Herodianischen Tempels«, Theologische Studien und Kritiken, vol. 51, 1878, pp. 608—626.

—, Geschichte des jüdischen Volkes im Zeitalter Jesu Christi. 4 vols. 3rd and 4th ed. Leipzig, 1901—1911; Engl. trans. A History of the Jewish People in the Time of Jesus Christ. 5 vols. Edinburgh, 1885—91; The History of the Jewish People in the Age of Jesus Christ, revised and edited by G. Vermes and F. Millar, vol. 1, Edinburgh, 1973.

Schwartz, E., »Aporien in vierten Evangelium«, Nachrichten von der kgl. Gesellschaft der Wissenschaften zu Göttingen, phil.-hist. Klasse, 1907, pp. 342—379; 1908, pp. 115—148, 149—188, 497—560; Berlin, 1907—08.

Schweizer, E., »Der Menschensohn«, ZNW, vol. 50, 1959, pp. 185—209.

Sherwin-White, A. N., Roman Society and Roman Law in the New Testament. Oxford, 1963.

Sjöberg, E., Der verborgene Menschensohn in den Evangelien. Lund, 1955.

Smith, J. P., St. Irenaeus' Proof of the Apostolic Preaching, translated and annotated by J. P. Smith, Ancient Christian Writers, vol. 16, Westminster, Md., 1952.

Smith, M., »Zealots and Sicarii, Their Origins and Relation«, HTR, vol. 64, 1971, pp. 1—19.

Stauffer, E., Jerusalem und Rom im Zeitalter Jesu Christi. Bern, 1957.

Strack, H. L., and P. Billerbeck, Kommentar zum Neuen Testament aus Talmud und Midrasch. 6 vols. Munich, 1922—61.

Strobel, A. F., »Die Passa-Erwartung als urchristliches Problem«, ZNW, vol. 49, 1958, pp. 157—196.

—, »Passa-Symbolik und Passa-Wunder in Apg. xiii 3 ff.«, NTS, vol. 4, 1958, pp. 210—215.

Taylor, V., The Gospel according to St. Mark, London, 1952.

Testuz, M., ed. Méliton de Sardes, Homélie sur la Pâque. Cologny-Geneva, 1960.

Tödt, H. E., Der Menschensohn in der synoptischen Überlieferung. Gütersloh, 1959; Engl. trans. The Son of Man in the Synoptic Tradition. London, 1965.

Torrey, C. C., »The Name Iscariot«, HTR, vol. 36, 1943, pp. 51—62.

Trilling, W., Das wahre Israel: Studien zur Theologie des Matthäus-evangeliums (Erfurter Theologische Studien, VII). Leipzig, 1959.

Tzaferis, V., »Jewish Tombs at and near Giv'at ha-Mivtar, Jerusalem«, Israel Exploration Journal, vol. 20, 1970, pp. 18—32.

Unnik, W. C. van, »Jesu Verhöhnung vor dem Synedrium (Mc 14, 65 par)«, ZNW, vol. 29, 1930, pp. 310—311.

Vermes, G., The Dead Sea Scrolls in English. Harmondsworth, 1962, 1968.

—, »The Use of bar nash / bar nasha in Jewish Aramaic«, Appendix E in M. Black, An Aramaic Approach to the Gospels and Acts, 3rd ed. Oxford, 1967, pp. 310—328.

—, Jesus the Jew. A Historian's Reading of the Gospels. London, 1973.

Vollmer, H., »Der König mit der Dornenkrone«, ZNW, vol. 6, 1905, pp. 194—198.

Weiss, J., Das älteste Evangelium. Göttingen, 1903.

Wellhausen, J., Die Pharisäer und die Sadducäer: Eine Untersuchung zur inneren jüdischen Geschichte. Greifswald, 1894.

—, Das Evangelium Marci. Berlin, 1903.

—, Das Evangelium Matthaei. Berlin, 1904.

—, Erweiterungen und Änderungen im vierten Evangelium, Berlin, 1907.

—, Das Evangelium Johannis. Berlin, 1908.

—, »Kritische Analyse der Apostelgeschichte«, Abhandlungen der kgl. Gesellschaft der Wissenschaften zu Göttingen, phil.-hist. Klasse, neue Folge XV, 2, Berlin, 1914.

Wendland, P., »Jesus als Saturnalien-König«, Hermes, vol. 33, 1898, pp. 175—179.

Wieder, N., »Notes on the New Documents from the Fourth Cave of Qumran: The Term TLH ḤY«, Journal of Jewish Studies, vol. 7, London, 1956, pp. 71—72.

Wilson, R. M., The Execution of Jesus. New York, 1970.

Winter, P., »The Treatment of his Sources by the Third Evangelist in Luke, XXI to XXIV, Studia Theologica, vol. 8, Lund, 1955, pp. 138—172.

—, »Luke XXII 66 b—71«, ibid., vol. 9, 1956, pp. 112—115.

—, »Ṣadoqite Fragments IV, 20, 21 and the Exegesis of Genesis 1, 27«, ZAW, vol. 68, 1956, pp. 71—84.

—, »I Corinthians XV 3 b—7«, NovT, vol. 2, 1957, pp. 142—150.

—, »Genesis 1, 27 and Jesus' Saying on Divorce«, ZAW, vol. 70, 1958, pp. 260 f.

—, »Tacitus and Pliny: The Early Christians«, Journal of Historical Studies, Princeton, N. J., vol. 1, 1967—68, pp. 31—36.

—, »Ṣadoqite Fragments IX 1«, Revue de Qumran, vol. 9, 1967—68, pp. 131 ff.

Winter, P., »Josephus on Jesus«, *Journal of Historical Studies,* vol. 1, Princeton, N. J., 1967—68, pp. 289—302.

Yadin, Y., »Pesher Nahum (4Qp Nahum) Reconsidered«, *Israel Exploration Journal,* vol. 21, 1971, pp. 1—12.

—, »Epigraphy and Crucifixion«, *ibidem,* vol. 23, 1973, pp. 18—22.

Zeitlin, S., *Megillat Taanit as a Source for Jewish Chronology and History in the Hellenistic and Roman Periods.* Philadelphia, 1922.

# INDEX

(See also the two Lists and the Bibliography
indicated in the table of contents)

# Walter de Gruyter
# Berlin · New York

## Studia Judaica

Forschungen zur Wissenschaft des Judentums
Herausgegeben von Ernst Ludwig Ehrlich
Groß-Oktav. Ganzleinen

Michael Avi-Yonah

## Geschichte der Juden im Zeitalter des Talmud

In den Tagen von Rom und Byzanz
XVI, 290 Seiten. 1962. DM 38,–
ISBN 3 11 001344 4 (Band 2)

Gershom Scholem

## Ursprünge und Anfänge der Kabbala

XI, 434 Seiten. 1962. DM 48,–
ISBN 3 11 001345 2 (Band 3)

Abraham Schalit

## König Herodes

Der Mann und sein Werk
XVI, 890 Seiten. Mit 1 Frontispiz, 8 Bildtafeln, 4 Karten
und 1 Stammtafel in Tasche. 1969. DM 148,–
ISBN 3 11 001346 0 (Band 4)
Die Übersetzung der hebräischen Originalfassung des Werkes
wurde von Jehoshua Amir besorgt

Arnold M. Goldberg

## Untersuchungen über die Vorstellung von der Schekhinah in der frühen rabbinischen Literatur

– Talmud und Midrasch –
XII, 564 Seiten. 1969. DM 72,–
ISBN 3 11 001347 9 (Band 5)

Chanoch Albeck

## Einführung in die Mischna

Aus dem Hebräischen übersetzt von Tamor und
Pessach Galewski
Enthält ein neuartiges Lexikon von 192 Seiten.
VIII, 493 Seiten. 1971. DM 68,–
ISBN 3 11 006429 4 (Band 6)

Hermann Greive

## Studien zum jüdischen Neuplatonismus

Die Religionsphilosophie des Abraham Ibn Ezra
X, 225 Seiten. 1973. DM 72,–
ISBN 3 11 004116 2 (Band 7)

Preisänderungen vorbehalten

# Walter de Gruyter
# Berlin · New York

Beihefte zur Zeitschrift
für die neutestamentliche Wissenschaft
Herausgegeben von Walther Eltester

Ulrich Becker

## Jesus und die Ehebrecherin

Untersuchungen zur Text- und Überlieferungsgeschichte
von Joh. 7₅₃–8₁₁
Groß-Oktav. X, 203 Seiten. 1963. Ganzleinen DM 28,–
ISBN 3 11 005593 7 (28)

Martin Hengel

## Nachfolge und Charisma

Eine exegetisch-religionsgeschichtliche Studie
zu Mt 8,21 f. und Jesu Ruf in die Nachfolge
Groß-Oktav. VI, 116 Seiten. 1968. Ganzleinen DM 36,–
ISBN 3 11 005600 3 (34)

Martin Lehmann

## Synoptische Quellenanalyse
## und die Frage nach dem historischen Jesus

Kriterien der Jesusforschung untersucht in Auseinanderset-
zung mit Emanuel Hirschs Frühgechichte des Evangeliums
Groß-Oktav. XII, 218 Seiten. 1970. Ganzleinen DM 42,–
ISBN 3 11 002588 4 (38)

Klaus Berger

## Die Amen-Worte Jesu

Eine Untersuchung zum Problem der Legitimation
in apokalyptischer Rede
Groß-Oktav. XII, 182 Seiten. 1970. Ganzleinen DM 42,–
ISBN 3 11 006445 6 (39)

E. Gräßer-A. Strobel-
R. C. Tannehill-
W. Eltester

## Jesus in Nazareth

Groß-Oktav. VIII, 153 Seiten. 1972. Ganzleinen DM 64,–
ISBN 3 11 004004 2 (4o)

Preisänderungen vorbehalten

# Walter de Gruyter
# Berlin · New York

Ernst Haenchen

### Der Weg Jesu

Eine Erklärung des Markus-Evangeliums
und der kanonischen Parallelen
2., durchgesehene und verbesserte Auflage.
Oktav. XVI, 594 Seiten. 1968. Ganzleinen DM 38,–
ISBN 3 11 0026505 3 (de Gruyter Lehrbuch)

Martin Dibelius

### Jesus

4. Auflage, mit einem Nachtrag von Werner Georg Kümmel
Klein-Oktav. 140 Seiten. 1966. Kartoniert DM 4,80
ISBN 3 11 006248 8 (Sammlung Göschen, Band 1130)

Emanuel Hirsch

### Betrachtungen zu Wort und Geschichte Jesu

Oktav. VI, 241 Seiten. 1969. Ganzleinen DM 19,80
ISBN 3 11 001192 1

Konrad von
Fußesbrunnen

### Die Kindheit Jesu

Kritische Ausgabe von Hans Fromm und Klaus Grubmüller
Oktav. VIII, 181 Seiten. 1973. Ganzleinen DM 112,–
ISBN 3 11 003332 1

### Zeitschrift für die neutestamentliche Wissenschaft und die Kunde der älteren Kirche

In Verbindung mit Erich Gräßer, Günter Klein
und Martin Tetz herausgegeben von Eduard Lohse
Erscheint bandweise. Jährlich 1 Band mit
2 Doppelheften. Bandpreis DM 58,–, Einzelheft DM 32,–
1974: Band 65.

Preisänderungen vorbehalten